# HIDDEN FROM HISTORY

## VOLUME I

*Voices Against Suffrage
From The
Silenced Majority*

DANICA DE LA MORA

Hidden From History: Voices Against Suffrage From the Silenced Majority, Volume 1.

Copyright © 2024 by Danica De La Mora.
All rights reserved.

It is illegal to copy, distribute, or create derivative works from this book in whole or in part or to contribute to the copying, distribution, or creating of derivative works of this book.

No portion of this book may be reproduced, stored in a retrieval system, or transmitted in any form or by any means—electronic, mechanical, photocopying, recording or otherwise—without written permission from the publisher.

Cover images by Freepik and Danica De La Mora
Cover design by Danica De La Mora
Book design, layout, and illustrations by Danica De La Mora

Public domain images and texts courtesy of Google Books, Internet Archives, Harvard University Library, Tennessee Virtual Archive (teva.contentdm.oclc.org), docsteach.org, and uncommonwealth.virginiamemory.com.

Special thanks to Nancy Stroupe, MAV, Neil and Nancy Schaffel, Tom Reece, Douglas Gallo, Linda and Al Colangelo and Patricia Sahm.

Published by Timeless Treasures Publishing
P.O. Box 278
Crossnore, NC 28616
www.TimelessTreasuresStudio.net
info@TimelessTreasuresStudio.net

First Edition: January, 2024.

Paperback ISBN: 978-1-953940-46-9
Hardcover ISBN: 978-1-953940-45-2

Manufactured in the United States of America.

Disclaimer: The information in this book is intended for the purpose of enlightenment and self-improvement. This work does not intend to pass judgments on any minority group or person of any race, color, personal denomination, sexual orientation, or belief system. This work is a referential representation of the research conducted by the authoress and does not directly reflect or represent any other entity or institution. It is not intended to diagnose, prescribe, or cure any specific type of psychological, emotional, or physical problem.

*This book is dedicated to God . . .*

*. . . and to the countless men and women who
placed the importance of the family, freedom, and the
American Constitutional Republic directly under God.*

*Although they were hidden from historical remembrance, they
were the brilliant souls who knew the real reasons for the feminist
agitation and indefatigably warned against the perils of
socialism, feminism, and woman suffrage.*

*They were the incredible men and women who fought tirelessly
to protect our institutions and enlighten the many of the
corruption of the few.*

*Together, we bridge centuries and generations
to join forces against evil.*

# Preface

What you hold in your hands is one volume in a series of books comprised of the extensive research I have collected for nearly a decade. What began as a few short questions and curiosities, ended up leading in one strange direction after another through complete darkness in a fiercely dangerous jungle. Slowly, I moved through the secluded and treacherous terrain, attempting to make sense of our societal dysfunction. The souvenirs I collected along the way are the basis for this work.

Why are these volumes called *Hidden From History: Voices Against Suffrage From the Silenced Majority*? When I started my research, I realized that I needed to learn more about feminism. Those people who blamed feminism for many of the problems society is experiencing today pointed their fingers at Women's Liberation and the Sexual Revolution of the 1960s, or what is now known as the second wave of feminism. The 1960s, I also believed, were when real feminism started. I had not given much thought to what is now designated as the first wave, which took place in the nineteenth century. Like most people, I held the misconception that American women simply wanted to be equal and to have the same rights and freedoms that men experienced. I even believed that women were oppressed by some patriarchy. All of these beliefs are socialist lies and methods of division. I was shocked to learn how well women were treated, that they had protections and privileges that men did not grant even themselves. I had absolutely no idea that there were anti-suffragists or that there was a powerful anti-suffrage movement. I did not know that there was a constant battle between an overwhelming majority of conservative American women and a very loud, forceful, and violent minority of women who were clamoring for suffrage that rational women vehemently opposed. My journey has been an incredible eye-opener through the sobering realization of the deafeningly loud and constant repetition of lies and deception to which we have been exposed for our entire lives. History has practically silenced a large majority of the women who resisted the burdens they did not want, and sounded the alarm against unmitigated evil, which ultimately resulted in history giving notoriety and false numbers only to the small number of women who forever changed history by illegal and nefarious means.

In order to fully understand *feminism*, not only is it necessary to do some time traveling through historical documents, but it is also extremely important to understand *socialism* as well as *globalism*. All three conceptualizations are necessary in order to understand women's suffrage—because it was not at all about allowing women to vote or about freeing women from their imaginary bondage; it was one nail in the coffin that has entombed our most important institutions, including religious faith and the nuclear family. A dark globalist agenda has been run by a small group of people on a global scale for many centuries, patiently operating behind closed doors of secret societies, powerful organizations, societal divisions, endless propaganda and wars, numerous psychological weapons, and more. It has been a continual subterranean current wreaking havoc on all of humanity. The onslaught of feminism is one of the many systems that misanthropic globalitarians have used to wage a war on Christianity, and to enslave and depopulate humanity. Globalism is an anti-human and anti-God agenda that seeks to injure God by destroying His loving creation. When the larger picture is realized, it becomes easy to see that women's suffrage of itself was insignificant, but it played an integral role in weakening our strongest institutions before detonating our entire civilization, causing it to collapse in its own footprint.

While it may take a little knowledge to have a good grasp of *socialism*, *feminism*, *globalism*, and *suffrage* in order to understand their relation to each other, it is relatively simple to recognize foul play. The reason these documents are as important today as they ever were is because they expose the corruption of their time and the evil agenda that is still being implemented. Those groups who were pushing evil in the 1700s are the same groups that are pushing evil in the 2000s.

In regard to women's suffrage itself, the suffragists never had the numbers to pass the 19[TH] Amendment. Women everywhere were rejecting suffrage and almost all of the states were constantly defeating women's suffrage in impressive numbers. The suffragists continually rejected requests for referendums by anti-suffragists who merely wanted to prove the numbers. Soon, the suffragists decided no longer to bother with attempts at persuading the public, but instead to harass

Congress. They threatened, stalked, and assaulted legislators and the President. Only when the socialists overtly stepped in with money and power did the suffragists see success with their goals. Long-time anti-suffrage legislators, as well as the President, suddenly supported the federal amendment for suffrage, all at once, causing the anti-suffragists great suspicion. The fact that the suffragists suddenly received the support that they needed is enunciated by President Wilson's *Fourteen Points,* proposed in Versailles, France, in 1919, when he mentioned the creation of a world government and a League of Nations, which vehemently opposed Congressional representation of the American people. Prominent suffrage leaders we champion like Susan B. Anthony and Elizabeth Cady Stanton, for example, and most of the people in their societies, were self-proclaimed radical communists. The reality of history is very different from the version we are spoon-fed from a very young age, as the documents in this series effectively will prove.

The brilliant men and women who penned the following documents and publications knew exactly what was going on and they attempted to expose feminist-socialist-suffragists through their plans, actions, and quotes every step of the way. They brought attention to their violence and criminality. They warned against the perils of woman suffrage, socialism, and feminism, how it would destroy the family and the home, yield masculine women and effeminate men, and much more. They painted a clear picture of the type of woman who would result from being uprooted from her husband and family, and upending all of the elements of the home. Their picture was extremely prophetic, considering that the woman their projections showcased is the only type of woman we know today.

The quality and size of these documents vary, but we are very fortunate to access their messages. Collecting these documents was not easy for me, which was equally surprising. One would think that, because woman suffrage was added to our Constitution more than 100 years ago, the history surrounding it would be available for all who had any interest in the subject. My experiences have refuted that idea, however. The beginning of my research included only pro-feminist publications, because they were the easiest to access and I had no awareness of any opposition. Eventually, I started to discover that there were antis and that they, too, had published information. Almost every online search for the anti-suffrage publications that were referenced in other books produced no results. Most of the time, there were listings and information about the published works, but no copy available to read. The interesting part was that most of these authors had published additional works on unrelated topics. Usually I would find that all of those were available—just nothing that contradicted suffrage or socialism. Why would that be? That discovery further piqued my interest, so I continued the search. Often the results I desired were hidden, maybe with a tease of a title page or introduction. Some universities claimed to possess a number of these publications in their libraries, but access was denied unless I was a member of their network, and I was not.

Fortunately, after years of countless attempts, I have gathered a collection of obscure printings that encapsulate their message and are now in the public domain. There are still many hidden documents that I eventually hope to find. I have created this series because I would like to make the quest for answers much easier for those who come along later. I also would like to make them accessible to those who wish to extend respect by humoring the wonderful men and women who attempted to fight with incredible resilience what has continually and incrementally worked to destroy us. The remarkable foresight of the writers who have penned many of these documents are worth every reader's time and interest. Some of the information in these publications may be surprising, as it was for me, since it may challenge many of the "truths" that long have been embraced. I have learned that the truth has been gagged and suppressed, only to have lies cooked and reheated with each subsequent wave and ill-informed generation. Constantly, we are wading through turbulent waters of feminism, frequently withstanding many smaller waves, only to encounter tsunamis every few decades. The devastating effects of feminism and socialism on society are no longer deniable.

It is time for the truth to be exposed and widely accessible to all who are interested, to learn that our trials and tribulations were deliberately planned and orchestrated for definite objectives, and to understand that almost all that we have become and believed, and all of the dysfunction we have experienced and can never seem to escape, have been the planned results and the influences of extremely nefarious individuals throughout history. First, it is necessary to bring public awareness and to oust them, and then to work on deprogramming ourselves and on rebuilding society.

It is my hope that these works awaken and enlighten our people and assist in correcting our course.

May the truth set us free from our real bondage,

Danica De La Mora

# Contents

Joint Resolution Proposal for the 19TH Amendment to the U.S. Constitution ................... 1
A Defense of the President and Congress of the U.S. Against Suffrage and Socialist Canards (1918) ............ 2
A Help or a Hindrance? (By Priscilla Leonard) ................... 3
A Leaf From History ................... 11
A Moment with Ruskin ................... 14
A Suffrage Lesson ................... 15
A Word of Appreciation to Mrs. Pruyn ................... 16
A World Without God ................... 19
Address Before Committee of New York Constitutional Convention by Francis M. Scott (1894) ............ 23
Address by Mrs. Francis M. Scott Delivered Before the Judiciary Committee of the N.Y. Senate (1895) ..... 36
Address of Hon. John Lowell Delivered Before the Committee on Woman Suffrage, Boston (1885) ............ 40
Address by Emily Bissell Before the U.S. Senate Committee on Woman Suffrage (1900) ................... 44
Address of Hon. Horace J. Canfield Delivered Before the M.A. House of Representatives (1877) ................... 48
Address of Mrs. W. Winslow Crannell Before the Committee on Resolutions of the R.N.C. (1896) ................... 64
Address of Mrs. W. Winslow Crannell Before the Committee on Resolutions of the D.N.C. (1896) ................... 68
Address to the Judiciary Committees of the Senate and Assembly of New York (1899) ................... 76
Aims of the Massachusetts Association Opposed to the Further Extension of Suffrage to Women ................... 83
America When Feminized (circa 1920) ................... 84
American Women and the Ballot (1909) ................... 85
An Economical Woman Who Thinks Men Need No Help From Others In Politics (1909) ................... 92
An Open Letter To A Temperance Friend by F. Parkman ................... 93
Analysis of the Vote on Wellman Bill of Massachusetts (1895) ................... 94
Anti-Suffrage Answers ................... 95
Anti-Suffrage Arguments ................... 96
Anti-Suffrage Arguments: Danger! ................... 97
Anti-Suffrage Arguments: What Votes Cannot Do ................... 98
Anti-Suffrage Postcard ................... 99
April Fool's Day Cartoon (1920) ................... 100
Argument Against Woman Suffrage: A Petition Request ................... 101
Argument Against Women's Suffrage by J. B. Sanford (1909) ................... 102
Argument of Hon. George G. Crocker at Hearing Before the Committee on Woman Suffrage (1884) ...... 103
Argument Against Woman Suffrage by Mrs. Kate G. Wells Before Special Legislative Committee ............ 110
Argument of Author Lord Before the Legislative Committee on Woman Suffrage (1889) ................... 114
Argument of Author Lord Before the Legislative Committee on Woman Suffrage (1890) ................... 138
Argument of Clement K. Fay, Esq. for Remonstrants on Municipal Woman Suffrage ................... 163
Argument of Mrs. A. J. George Before the U. S. Senate Committee on Woman Suffrage (1913) ................... 184
Arguments for Woman Suffrage Considered ................... 203
As to Suffrage in New York State ................... 211
As to Women (From the Seattle Daily Times, 1898) ................... 214
Ask Suffragists to Explain This ................... 215
Beware! ................... 219

Bishop Seymour on the New Woman: God Created Man and Woman Somewhat Differently ................. 220
Can Anybody Terrorize Tennessee Manhood? ............................................................................................ 223
Cardinal Gibbons Says Women Should Keep From the Polls .................................................................... 226
Sinister Feminism is Due to the Abdication of Man, Says Cardinal O'Connell (1920) ......................... 230
Chicago Chronicle, July 10, 1896: Oppose Woman Suffrage...................................................................... 232
The Consent of the Governed by Munroe Smith, Professor of Jurisprudence, Columbia University ......... 234
Declaration of Principles by the Southern Women's League ..................................................................... 241
Defeat of Woman Suffrage in the State of Washington (From Portland Oregonian, 1898) ................. 242
Cartoon of the Day: What They Are Breaking ............................................................................................ 243
Diagram of Official N.Y. Vote, Proving Suffrage Converts to Socialism, Majority Against Suffrage ......... 244
Dignity of Womanhood (1912) ..................................................................................................................... 250
Do Not Want the Ballot (1896) ..................................................................................................................... 254
Do We Want It In Massachusetts? By James T. Gardiner ........................................................................... 256
Do Women Want the Vote? By William M. Bray (1916) ............................................................................ 257
Does Suffrage Work Pay? (1896) .................................................................................................................... 268
Equality by Mrs. Caroline F. Corbin (1910) ................................................................................................. 270
Extract From an Address on Taxation Without Representation by Mrs. H. A. Foster ......................... 274
Extracts From an Article by the Rev. J. M. Buckley on the Wrongs and Perils of Woman Suffrage ........... 275
Extracts From an Article by the Rev. J. M. Buckley on the Wrongs and Perils of Woman Suffrage ........... 276
Extract From an Address Before M.A. Federation of Women's Clubs by Horace Wadlin (1903) ............. 277
Extracts From an Address on Co-Education by Andrew S. Draper Before Twentieth Century Club ......... 279
Extracts From the Address of Rt. Rev. William Croswell Doane to St. Agnes' Graduates (1894) ............... 282
Extracts From the Address of Rt. Rev. William Croswell Doane to St. Agnes' Graduates (1895) ............... 286
Extracts From Remarks of Judge Aldrich in the N.H. Constitutional Convention (1902) ....................... 289
Facts and Fallacies About Woman Suffrage (1911)..................................................................................... 296
Female Suffrage: A Letter from the Rt. Hon. W. E. Gladstone to Samuel Smith (1892) ...................... 304
Fifteenth Annual Report for the Illinois Association Opposed to Woman Suffrage (partial) ................... 311
From New York Mail and Daily Express (1897) ......................................................................................... 317
From The Outlook............................................................................................................................................ 319
From "The World," London: Woman and Whine (1899)........................................................................... 322
Household Hints: Vote NO on Woman Suffrage ........................................................................................ 324
How Suffrage Pickets Were Suppressed by Real Men.................................................................................. 326
How Women Can Best Serve the State by Mrs. Barclay Hazard (1907)................................................... 238
James T. Gardiner on Woman Suffrage ........................................................................................................ 336
Joint Resolution of Maryland, Rejecting Ratification of the 19TH Amendment.................................... 338
Letter from Mrs. Sarah Calhoun Winter to Mrs. Cameron........................................................................ 341
Letter from the Citizens of Georgia to Georgia Senators (1918) .............................................................. 342
Letter from Mrs. Clara T. Leonard in Opposition to Woman Suffrage (1884) ....................................... 344
Letter from the Alabama Male Association Opposed to Woman Suffrage (1918) ................................. 348
Letter to the U. S. Congress from the Women of Georgia Opposed to Woman Suffrage (1913) ......... 349
Letter from the Iowa Association Opposed to Woman Suffrage (1918) .................................................. 355
Letter from the New Jersey Association Opposed to Woman Suffrage (1918)........................................ 356

Letter to Hon. Henry W. Blair from Caroline F. Corbin (1887) ...................................................................... 357
Letter to U. S. Congress from the Massachusetts Anti-Suffrage Association (1916) .................................... 364
Letter to Rev. Dr. J. M. Buckley from Bishop John H. Vincent (1894) ......................................................... 366
Liberty Above Equality by John Corbin ........................................................................................................ 367
Massachusetts Women Opposed to Woman Suffrage: Appeal for Consideration ....................................... 380
Massachusetts Association Opposed to the Further Extension of Suffrage to Women: By-laws (1897) ..... 384
Massachusetts Association Opposed to the Further Extension of Suffrage to Women: Circular ................ 387
Massachusetts Association Opposed to the Further Extension of Suffrage to Women: Officers ................ 389
Matrimony and the Building of Homes (1913) ............................................................................................. 393
Men! Are You Politically A Subject Sex? (1915) ............................................................................................ 397
Men and Women (1910) ................................................................................................................................ 398
Men for the State, Women for the Home (1911) .......................................................................................... 402
Minority Report of Committee on Woman Suffrage by William H. Tappan (1895) ................................... 408
Modern Thought (1912) ................................................................................................................................ 412
Mr. Depew Answered: A Flight of Imagination by Mrs. W. Winslow Crannell (1896) .............................. 416
Mr. Gladstone on Woman Suffrage ............................................................................................................... 420
Mrs. Creighton's Appeal ................................................................................................................................ 421
Mrs. Lyman Abbott on Woman Suffrage ...................................................................................................... 424
Municipal Suffrage for Women—Why? By Frank Foxcroft (1902) ............................................................. 430
Noblesse Oblige by Mary A. Jordan .............................................................................................................. 432
Objections to License Suffrage From a No-License Point of View by Frank Foxcroft (1898) .................... 439
Of No Benefit to Woman: She is a Far Greater Power Without Suffrage by Mary A. F. M'Intire ............... 441
Of What Benefit to Woman? (1910) .............................................................................................................. 449
Opinions of Eminent Persons Against Woman Suffrage ............................................................................. 456
Ought Women to Vote? From The Guidon of Manchester, N.H. ................................................................ 464
Paper by Newton Fiero at Anti-Suffrage Meeting (1894) ............................................................................. 468
Petition From Citizens of Newport, N.H. ..................................................................................................... 472
Petition From the New York State Association Opposed to Woman Suffrage (1918) ................................ 478
Petition From the Women Voters Anti-Suffrage Party of New York to U.S. Senate (1917) ........................ 479
Petition From the Women Voters Anti-Suffrage Party of New York to U.S. Senate (1918) ........................ 480
Petition From the Women Voters Anti-Suffrage Party of New York to U.S. Senate (1918) ........................ 481
Protest Against Woman Suffrage: Address Delivered by Rev. Father Walsh ............................................... 484

H. J. Res. 1.

# Sixty-sixth Congress of the United States of America;

## At the First Session,

Begun and held at the City of Washington on Monday, the nineteenth day of May, one thousand nine hundred and nineteen.

## JOINT RESOLUTION

Proposing an amendment to the Constitution extending the right of suffrage to women.

*Resolved by the Senate and House of Representatives of the United States of America in Congress assembled (two-thirds of each House concurring therein),* That the following article is proposed as an amendment to the Constitution, which shall be valid to all intents and purposes as part of the Constitution when ratified by the legislatures of three-fourths of the several States.

"ARTICLE ——————.

"The right of citizens of the United States to vote shall not be denied or abridged by the United States or by any State on account of sex.

"Congress shall have power to enforce this article by appropriate legislation."

*F. H. Gillett*
Speaker of the House of Representatives.

*Thos. R. Marshall*
Vice President of the United States and
President of the Senate.

# HIDDEN FROM HISTORY

## A Defense of the President and Congress of the United States against Suffrage and Socialist Canards

*Washington, January 3, 1918.*

*To Members of the House of Representatives of the United States.*

*Gentlemen:*

We have learned that **suffragists and socialists**, who desperately desire to secure the passage of the Federal suffrage amendment and thus **destroy the right of each State to settle this question for itself by popular vote**, have resorted to the lowest political methods.

**They have insulted President Wilson**, the most distinguished **friend** of woman suffrage, because his well-known preference for the State **referenda** plan does not satisfy them.

They are spreading and syndicating throughout the country **the canard that the President sent a secret representative to see Miss Alice Paul while she was in jail**, who, they say, promised her that:

> "Although the President would **not mention suffrage in his message at the opening** of Congress, he would **make it known to the leaders of Congress** that **he wanted it passed and would see that it passed.**"

This canard was first put out in a public statement by **Miss Maud Younger**, at the recent "**pickets**" **meeting** in Washington. It has been circulated industriously by the SOCIALISTS; Victor Berger, editor of the Milwaukee Leader, featuring it as a proof of "**effective picketing**" and declaring that it shows that the President "**secretly favors**" the amendment. (Editorial, Milwaukee Leader, December 18, 1917.)

It is also being stated by suffragists here in Washington that this "**secret**" assistance will take the form of a **request from the President that opponents** of the amendment **remain at home on the day it is voted upon in the House of Representatives, January 10.**

These allegations that the President of the United States would "**secretly favor**" by such means suffrage methods **he has publicly condemned** are **insults to his character** which this organization cannot allow to go unchallenged.

President Wilson has **repeatedly asserted** that he believes that **it is a matter to be fought out in the individual States.** He won his election on this platform against a Federal amendment candidate. He taught this doctrine for many years to **thousands** of students of American Government. No one has defended **the rights of the States** in this connection more ably than **President Wilson**. In his textbook, entitled, "State and Federal Governments of the United States," extracts from which are submitted herewith for your consideration, Mr. Wilson has **clearly and conclusively stated his position on this question.**

The canards that suffragists and socialists are circulating **about the President** in this matter are not only an **insult to him**, but **to every Member of Congress**.

We therefore deem it our duty to bring these outrageous insinuations to the attention of the President and Congress.

We believe that they will be **refuted in the House on January 10th by a large and emphatic vote against the Federal suffrage amendment, at which every Member will be in his seat and vote his convictions.**

*Respectfully,*

THE NATIONAL ASSOCIATION OPPOSED TO WOMAN SUFFRAGE,
Mrs. James W. Wadsworth, Jr., President.

## A HELP OR A HINDRANCE?

There is no wise woman who does not want her sex to have the best opportunities that life can give, the freest and highest education, the widest choice of occupations, the largest social activity, the truest culture, the most commanding and permanent influence that are possible in the world to-day. Young or old, rich or poor, educated or ignorant, we are all women, and we want what is best for all womanhood.

Do you want the ballot? If so, why? and if not, why not? It is a real question and an important one, a question on which every thinking woman to-day ought to have an opinion, and know what her reasons for that opinion are. It is well for you to ask yourself, seriously, do I want the ballot? and would it be a hindrance or a help to me as a working-woman?

Suppose we begin with a few facts about that great body to which any girl may be proud to belong, that army of intelligent, conscientious, capable workers who are so necessary in every field of occupation to-day. Do you know that out of the 369 groups of industries in the United States only nine have no women employed in them? There are about 2,000,000 working-women in the United States, (of these, by-the-way, more than half are in the New England and Middle States) and their number increases steadily every year. Besides these two million, more than a million and a half women are employed in domestic service, and half a million more are teachers, thus making about four million in all.

This great army of two million workers, is not detached from the ordinary life of womankind. Ninety-five per cent. of the two million live at home, and the average length of their outside occupations is less than five years. The average woman works only from about eighteen to twenty-two years of age, after which she returns to domestic life, usually to preside over a home of her own. During these years of outside work, half of the workers give their earnings to the home life, and nearly two-thirds not only work at their regular occupations, but assist in the housework at home. Working girls seldom change from one occupation to another, and are peculiarly steady and conscientious in their work. Their wages, however, are less than those of men, except in piece-work, where they often earn more than men can. In some fields of occupation, they have already driven men out, and are rapidly displacing them in others.

"But," you say, "what have these facts—most of which I know already—got to do with the ballot?" Suppose we take them separately and see.

What does the equal suffragist promise that the ballot will give the working-girl? A larger field of labor? well, 360 occupations already conquered, out of a possible 369, does not seem to need much improvement, does it? More permanent work? but does the woman who only works five years on an average require more permanent employment? These two promises, surely, we need not consider seriously.

The great question of wages, however, is a different thing. The suffragists make a point of assuring us that the ballot will raise wages, shorten hours and equalize conditions; and if this were true, the ballot would certainly be a good thing for the working-woman. But, is it true? is it backed up by facts? or is it just a mere catchword? The only way is to study up the facts, and see for ourselves.

It is hardly worth while, here, to set forth the laws of supply and demand, the position of woman as a new economic factor, etc. Political economy is a dry subject; so, beyond the mere statement of the acknowledged fact that the supply of women ready for work is greater than the demand for their labor, and that woman, as a mere factor in the field of occupation will take some time yet to find her right place and her fair wage, we will not consider these points. One thing, however, may be affirmed that voting can no more influence supply and demand than it can change the phases of the moon. When there are two men to every job, wages are low, whether men vote against the lowering of wages or not; and when there is only one man to two jobs, he can ask his own price and get it. And another thing is also certain, that where untried labor comes into the field against skilled labor, skilled labor will always command the high wage, and unskilled labor sink to the lower one.

Just think about it. If you go into a factory or a store as a beginner, say, at sixteen years of age, you do not look at that work at all in the same way that a boy of sixteen would do. You only work because, at present, you have no necessary home duties, and you want the money for your support or for the support of others at home. No girl works outside her home for the pleasure of it, or deliberately expects and hopes to work thus all her life long. She expects, and she is right to expect, for the vast majority of all working-girls realize this expectation, to work only for a limited term of years, until she has a home of her own, or until the present necessity for her wage-earning is over. It would be a most unnatural and wrong state of things, and a peril to any community, for such an immense number of girls, in the flower of their youth, to renounce the thought of marriage and devote themselves absolutely to their work. For this obvious reason, no working-girl does or can, or ought to, enter any field of occupation on the same level as a working-man, because marriage does not stop a man's work but rather stimulates him to become more skilful in it, and therefore, though he also expects to marry, he is a permanent worker from the beginning.

The average age of the working-woman is only twenty two. Few remain after twenty-five, and fewer still after thirty. In other words the woman-worker must either choose a trade which can be learned quickly and such trades are always poorly paid, or she must drop out just as she becomes skilful, thus losing her only chance of a high wage. Don't you see that all the voting in the world cannot make a high wage for woman's work, if it is temporary and unskilled? On the other hand, when a girl remains in higher grades of work, after becoming skilled, as in piece-work, for instance, she earns a wage equal to and sometimes larger than a man's. I know, and I daresay you do, many a girl who makes larger wages than her father does in the same mill, and who is surer of her position, as long as she wants to keep it, than he is. And in trades where men are principally employed, but where there is overcrowding and the grade of work required is not especially skilled, wages and conditions are no better, and often are far worse, than in the case of women.

The best illustration of the whole thing can be found in the case of the million and a half of women engaged in domestic service. Here is a vast class of women, generally foreigners, often uneducated, entirely without organization or influence, whose wages are yet raised, year after year, without a struggle. Why? The answer is evident, there are never enough good domestic servants to supply the demand, and therefore even the unskilled emigrant gets a high wage at once. The plain fact is that the ballot has no more connection with wages than the Statue of Liberty has with the tides in New York Harbor.

But suppose, just for the sake of argument, that voting was a sort of miraculous process, and could work the impossible wonders the suffragists promise. Suppose that the ballot, in the hands of working-women, meant higher pay for skilled work, shorter hours, longer vacations, and yet more wages. Suppose all these fairy tales were true, how would the working-girl gain control of the ballot? Could she grasp the talisman, or would it remain tantalizingly outside her reach?

In the first place, the majority of working-girls could

not vote. They are too young. More than half are under twenty-one, the legal voting age at present. Even if eighteen were fixed as a voting age for women there would yet be many who could not vote. And the remainder would not be a large enough body, for the proportion of working women to women in general, as shown by the last United States census, is only one in ten—to make even the smallest impression upon politics unless they were closely organized, well officered, and all of one mind as to what should be done. It would take a tremendous amount of determined work and steady perseverance to organize such a party, and each member would have to give her leisure to it. The closest organization, the most arduous work, the largest expenditure of time and thought would be necessary to form and guide a Working-Woman's Party. It must have its primaries, its delegates, its conventions, its candidates, its district leaders and workers, and, naturally, its expenses. It would mean a great deal of hard work for both leaders and members, and it would be so small, in comparison with other political organizations, that it would never be an appreciable factor in a general election. The ordinary women's vote, nine time as large, would overshadow it completely, and it could not command the needed influence to accomplish the hoped for results, even if the ballot could bring them.

Even if it could bring them! Some of them if we will stop and think about it, have come already, without the ballot. A girl employee has the right to be paid where a man's claim must wait. A married woman's earnings are her own property, her husband's must be shared with her. The hours of labor for women have already been restricted by law, while men's are not. Girls in stores must be provided with seats, and given a certain length of time to eat their noonday meal. The wages of a wife cannot be attached for her husband's debts. If any employer fails to pay the wages due to a woman, up to $50, not only is none of his property exempt from execution, but he is liable to be imprisoned without bail. No woman can be arrested in a civil action, or held by an execution, unless it is clearly shown that she has committed a wilful injury to person or property, or is in contempt of court. It would be hard to mention any injustice to women that the law has not tried to prevent, as far as such injustice lies within the power of law. But the trouble is that law cannot help most of life's problems. The majority of voters have wives, sisters and daughters, and are anxious as to their welfare. As far as the ballot can help woman, it is helping her now, though cast only by man in her behalf. It is because the ballot cannot help her in certain directions, and against certain economic laws, that she continues to struggle with low wages and overcrowded trades.

The voter would help his wife, his sisters, his daughters, if he could but, alas! he cannot even help himself by his vote to steadier work or a better living. Recognizing this powerlessness of the ballot, he has organized instead, the Labor Union, and the Labor Unions, with all their mistakes, are far better and more available channels of influence than the voting-booths. In several cases they have succeeded in raising the wages of women to a level with those of men; and if a woman is to give time and energy, she had better spend it in the promotion of such organizations among women than in a fruitless struggle for political power. The working-girls' clubs are also a splendid force for good, and time is never wasted in joining and working in them. But the ballot, which has never yet raised wages for men, and never will for women, is a delusive light which is not worth while to follow. Equal suffrage has not raised the pay of women workers in Colorado, during its three years of trial there, nor in Wyoming, where it has been in force for a quarter of a century; a fact which its advocates agree to ignore, but which is convincing to any intelligent mind.

In fact, instead of being a help, the ballot, in several ways, might become a decided hindrance. Many laws have already been made, as we have seen, to protect women. Would men continue to make laws which discriminate in favor of women, if women had the vote? It would be only natural for them to say, " You asked for the vote so that you could arrange better things for yourselves; now that you have the vote, use it, and do not trouble us to legislate for you. Your vote gives you an equal chance and we are no longer responsible." In that case, the working-girl's chance would be a poor one indeed.

And, above all, we must remember that a vote is a very poor and mechanical substitute for true womanly influence. The girl who only has the power in the world represented by one vote out of 26,000,000 is a cipher indeed; while the intelligent and womanly girl who influences all those who know her is a queen in her own right. Do you suppose a vote would have added anything to Martha Washington, or rendered Mrs. Cleveland a whit more popular? The women of America, without a vote among them, abolished slavery. The great temperance movement of to-day, which grows stronger and spreads wider every hour, is the work of women with no aid from the ballot. If we were all the right kind of women, thoughtful, wise, loving, helpful, striving to understand and do the best things, the world would move onward as fast as we could lead. The ballot is only a hindrance to such progress, for it tempts the weak and useless woman to think that it would give her power in an easy an irresponsible way.

No! true womanhood does not need the ballot to influence the world. And the working-woman is not an abstract woman, one cut off from normal, womanly life, no longer restricted by its natural limitations, or out of sympathy with its sphere of love and home. She is just a woman, who, for awhile, happens to be working outside the home, but who, later, will be a home-maker and a home-lover. Votes, politics, office-holding, primaries and ward meetings, the pulling of wires, the making of speeches, the manipulation of candidates, what useful wife and mother has room in her life for these? what active, hard-working, home-loving girl can make a place for them in her busy existence? Education? yes, let a woman strive for the best and most of it that she can get; it will make her home brighter and her life more of an influence upon her husband and her children. Social opportunity? yes, the more of it the better. Choice of occupations? yes, while she is working, let her work be as congenial and as wide as possible. All these are good; but political activity is a barren gain, it cheapens womanhood in a vain struggle for the wrong kind of influence. As in England centuries ago the "King-maker" was far greater than the kings whom he made and unmade, so woman, with the training of voters in her hands, is greater than the voter, if she but knew it. She supplements man best by keeping in her own higher, more disinterested sphere of love, sympathy, purity and righteousness in daily life and thought, and leaving him to translate that influence into action upon the world outside, into whose work she never throws herself except from necessity, and from which she returns gladly, as soon as she can, into the higher life of the home again. "Every wise woman," said the greatest of ancient sages, "buildeth her house, but the foolish plucketh it down with her hands." It is the foolish woman, to-day, and not the wise one, who asks for the ballot, that she may pull down, with her own hands, the protection and the sanctity of her womanhood and her home.

PRISCILLA LEONARD.

*Printed by the New York State Association Opposed to the Extension of the Suffrage to Women.*

# A LEAF FROM HISTORY.

In July, 1848, Elizabeth Cady Stanton, Lucretia Mott, Martha C. Wright and Ann McClintock issued an unsigned call for a convention, which was " to consider the social, civil and religious condition and rights of woman." They framed a "Declaration of Sentiments" for " the inauguration of a rebellion such as the world had never seen before." This " Declaration " travestied the Declaration of Independence, summing up, after many verbose statements, their sentiments in these words:

" The history of mankind is a history of repeated injuries and usurpations on the part of man toward woman, having in direct object the establishment of an absolute tyranny over her."

From that date until the year 1894 the women suffragists, acting in accord with the " Declaration " and its eighteen grievances, beseiged Legislatures to give women the right of suffrage, this being the crux of their argument: That women had an inalienable right to the ballot, and were subject to taxation without representation.

No great opposition was made to the suffrage clamor.

Legislators treated the annual visit of the women suffragists as a sort of " field day," and the women who were opposed made no outward sign, resting their cause in the common sense and justice of the men who made the laws of the State to govern and protect alike male and female citizens.

In the winter of 1893 Miss Susan B. Anthony, in an address made in Albany, N. Y., stated that at the Constitutional Convention, which was to be held in May, 1894, there would be an amendment demanded striking out the word " male " from the Constitution, thereby allowing women to vote; and, that in order to effect this, the women suffragists were going into every town, village and city of the State to secure the names of 1,000,000 women over 21 years of age to a petition for such an amendment.

In answer to a question as to whether all women of the State desired the suffrage, she said: " They do not oppose it."

It seemed then, to the women who had hitherto been silent, that this was a time when they must, of necessity, make themselves heard. In Massachusetts there had been for years a silent organization which worked to defeat the suffragists, and which was ready to take open action if the New York State women should decide to do likewise. In Illinois there was the same feeling.

Brooklyn, N. Y., took the initiative, and following in line, on the 27th of April, 1894, a meeting of women opposed to woman suffrage was held at the residence of Mrs. John V. L. Pruyn, 13 Elk street, Albany, N. Y. An organization was perfected, and the work of securing signatures to a protest against striking the word "male" from the State Constitution was undertaken. In less than a month more than 8,000 names of women over 21 years of age were enrolled upon the protest, which was presented to the Convention on June 12th.

It is of interest to note that the suffragists failed in their effort to secure 1,000,000 names to their petition, though every county in the State was canvassed during the year preceding the Convention, by women engaged for the purpose, some of whom were paid for each signature procured. In one town there were more names sent in than there were women and girls in the town. Rooms were secured in the Capitol, and a banner flung out: "Come in and sign the 1,000,000 petition." Finally men were urged to sign, messenger boys getting much amusement filling up the pages, one lad signing "Mike Dolan, Paris, England." It was claimed that two labor organizations had sent in 250,000 names through the votes of their respective secretaries, and that the secretary of the W. C. T. U. had signed for its membership of 75,000, though many persons of each organization were known to be opposed to woman suffrage. Their petitions as presented to the Convention were published in the daily press, and with the foregoing additions only reached 397,055 names. It is well to bear in mind that, at that time, there was a population of over 7,000,000 in the State.

After full and free discussion before the committee appointed by President Choate, on the proposed sufferage amendment, the Constitutional Convention decided that: "Until it is shown that woman may become a politician without losing something of the precious charm of her personality, and that the State may exact her services in that capacity without imperiling its stability and tranquility," and "until the time also come when party politics shall be so pure that the presence of women at the polls would not be incongruous; and party feeling so subdued that opposition from those we love could be freely tolerated by our better natures," the experiment of woman suffrage should not be tried and so refused to submit the question to the people.

# HIDDEN FROM HISTORY

The anti-suffragists went back to the duties laid aside for the while and forgot that there was an opposing faction.

But that faction is noted for its tenacity of purpose, and so at the next legislative session they appeared with the amendment framed as a concurrent resolution of the Legislature and asked that it be passed.

To defeat this the women of Albany, who had been active in opposition, reorganized as a permanent association, at a meeting held at the residence of Mrs. J. V. L. Pruyn, on May 14, 1895. At this meeting a board of officers, consisting of a president, first vice-president, secretary, treasurer, an executive committee of seven, and 100 vice-presidents were elected, with a membership classified as sustaining, active, and associate. The name adopted was: " The Anti-Suffragists of Albany and Vicinity."

At a meeting held subsequently it was decided to work in unison with the New York and Brooklyn Associations, as an auxiliary to a State Organization, the field of work for Albany being the Third Judicial District of the State.

But Albany did not confine her efforts to the State of New York alone. In unison with other associations she sent a representative both to the Republican National Convention held at St. Louis in 1896, and to the Democratic National Convention held at Chicago the same year, to oppose the introduction of a suffrage plank in the National Platforms. Later the Albany Society joined in sending at the request of many women of the State of South Dakota and of the State of Washington, a representative to help the resident women defeat amendments to their State Constitutions which would force suffrage upon them. The amendments were lost in both States.

In this way the women of the other States of the Union came to know of the organized opposition to woman suffrage; and, as a result, many requests were made for information and literature.

Since the organization of the Albany Association 153,050 leaflets have been published and sent out through the energy and liberality of its honorary president. Thousands of personal letters have been written, and hundreds of letters have been published through the courtesy of the press. Later, a request came from the libraries for literature on the subject, and for that reason the honorary president has caused the leaflets published by the Society to be bound in book form and placed in libraries where the public may have access to them.

# A Moment with RUSKIN.

"In a recent conversation with Ruskin, touching "our Republican experiment," as he was pleased to call the United States, he said, "The fact of women being elected to mayoralties in Kansas makes me think of certain African tribes that exalt their women into warriors—you want your women to fight your political battles?"

"You evidently hold the same opinion on the subject of equal rights that you expressed some years ago," interposed a listener.

"What did I say?—really I have forgotten."

"You replied to a correspondent, saying: "You are certainly right as to my views respecting the female franchise, so far from wishing to give votes to women I would fain take them away from most men."

"Truly that was a sensible answer. My respect for woman is too great to force upon her increased responsibilities. Then, as for restricting the franchise with men, I am of the firm conviction that no man should be allowed to vote that does not own property, or who cannot do considerable more than read and write. The voter makes the laws, and why should the laws regulating the holding of property be made by a man who has no interest in property beyond a covetous desire, or why should he legislate the education when he possesses none? Then again, women do not bear arms to protect the state."

"But what do you say to Mrs. Carlock, who answers, that inasmuch as men do not bear children they have no right to vote, going to war, possibly being necessary and possibly not, but the perpetuity of the state demanding that someone bear children?"

"The lady's argument is ingenious but lacks force, when we consider that the bearing of arms is a matter relating to statecraft, while the baby question is Dame Nature's own and is not to be regulated even by the sovereign."

Apply for more papers to Anti-Suffrage Association, 13 Elk Street, Albany, N. Y.

# HIDDEN FROM HISTORY

# A SUFFRAGE LESSON.

The Pittsburg "Chronicle" of January 19, 1897, contains the following:

Now that the women of Colorado have the ballot, they are wondering whether it is worth much. A Colorado woman is quoted as saying:

"The great advantage of suffrage is that it teaches women that they are not one bit better than men. We've sat for years and told men how corrupt their politics were, and men have smiled up at us and told us how superior we are and how we should have suffrage. We've had a large and enthusiastic surprise party. We women have found that our politics are just as corrupt as men's politics and they're just a little trickier. We've been at it two years, and we're scheming and making combinations and doing all the very things we've been finding fault with the men for doing all these years.

"The women of the better classes are getting disgusted and drawing out of politics, just as our men have done, and the women of the other classes have become enthusiastic and have gone into politics just as their mankind have done."

Well, Well, Well! This is most suprising reading. So, woman suffrage does not bring all the reforms, the joy and the purity that were to be expected from the roseate views which were expounded by advocates of giving women the right to vote.

Instead of exalting politics it seems according to this authority, that woman suffrage has developed even a trickier phase of politics than was known when the game was played exclusively by men.

This is very sad. If it be true, it is manifest that the persons who acted as though they were inspired when they arose to advocate granting women the divine right to vote were not inspired at all, but were singularly at fault in all their vaticinations.

Man is inclined to place woman on a pedestal and there adore her, but if women will persist in going about predicting that granting them the privilege to vote will effect the world's regeneration and then come out when the privilege is accorded with the confession that politics under woman's influence has gone from bad to worse, it is feared that man will lose that absorbing affection he has always felt for the other sex and will regard it as composed of very weak and very foolish sisters.—*Albany Evening Journal, January 27, 1897.*

# A Word of Appreciation to Mrs. Pruyn.

The Woman's Association opposed to the extension of suffrage to women, of the Third Judicial District of the State of New York, sincerely appreciating the invaluable services of one who for years has been the foremost leader in the cause of anti-suffrage, whose enthusiastic energy and rare ability have been chiefly responsible for the uniform success and repeated achievements of the association in the interest of womanhood and the home, desires to express its great indebtedness to its honorary president, Mrs. John V. L. Pruyn, of Albany.

Mrs. Pruyn was the president and active leader of the association from 1894 to 1900. During that time she was the moving spirit in the work, ingeniously planning many aggressive measures that were carried out effectively under her personal supervision. The results thus achieved had great influence not only in this State, but also in nearly every other State in the Union where the woman suffrage question was pending.

When in 1894 it became necessary for the home-loving women of this State to demonstrate to the Constitutional Convention that they resented the efforts of female agitators to thrust women into the political arena, it was under Mrs. Pruyn's guidance that our association enrolled over 8,000 members in a single month.

Again, when it became apparent that the woman suffragists would besiege the Republican National Convention at St. Louis in June, 1896, to obtain a declaration favorable to female suffrage in the party platform, it was Mrs. Pruyn's idea to discount the suffragists by sending to the convention a representative of the anti-suffrage association to protest.

The protest was heeded. It was as one of the leading suffragists present at the convention said: "A protest more forceful than the protest of a thousand men;" and continued, " it will require years to regain the lost ground."

The plan of the suffragists being frustrated at St. Louis, where the Republican party refused to give the desired recognition, the suffragists, a few weeks later, went to the Democratic National Convention in Chicago to urge the adoption of a woman suffrage plank for the Democratic platform. But it was again due to Mrs. Pruyn's forethought that a representative of the anti-suffragists was present to protest.

The result of this opposition was electric. Immediately the attention of the press was attracted, and the fact was heralded throughout the land that an effective organization had been perfected among women opposed to the extension of suffrage. Thus women in many States were roused to join the movement, and the cause of anti-woman suffrage became a matter of national concern.

It was Mrs. Pruyn's thought and her determination that sent a representative to the far western States of South Dakota and Washington to assist the women there in defeating woman suffrage amendments.

It has been due to Mrs. Pruyn's never-failing watchfulness that woman suffrage bills in State legislatures throughout the Union have been discovered and obstructed year after year. She has turned the searchlight of publicity upon them, and by distributing thousands of leaflets and sending hundreds of personal letters has awakened both men and women to a full knowledge of the many objections to such legislation. During this campaign of education there were nearly 100 suffrage defeats in about two-thirds of the States of the Union. No doubt the literature sent out by Mrs. Pruyn had much to do with the results.

No one save those who have been in actual touch with the work will ever know how great and how wide-spread has been her influence. She has been the most potent and vigorous apostle the anti-suffrage cause has ever had, and her enforced withdrawal from active work by order of her physician is a great lost to the anti-suffrage movement. Being devoted to the cause from a high sense of her duty to womanhood, she has not only contributed her time and her best thought to the work, but also has given the principal financial support to the association, using her own private means in a hundred different ways for the advancement of the work.

The members of the association, who have had the honor and pleasure of working under Mrs. Pruyn as leader, desire to give this testimony in recognition of her invaluable services to the cause; and to add an expression of keen regret that ill-health makes it necessary for her to sever her active connection with the association.

Mrs. William J. Wallace,
*President pro. tem.*
Mrs. William Bayard Van Rensselaer,
*Secretary.*
Mrs. Joseph Gavit,
*Treasurer.*
Mrs. W. Winslow Crannell,
*Chairman Executive Committee.*
Mrs. William Cassidy,
Mrs. J. Howard King,
Miss Lucy A. Plympton,
Mrs. Joel R. Reed,
Mrs. Frederick Townsend,
Mrs. William O. Stillman,
*Executive Committee.*

Albany, N. Y., April, 1901.

# HIDDEN FROM HISTORY

### BULLETIN No. 19

# A World Without God

---

Human society is constructed along divine and irrefragable principles; Socialism is man-made and proposedly takes no account of God's word or work. It is no wonder, therefore, that there is a perpetual and insoluble clashing between them. As for the latter being an improvement upon the former, that is absurd. In fact, it does not pretend to be so much an evolution as a revolution. An upsetment of all the ways of creation and a substitution of what the so-called philosophers of the eighteenth century asserted to be a better scheme.

It was more scientific, they said, that all men, all women also, should be equal, with equal duties, equal rights, equal opportunities, that one should produce as much as another, enjoy as much as another, and each and every one act with perfect freedom; yet not wholly for himself, but in an equal way and degree for the community at large, and this not by compulsion, but because of an innate sense of justice. That women should produce as much of national property as men, have the same liberty in kind and degree, should act, in fact, as though sex were one of the common properties and privileges of mankind, with no particular aim but that of pleasure, and that to it, child bearing was only an incidental drawback. The children being, however, of a certain sort of civic usefulness, the penalty of bringing them up and educating them should be turned over as soon as nature would permit to the State. whose duty it should be to assimilate and subordinate them to the new system of human existence, the product of the antecedent revolution, or so much of it as could not possibly be brought about by previous manipulation of the public mind. The parent has, therefore, in the new scheme. no preponderance over any other citizen; nor any more influence in the brand new government.

This leaves the way clear for every man and woman to be equally the possessor of the common property of the State, and the non-worker, and the full worker, the man or woman without capacity, the unit with only half capacity and the full ambitious soaring soul, if any such exists under Socialism, are all on a dead level of circumstance and opportunity. Variety there would be none. If two opposing opinions were held by two differing geniuses, there might or there might not be a battle, depending upon whether the socialization of such units were more or less complete. If two men had laid admiring eyes upon the same woman, or, let us say, two women had desired the same man at least for a season, or as a temporary test of rivalry, the anomalous "State" of which we hear so much and so weighty mention made, would be called upon to decide the question. Any law bearing upon the subject would be an infringement of personal liberty and, therefore, not to be tolerated.

Opinions, women, that perhaps is a fair sample of the most prominent causes of difference in the Socialistic government if it were to be adopted as a whole, by our race, as it is now constituted. At any rate, all are to be equally useful to the community, all equally receiving from it equal means of welfare and happiness. All made free of poverty with its blessings, with riches and their temptations, the whole race exempt from sin and sorrow, from want and woe, by the simple fact of equally good fortune and perfect liberty of action bestowed upon them by the State.

It seems to some old fashioned people, born before Socialism was widely known, that this "State" which is to have so much thrust upon it in the new and somewhat mysterious condition of things, is not unlike what children in the old time were taught to think of as God, wanting simply omnipotence and the moral and spiritual element. For it is to be understood that no good Socialist believes in God, or His power and providence over the world.

It would have been better for the philosophers if they could have had a brand new world on which to exploit their scheme of government, instead of having to exhibit it upon this same old world which has been spinning around the sun ever since chance or primal force, or whatever power it was that first set it in motion. It seems to have had some unchangeable principles impressed upon it which it is difficult for a beginner's first attempt to set aside, no matter how new and well devised it may be. One of these is sex. Socialists make little of it, as we have seen, but somehow, when one comes to work with it and make it over to meet the wants and ways of the new science, it presents its difficulties. For instance, how is the work of men and women to be made the same, or even equal in the bearing and rearing of those children who are so necessary to the continuance of the race, even after revolution shall have made all government so scientific and so simple? This is a question which men scarcely think it necessary to ask at present or they answer it by saying that women will be given all the political privileges which accrue to men, and as for the rearing of children, the State will assume all that responsibility. But still the intuitive women will be reluctant, and the educated women will ask questions. It may be conceded that a revolution will sometimes overturn the forms of human government, but scarcely any force known to man will change the settled laws of nature and of all the processes of natural evolution, that of child bearing, is the most fixed and unchangeable, and child bearing which comes before child rearing, is the most indispensable and inalienable work of woman. If, in the political world, women are to receive equal consideration with men, what service will men give to the State, which will compensate women for the daily cares, the night watchings, the long continued and often painful self-sacrifices of the prospective mother? We do not ask that man shall bear half the children, since that is a privilege which nature has peremptorily denied him. In fact, we should, having the best good of the race at heart, hardly permit this, lest it be found that, with his coarse and strong nature, he might not be worthy; but we do wish to be told what sacrifice he can possibly make, greater or worthier than that which present day civilization requires of him—namely, that he should be the faithful and untiring helper and protector of the woman who is spending her days and nights bringing his successor into being, and so renewing the life of the world. This is the old fashioned interpretation of sex. What has the new system of the philosophers to offer when it has achieved its revolution that is more sensible, more straightforward, of greater benefit to man, to woman, to the world as it was made in the beginning, than this, even though this simple system perpetuates the home, authorizes private property, makes political duties unsuitable to woman and upsets Socialism generally?

We women "pause for a reply"!

We maintain that Woman Suffrage is ever an element of weakness rather than strength to a State, for this reason:

Because it is an injustice to require of woman double duty, namely, the doing of her own and man's duty as well. If, for instance, she bears the warriors and then, as suffrage claims, either goes to war herself or does some other duty required by war, she is doing double duty. If she does not do this, where does her "equality" come in?

Doing a **commensurate** duty is not the demand of Socialism or woman suffrage, but of the old idea of sex created "in the beginning" when woman was made inalienably the "mother" of the race, and had her own duties given her which were from the first quite unlike those of men. That she should do both these duties was never expected nor required of her. Such injustice cannot possibly be the foundation of a stable State. Suffragists declare that when women vote there will be no more wars, but woman has ever been a good fighter— by proxy.

If women bear all the children as nature inevitably demands of them, and do half the work of the world besides, as Socialism requires, that again is a manifest injustice, which is even now resulting in a serious evil. When 6,000,000 of women and girls do the work which it belongs to an equal number of men and boys to do, all in pursuit of "equal work and equal pay"—though they never get the latter—at least that number of males are thrown out of employment. Homes thus become fewer and as statistics plainly prove, the children born of such homes are inferior, both mentally and physically; imbecility and general decrepitude increase alarmingly, and in the end ambition and incentive are taken from both men and women alike. The statistics of various of the States, notably of New York, have established this conclusion. If women are to keep up the standard of children, improving the race from generation to generation, the men must do the work which supplies the homes and carries on the enterprises of the world. Study and investigation prove that the original division of the labor of the sexes as ordained by the Maker of the world, is amply justified, even in this latter day, as opposed to the man-made schemes of Socialism.

Chicago, October, 1913.

Issued by Illinois Association Opposed to Woman Suffrage,

1523 Dearborn Avenue, Chicago

# HIDDEN FROM HISTORY

## Address Before Committee of New York Constitutional Convention by Francis M. Scott (1894)

At a meeting of the Committee on Suffrage of the New York Constitutional Convention, held at the Capitol in Albany, on Thursday, June 14, 1894, Mr. Francis M. Scott of New York city spoke as follows upon the amendment under consideration by the Committee, providing for the elimination of the word "male" from Article 11, Section 1, of the Constitution : —

I appear before this Committee as the spokesman of a large body of women resident in the county of New York, who are seriously and sincerely alarmed at the mere possibility that this Convention may be induced to take the first step toward the imposition upon the women of this State of new and onerous duties and responsibilities.

In the opinion of those who send me here, the experiment which you are asked to indorse would be a most dangerous one, not only for the State, but for woman herself, and they have therefore come forward most unwillingly, but in fulfillment of what they regard as an imperative duty, to protest publicly against so radical and revolutionary an amendment of our fundamental law, as would be implied in the unlimited extension of the suffrage to women.

It is proper at the outset that I should state as briefly as possible how it has happened that these women whom I represent, and who shrink from active and personal participation in public affairs, have, in apparent contradiction to their own professed principles and beliefs, been moved to take part in the public discussion of a question of this character.

The agitation for woman suffrage is no new matter in this country, and there are few of us present to-night who can remember the time when there were not some women, with active, restless minds, who clamored for the right to vote.

Never, until the present year, however, has the agitation for this extension of the suffrage made sufficient headway in this State to appear really dangerous, or to seem to warrant active opposition.

Early in the past winter, indeed almost as soon as the members of this Convention had been elected, certain very well known, very estimable, and very able ladies in the city of New York began to solicit petitions addressed to this Convention, asking it to recommend to the people an amend-

---

ISSUED BY MASSACHUSETTS MAN SUFFRAGE ASSOCIATION, 7A PARK ST., BOSTON.

2

ment to the first section of Article 11 of the Constitution, to consist of the elimination of the word "male" from that section.

At a time like the present, when the unrestful spirit of Socialism is abroad throughout the land, it is not surprising that they were able to attract to their support many men and women of acknowledged intellectual capacity, many of the women who have acquired a certain kind of prominence by their constant participation in all kinds of public discussion, some women, who by means of their husbands' wealth and their own social prominence had become well known by name in the community, and not a few of that always considerable body of people who constantly seek some change in the existing condition of affairs, and who, unthinkingly, believe that whatever is new must, for that reason alone, be progressive and desirable.

A large number of public and quasi-public meetings were held, many speeches were delivered, and pamphlets written, and a vast amount of newspaper prominence was obtained.

For a long time the suffragists, as they have come to be called, had the field to themselves,—the subject became the theme of discussion in drawing-rooms and over dinner-tables, and woman's suffrage became the "social fad" of the hour.

At length, only about three weeks before this Convention met, a few earnest and thoughtful women in the city of New York became aroused to the possible danger that unless some positive steps were taken to present the other side of the question the agitation in favor of the amendment might succeed by default. They realized how difficult it has become in these days for man to refuse to woman anything that she asks at his hands, and they feared that if this Convention heard only from the women who wished to participate in the politics of the State, it might be misled into the belief that these petitioners represented the sentiments of the women generally.

They also appreciated the fact that many of the advocates of female suffrage were women of signal ingenuity and ability, well primed with specious and plausible arguments, and that you gentlemen, having many matters of great importance to consider and act upon within a very limited time, were entitled to all possible assistance in reaching a conclusion upon a question of such vital importance, not only to womankind but to the community.

These women, therefore, who were opposed to the extension of the suffrage, and who felt very strongly and seriously

3

upon the subject, quietly prepared and circulated the protest which has been laid before you.

They refrained from imitating the methods adopted by the suffragists. They held no meetings, made no speeches, conducted no campaign.

They made no effort to impress the Convention by the mere number of names attached to their protest.

They accepted the signatures of no men, of no women under twenty-one years of age, of no aliens or non-residents of the State.

The results have exceeded their most sanguine expectations.

Notwithstanding the very short time allowed for the circulation of their protest, notwithstanding the unaggressive methods adopted by them, notwithstanding the reluctance of many women to take even so much part in public affairs as would be involved in signing a document of this character, they have already been able to lay before you from the city of New York the names of nearly as many women — within three or four thousand as many — as the suffragists have been able to present from that city after months of effort and an elaborate and aggressive campaign, and to-day I have brought to Albany the names of nearly a thousand women in addition to those already presented.

Nor had these women of New York, until within a very few days, contemplated the presentation of any oral arguments or addresses to you.

They have selected and sent to each member of the Convention some of the best literature upon the subject, in which the unanswerable arguments against female suffrage are ably and convincingly stated.

At the very last moment, however, it has been deemed due to yourselves that the side of the Anti-Suffragists, as they are termed, should be orally and formally presented to you.

I shall, however, be very brief in what I have to say, contenting myself rather with suggesting than elaborating a few of the most serious and apparent objections to the proposed amendment.

You will not accuse me of seeking to instruct you in your duties if I begin by quoting from the leading advocate of the amendment a sentence which, in my opinion, every member of this Convention should keep ever clearly in mind.

Mrs. Jacobi very justly said to you a few evenings ago that "this Convention is no revolutionary tribunal assembled to sap the foundation or overthrow the structure of existing society."

If, then, it can be made clear to you that this proposed amendment is essentially revolutionary; that its inevitable tendency must be to sap the foundations and overthrow the structure of existing society; that it would bestow apparent authority upon those who lack the power to enforce respect for their authority; that it would tend to destroy that interdependence of men and women for which nature has wisely provided, and which alone makes social development and progress possible; that it would be, to quote the report of Horace Greeley to the last Constitutional Convention, "An innovation revolutionary and sweeping, openly at war with the distribution of functions between the sexes as venerable and pervading as government itself, and involving radical transformations in social and domestic life," —

If you shall be convinced that this proposed amendment is of this character, then your duty with respect to it will be clear and easy.

What, then, is the proposition now laid before you and for which your approval is demanded?

It is that man, upon whom from time immemorial has devolved the duty of making and enforcing laws for the protection of society, shall now abdicate his position, and, potentially at least, turn over to the women the power of making the laws, reserving to himself only the responsibility of enforcing those laws which she may make, for while it is possible by amendment of the Constitution to confer upon women the power to make laws, a higher power than even this Convention has denied to her the power of enforcing the law.

I have said that the adoption of this amendment involves man's abdication of his right to make laws, and the statement is none too strong. The women always outnumber the men, and owing to the itinerant character of many of man's avocations the voting women would always largely outnumber the voting men.

It may be that we should seldom see all the women on one side of a political question, but we might easily do so, especially upon a question that appealed to sentiment or emotion, and so, as I have said, potentially at least, the proposed amendment involves the abdication by man of the power of government.

If that be not revolutionary in its tendencies, I know not what could be.

We have all become so accustomed to defer to woman —

to accede to her slightest wish — to extend to her all the privileges that her sex seems to demand — to share with her everything in which she desires to share, that we approach this question with a sort of half formed feeling that we may, in some way, be deemed ungracious and ungenerous if we refuse to admit her to participation in the suffrage.

But as upon man devolves the power to change the fundamental law of the State, so upon man rests the responsibility of exercising that power in the interest and for the benefit of the community, and it is his duty to approach the consideration of this question with all seriousness and without a trace of sentimentality.

Before the men of this State consent to surrender to women the responsibility for government and the power to change at will its fundamental law, before even we consent to share that power and responsibility with them, we are bound to be fully assured: —

*First:* That to do so will be of benefit to the whole community, and

*Second:* That there are certain definite benefits to be secured through woman's suffrage, which cannot otherwise be secured.

The great and insuperable objection to the extension of the suffrage to women is fundamental and functional.

It rests upon the difference that nature has established between men and women.

The basis of government is force; its stability rests upon its physical power to enforce its law. Since the world began no government has ever sustained itself for any length of time unless it controlled the physical force of the nation.

To imagine a government unbacked by the physical power necessary to enforce its laws is to imagine an anomaly, — which must soon develop into anarchy.

And it is for this reason that in all times and all countries the government has been intrusted to the men, because they alone are able, if necessary, to fight for its maintenance.

I am well aware that the advocates of female suffrage refuse to admit the truth of the proposition that the stability of government is dependent upon physical force; they cannot admit it, since to do so would be to admit the weakness of their cause. But it is true, nevertheless, and the more you think of it, the more you turn it over in your minds, the more you consider it from every side, the more certainly must you come to recognize its truth.

The suffragists characterize such a proposition as brutal

and revolting. They assert that with the advent of female suffrage human nature and the whole theory of government will change; that a government of reason will supersede a government of force; that bad men and women will consent to be persuaded to observe the law, and that it will no longer be necessary to compel them to do so.

Indeed, one of the most enthusiastic, and least logical, of the advocates of female suffrage ventures the assertion that already there is going on all over the civilized world "a continuous evolution in the form of government from the military type to the industrial type, — from government by involuntary coöperation to government by voluntary coöperation, from government by force to government by discussion."

Fine words indeed, but far at variance with the facts.

This is still the age of Bismarck; Europe still resembles nothing more than an armed camp; the echoes of the rebellion have not yet died away, and the pension list still remains to remind us that the government, even of pacific America, can, upon occasion, maintain itself by force.

If we are passing beyond the age when government must rely upon force for its stability, why do we go on year by year developing and improving our militia? why do we erect armories, and not debating halls, why in all the centres of population do we continue to organize and drill bodies of police?

Because we know — you and I know — that laws that cannot be enforced are worse than useless; that to make laws, and not provide at the same time the means of compelling obedience to them, would be to bring government into contempt, — to invite a condition of anarchy, — to endanger the safety of the individual, the sanctity of the home, the permanency of all our most cherished institutions; in short, to call down destruction upon the community that it is our duty to defend.

Herein, therefore, lies the fundamental difference between men and women; herein is to be found the ultimate and immutable reason why men should vote and women should not: it is simply because men can fight and women cannot.

This fundamental fact may be momentarily lost sight of in the clouds of emotional and sentimental rhetoric, but it is your duty as serious men, charged with a grave responsibility, to see to it that you do not permit your vision to be obscured by either emotion or sentiment. You are bound to look the facts in the face, and to legislate in the light of the facts, for the benefit of the whole community.

7

The interests of the community clearly require that the law should have behind it sufficient force to compel respect and observance.

We talk about the "strong arm of the law," — where would be the strength of that arm, if it were only that of weak, non-combative woman?

The reason why you and I, Mr. Chairman, are entitled to participate in the government, is not because we are intelligent, or educated, or able to pay taxes. We may be none of these and still be entitled to vote. It is because we have back of our votes the physical force necessary to enforce the laws we help to make.

But laws passed by the vote of women would have no force behind them, and consequently could be disregarded with impunity.

The reason why we have adopted, as the foundation of our political system, the rule that the will of the majority must prevail over that of the minority, is that both majority and minority recognize the fact that the majority can, if the minority rebel, force them into acquiescence.

But if the majority were all women and the minority were all men, this would not be true; the minority would soon cease to pay any regard to the will of the majority, and our whole theory of government would be overturned, and government itself cease to be government.

The exception to the general rule that man is combatant and woman non-combatant in no wise affects its application.

I concede that some women are physically able to fight, and that some men are not. I recognize the existence of mannish women, and of womanish men; but in discussing a question of this character we must consider the rule, rather than the exceptions, and even the most ardent suffragist will not venture to assert that the average woman equals in physical power the average man.

I repeat that the only question you have a right to determine is whether, in the interest of both the sexes, it would be conducive to good government to bestow the franchise upon women.

In considering that question you cannot close your eyes to the fact that the result of such a measure would practically be to bestow upon women power without responsibility, leaving to the men merely the responsibility without power.

I am sure that you must conclude that an experiment so revolutionary as that must endanger the welfare and very existence of the State.

8

If there were any advantages to accrue either to the State, or to woman herself, from the adoption of this amendment, which cannot be obtained without it, it might be your duty to weigh those advantages against the very many and palpable disadvantages.

If there be in fact any such advantages, the burden of pointing them out, and proving them, clearly rests upon the proponents of this radical measure.

I have read with some care all the obtainable essays and speeches in behalf of the amendment, and have sought in vain for the statement of a single certain, well defined benefit which is to result either to the State or to womankind. Glittering generalities, fantastic speculations, socialistic theories, populistic fallacies, I find plenty, but I find the statement of no wrong to woman that man has refused to redress, of no provision for her benefit that he has refused to make. I find no business or profession closed to her, no barrier interposed to her development and advance in any direction in which her sex permits her to direct her footsteps.

The law of this State already accords to women, as it rightly should, many special privileges and immunities, and has removed the trammels which in years gone by confined her freedom of action.

If there still be grievances to be redressed, of which we hear no mention, it is to the Legislature that appeal should be made, and until it has shown, as it has not yet done, an indisposition to act upon any reasonable complaint, there will be no necessity for an appeal to the ballot-box.

It is true that it is said by some theorists that the possession of the privilege of voting would enable working-women to command higher wages and greater consideration from their employers.

If that were true, it would seem that the possession of the franchise by men should by this time have raised to a satisfactory figure the wages of working-men. But we all know that it has not yet had that effect.

To-day the newspapers are filled with accounts of labor strikes all over the country, and every striker is a voter.

It is true that among male workers organization and co-operation have in many industries increased wages and lessened the hours of labor, but these concessions have been compelled because the male workers have possessed that which female workers do not and cannot possess, physical force to back up their demands. Practically all these concessions have been gained by strikes, or the fear of strikes, and

## 9

back of every strike is a possible resort to physical force; not perhaps sufficiently strong to defy the law for very long, but in many cases strong enough to make compromise cheaper and safer than battle.

But it is claimed that the exercise of the suffrage is a natural right inherent in every individual, and that to deny it to woman is to refuse arbitrarily that which she has a right to demand.

No proposition can be more at variance with the theory and history of political government. There is no such thing as an inherent natural right of an individual to vote. The right to say who may and who may not vote has always remained, and must always remain, with the State, and, in the nature of things, must be exercised with reference to the interest, not of the individual, but of the State.

In no proper or exact sense is the suffrage a right at all, or even a privilege.

It is a duty imposed upon the individual citizen because it is believed that its exercise by him will make for the best interest of the whole community.

And even if it were, as it is not, a personal, natural, individual right, it would still be perfectly competent and proper to deny it to woman, if by granting it to her the safety or stability of the State would be imperiled.

There is no individual right so sacred that the State may not, for the benefit of the whole community, deprive the individual of it.

The right of property, of liberty, of life itself may be destroyed if the interest of the community demands it. Private property may be taken for public use; the writ of habeas corpus may be suspended; men may be drafted into the army and sent, unwilling, to meet death upon the field of battle, if the welfare of the State — of the whole community — needs the sacrifice.

It is urged that to refuse the ballot to women is to render them liable to taxation without representation, and this is proclaimed as a gross injustice. To sustain this plea, the Committee has, as I understand, been furnished with elaborate tables purporting to show the amount of property in various countries owned by women and subject to tax.

But those who advance this argument exhibit their entire lack of understanding of the theories, both of taxation and of suffrage, and thus demonstrate that they, at least, are not yet prepared to participate in the suffrage.

The duty, or right if you prefer the word, of voting is in

10

no sense dependent in this State, and has not been for many years, upon the fact that the voter pays taxes or owns taxable property.

We have founded our government on manhood suffrage, and have conferred the voting power upon our male citizens, not because they own more or less property, or any property at all, but because they are men.

The women would, indeed, have a right to complain if we so far differentiated them from their husbands, their brothers, and their sons as to confer upon them alone a limited right of suffrage restricted by a property qualification.

Nor do we levy taxes as an equivalent for the suffrage, or even in proportion to the population. New York pays more taxes than Albany, not because New York contains a larger voting population than Albany, and is represented by more senators and assemblymen, but because the value of the taxable property in New York is greater than the value of the taxable property in Albany.

Taxes are the involuntary contributions levied and collected by the State for the protection, benefit, and advancement of the whole community. They are levied alike and in the same proportion upon the property of voters and non-voters, of aliens and citizens, of infants and adults, of men and women.

In short there is no relation whatever in fact or theory between taxation and the voting power.

I have already pointed out that the advocates of the amendment now before you have failed to indicate any positive definite advantage to be gained by the extension of the suffrage to women.

They refuse to assume the burden of proof which justly should rest upon their shoulders, and content themselves with arguing that no harm is likely to follow upon the proposed experiment.

They undertake to wage an affirmative contest by assuming a negative attitude.

But if needs be we are prepared to meet them upon this field.

The change in our political system contemplated by this amendment is the most far-reaching and radical that has ever been attempted in this State.

It is proposed to interject into the political life of this State a body of voters, larger than the whole number now entitled to vote, and composed, for this main part, of persons wholly untrained and inexperienced in public affairs, and who

## II

from the very nature of their duties and occupations have had, and will have, little opportunity to educate themselves in the many complex questions that must constantly arise in the government of a State like ours.

I beg you to remember that you must consider the probable effect of extending the franchise to all women, not alone to the exceptionally intellectual and brilliant women who have addressed you on this subject.

They constitute but a small fraction of their sex, and are by no means representative, intellectually, of the great body of women in this State — of the women who are engrossed by the cares and duties of maternity and wifehood — of the women who find their home duties so exacting that they have little time for political reading and discussion — of the women whose waking hours are fully and happily filled in rearing their children for the State, and keeping homes attractive for sons and husbands.

Should we not find the average woman divided into two classes? — one which, holding on to her home work, voted unintelligently and blindly, and the other gaining, perhaps, political intelligence at the cost of a neglected home.

Would the State derive benefit from either of those classes?

I know that I am referring to what is an unpopular fact with some female suffragists, when I speak of the home duties of woman as a possible barrier to her intelligent participation in politics. I have observed a disposition on the part of many of their writers and speakers to resent the suggestion that woman's especial duty in the world lies within the confines of the home.

But we must deal with the facts of life as nature has made them for us, and nature has imposed upon women certain burdens and duties, which we men cannot relieve them of, even by an amendment of the Constitution.

The chief of these is maternity, and upon the heels of maternity follows the care of children.

The very existence of the State depends upon the birth and care of children, and nature has devolved that function upon woman, while the law, following nature, has imposed upon man the duty of supporting and protecting the mothers and the children. Hence if any advocate of female suffrage is disposed to quarrel with the arrangement which relegates woman to the home duties, her quarrel must be with nature, — not with man.

And then there is another large class of women who cannot be left out of account, — the densely ignorant, who have neither the education, the mental capacity, nor the desire to acquire political intelligence. Will the extension of the suffrage to them make for the benefit of the community?

It is no answer to say that there is a correspondingly large body of ignorant and unintelligent men who are now entitled to vote. It surely cannot be seriously argued that there is less to be apprehended from two unintelligent votes than from one, — from two purchasable votes than from one, — yet that proposition must be accepted to justify the extension of the suffrage to such women as these.

And then we have, at least in the cities, that large class of unfortunate women who live outside the law, numbering from forty to sixty thousand in New York alone. Would municipal politics become cleaner and better if all these women were permitted to vote? — and you may be entirely sure that every one of them would vote — would be compelled to vote.

You gentlemen of the Constitutional Convention know already, better than most of us can, that there are yet many unsolved problems arising from universal manhood suffrage, especially with regard to the government of large cities.

That they will all be solved in time I presume none of us doubt.

Some of them you will doubtless solve, or at least suggest a solution for, before you adjourn.

Do you think that you would be fulfilling the trust imposed upon you by the people, if you were now to complicate and multiply these problems by doubling the suffrage, — by extending it to a large body of untrained and unready persons, wholly lacking in political experience?

I have endeavored to point out to you some of the dangers to the State and to woman herself which would attend the adoption of this amendment, and I have called your attention to the fact that no one has yet been able to indicate one single positive, certain advantage to either that may be expected to result from it.

I cannot help thinking, however, that all the discussion and consideration now given to the subject is premature.

Surely nothing but an overmastering public necessity could justify the imposition of political duties upon the women of this State, until they themselves have expressed a desire to undertake those duties.

No such necessity exists, and there is no evidence whatever that the majority of the women, or even a respectable minority, have the slightest desire for the ballot.

The total male vote of the State at the last presidential

13

election was over 1,300,000. We all know that a considerable number of men neglect their political duties, and refrain from voting at all, and we also know that the women exceed the men in number by an appreciable percentage. It is fair to assume, therefore, that this amendment would affect not less than 1,500,000 women.

Up to June 1, the whole number of women's signatures attached to petitions in favor of this amendment, including those from the city of New York, was barely 44,000, even allowing the claims of the suffragists, for I do not suppose that any one else has counted them, — not more than three per cent. of the whole number of women to be affected. And this, too, after months of a most vigorous and active campaign.

Does this serve to convince you that the women of this State are really anxious for the adoption of the amendment?

Is it worth while to spend valuable time upon the consideration of an amendment of this character, when only an insignificant minority of the women of the State care enough for it to ask for its adoption?

Will it not be time enough to consider the question seriously when we find at least a majority of the women asking for the imposition of the suffrage?

I beg that you will not be led away by the specious plea that it can do no harm to submit the question for determination by the people.

It would do much harm.

There will be other questions of really serious import to the welfare of the State, upon which the people will have to vote. It would be little short of a crime to distract their attention from the consideration of these subjects by laying before them a fanciful proposition, foredoomed to defeat.

You cannot shift your responsibility upon the shoulders of the people; to attempt to do so would be cowardly.

Your clear duty is to recommend, not merely to suggest, and unless you are convinced that the public interests require the adoption of this amendment, you cannot in good conscience dignify it with your indorsement.

I cannot more fittingly close than by again reminding you of the wise words of Mrs. Jacobi, that "this convention is no revolutionary tribunal assembled to sap the foundations or overthrow the structure of existing society.

# Extension of the Suffrage to Women

## ADDRESS

BY

## MRS FRANCIS M. SCOTT

DELIVERED BEFORE THE JUDICIARY COMMITTEE
OF THE NEW YORK SENATE

*APRIL 10, 1895*

ISSUED BY MASSACHUSETTS MAN SUFFRAGE ASSOCIATION,
7A PARK STREET, BOSTON.

WE women who are opposed to the Extension of the Suffrage have felt constrained to appear before this Committee, because we believe the legislative bodies to be under a misapprehension as to the attitude of the majority of our sex toward this, one of the most important social questions of the day.

Every extension of the suffrage has been a subject of grave debate, but the general feeling of a fundamental similarity between men has led to Universal Male Suffrage.

Now comes the question of the extension of the suffrage to women, and we can no more call it a *like* question to those earlier ones than we can call women *like* men. Equal they may be — different they certainly are. I shall very briefly touch upon the points which appeal most strongly to the body of women whom this committee represents.

The question of the *right* of suffrage is disposed of by the fact that the State *alone* holds the power to extend the suffrage, and she is only justified in extending it when her own best interests can be served thereby.

That the best interests of the State would be served by the extension of the suffrage to women, we do not believe. Think for a moment of giving the voting power to a majority (we women are in the majority, you know), unable to coerce a troublesome minority by physical power. A government unable to compel is no government at all; it is a mere travesty, a farce. We cannot be blind to the fact that civilization in the nature of things progresses by the *force* of the law, not by its moral suasion.

But civilization goes forward by two roads; one I have mentioned, the other is philanthropy, and I use the word broadly. By it I cover educational, municipal, and charitable work of all kinds, and it has a most important bearing on this question. The fact that women have no political prizes to gain, no offices in view, no constituencies to please, has made them of special value in all this wide field of work. Their ends are more quickly achieved, since their singleness of purpose cannot be questioned. Let them be plunged into the arena of political strife, and there will be no one left to carry on the work they now sustain so bravely.

There is a ridiculous side to this whole question, which is tacitly avoided in these public hearings, as are other more serious views of the subject; but brief as the time is, I propose to touch upon both.

A very slight mention of the ridiculous side will suffice. We women are not supposed to be humorous, I know, but even the most serious of us are obliged to smile when we ask ourselves who will do our work when we are doing the men's!

The obvious reply to that is that all women will not want to go into political life, if they have the ballot, any more than all men do; but all men *may* and *can*, it is a matter of choice. Legislation is for the majority, and the majority of women are mothers, whose health and strength must be given to the State, during their best years, only through the medium of those lives in whose preservation and upbringing lies the future of our country. It is these women — the great majority — whom we beg you to protect; the chivalry of men belongs to them. So sure are thousands of them that you will never place the burden of government upon their shoulders, that it is difficult to persuade them that there is any danger of your mistaking the clamor of the suffragists for truth, or that their still small voice should be heard above the din.

It is true that last spring, in less than three weeks, without solicitation, 7000 names, nearly half of which were those of self-supporting women, were collected and sent to the Constitutional Convention to protest against the amendment you are now considering, but I cannot give you an idea of how difficult it was for many women to gather sufficient courage even to put their names to a public paper. They confessed to a struggle before they could make up their minds to come forward. That may have been a foolish feeling — it is not for me to criticise — it is at least one which most women understand. These women do not want publicity, they do not want to be mixed up in politics; they just want to be women, and do a woman's work, and they are the great majority of our sex, and they should be respected.

This question is often confounded with that of the higher education. Believe me, they have nothing whatever to do with one another. The ballot in itself is not an educational force, as you men very well know, nor is it a wand with which to turn all vileness into purity. It is simply a part of the machinery of the State, a very cumbersome part, costing an enormous amount, but the only way we know of giving to a few representative men the power to legislate for all. The laws of the State have given women so much, that any attempt to alter her position would in the cause of justice have to begin by taking away, not adding to her rights.

The gradual changes in the laws of this State during the last quarter of a century have taken away every cry of the suffragists of that earlier time, and what women have asked, men have done, time and time again.

Now, in closing, I wish to be very serious. To many young persons, to many emotional persons, change is mistaken for progress. Thus in the train of the women so long identified with the demand for suffrage, who do not realize that the times have outgrown their cause, have followed many who, full of the unrestful spirit of the end of the century, are hurrying along, eager only for something different, something more, forgetting the inexorable law which science has laid down — the law we know as the Specialization of Function. In every line of life we see this law ruling development. Where there is specialization, there comes to be greater and greater perfection; nowhere is progress accompanied by a diffusion of force, but always by a concentration of effort in special directions. So, since the first development of sex, has specialization of the male and female types gone on; men have grown more manly, women more womanly. Are we alone of all nature to forcibly destroy the work of untold ages, and, thrusting men and women together, demand that the work that each is beginning to be perfect in shall be indifferently done by both? And then, there are the assertions of greater virtue made for our sex without foundation. Again, in being equal, we differ. Born as we are of man and woman, inheriting the mental and moral characteristics of both parents, we differ from our brothers only in so far as our physical limitations affect our organizations. Theirs are the robuster virtues, called to growth and strength by rough contact with the world. Theirs the word which serves for the bond; the responsibility which is the foundation of business life; the integrity on which justice rests; the broad mindedness, which gives each man his chance. And to balance all that, women have the spirit of self-sacrifice, the charity which forgives, the personal purity, all of which are essential to the existence of the home, and cause their sons to rise up and call them blessed.

I approach this question of morality with natural hesitation. It and our physical disabilities are the points I spoke of earlier as being ignored when this question is seriously discussed, and yet, unless considered, this question cannot be properly dealt with.

Who does not realize the present disinclination for motherhood which possesses so many of our younger generation; and who can see it without alarm? It can be traced to this unrestful desire for life outside the home. When motherhood is spoken of with contempt, when a home-life is considered too dull to be endured; when the ambition of the intellectual life becomes so warped as to be dissatisfied with any outlet but that of public life — what is to become of the future?

Do what we may, say what we can, we cannot break down the barrier of sex which indicates the parting of the ways.

Build up the wall of the law about us, seeking and accepting our counsel meanwhile; protect the homes, which we women alone can make for you; open to us every door for our education and advancement, but do not put upon the shoulders of women the muskets they are too weak to carry, nor the burden of the government which was constituted to protect them; do not force them to undertake an undue share of the world's work.

I leave this matter in your hands with confidence. I am a woman speaking for my silent sisters, appealing to you to leave us the liberty we might demand, begging you not to give your sanction to a retrogressive action, by breaking down the barrier experience has built between our sexes, but, as you go on becoming nobler, finer men, carrying on the active part of the world's work; to let us too progress, becoming every decade abler and more intellectual women, better and better fitted to help and counsel, but never your rivals, never partakers in the eager strife of public life.

# ADDRESS OF HON. JOHN LOWELL.

*Delivered before the Committee on Woman Suffrage, in Boston, March 9th, 1885.*

PRINTED BY THE REMONSTRANTS.

I have been asked to say a few words on the question whether, under our free Constitution, our Bill of Rights, and our Declaration of Independence, the right of suffrage is one of those rights which are declared to be inalienable rights.

Of course, it is hardly necessary to say that the Declaration of Independence and the Article of the Bill of Rights which refers to inalienable rights have nothing whatever to say about suffrage. That would seem to be a pretty sufficient answer. But there is in our Constitution something about suffrage which shows clearly the opinion of the founders of the Republic that it was not one of those " inalienable rights." Under the Constitution, as adopted, every male citizen, inhabitant of the town, who had a freehold estate worth three pounds a year, or personal estate of sixty pounds (which at five per cent. would be three pounds a year), had a right to vote. That Constitution, of course, was framed by the same people who framed the Bill of Rights. They were persons, John Adams and others, who had very thoroughly considered these "inalienable rights;" some of whom had periled their lives for them.

Suffrage has been very much restricted in the freest country in the world except our own, — England. They are enlarging it now, and I believe they are doing well. But England was a free country with a very restricted suffrage. In France universal suffrage was made the chief prop of despotism under the second emperor. Napoleon III. was kept in office by universal suffrage.

Suffrage is a political and not a natural right. As our Consti-

2

tution has it, it is the right of every person to elect and be elected according as the same is established "by the frame of government," — that is the way these men put it, who required a property qualification. That property qualification was done away with in 1820, though Mr. Webster thought it had better be preserved. But it was argued on the ground of expediency, and not of inalienable rights.

I think it must be conceded by any one who has read our Bill of Rights, or who thinks upon the subject, and believes that the Bill of Rights is sound, that suffrage is a political right, a political privilege, or whatever you may choose to call it, which is to be established according to high expediency.

The chief point, which is almost his fundamental one, upon which my friend and neighbor Mr. Bowditch made a very earnest argument to you, is that unless women can vote you have no right to tax them. That is not quite fundamental, because you can abolish, of course, the taxes on the property of women, and leave the right of suffrage where it is; but he says men are so mean they will never do that, and therefore he thinks they will rather establish the right of suffrage. He says that taxation without representation is "robbery." He does not give any reasons for saying that it is "robbery," — he says that Lord Camden said so, and that James Otis thought that taxation without representation was robbery. Well, he admits that James Otis and Lord Camden did not mean what he means. James Otis and his associates made this Bill of Rights and this Constitution, and in that they provide for this very thing that they had been fighting for. They say no one ought to be taxed without the representatives of the people, and they say the representatives of the people should be chosen by those who have a freehold estate of three pounds a year or sixty pounds in money. That shows exactly what James Otis and those who fought with him against "taxation without representation" meant by it. Therefore Mr. Bowditch takes a maxim, and, giving a new meaning to it, makes it the foundation of a very earnest, very able and impressive, but yet a very peculiar speech. He brings up an example: he says, "I know a woman in Brookline who pays nearly $11,000 of taxes a year, and she cannot vote. Isn't that robbery?" Or rather, "I say that is robbery," says Mr.

### 3

Bowditch. Well, I hope Mr. Bowditch pays $11,000 taxes. If he does, he pays it for precisely the same reasons, and he gets for his money precisely the same things that this lady gets, exactly. He gets his roads, his gas, his water, etc., and he pays on exactly the same property. Where is the robbery? How is that tax "robbery" from a person who has for that tax precisely the same equivalent that he has, and who pays that tax on precisely the same property that he pays it on?

There is no such universal maxim in morals or in anything else as that everybody who pays a tax shall vote. It must have been a slip of the tongue in which he said that if a man was refused his vote the law would not compel him to pay his taxes. There is no such law, of course. If a man is refused his vote, he may have some action against the selectmen, but I do not think he will find the tax bill on his property is any smaller. He means to say it ought to be so, perhaps, but I really do not know what he does mean. But he says this taxing is "robbery," and therefore that the governor, legislators, and judges, when they draw their salaries, are receiving stolen goods. "And," says Mr. Bowditch, "if I were a judge, I should feel every time I sentenced a thief that I was sentencing a brother, for I am receiving stolen goods all the time, because I receive my salary." The remark was received with applause, the reporter says, and I don't wonder at it. It is the funniest thing that has been said for months; it would make the fortune of Gilbert in the Pirates of Penzance!

"Receiving stolen goods"? Why, every citizen, of course, has some benefit from the taxes; Brother Bowditch has,—he walks on the common roads. Why does he not go through the fields? He uses the water the town of Brookline taxes him for. He uses the gas. Why does he not go and put out the gas? "Receiving stolen goods"!—it is not worth while to say much about that. But the way he reconciles himself to it is this, I suppose: no one can be a thief against his own will; it is against my will that we do not give women the vote, and therefore I am not a thief, and the people who think with me are not thieves. Or, in other words, everybody who thinks differently from me is a thief, and those who think with me are honest folks,—that is the amount of it.

It is evident a great many persons pay taxes who have no vote.

4

Our corporations have no vote, — they pay taxes pretty liberally. I do not mean to say they ought to have a vote, — I am not advocating that side of the question, — but they have no votes. Some of their stockholders may have or may not, according to where they live, etc., but the majority of them may not, of course. Corporations have no votes, and a foreigner who has lived here less than five years has no vote, however rich he may be, and however much he may be taxed. The richest man in the Commonwealth has no vote, if he cannot read and write.

The truth is, that maxim had nothing to do with individual voters at all. It was a good maxim, and it was intended to say that in a free government there should be representation of the people, in order that the taxes may be voted by the people, and not arbitrarily by a king or a foreign parliament, or persons who have no interest whatever in the matter. The male taxpayers have the same interest, of course, that female taxpayers have in all these matters.

If you are talking about "robbery," the woman in Brookline who pays $11,000 tax would be more robbed by allowing two people who pay only a poll tax to vote away her taxes than she is robbed by not being permitted to vote. Universal suffrage is a robbery in that sense. I am not saying that, — that is not my point; I do not believe it; but it would be so upon their theory. The "robbery" would be in allowing people who pay no taxes to vote away the money of those who pay all the taxes. It would strike directly at universal suffrage. It would lead directly to a plutocracy. If people were to vote in Massachusetts as they vote in a corporation, according to the stock they hold, then the "robbery" that Mr. Bowditch speaks of would not be committed.

I am not arguing for or against the suffrage. I have not fully made up my own mind upon it. But I say that the right to vote by man, woman, or child, above the age of intelligence, is a political right, to be established on grounds of high expediency for the good of the Commonwealth, for the good of the people themselves, for the good of the women themselves, the children themselves, the foreigners themselves, and all who are subject to our laws. On these grounds it must be argued and on these grounds it must be decided.

# ADDRESS

BY

## MISS EMILY P. BISSELL OF DELAWARE,

BEFORE THE

### U. S. SENATE COMMITTEE ON WOMAN SUFFRAGE, FEBRUARY 13, 1900

MR. CHAIRMAN AND GENTLEMEN: It is not the tyranny, but the chivalry of men that we American women have to fear. The men of America want to give us everything we really need, and the danger is that they will mistake a minority for a majority. That is why we are here to-day. We hold a brief for the silent majority who do not want the ballot. There may be thousands of women who wish the ballot, and wish it earnestly, but certainly there are millions who do not desire it.

The proof that we represent this majority may be asked for. It lies in this, — that the suffrage movement must be against the opinions of most of our sex, since it has been pushed for fifty years by as able a woman and as popular a one as Miss Anthony, and yet still remains a minority movement. In these fifty years every other woman's movement really desired by women has succeeded. The educational movement (not necessarily the coeducational) is a magnificent success. And, by the way, I may mention here that the heads of four of the most prominent women's colleges are all antisuffragists. The movement for property rights is so successful that even married women now have more property rights than married men. The entrance of women into all occupations and professions has been so great that out of a possible 369 occupations over 360 had been conquered for our sex, according to the census of 1890, while a suffragist speaker at the conference this week claims that we are now represented in over 400 trades and occupations. And the club movement — well, gentlemen, wherever there are two women nowadays, there is a club. The remotest hamlet is no exception to this rule. These movements have had no trouble in winning their way, and they have not taken half a century to do it, either. The woman-suffrage movement is the only woman's movement in existence that after fifty years' hard work finds itself not only in the minority, but with strong associations of women banded against it.

The suffrage movement is a minority movement even where it has succeeded. In Colorado, where I have been twice since the equal-suffrage law was passed, and where I have friends who are old residents, I have been assured that the majority of women did not desire to vote, and have been indifferent ever since as to casting their ballots. When I was going to Oregon last year, I had a most interesting talk with an Oregon suffragist, who sought to dissuade me from opposing suffrage. I asked her if she did not think that I represented the majority, and she said: "Why, of course; the majority of women here in the East are against us, and you will find the majority out there against us, too; but when they have to vote, they will vote." And when I reached Oregon I found that she was right in her first remark, at least. The great majority of all the women I met there did not care a button for the ballot, and a strong organization has been formed there against it. In this connection I may add, as the success of municipal suffrage in Kansas is often spoken of by the suffragist, that one of the members of the standing committee of this Oregon State association opposed to the extension of the suffrage to women, came upon that committee because, as she said, she had been living in Kansas under municipal suffrage, and was so disgusted with it that when she moved to Oregon she wanted no more suffrage.

The suffrage movement is a minority movement, too, in that the four States which have accepted suffrage are not representative of our large communities. Colorado by the census of 1890 had less inhabitants in the whole State than the city of Baltimore; by the last estimate, made by its governor, it had just about 20,000 inhabitants in the whole State more than Baltimore, which is not much of a margin. Wyoming's total population is less than the foreign population of Maryland, and Maryland is not a land of immigrants by any means. The population of Idaho is far below the number of colored people in Maryland. Utah (where the admission of women to the suffrage can hardly be said, in view of the recent events, to have elevated the character of the candidates) has less population than there are negroes in Arkansas; and altogether the four States that have equal suffrage, all put together, have fewer people in them (700,000 fewer) than Chicago, and not half as many as New York City. Gentlemen, results from such States, even if they were conclusive and positive, would still be minority results.

But even in these States the results are negative. Colorado has no advance in legislation to speak of, no purification of politics, no improvement of municipal conditions, no raising of working women's wages, no tokens of the millennial dawn whatever. Utah has sent Mr. Brigham Roberts here, but he has been returned with thanks (through the efforts of the women without the ballot), so that Utah's effort to uplift the country goes for nothing.

Wyoming has had equal suffrage for thirty years, yet nothing important has happened any more than in Idaho, which has just begun the experiment. Negative results such as these speak powerfully against suffrage, to our mind.

I may be asked by what authority I speak for Colorado. I have here letters from Colorado men, signed with their names and giving their opinion as to the negative or evil results of suffrage in Colorado. It may be said that you would prefer to hear from the women, and I also have a letter from a Denver woman who signs her name to it and who shows up the same evils.

I will read extracts from some of the letters I have received. I have here a letter from R. S. Morrison, of Colorado, in which he says: —

> One problem in the local politics of Denver to-day is the large number of "women who vote under police surveillance," and he adds: —
>
> "I have conversed with a large portion of the politicians of this city and they are unanimously against it. Still, in public utterances and in private letters they are not willing to commit themselves to that view. They have talked with me fully because they know I will reveal no names, but they recognize the danger of provoking a vindictive vote when there is no issue on the subject to bring out the vote on the other side. . . .
>
> "Women are fit to vote; no one denies their fitness. They are fit just as a silk dress is fit for a mop — but the silk dress was made for something better than a mop, and a woman was made for other purposes than those of political contentions. . . .
>
> "The phrase 'purity in politics,' as produced by the woman vote, will raise a laugh wherever mentioned. They have quickly brought to the polls the power to ape the vices of men and have produced no countervailing virtues. They have been indicted for ballot stuffing and charged with repeating, and when the subject is mentioned to that class of women who still advocate the right, because to them the right means power, the common answer is, 'We are no worse than the men.'
>
> "This answer is doubtless true, yet, madam, it is a fearful fall from the promises they made when they appealed for the ballot, that they would elevate and purify the polls.
>
> "If the question were to be resubmitted to-day, it would be overwhelmingly defeated.
>
> "Yours respectfully, R. S. MORRISON."

Now, they will say that that is a Denver man. I have just one word to read from a Denver woman's letter to me — Mrs. Joel T. Vaile. She says: "He would be a bold man, indeed, who should claim that the municipal affairs of the city of Denver are to-day in the hands of cleaner or more disinterested politicians than before the days of woman's suffrage;" and she adds, with regard to the "testimonials" signed by Colorado legislators

3

and officials, of which the suffragists boast, that they are not by any means spontaneous expressions of real opinion, but have been framed and urged through by committees of women, and personally presented for signature by them, the names being in some cases, to her positive knowledge, "signed with strong mental reservations and some after-grumbling as to the kind of pressure to which the signers had been subjected."

In conclusion, gentlemen, if you will excuse a personal detail, I wish to say that if any woman in the United States needs a vote, I ought to be that woman. The suffragists ask for the ballot in the name of the self-supporting woman, who must be a bread-winner, not only for herself, but often for others; they ask it for the property-owning woman, who needs it on account of taxation; they ask it for the temperance woman, so that she can save those nearest and dearest to her from the saloon; they ask it for the club woman, because her intelligence and interest in public affairs deserve it. And above all, they ask it for the poor downtrodden single woman, who has no one to look out for her or take care of her interests. Well, gentlemen, by a freak of coincidence I happen to be a single woman myself, a club woman, a temperance woman (though not a prohibitionist), a small property owner, and a self-supporting woman these many years. And yet, though I ought to have thus a fivefold longing for suffrage, I have never yet been so situated that I could see where a vote could help me. If I felt that it would, I might become a suffragist, *perhaps*, but as it is I remain with the majority of my sex, and I beg you to believe that we do not want to vote, and that Miss Anthony, whose courage, whose devotion, whose interest, whose determined perseverance we sincerely admire, is nevertheless not backed by the women of America, but is leading a minority movement only.

*Printed by the Massachusetts Association opposed to Extension of Woman Suffrage.*

Pamphlets and leaflets may be obtained from the Secretary of the Association,

Mrs. Robert W. Lord,
P. O. Box 2262, Boston.

# HIDDEN FROM HISTORY

OPPOSITION TO WOMAN SUFFRAGE.

# ADDRESS

OF

## Hon. Horace J. Canfield,

OF STOCKBRIDGE,

DELIVERED BEFORE THE MASSACHUSETTS HOUSE OF REPRESENTATIVES, MARCH 30, 1877.

BOSTON:
ALBERT J. WRIGHT, PRINTER,
79 MILK STREET (CORNER OF FEDERAL).
1877.

# PREFACE.

In offering this little pamphlet to the public, I have faith to believe it will meet with a warm reception. Annually, the Women Suffragists come to the Legislature asking for a constitutional amendment, granting to women the right to vote. Often, very often, are speeches delivered both in favor and against the proposed measure. Never within my experience of legislative matters,—some eight years,—has there ever been such a universal demand for the speech of a member, as has been manifested for this one. Therefore I have, at considerable expense, presented it in this form.

When the bill giving women municipal suffrage was reported to be acted upon, Hon. Horace J. Canfield arose in his place, and delivered the remarks which will be found in the following pages. Members who seldom take interest in debate crowded around him, and listened with rapt attention from the opening to the close.

Mr. Canfield is a rising man, and all good and true women will feel grateful to him for his earnest endeavor to protect and defend them from this innovation that a few fanatics seek to thrust upon them.

MRS. E. A. LANE.

# ADDRESS.

To the English-speaking man, the term *woman* was wont to call up a vision of something lovely and enchanting, which appealed in some mysterious way to his deepest feelings, and was all-powerful in influencing him for good or evil. Now, however, the notions conveyed by the term seem to be suffering a subtle change. The vision is not so clear; its influence not so decisive; it is blurred and distorted; it is even grotesque and absurd. For one cannot mention "woman" now without that ominous and angular word "rights" erecting itself grimly before the mind's eye, and along with it is conjured up that weird and uncanny throng of beings who have caused all this confusion and distortion.

The old notion, the peculiar, special, poetical (and that is the natural and philosophical) notion of woman, does not include this threatening substantive. The poetical and natural idea has found no better expression than in Milton's picture of Eve, the primitive mother of us all: "Grace was in her steps, heaven in her eye, in every gesture dignity and love." But the finest thing that poet ever sung, or painter drew, is yet short of the reality.

> "To gild refined gold; to paint the lily;
> To throw a perfume on the violet,
> Is wasteful and ridiculous excess."

Leaving, then, the region of compliment, which, in this case, is also the region of truth, let us turn to the practical side of this discussion. And here, too, we need not abandon the poet,—the true interpreter of nature. Wordsworth understood the subject, when he wrote,—

> "A perfect woman, nobly planned
> To warn, to comfort and command."

The possession of power, the idea of power, are both dear to the feminine nature. Women, notwithstanding their cry for "rights," do now, and always have, ruled the world. Both poets and historians bear us out in this. From Moses to Homer, and so down to the latest thinkers of the world, all bear the same testimony. Everywhere the feminine influence is paramount, and, perhaps, in the good time coming, it will always be exerted for good. But it never has been in the past. Strange to say, in the past,—in the great crises of men and nations,—the feminine influence has been fatal. Why? Who can answer? Perhaps because man is so weak and woman so undeveloped.

There is a theory that woman *is, or is to be*, the moral savior of the race. This I am not inclined to doubt; but she never can exert her saving influence on the stage of public and official life. Nothing has ever been written upon the natural relation of the sexes so beautiful and philosophical as the narrative of the Hebrew Moses. I refer to it, also, because it is so universally known; and I ask your attention for a moment to that important and fascinating story, considering it not from a religious point of view, but as a subtle philosophical treatise.

Adam appears alone in Paradise. Like *other animals* by which he was surrounded, he was a social being, with capacities for higher wants, desires, and aspirations; and yet he was *alone in Paradise*. One day the animals went trooping past him, and he gave them names. He noticed that—

> "The rabbits and hares,
> They all went in pairs,
> And even the bears
> With each other agreed."

Adam felt very much alone. We may suppose that it was with a feeling of vague and undefined unrest that he fell asleep. What were his dreams we know not, and, in point of fact, we do not care. For no vision of the night, nor poet's ecstasy, ever gave to "airy nothing" such loveliness as then took palpable form and shape while Adam slept. Then womanhood became incarnate! Nature had completed the circle of her works, and given her last, best gift,—"Earth's noblest thing, a woman perfected."

Adam was quick to see this. He recognized at once the best image of himself, and dearer half. Still the story will not let us forget that she was "bone of his bone, flesh of his flesh." Not from the original elements came she, but she was the creature of a creature. If we stick to the text, then, man was not made for woman, but the woman for the man. When Adam reviewed the beasts, he saw that he alone was not mated. And yet he was of a higher order than they! He had work to do; he needed help, and there was no helpmeet for him, no sufficient helper; so the woman came.

This story has given rise to a great deal of beautiful writing. St. Augustine says: "Woman was not made out of man's head, to be his ruler; nor was she made from his feet, to be his slave; but out of his side, to assist him, and from under his arm, and from near his heart, to be defended and beloved by him." This theory is all true to nature, to experience, and to philosophy, and Moses has wrought his work with exquisite simplicity, and yet with the skill of a master. On one occasion Eve forgot herself, and ate of forbidden fruit. Now, what is the inference? Nothing but this: that Eve assumed the leadership. She was no helper here, but a leader. Adam was by her side, but there was no consultation; she did not act as a helpmeet for him, but as one all self-sufficient, and so, according to the Mosaic story, came woe and sin and death. But what did Adam do? The Mosaic narrative is rapid and dramatic. She gave to the man; and he did eat. No persuasion was necessary. He must follow Eve, or she was lost to him. He saw her standing before him, beautiful, modest, winning, unchanged,—just as she was on the morning of her creation, when—

> "Grace was in all her steps; heaven in her eye,
> In every gesture dignity and love."

He saw her take the fatal plunge, and resolved, in the fullness of his passion for her, to die *with* her.

We have no concern here with the religious aspect of the story, but one point comes out with extraordinary clearness. We cannot fail to see what conception the author of Genesis had of the strength of feminine influence upon man. If the Old Testament had been written by one author for the purpose of developing this truth, there could not have been a greater consistency on this subject than now exists in it. David yielded in the most humiliating and criminal manner; and through Solomon's susceptibility to female influence, came the separation of the Hebrew kingdom. A well-known commentator observes: "They who have noted in history or in society the influence of intriguing women over the greatest and wisest of men, will readily perceive that it was almost impossible that Solomon should stop short of extreme folly and wickedness when he had once suffered himself to be entangled in the fatal net."

Ah! Mr. Speaker, it will be a sad day for Massachusetts and for civilization when women are seen in their places on this floor, urging their pet schemes with "speaking eyes" upon the attention of bewildered male members. We can scarcely hope that a wiser than Solomon will ever be here.

But if woman cannot contribute moral force to public life, can she, by acting the part of a voter and stateswoman, contribute anything of superior intellectual value? An able English writer remarks that "women have at times ruled like men." The reigns of Queen Elizabeth and Catherine II. are among the most brilliant in the history of their country, but they are exceptions to the rule.

Woman is not made to govern; she is incompetent to carry out strict justice; and the reigns of women are generally marked by precipitation, by a tendency for arbitrary undertakings, and more especially by a martial spirit. The heart is woven up in politics; it calculates less than it craves, and hence originates the rule of favorites who are summoned to their posts rather by the woman's heart than by their own talents and merits. On one of these reefs the reigns of nearly all women have stranded. Such were the reigns of the Spanish Isabella, Margaret of Denmark, Queens Elizabeth and Anne, the Empress Maria Theresa, and the Russian empresses, and among the records of those brilliant reigns we seek in vain for deeds and institutions which later history has declared to be valuable.

Women, by a participation in public affairs, Mr. Speaker, can contribute nothing of value to the State, but they can bring incalculable injuries on society. If women were granted a place in public affairs, by the side of their husbands, or if too great scope were allowed to their radiant influence, they would only become estranged from their families, and thus an incurable wound would be dealt to the social as well as the political order of things. This lesson history has often taught us with a warning voice. France furnishes a striking proof of the assertion. In that country women have always sought to exert an influence beyond the family circle, and a still current proverb says that in France they are the real men.

But, Mr. Speaker, to come more nearly to the subject in hand. In answer to the petition for "suffrage, irrespective of sex," the remonstrants claim that women have burdens enough,—burdens imposed by nature and by circumstances which suffrage cannot alleviate,—that they do not want this burden of the ballot to be superadded, that it would cause trouble in the domestic relations, and increase divorces. When, more than a quarter of a century ago, this agitation began, the purpose was to correct the laws; they did then bear heavily upon women. Men were astonished, when the subject was presented to them from a female point of view. Did they refuse to listen? Has not the whole current of legislation, since that time, set in favor of the sex? To-day, women stand better before the law than men. Do you dream that this would have been the case if woman had been endowed with the franchise of the ballot? Would she have dared to vote herself those privileges which man, in his generosity, has granted her? Why, the moment she seized on these immunities as rights, the most chivalrous man on earth would resent such usurpation. Woman stands better before the law to-day than man does, and the woes which she complains of are incident to the conditions of human existence; they belong to the "ills that flesh is heir to," and no mere legal enactments, no granting of political franchise can remove them. Nothing can ameliorate them but self-government, self-improvement, the patient, personal melioration of the individual men and women who constitute society; and this cannot be accomplished by the ballot.

Colonel Conwell demonstrated very ably before

the committee, that the laws made by men were more than just, that they were generous towards women, and the replies made by Mrs. Campbell and Mrs. Howe were merely charges brought against human nature, and not against laws. What, asked Colonel Conwell, have the women to gain in Massachusetts by the ballot? Higher wages? No; because in Massachusetts women are very numerous, and wages are consequently low; while in the West, women are fewer and wages higher.

Has suffrage given to women higher wages in the West? No; and neither could it increase them here. In Massachusetts there are 62,000 more adult women than men,—52,000 widows, and 10,000 spinsters. It is excess of numbers, and not because men vote and women do not, that makes female labor cheap. Would suffrage give more public offices to women? Why, the fact is, that the women employed as teachers outnumber all the masculine officeholders in the State. There are more women than men in public offices to-day in Massachusetts. This is Colonel Conwell's statement, and if they should go further than this, they would create a tyranny which men might justly resent.

And another point, Mr. Speaker: if Massachusetts should give the ballot to women, she might justly lose the respect of other States; yes, the respect of the civilized world. The female vote would then outnumber the male vote by 60,000! The Commonwealth would virtually be turned over to the women, a condition of things revolting to the virile, the manly nature, and, as I believe, abhorrent to every healthy, to every normally-constituted woman. Ah! Mr. Speaker, we should then have reached the degenerate condition of ancient Israel, when the prophets were dumb dogs, and the women ruled over them!

But what has woman to lose by suffrage? Why, all of those peculiar privileges which she now enjoys through the chivalry and generosity of man.

Those privileges would then be revoked. Man is the stronger animal, and the best man can be discourteous, when the question of right is involved. A brutal husband may now abuse his wife, but that is a fault of human nature, and not of the laws. But let all things become questions of right, and woman's special privileges will be cancelled. Both will then stand as equals before the law. If she assaults him, he will then have the same remedy as she now has if he assaults her. Now, he has no remedy.

Miss Lucy Stone desires that a woman may have a right to possess her own clothing. In point of fact, answers Colonel Conwell, she can hold all her husband's property against his creditors.

Now, Mr. Speaker, what have men done for women in Massachusetts? Married women can hold all their property, real and personal, under all circumstances. They are not liable for their husbands' debts. Women are exempt from arrests for debt; men are not. If the two are engaged in an assault, she is exempt, he is not. She can assault him, not he her. He may starve, but must support her. He must pay her debts, and, in Massachusetts, by law, the husband must *love, honor,* and *obey* his wife, but she is exempted from all these obligations. There are *twenty-seven* excuses, for any one of which a wife may leave her husband, but not one which will permit him to leave her. I am glad, Mr. Speaker, I am rejoiced, that the laws of Massachusetts are so favorable to woman, and it is evident, that if a woman is wronged, the fault lies in the defects of human nature, and not of the laws.

Mr. Speaker, one lady appeared before the Committee for the remonstrants, who would shrink, I am sure, from public mention here. If I had the power, I would even then feel debarred from paying that tribute to her eloquence, her culture, her intellectual breadth, and perfect womanliness, which she so justly merits. I am sure that her words fell with convincing weight upon the ears of every gentleman then in this house. I am sure that every man who heard her would have blushed to proclaim himself her superior in anything but mere brutal strength. I am sure that every man then present was sad to think of the cruel humiliation and anxiety to which the petitioners for female suffrage subject all of her sex who think like her; and, Mr. Speaker, *they are a majority of the women of this State.*

While she was speaking, I could not but recall the quaint phrases of old Sir Thomas Browne, in his essay on the transmutation of sex in hares. "As for the mutation of sexes," he says, "we cannot deny it in hares, it being also observable in man. For hereof, there are not a few examples, and though none of men who have turned women, yet very many, who, from a reality of being women, have infallibly proved (to be) men."

This, truly, is something startling, and may we not fear that a devotion to masculine pursuits, as some women have this tendency and hankering to become men, may unsex the whole race, and that, by and by, we shall, in effect, be as much alone, as truly without a helpmeet, as Adam was in Paradise.

And again, this wise old Thomas Browne remarks that "The wisdom of God hath divided the genius of mankind according to the different affairs of the world; while they who consider not, rudely rushing upon professions and ways of life unequal to their natures, dishonor, not only themselves and their functions, but pervert the harmony of the whole world."

Herodotus has immortalized Candaules, as the man who loved his own wife. This was exceptional among the Asiatic Greeks. There are many such now, and, Mr. Speaker, I am not ashamed to be counted among the number. In opposing female suffrage, this large class does not oppose the wishes or the best judgment of the women whom they know the best. It is in the interest of those remonstrating ladies that I have spoken.

# ADDRESS OF MRS. W. WINSLOW CRANNELL,

CHAIRMAN OF THE EXECUTIVE COMMITTEE OF THE 3RD JUDICIAL DISTRICT OF THE STATE OF NEW YORK, BEFORE THE COMMITTEE ON RESOLUTIONS OF THE REPUBLICAN NATIONAL CONVENTION, AT ST. LOUIS, JUNE 16, 1896.

---

*Mr. Chairman and Gentlemen of the Committee on Resolutions.*

I appear before you with reluctance and trepidation. I am here to represent a large body of women who do not crave publicity or notoriety, and who, until recently, were content to submit in silence to the demands presented by a few women for the extension of suffrage to their sex; but when the issue was forced upon us either to speak or to become implicated in the suffrage movement through our silence, we felt that we must be heard; and so I was asked to present our protest to your honorable committee.

In the name of nearly one million and a half of women of the State of New York, I protest against any such action being taken by your honorable body as is asked for by Mrs. Blake.

I protest in the name of the Constitutional Convention of New York State, in 1894, a body largely Republican, who, after mature deliberation, decided that "until it is shown that woman may become a politician without losing something of the precious charm of her personality, and that the State may exact her services in that capacity without imperiling its stability and tranquility, it is surely the conservative course of wisdom to retain the existing conditions under which we have achieved our great happiness and prosperity."

I protest in the name of South Carolina, as shown by her action in 1895; of the Commonwealth of Massachusetts, as shown at the November election in 1895; of Rhode Island's Legislature of 1896.

All the best civilization opposes forced changes; and I take it that such a radical change as adding to the 1,500,000 votes of New York State over 1,500,000 votes more, in direct opposition to the wishes of her people, is something that you are hardly prepared to father; but if you were, there would then be these questions to be answered affirmatively:

Will it be for the best interests of the country to grant the suffrage to women?

Are these certain definite benefits to be secured through women's suffrage which cannot otherwise be secured?

And men of your intelligence, gentlemen, do not need to have me point out the fallacy involved in an affirmative answer.

Permit me to state briefly our objection:

We object to any woman who has only a backing of one thousand six hundred enrolled suffragists in New York State to say that she represents the million and one-half of home-loving women of that state.

We believe that the extension of suffrage to a people more than as large again as the present voting population would be to increase the evils that already threaten to overcome the principles for which our fathers fought.

We assert that women to-day are so protected by laws made by men, that they have nothing more to ask for legally. The question of wages never has been, nor never will be, governed by the question whether the wage-earner has a vote; wages are always governed by demand and supply. The question of taxation without representation, as applied to women who have no vote, is absurd. Taxes are not conditioned upon a right to vote. When our forefathers complained it was because taxes were imposed upon them by a Parliament sitting 3,000 miles away, in which there was no representation whatever of the colonies. They did not ask for individual representation.

There is no discrimination against women in taxation. Every tax-paying woman in the city of Albany, N. Y., who could be found, signed a protest against striking out the word "male" from the State Constitution. Many men are taxed who have no vote—the wealthy minor and the man who, living in one town, owns property in another. Taxation is the price the citizen pays for the protection of his property, his life and his liberty.

The value of the ballot in itself is largely overestimated. It is but a simple piece of paper, were it not for the force lying behind it.

3

The truth of Horace Greeley's terse statement to Miss Anthony many years ago, that "behind the ballot lies the bullet," is as powerful to-day as it was when uttered. To imagine a government unbacked by the physical power to enforce its laws, is to imagine an anomaly, or something which must of necessity develop into anarchy. The advocates of female suffrage refuse to admit that the stability of government is dependent upon physical force, because they dare not admit it; since to do so would be to admit the weakness of their cause.

But you will recognize its truth, I am sure, gentlemen; otherwise why do you develop and improve your militia; why do you erect armories and organize and drill bodies of police in all the centres of population? To make laws that cannot be enforced is worse than useless; and to grant the right of embroiling the nation in war to a people wholly incompetent to carry it on, would be to bring our government into contempt.

Without doubt I shall be stigmatized as absurd by the women suffragists, but ridicule is not argument; and it is your duty as serious men, charged with great responsibility, to see to it that your vision be not obscured by chivalry, emotion or sentiment.

We are in the midst of hard times. Every industry languishes. Our farmers fail in the markets, and our merchants and bankers go into bankruptcy. There is an undercurrent of anarchy that roils the waters of our social and political life. Everywhere men and wise women are asking, What will be the end? The cry goes up all over the land, How shall we regain our prosperity? To-day you were told that the people were going to ask the Republican party to lead them back to green pastures. Do you think that a solution of the problem that is vexing men's minds and casting shades of gloom over the whole country can be found in adding to the already unwieldy and uncertain quality called male suffrage, the vote of every woman in this land?

For suffrage is not asked only for the women who are here to-day, but for every woman in our land, without regard to intelligence or morality.

If there be any among you who believes at all in the extension of suffrage to all women, I ask you, seriously, is this the time for its inception? Have you not to face such problems as have not often vexed men's souls, and do you think it would be wise, at this time,

4

to throw into the boiling mass of unrest and disquiet the uncertain element of woman suffrage?

Gentlemen, without taking up more of your time, in the name of your mothers, who served their country best by being home makers and keepers, and by educating sons to care for their country; in the name of your wives, who are living up to the full the sweetness of the quality of help-meet; in the name of your daughters—I am sure you would wish to keep them out of the mire of political life—in the name of the many hundreds of thousands of women who are silent to-day because they are loving, home women and have confidence in you, and in the name of the many thousands of women in New York State whom I, personally, represent, I ask you to refuse to take action on the question of woman suffrage.

Officers of the Anti-Suffrage Association of the 3rd Judicial District, of the State of New York.

    MRS. J. V. L. PRUYN,
        *President.*

    MRS. WILLIAM J. WALLACE,
        *1st Vice-President.*

    MRS. WM. BAYARD VAN RENSSELAER,
        *Secretary.*

    MRS. JOSEPH GAVIT,
        *Treasurer.*

    MRS. W. WINSLOW CRANNELL,
        *Chairman.*

    MRS. ERASTUS CORNING,
    MRS. WILLIAM CASSIDY,
    MRS. J. HOWARD KING,
    MRS. JOEL R. REED,
    MRS. WM. O. STILLMAN,
    MRS. FREDERICK TOWNSEND.
        *Executive Committee.*

Apply for more papers to Anti-Suffrage Association, 13 Elk Street, Albany.

# Address of Mrs. W. Winslow Crannell,

Chairman of the Executive Committee of the Anti-Suffrage Association of the 3d Judicial District of the State of New York, before the Committee on Resolutions of the Democratic National Convention, at Chicago, July 8th, 1896.

---

*Mr. Chairman and Gentlemen of the Committee on Resolutions:*

I scarcely expected when I heard the cause of Woman Suffrage presented at St. Louis to the Republican Convention, that I should be forced to protest against it before your honorable body; for it was distinctly stated at that time that the suffragists either were, or were willing to be, Republicans; and that women suffragists everywhere, had worked to save the country from what they then termed "Democratic and Populistic misrule." This fact is substantiated by the plank that they succeeded in getting into the Republican platform; which was written by a prominent suffragist, was approved by all of the suffragists present, and which runs:

"The Republican party is mindful of the rights and interests of women. Protection of American industries includes equal opportunities, equal pay for equal work, and protection to the home. We favor the admission of women to wider spheres of usefulness, and welcome their co-operation in rescuing the country from Democratic and Populistic mismanagement and misrule."

And now they ask you, who they claim have mismanaged and misruled the country, to give them the franchise that they may still further work against you. If they were honest in their wording of the Republican plank, then they would have no right to appear before you; if they were *not* honest, then they certainly have no right to appear, because one of the reasons for which they ask the franchise, is that they intend through it to purify politics; and if this be the manner of purification, it must be based upon the homeopathic principle of *Similia Similibus Curantur*.

You know enough about politics, gentlemen, to take at its true value the assertion that women, by voting, could change the existing condition of things. But if they could, would you want your wives or your daughters, your mothers or your sisters, to take active part in the primaries and caucuses, at the polls, and even in the conventions, for the purpose of making them what it is claimed they would be "social centers?" And after politics were purified by women, who would purify the women? Is it not true that womanhood would suffer more than political morality would gain? And while the purification is going on who is going to do the home work, and the charitable work, that now so fills the lives of good women that they are often overburdened, and break down beneath the strain? It is to build up homes, not to break down their walls, and quench the light upon the hearth stone, that women's best energies should be directed.

Mrs. Stanton-Blatch, daughter of Elizabeth Cady Stanton, said in a published article, that it was better to let home suffer in order that women should gain economic freedom. "Let the women" she said, "who have not the taste for domestic work turn their children over to other women's care." We have too many servant mothers to-day; and the true duty of woman to woman, as well as to man, is to encourage and upbuild the home life from which we are so sadly drifting; and it is only as women yield themselves to the elevating and purifying influence of Christian teaching concerning marriage and home, that they rise to a higher moral level, and bring men up to that plane with them.

I appear before you unwillingly; but as the representative of the many millions of women who have hitherto proved the "silent majority." I come from New York State where there are only 1600 enrolled suffragists out of nearly 7,000,000 people, or, 29 organized suffragists to every 100,000 of her population. I have also been asked to represent the home-loving women of Massachusetts where there are but 51 organized suffragists to every 100,000 of her people; of Pennsylvania where there are only 14 organized suffragists to every 100,000 of her population; of New Hampshire where there are but 5 suffragists to every 100,000 of her inhabitants; of Connecticut where there are only 23 suffragists to every 100,000 of her inhabitants; of South Carolina where there are but three suffragists for every 100,000 of her people; of Arkansas where there are only three suffragists to every 100,000 of her people; besides being asked to speak by women of prominence in California, where there are but 33 suffragists to every 100,000 of her people; in Illinois where there are but 13 suffragists to every 100,000 of her people; in Michigan where there are only six suffragists to every 100,000 of her people; in Kentucky where there are but 32 suffragists to every 100,000 of her people; in Iowa where there are only six suffragists to every 100,000 of her people; in Virginia where there is but one suffragist to every 100,000 of her people; in Maryland where there are only six suffragists to every 100,000 of her people; in Maine where there are but 12 suffragists to every 100,000 of her people; in Ohio where there are only 11 suffragists to every 100,000 of her people, and in New Jersey where there are but eight suffragists to every 100,000 of her people. All these requests coming to me unsolicited.

These statistics are taken from an address delivered by Mr. Catt, husband of the National Suffrage organizer, before the National Society, at their annual meeting last January; and published in the Woman's Journal, the suffrage organ edited by Henry B. Blackwell,—better known as the husband of Lucy Stone,—and his daughter, Alice Stone Blackwell. I make this statement so that it may not be subject to contradiction by anyone present.

What are the reasons given for asking you to help the cause of Woman Suffrage?

First; That women who pay taxes should have a ballot. In answer we assert that the women who pay taxes do not want the ballot. That taxes are not conditioned upon the right to vote. That there is no discrimination against women in taxation. That taxation is the price the citizens pay for the protection of their property, their life, their liberty. That many men are taxed who have no vote,—the wealthy minor, and the man who living in one town owns property in another. That the woman who pays taxes will receive no benefit from the ballot which will not be an hundred times counteracted by the ballot of the women who do not pay taxes. That what is needed for the benefit of the tax-paying woman is not an increased but a restricted ballot. That while there are in New York State 144,000 women who pay taxes, there are at least 1,500,000 women who do not pay taxes; and the granting of suffrage to these women would more than duplicate the evils from which the tax-payer now suffers.

Second: That when women have the ballot, they will be employed constantly and at higher wages. The answer is shown in the fact that men vote and are yet unemployed. That no employer is going to pay an increased wage because the employee has the franchise. That while there are, as in the factories everywhere, long lists of girls waiting to be employed at nominal figures, no employer is going to raise the pay of his employees because they ask an hour off to vote on election day.

Third: That the cause of temperance will be helped when women vote. I admire the women who are working for temperance, and wish them God speed, but feel perfectly sure that they are mistaken if they expect to be helped by the granting of suffrage to all women North, South, East and West. Statistics tell us that while the population of the United States has increased but 20 per cent in the last two decades, the dram drinking and drug taking women have increased 500 per cent. The Christian Advocate is my authority for the statement that before the high license law in Philadelphia, Penn., out of 8,034 saloon licenses 3,696 were granted to women. In Boston, Mass. last Spring, out of 1,100 liquor licenses 491 were applied for by women. The same condition of things prevails nearly all over our country. Would these women work for prohibition?

Let us look carefully at what is asked for: "Equal pay for equal work." That sounds equitable and consequently reasonable. But if the question of wages were to become a matter of legislation, would you be willing to say to the already overburdened and unemployed workman that you believe that his wages should be cut down to those received by women? For it is a fact beyond dispute that the wages paid is always a question of demand and supply; and women have entered nearly every field of labor once a man's sole province; and, by being willing and able to work for lower wages than men, who have families to support, have crowded them out. Now if equal wages for equal work means anything at all, it means that no man shall be paid more for his work than the women are begging to receive. For instance, if that law could be passed and enforced, the merchant could say to his male employe that he could fill his shop with girls at half the price he was paying him, and while he preferred keeping the man at the higher rate, he must either discharge him or lower his wages to that which women were asking to receive. But the whole thing is a farce. You do not ask, in fact, I doubt if any of you care, how much the workman is paid who makes your clothes. I know that women do not; otherwise they would not haggle over prices, and gloat over bargains. This is hard common-sense. It isn't poetic nor imaginative. It is more, it is truth, and you are here to deal with truths and not with fallacies.

The number of votes cast at the general election in 1892 was 12,034,858. To grant suffrage to women would be to more than double that number. Do you believe that at this time, if at any time, when industries languish, and our farmers are being pushed to the wall, while our bankers and merchants go into bankruptcy, that it would be wise to add this immense increase to the voting population?

The facts for the suffragists to prove are that suffrage is necessary for the protection of women, and that it would be beneficial to the State. They have not and cannot prove either. To-day in New York State, and in many of the other States, a woman is protected better by the laws that men have made, than by any she could make herself. A husband cannot sell his real estate unless the wife joins in the deed. He cannot deprive her by will of right of dower. The wife can by deed or will dispose of her entire estate, real or personal, whether the husband consents or not. A father cannot now apprentice his child or make a valid appointment of a testamentary guardian without the consent of the mother, if she be living. The wife can carry on business on her own account, and is entitled to all the profits and earnings in that business, and may contract as if she were unmarried. Every profession is open to women, and every occupation also. Then what do they want, what will they gain by having the ballot? If men are not capable of managing the affairs of the State and the Nation according to the highest and best ideas of the race, that is of both men and women, will you permit me to respectfully inquire what proper and adequate share of this world's work you can perform? What is your natural place in the order of society? Are you mere hewers of wood and drawers of water? You cannot bear citizens; you cannot care for them in infancy and rear them to manhood. If you cannot govern them with wisdom and justice when they are given into your hands, what is your reason for being? It strikes me that these women who want to retain all the privileges of their sex, and secure besides those, all that they think a man has; who want to be men and yet remain women; have much hardihood in coming to you and saying: "You do not know how to make laws; how to govern the people; you are corrupt and misrule the nation. Give us the suffrage that we may supplant you" And they say this not for themselves alone, but for all the women in this great nation, North, South, East and West, without regard to education or morality! They are to purify politics!

Gentlemen, a large number of the leaders of the suffrage party became a revising committee to give to the world what is known as the Woman's Bible. At the present time they have only dealt with the Pentateuch. I need only to quote from its columns to show you its character. It is said: "The utter contempt for all the decencies of life, and all the natural personal rights of women, as set forth in these pages"—the Bible—"should destroy in the minds of women, at least, all authority to superhuman origin, and stamp the Pentateuch at least as emanating from the most obscene minds of a barbarous age." The story of the creation is said to "have been manipulated by some Jew in order to give heavenly authority for requiring the woman to obey the man she married." When it was found that the Christian women all over the land raised their voices in protest, at the National meeting of the suffragists, it was voted to repudiate the Woman's Bible as a suffrage work, but only by a majority of twelve. They then cast the onus of revision upon Elizabeth Cady Stanton, who is more to be honored for her truthfulness, than are the many women whose names are found among the revising committee, and who betray their leader. Nearly as many of the articles are written by Lillie Devereux Blake as by Mrs. Stanton; and the character of

5

them will be seen when I tell you that she covers much space to prove that "the chief point of interest in the parable of Balaam and his ass, is that the ass belonged to the female sex."

These are the women who are going to give us better laws than those founded on the Mosaic code, and who are going to purify politics! Do you wonder, gentlemen, that the mothers appeal to you; the mothers who have builded their homes upon the truths laid down in the Bible; and who have taught you to reverence it? There is little enough of reverence left in the world to-day. Take away from men and women that belief in the Bible that causes them to strive to do right for righteousness sake, and what have you? History tells you.

The suffragists speak of what has been accomplished by woman suffrage in a hazy sort of way. Let us have facts:

Cheyenne, the capital of Wyoming, where women have voted for a quarter of a century, has a population of less than 12,000. I am told that in Cheyenne there are 25 licensed gambling houses, and that saloons are as numerous as any other kind of stores; and it has been officially stated that not a single act of legislation aimed at the betterment of the human race, has been passed in Wyoming through woman's influence. Gen. Thompson, who managed the Democratic campaign in Wyoming, in 1892, said:—"The women's vote is the easiest thing in the world to get, and the easiest thing to keep, and the easiest thing to manipulate of any element in politics." After six months residence in Wyoming, divorce may be obtained for any one of eleven reasons!

The history of woman's influence in the legislative halls of the other States where woman suffrage obtains, is not a glowing tribute to their intelligence or probity, and has been in existence too short a time to be given as precedent for the States East and South. The partial suffrage referred to is also a thing not to be boasted of by the women who desire the suffrage. The record of the Massachusetts vote is that in Boston in 1888, 20,252 women registered in the interest of school suffrage, and most of them voted, for it was a warfare of religious sects; a Protestant and a Roman Catholic fight, such as would appeal to most women. The next year the number of women registering was reduced nearly one-half. In 1891, 6,008 women registered and 5,428 voted. The same thing was tried in Connecticut and not two and one-half per cent of the women entitled to vote exercised that right. Do you imagine for a moment that they would do better if a full franchise were given them? Who are the women who would go to the polls in stormy weather? I do not need to prove to you gentlemen that the women who would vote "early and often" are not the women to whom you would trust the ballot in case of need.

# HIDDEN FROM HISTORY

It has been stated to you that I have no right to claim that I represent 1,500,000 women of New York. It has also been stated that 400,000 women of New York had signed the suffrage petition. The truth of the matter is, gentlemen, that two years ago when the suffragists made an effort to strike out the word "male" from the Constitution of New York, Miss Susan B. Anthony promised to offer a petition signed by 1,000,000 women of New York; and with that end in view, the suffragists canvassed New York State with that energy for which they are noted. I should not be surprised to learn that not one woman over 21 years of age had escaped having been tried to be cajoled or coerced into signing the petition. The result was a failure so great that they abandoned the idea of getting the women to sign, and so they asked men to come to their help. They paid for signatures sometimes as high as three cents. In one town there were sent in the signatures of more women than there were women in the town, over 21 years of age. They did not succeed even then; so they claimed to have the signatures of 200,000 members of the labor organization, and 50,000 grangers through their respective secretaries. Many members of both of these organizations have denied since then having known of the petition, and also denied having any sympathy with the woman suffrage movement.

They claimed also 75,000 W. C. T. U. members. I have personal friends who are members of the W. C. T. U. and who are bitterly opposed to the granting of suffrage to all classes and conditions of women.

But allowing for the sake of the argument that all these persons signed the petition, they then only claimed 426,000 names; as reported at the time. I quote from an article written by one of the leaders after their defeat before the Constitutional Convention. "We have 200,000 women's names encircled by the great arms of labor and clasped together by the strong arms of the farm", which is poetic at least, but which only claims 200,000 women.

There are 7,000,000 of people in New York State. It is fair to believe that one-quarter of that number are women over 21 years of age, that is 1,750,000. The truth is, that there are several thousand more women than men in New York State. But granting them those figures, I lay claim to only those women who refused to be enrolled as suffragists, when I say I represent 1,500,000 women of voting age in New York State, who do not desire to have suffrage thrust upon them. I am sorry to take up your time to prove my assertion: One more fact and I will close.

The Anti-suffragists have not tried to organize until recently; and then only because we were forced to protest against the cry of this very small minority that claimed "women do not oppose suffrage even if they do not ask for it". In the city of Albany, N. Y., in one month's time 8,320 women signed the anti-suffrage protest. This will give you an idea of the feeling of the women. In this number were nearly every tax-paying woman in Albany as well as women who work for their daily bread. On my return home from St. Louis, I was delighted beyond expression when I went into one of our largest dry-good shops to have one of the women clerks thank me for the position I had taken at St. Louis, and before I left the shop every girl in the department had expressed her thanks. One of them said: "We signed the suffrage petition; we did not understand what it meant; but when we did we signed the anti-suffrage protest. When I marry I expect to get a husband who can be trusted to make the laws that are to protect me and my children, and until that time, my father will look out for me better than I could for myself."

It is said by the suffragists that I represent women who are slaves; and that we boast of our bondage. Well, gentlemen, if it is to be a slave to be a woman in this part of the 19th century, in the United States of America, where women are so protected by laws made for them by men, that they may enjoy every privilege a man enjoys without annoyance or effort; where men toil from morning till night to provide the women of their households with the luxuries of life as well as its necessities; where ninety-nine men stand ready to chastise the one man who may dare to insult a woman; where nothing that the womenly women ask for legally is denied them by men; then I am proud to belong to that class of women whom the suffragists dub "slaves"; and it is in the name of these women who are living the lives God intended them to live, whose even wholesome existence in the charm of youth, in the bloom of maturity, and in the calm decline of age, proves the wisdom and beneficence of the Creator,—your mothers, your wives, your daughters,--I ask you not to embody in your platform any resolution, that even by the greatest stretch of imagination, could convey a belief that you approved of and favored woman suffrage.

Officers of the Anti-Suffrage Association of the Third Judicial District of the State of New York.

MRS. J. V. L. PRUYN, *President.*
MRS. WILLIAM J. WALLACE, *1st Vice-President.*
MRS. WM. B. VAN RENSSELAER, *Secretary.*

MRS. ERASTUS CORNING,
MRS. J. HOWARD KING,
MRS. WM. O. STILLMAN,
MRS. WILLIAM CASSIDY,
MRS. JOEL R. REED,
MRS. FREDERICK TOWNSEND
MISS LUCY A. PLYMPTON,
*Executive Committee.*

MRS. JOSEPH GAVIT, *Treasurer.*
MRS. W. WINSLOW CRANNELL, *Chairman.*

Other leaflets may be obtained by applying to the Anti-Suffrage Association, 13 Elk Street, Albany, N. Y.

# ADDRESS

TO THE

## JUDICIARY COMMITTEES OF THE SENATE AND ASSEMBLY OF THE STATE OF NEW YORK

FEBRUARY 22, 1899

PRESENTED BY

### THE ASSOCIATION OPPOSED TO THE EXTENSION OF THE SUFFRAGE TO WOMEN

The Address was prepared by a Sub-Committee consisting of Mrs. Rossiter Johnson and Mrs. Winfield Moody, and was read by Mrs. Arthur M. Dodge

# ADDRESS.

GENTLEMEN: We come before your honorable body as representatives of the New York State Association opposed to the Extension of the Suffrage to Women.

We come to speak concerning three bills which have been introduced into the Legislature by advocates of woman suffrage. They refer to a tax-paying vote for women.

Of two presented in the Senate, one provides that "A woman who possesses the qualifications to vote for village officers, except the qualification of sex, who is the owner of property in the village, be entitled to vote upon propositions authorizing the expenditure of money."

The other provides that "Every other person" (except married women) "twenty-one years of age, who shall have resided in the village thirty days next preceding such election, and is the owner of property in the village, shall also be entitled to vote upon a proposition for or against the expenditure of money."

The new one introduced in the Assembly provides that in all towns and villages, when questions of local taxation or the issuing of bonds for municipal improvements are submitted to the tax-paying citizens, women shall have the right to vote on equal terms with men.

The most specious of suffrage cries is: "Taxation without representation is tyranny," and the claim that appeals most strongly to those who would otherwise feel no sympathy with suffrage is: "We pay taxes, and yet have no voice as to how our money shall be spent."

Before discussing these bills, we wish to call your attention to a singular fact. Suffrage advocates appear to know that the din concerning taxation rings hollow; for they do not make it a legislative issue. It has not been pressed here before for twenty-five years, at least. During the last three years suffrage propositions have met with thirty-seven defeats in twenty States, and of all these only two concerned taxation. In Connecticut, in 1897, the Legislature rejected a bill to permit tax-paying women to vote on questions involving the laying of taxes; and in Kentucky, in 1898, the House rejected a proposition to exempt from taxation the property of women while they are not permitted to vote.

The bills before you may or may not encroach upon constitutional suffrage. If they do so, we believe that you can be trusted to defeat them; but even if they represent only delegated power, as does the school vote, we have profound objections to them. They would give special privileges to some, and equal rights to none. They would establish a special privilege for the woman who has property, against the rights of the woman who has none. They would also establish injustice as between women of property; for the millionaire would have no more votes as to her thousand acres than the wage-earner would have as to her grass-plot.

If you are going to establish or extend a property vote at all, it should be proportional. Where will you stop? If the woman who has five thousand dollars has one vote, then the woman who owns a hundred thousand dollars' worth of property must have twenty votes, or she is wronged.

These bills are based upon such undemocratic and exceptional conditions as to lead one to believe that they are intended as mere entering wedges for a cause that is desperate. One of them asks this vote for widows and spinsters; the other asks it for married women as well. The first restriction belongs only in Europe, while any tax-payer's vote is an anomaly in a free land.

*Unmarried* women have always stood, as to property rights, on a par with men. Will anybody believe that man intended to favor his sister, and to wrong his wife and his mother? The laws that once bound a woman's property rights with her husband's were meant to be protective. But, whether unmarried or married, woman cannot vote "on equal terms with men," for reasons that will be given later in the course of our argument.

It is quite generally thought that the advocates of woman suffrage secured the passage of the laws giving property rights to married women in this State and country. But the "His-

5

tory of Woman Suffrage," edited by Mrs. Stanton, Miss Anthony, and Matilda Joslyn Gage, tells a different story. That work was published in 1881-85. In setting forth the causes that gave rise to the suffrage movement the editors mention as:

First. "The discussions in several of the state legislatures of the property rights of married women."

The suffrage movement began in 1848. In 1844 Rhode Island had passed a law securing property rights to married women. In 1848-49 Connecticut, Massachusetts, and Texas passed such laws. In 1850-52 Maine and Alabama passed such laws. In 1853 New Hampshire, Indiana, Wisconsin, and Iowa took the same step. In 1849 Ohio, Maine, Indiana, and Missouri passed laws giving married women the right to their own earnings. Suffrage agitation had not even been dreamed of in most of these widely separated States. As to New York State, we quote the following from the Suffrage History: —

When preparing their first volume, Mrs. Gage wrote to the Hon. George Geddes to ask who was responsible for the married woman's property rights bill that was passed in 1848, and whether any debates had preceded it. He wrote in reply, in part, as follows: "I believe this law originated with Judge Fine, without any outside prompting. Only one petition was presented in favor of the bill, and that came from Syracuse, and was due to the action of my personal friends. I know of no debates that preceded it, and I am quite sure that in our long discussions no allusion was made to anything of the kind."

So it appears that suffrage advocates had no connection with this bill, which opened the way for all the liberal legislation that has ended in making laws far more favorable to women than to men.

In a pamphlet published by the New York State Woman Suffrage Association, to report their proceedings during the Constitutional Convention of 1894, it is recorded that Mr. B. F. Church, in presenting an appeal from his county, asking for the submission of the suffrage amendment, said: "Sir, beginning in 1848, the male citizens of the State of New York, not at the clamor of the women, as I understand it, but actuated by a sense of justice, began to remove the disabilities under which women labored at that time, until, in 1891, I believe, the last barriers were stricken away."

A prominent suffrage advocate said: "When any community

is civilized up to the point of enfranchising women, it will be civilized up to the point of sustaining their vote, as it now sustains their property rights, with the whole material force of the community."

We offer the foregoing as testimony that woman does not need the property vote in self-defence.

These bills ask for the ballot in behalf of women who hold property in their own right. But the owner always adds the taxes to the rental; therefore, tenants and occupiers are as truly tax-payers, and this bill, which is urged in behalf of woman suffrage, and not of tax-payers, may soon be followed by another demand for the ballot.

Virtually there is no connection between voting and tax-paying. When a millionaire becomes a bankrupt, he does not lose his vote. This is because he does not lose capacity for the things the government counts on equally whether he is rich or poor, a tax-payer or a non-tax-payer. These are: police duty, jury duty, riot quelling, property guarding, and law defending, in peace or in war.

The property of man, woman, and child is alike taxed; and in return for the payment of the tax they all get the same things: schools, roads, gas, water, police protection, etc. But there is another tax — the service tax — which is necessary to make the property of all tax-payers of any value. It is the service tax that gives security, and this tax is laid upon men alone. With this tax goes the vote. To give woman a tax-paying vote when she is exempted by nature and civilized usage from forming part of the defence of even her own property, is to work injustice. It is not true that woman has no voice in regard to her property now. Practically she is likely to have more voice than her masculine neighbor with his one vote. Besides, the majority of women are not direct tax-payers.

Again, the property interests of women are so bound up with those of their husbands, sons, and friends that they are represented by men. If a woman cannot trust any of these to vote as she could wish, how can she trust them to carry out her wishes after she has voted? For we must remember that the execution of laws must always be left to the men.

The final vote concerning laws should rest in the hands of those who alone can enforce the laws. In a republic the defence depends only on the individual men, and the wisest states-

## 7

men have seen that the ballot must therefore be theirs alone, if the government is to be stable. The ballot is not a reward to man for standing ready to give this defence. It is merely the symbol that civilized usage employs in order to learn what strength could be arrayed to support opposing votes. If man's strength ceases to stand behind the symbol, the ballot is of no value to anybody. Man is as much controlled by the limitations of his nature as woman is by hers. He cannot "make over half the voting power to women" without endangering all voting power. So long as human nature remains what it is, and so long as man cannot make over his larger brawn and muscle, he cannot make over the voting power. He might hand over the symbol; but the symbol without the thing symbolized would prove a delusion.

That the sovereign power is man's only while he is able to exercise it, we realized during the glorious and tragic summer of 1898. Man would fain have *voted* freedom to Cuba and the islands of the sea, but found that only his sword could win it. This is as true, though not as evident, of every law's enactment and every poll's decision. For this reason women cannot vote on equal terms with men.

Woman's right to life, liberty, and the pursuit of happiness is inalienable; and man commits a moral wrong when he endangers these by attempting to extend the symbol of his protective power where he cannot extend the power itself.

Nature, not man, has exempted woman from the fighting line where rests the ballot-box. Frederick Douglass said: "American freedom depends on the ballot-box, the jury-box, and the cartridge-box." The advocates of woman suffrage demand complete use of the first, partial use of the second, and entire exemption from use of the third, on which both the others rely for existence. And this they do in the name of "equal rights to all, and special privileges to none." The request would be ludicrous if it were not dangerous.

We have other grave objections to offer, gleaned from experience. Woman tax-payers are among the most numerous signers of anti-suffrage petitions. Women do not now vote concerning their money affairs where they have opportunity. They do not use the school, or even the constitutional suffrage, except to a very limited degree. The social and moral initiative is theirs, and stated voting does not belong to the genius of their life.

8

Gentlemen: Woman suffrage and woman's progress are founded on distinct and, as we believe, on antagonistic principles. As proof that law-makers have recognized this truth, we point to the fact that while for fifty years New York has steadily denied appeals for woman suffrage, her statesmen have made laws so largely in our favor that, if we want legal equality, we must begin with a surrender of great privileges. We believe that these privileges have been granted in recognition of the fact that our life and work are as valuable to man and to the government, and as much respected by both, as man's more evident service. Such privileges appear to be our equal rights, and we pray you not to endanger them by the passage of these bills. We also believe that their passage would result in serious injury to the general welfare.

Issued by the New York State Association opposed to the Extension of the Suffrage to Women.

*Reprinted, with slight adaptation, by the Massachusetts Association opposed to the further Extension of the Suffrage to Women.*

Pamphlets and leaflets may be obtained from the Secretary of the Association.

Mrs. Robert W. Lord,
P. O. Box 2262, Boston

## MASSACHUSETTS ASSOCIATION

### OPPOSED TO THE

## FURTHER EXTENSION OF SUFFRAGE TO WOMEN.

---

*The aim of this Association is to increase general interest in this subject, and to educate and stimulate public opinion to an opposition based on intelligent conviction.*

*The method of work is to collect and distribute literature which the discussion of this subject calls forth, to encourage the writing of articles and giving of lectures setting forth the reasons for opposing female suffrage, to present, when necessary, remonstrances to the Legislature to counteract the influence of petitions presented by advocates of female suffrage.*

*The suffragists, in the face of the decisive vote of November, 1895, when only four per cent of the women of Massachusetts called for the suffrage, continue to demand this undesirable and undesired privilege. While they remain active and aggressive, it is important that women opposed to female suffrage should also testify to their opinion.*

*Printed by the Massachusetts Association opposed to Extension of Woman Suffrage.*

Pamphlets and leaflets may be obtained from the Secretary of the Association,

Mrs. Robert W. Lord,
P. O. Box 2262, Boston.

# America When Femininized

SUFFRAGIST—FEMINIST IDEAL FAMILY LIFE.

The More a Politician Allows Himself to be Henpecked
The More Henpecking We Will Have in Politics.

A Vote for Federal Suffrage is a Vote for Organized Female
Nagging Forever.

"American pep which was the result of a masculine dominated country will soon be a thing of the past. With the collapse of the male ascendancy in this country we can look forward to a nation of degeneration. The suppression of sex will ultimately have its harvest in decadence, a phenomenon already beginning. The effect of the social revolution on American character will be to make "sissies" of American men—a process already well under way."—Dr. William J. Hickson, Chicago University.

**WOMAN SUFFRAGE** denatures both men and women; it masculinizes women and femininizes men. The history of ancient civilization has proven that a weakening of the man power of nations has been but a pre-runner of decadence in civilization.

**Will you stand for this? Prove that you will not by** voting to **Reject** the Federal Woman Suffrage Amendment to the Constitution of the United States.

SOUTHERN WOMAN'S LEAGUE FOR REJECTION OF THE
SUSAN B. ANTHONY AMENDMENT

WE SERVE THAT OUR STATES MAY LIVE, AND LIVING, PRESERVE THE UNION

# American Women and the Ballot.

THE great Anti-Suffrage movement which is sweeping over the country, with quiet but irresistible force, is causing such agitation in the Suffragist ranks as they have never manifested before. Unable in spite of heroic efforts for the past twelve years to gain a noteworthy legislative advance, they have been at last impelled to call in the aid of the militant Suffragists of England, and in New York and Massachusetts are adopting, to a certain degree, their noisy and ill-mannered tactics.

It is time, therefore, that the claims of the Anti-Suffragists, hitherto prosecuted by quiet though persistent means, should be clearly and forcibly stated that the public may have a true understanding of the nature of their campaign. In presenting their claims, therefore, (see accompanying documents) we ask leave to state respectfully the keynote of our contention.

The unfailing reply of men to the petitions of Suffragists has been, "When the majority of women ask for the right to vote it will be granted them!" To this we add that the converse of the proposition ought to hold true; that so long as an overwhelming majority of women for good and sufficient reasons actively oppose this revolutionary change in our social, domestic and political order, it ought not to be imposed upon them. That such opposition is felt and exercised by the great majority of American women, we propose to show in these pages.

### Women Do Not Want To Vote

It is now more than sixty years since the first Woman's Right Convention was held in the state of New York. Until after the Civil War the cause received little serious attention, being generally treated with indifference on the part of women, and ridicule from men. But the services of women in the hospitals in connection with the Sanitary Commission during the war emphasized the civic possibilities of women, while the loss or disability of more than a million of our most active and energetic young men upon the battlefields left many women dependent upon their own exertions, and opened to them new and unaccustomed fields of labor, all of which facts were favorable to the consideration of the new doctrine about women. Many of the early Abolitionists also were believers in woman's rights, and one of them had left a considerable sum of money for the maintenance of the cause. To this fund additions have been made from time to time so that the Suffragists have always been well supplied with money.

The opposition of the best women, educators, philanthropists and social leaders—using that term in its truest sense—to the addition of political duties, to those already borne by women, had been from the first pronounced. Such women as Emma Willard of Troy Female Seminary, Mary Lyon of Mt. Holyoke Seminary, Mrs. Almira Lincoln Phelps, Mrs. Admiral Dahlgren, Mrs. W. T. Sherman, said emphatically that the duties of wife and mother were more important than any that women could render in the political field. In 1870, only five years after the war closed, a petition, written and circulated by women was sent to Congress. Fifteen thousand women in all were enrolled, but no organization was formed, and the work was not continued, mainly because it was supposed, that as the number of women signers was at least ten times greater than the number which the Suffragists could then rally, this expression of opinion would be conclusive.

The agitation however, was kept up, drawing its main energies, as is now apparent from history, from that revolutionary impulse which followed in the wake of the Communistic Manifesto of Karl Marx and Frederic Engel, which, published in nearly all the languages of Europe, in 1847, had been largely instrumental in bringing about the uprisings of 1848. Against this revolutionary offshoot from the European movement conservative American women continued to struggle. A very lively correspondence was kept up between the women of different states, but it was not until 1880-85 that concerted public measures began to be taken, and committees formed to take charge of the work. When petitions were presented to legislatures, counter petitions, often with only a few well-known names appended, were presented; arguments were met with counter arguments; in certain cases newspaper and magazine articles were prepared which did good service. And so far the cause had made almost no legislative gains. Wyoming had indeed given full suffrage to women in 1869, but the state was of so little importance at that time that not much notice was taken of the fact. Men in general regarded it as more of a joke than otherwise. But when, under the brief but excited sway of Populism, joining forces with Mormonism, Utah, Idaho and Colorado were added to the Suffrage states, it was felt by Anti-Suffrage women that the time for decisive action on their part had arrived. In 1895-97 the three State Associations of Massachusetts, New York and Illinois were formed, and a determined and co-operative plan of action was inaugurated. Other states gathered around these three by forming committees or associations, until now every section of the Eastern, Middle and Western states is powerfully represented in the Anti-Suffrage ranks, and the movement is still increasing. Since that date not one noteworthy gain has been recorded for suffrage, while the legislatures of almost every state have again and again defeated their measures, in response to the pleas of the Anti-Suffragists, by decisive and increasing majorities. This fact alone is proof that the great body of American women is opposed to the imposition of political responsibilities upon their sex. But we have much more proof to offer.

## The Massachusetts Referendum

Massachusetts was for many years the state most inclined to suffrage views, and the conservative women had for more than a decade been constantly occupied with refuting them. Year after year they had appeared before the legislatures in opposition, and the agitation had extended all over the state. At last the legislature, with a view of settling the vexed question forever, submitted the whole matter to the people, women as well as men being empowered to register and vote upon it. The result was the most general and overwhelming defeat for the Suffragists that any proposition had ever received in the state. The male majority was overwhelming, while in spite of the frantic efforts of the Suffragists to bring their forces to the polls less than four per cent of the number of women entitled to register and vote, voted "Aye."

## School Suffrage

There are now more than twenty states in the Union which have given school suffrage to women. It was supposed that their interest in education and in the facilities afforded to their own children, would ensure their vote in large numbers; that in fact they would be eager to use the privilege accorded them. It does not require statistics to prove that the reverse of this is true. School suffrage is notoriously a failure, scarcely two per cent of the women in most states availing themselves of it. They evidently feel that their best power lies in home influence, and prefer to use it in accordance with the principles of our Constitution, which has from the beginning recognized the husband and father as the political head of the family.

## Do Club Women Want to Vote?

On page 6 of the LADIES HOME JOURNAL for February, 1909, is an editorial article somewhat more than a column in length, which gives the results of a series of investigations made by the editor, to ascertain the percentage of women who really desire the ballot. It should be premised that the LADIES HOME JOURNAL is a magazine having the largest circulation among women of any in the country, amounting to more than a million of copies a month; and this enormous circulation has been built up mainly by the untiring energy of its editor, Mr. Edward J. Bok. He has studied the nature and wants of American women, as he would study a problem in Euclid, and has reduced the art of pleasing them to an exact science. It being thus a matter of vital importance to his business, Mr. Bok has made a special point of finding out how women stand upon the suffrage question. He gives his readers the results.

The first testimony which he cites is the test made by a former president of the United States, not many years since. Receiving the customary petition from the suffrage agitators, that he should incorporate in his message to Congress a recommendation that woman suffrage should be favorably considered by that body, **"as it was practically the desire of the whole body of American women,"** he carried the request to his wife. She replied that it was a matter to which she was wholly indifferent, but if he really wanted to know how other women felt, why not ask them? It was finally decided that he should write to fifty women of his acquaintance, impartially selected, each one a woman of good sense and high character, asking them if they wanted to vote, and be guided by their replies. He did so and received forty-six answers, four of the ladies being ill or out of the country. Thirty-four had no desire to vote; eleven were utterly indifferent; one solitary lady thought she would like to vote, if permitted, but added, "probably, when the time came, I should not bother about it." The president omitted the recommendation from his message.

But these were just plain home and society women. So our editor set about investigating the clubs. With club women it might be different. His experience was singularly like that of the president. He thought he must be unfortunate in his choice of clubs. So, armed with introductions, he betook himself to the meeting of the General Federation of Women's Clubs, at Boston, last summer (1908). Like the astute purveyor of news that he is, he "took particular pains to ask the leading officers and workers of the movement, how they believed the Federation, as a whole, stood on the question of woman suffrage." We quote the editor literally.

"Said one of the principal officers: 'So overwhelmingly against it that I would not like to see the Federation place itself on record on the subject.'"

"You are in favor of woman's voting, then?" I asked.

'I am, decidedly!' she answered. 'But I know only too well how the Federation as a body would express itself!' I said to another officer standing by: "What do **you** think?" 'Just as Mrs. ——— does.' I have tried it on three clubs in different parts of the country and I have desisted from any further effort. "Would you mind telling me the ratio?" 'Oh! it was terrible—eighty per cent against! It was anything but encouraging.'

"I asked another leading worker in the movement--one who has perhaps traveled as extensively over the country as any officer of the Federation, and spoken before nearly every principal woman's club in America. "What would be the vote of the Federation on this question? Would you, from your experience, hazard an opinion?" 'It isn't hazarding an opinion. I know only too well it would be a Waterloo for me and mine,' she laughingly answered. "You are a Suffragist, then?" I asked. 'Well, yes,' she replied, 'I suppose I am. I have said so often enough in public. But somehow or other I am free to say that wherever I have spoken on the subject, I have not been surprised that my arguments have failed to convince. They do not seem convincing to myself!"

The article concludes by saying: "The field of politics **as a new excitement for a few restless American women** is barred to them by their own sex." If Mr. Bok had believed that the great body of American women desired the suffrage, can it be believed that he would have given more than a column of his valuable space to the elucidation of such a sentiment as this?

### Why Women Vote in Colorado

We are told that women vote in Colorado as generally as men, but we have excellent testimony from private sources, that it is under compulsion, to save the state from the calamity of being governed by the undesirable classes, who bring out their women voters to the last unit, and so necessitate the voting of the better classes to preserve the balance. Proof that the women of the slums and of the red light districts have not only generally voted in some elections, but have been forced to repeat their votes by the unprincipled politicians who were officially brought in contact with them, is recorded in the courts where such offenders have been tried and convicted. We know that the same thing would occur in Illinois, and especially in Chicago, if municipal suffrage were given to women. Who can imagine that the unscrupulous politicians who infest our down-town districts would see such a mass of votable citizens, lying under their hands, and not find means to use them for their own purposes? Then other women who have their hands full and more than full of home and social and philanthropic duties, would be called upon to take upon themselves, in addition, the burden of politics to counteract their votes. We sincerely and earnestly request to be spared this most unjust and humiliating service.

We will gladly do our duty in the state whereunto, as women, God has called us. We will study to improve our intelligence and enlarge our opportunities in this direction, but we believe that the supreme position of woman as the mother of the race, the guiding genius of the home, and the arbiter of social morals, however it may need to be re-emphasized and expanded in this generation, and under the light of modern science, is too grand and glorious a birthright to be disparaged and bargained away for such political rights as suffrage would bestow upon us.

CHICAGO, February, 1909.

ILLINOIS ASSOCIATION

OPPOSED TO THE EXTENSION OF SUFFRAGE

TO WOMEN

PRESIDENT:
Mrs. CAROLINE F. CORBIN

1st VICE-PRESIDENT:  2d VICE-PRESIDENT:
Mrs. S. M. NICKERSON  Mrs. RICHARD J. OGLESBY

SECRETARY:
Miss J. C. FAIRFIELD

EXECUTIVE COMMITTEE:

Mrs. GEO. W. SMITH   Mrs. RALPH N. ISHAM
Mrs. A. T. GALT   Mrs. WM. ELIOT FURNESS
Mrs. FRANCIS LACKNER   Miss MARY POMEROY GREEN

No. 4

# AN ECONOMICAL WOMAN,

## Who Thinks Men Need No Help From Others in Politics.

There is one thing I can never understand about the woman suffragists, and that is why they want men and women to do the same work. It seems so wasteful. I never can bear to see two people doing what one can do just as well. I may not be able to rise above the plain, practical common sense side of the question, but I know I have a love of economy, and I do not like to see time and strength wasted any more than I do money; in fact, time and strength are so much harder to get than even money, that I would rather throw away money. Of course, if the men can't possibly get along in politics without the women, that is a different thing. If they are unable any longer to take care of what has so long been considered their department, let them say so, and then, out of pity, and the spirit of helpfulness for which women are noted, perhaps we will turn to and help them. But it will have to be a beseeching and heartrending wail from our enfeebled men that will make the greater part of our women willing to use their time and strength that way. **Our women do not seem to have any superabundance of strength and nerves anyway, and what will they become if the woman suffrage reign should come in?** I love to see people work, and I love to work myself, but I would rather women should set men a good example, by doing their work well, than by pitching in to help the men and neglecting their own special duties. **Woman's work is the noblest in the world; her power and influence the strongest.** The homes, the babies, the charities, the schools need woman, and let our legislators consider carefully whether woman can attend to all these duties and a hundred others, as well as do their part in the political world. Let us hope and pray that these legislators of ours will not vote away so much of the time and strength of the women of this state in as thoughtless a way as they sometimes do its money.

AN ECONOMICAL WOMAN.

1909.

ISSUED BY
*THE NEW YORK STATE ASSOCIATION OPPOSED TO WOMAN SUFFRAGE,*
29 WEST 39TH STREET, NEW YORK CITY.

15 Cents per 100.

VIRGINIA STATE LIBRARY
RICHMOND

# An Open Letter to a Temperance Friend.

My dear Madam:

You and I agree in aim, though not in methods. You think that license-suffrage for women will help the temperance cause. I see in it nothing but a desire to gain by indirect means an entering wedge to universal woman suffrage, which, when asked for directly, the common sense of the great majority of both men and women will refuse.

Eager prohibitionists of both sexes, joined with the politicians who trade on them, are pushing this new stroke of the woman suffragists. If it succeeds, the advocates of extreme temperance legislation will no doubt gain some votes. Enthusiastic and unpractical reformers, among women even more than among men, will vote for what they are pleased to think radical legislation, whether it answers their purpose or not. They will bear their testimony though the heavens fall, and though all our large cities be subjected to the corrupting farce of a prohibition which does not prohibit, which in large communities does not prevent or even diminish drunkenness, but which is the fruitful parent of meanness, fraud, lying, and contempt of law. They forget that all women are not reformers, and that, for the sake of the votes of those who think with them, they call into action the vastly greater multitude of those who do not, those rude masses of their sex of whose votes nothing can be foretold except that they will reinforce that ignorant male vote which already puts our institutions to so perilous a strain.

Yours very truly,

F. PARKMAN.

*Printed by the Massachusetts Association opposed to further Extension of Suffrage to Women.*

Pamphlets and leaflets may be obtained from the Secretary of the Association. Mrs. Robert W. Lord,
P. O. Box 2262, Boston.

# The Vote of Massachusetts on Municipal Suffrage for Women at the State Election, November 5, 1895.

## OVER 100,000 MAJORITY AGAINST IT ON THE PART OF THE MEN.

**Every County and every Congressional, Councillor, Senatorial and Representative District votes "NO" on the Proposition.**

After twenty-five years of agitation by the suffragists, the question of municipal suffrage for women was brought to a test at the State election, November 5, 1895. The voters were asked their opinion, and gave a most emphatic reply.

**Never was there so full an expression of opinion upon any question submitted to the people of Massachusetts.** The vote for governor at the State election was 328,121. The vote of the men upon municipal woman suffrage at the same election was 273,946. Over 83 per cent of those voting for governor voted upon this question, while in 1891 only 62 per cent of those voting for governor voted upon the constitutional amendment abolishing the poll tax as a prerequisite for voting, and in 1896 only 72 per cent of those voting for governor voted upon the constitutional amendment providing for biennial elections.

**Never has any question submitted to the people of Massachusetts received so overwhelming a defeat. The vote of the men was, "No" 186,976, "Yes" 86,970, a "No" majority of 100,006.** The vote in 1889 on the prohibition amendment to the constitution was, "No" 133,085, "Yes" 86,459, a "No" majority of 46,626. The vote in 1896 on the biennial elections amendment was, "No" 161,263, "Yes" 115,505, a "No" majority of 45,758. So that the majority against woman suffrage in Massachusetts is more than twice as great as that against either prohibition or biennial elections.

The vote of the women on the suffrage question, "Yes" 22,204, "No" 861, is as significant as that of the men. By the census of 1895 the number of men in Massachusetts qualified to register and vote was 560,802. The number of women qualified to register and vote on this question was at least 575,000. Of these more than 550,000 declined to vote, and less than four in a hundred voted "Yes." In other words, more than 96 per cent of the women of the Commonwealth either prefer the present status of the suffrage or are wholly indifferent in the matter.

In 48 towns not one woman voted "Yes," and in 137 other towns the women voting "Yes" numbered fifteen or less. As the vast majority of the women opposed to the suffrage expressed their opinion by refusing to vote, the women's vote, for purposes of tabulation, has little value. In the following statement of votes, therefore, the votes of the men alone are considered.

Massachusetts, at the time of the election, had 31 cities and 322 towns. Of the 31 cities, every one cast a large majority against woman suffrage. The vote of the cities was, "No" 120,657, "Yes" 53,982, a "No" majority of 66,675. Many people have thought that the vote against woman suffrage was disproportionately heavy in the cities, but this is not so. The vote of the 322 towns was, "No" 66,319, "Yes" 32,988, a "No" majority of 33,331. The cities of Massachusetts contain two-thirds of the population of the State, and, in an even distribution of sentiment, should therefore contribute two-thirds of the "No" majority. That is just what they did, and the closeness of the figures to an exact two-thirds is remarkable. Of the 322 towns, 293 voted "No," 28 voted "Yes," and 1 was a tie. The 28 towns voting "Yes" were among the very smallest in the State, their vote averaging only "Yes" 51, "No" 42.

Every County and every Congressional, Councillor, Senatorial and Representative district in the Commonwealth cast a majority against the proposition.

# ANTI-SUFFRAGE ANSWERS

## SUFFRAGISTS SAY:

1. Taxation without representation is tyranny.

2. Women are deprived of citizenship because they may not vote.

3. Women belong to the disfranchised class of criminals and idiots because they have not a vote.

4. The welfare of children is woman's work. Why should not women vote for child welfare laws?

5. Women are wage-earners. Why should not women vote on laws governing the conditions under which they must work?

6. Property qualification, religious qualification, and also color qualification have been abandoned. Why should sex disqualification continue?

## WE SAY:

1. It is folly to use this Revolutionary War Cry as an argument for woman suffrage. Men do not vote because they pay taxes. Why should women?

2. Women are citizens without the ballot, but the State requires a different service from its men and women citizens. Man's political service to the State is counterbalanced by woman's service in the home. If there were no families and no homes, there would be no State. One service is fully as important as the other.

3. Only suffragists make such a classification. Criminals have been disfranchised by statute; idiots may not vote for obvious reasons. Women having never been enfranchised cannot be spoken of as a disfranchised class.

4. The best laws to protect working children have been passed through the influence of the National Child Labor Committee. Ohio, Massachusetts, New York and Wisconsin have better Child Labor Laws today than some of the States where women vote.

5. Some of the best laws regulating the employment of women have been passed in recent years in the great manufacturing Eastern States where women do not vote.

6. Because Sex is a distinction imposed by Nature which precludes men and women from doing similar work equally well. Government is **MAN'S** work. Voting is a part of the machinery of government.

New York State Association Opposed to Woman Suffrage.   37 West 39th Street, New York

# ANTI-SUFFRAGE ARGUMENTS

The vast majority of women of the State of Virginia do not desire the burden and responsibility of the franchise, believing in the decision of the Supreme Court of the United States, that the franchise is a privilege and not a right. They do not wish the franchise.

**Because.** Facts show indisputably that suffrage has done nothing that it's advocates claim for it in the States and Countries where women have the ballot.

**Because.** The best legislation affecting women and children is in the states where women do not have the ballot.

**Because.** Women cannot have the franchise without going into politics and the political woman will be a menace to society, to the home and to the state.

**Because.** Equal franchise will only double existing conditions in the electorate if all women vote and it will double election expenses.

**Because.** More can be done for the advancement of the highest interests of the race by the influence of women free and unfettered by political ties and obligations.

**Because.** It would be a calamity if woman suffrage were carried into law without the real consent and deliberate demand of the majority of the women of this state.

*Literature can be obtained free of cost at*

    MEYERS BOOK STORE, First and Broad Streets
    BELL BOOK AND STATIONERY CO., 914 E. Main St.

## Virginia Association Opposed to Woman's Suffrage

VIRGINIA STATE LIBRARY
RICHMOND

# Anti-Suffrage Arguments
# DANGER!

## WOMAN'S SUFFRAGE THE VANGUARD OF SOCIALISM

Proof.—See here—

1. What is Socialism?

    Socialism is against Christian marriage.
    Socialism is against the Christian family.
    Socialism is against the holding of private property.
    Socialism is against Christianity.
    Socialism is against the Bible.

2. If you hold your marriage, your family life, your home, your religion, as sacred, dear and inviolate, to be preserved for yourself, and for your children, for all time, then work with all your might against Socialism's vanguard—Woman's Suffrage.

3. In a parade in New York City last November they openly marched together. The Woman Suffragists as the vanguard, with their yellow flags. The Socialists behind with their red flags.

4. The Socialist red flag had this inscription: "Every Socialist is a Woman Suffragist."

    Does every Virginia Woman Suffragist intend to be a Socialist?

5. We hope not. But "There is a way which seemeth right unto a man, but the end thereof is death."

    Danger lies ahead of you.

*Do you not recognize the kinship?*
*Is not this Plain enough for you?*

*Literature can be obtained free of cost at*
*Meyers Book Store, First and Broad Streets*
*Bell Book and Stationery Co., 914 E. Main Street*

## Virginia Association Opposed to Woman's Suffrage

VIRGINIA STATE LIBRARY
RICHMOND

# ANTI-SUFFRAGE ARGUMENTS
## What Votes Cannot Do

*VOTES* cannot make work when there is no work.

*VOTES* cannot increase wages when there is no natural increase in business.

*VOTES* cannot stop the liquor traffic. The liquor traffic STILL FLOURISHES in Equal Suffrage States.

*VOTES* for women cannot lessen election expenses, it will double them.

The best safeguards for the working women are found in those states where the laws have been made by MEN VOTERS.

A woman's citizenship is now just as real and important as that of any man. The Anti-Suffragists stand for the true view of woman's place in the State.

Literature can be obtained free of cost at
Meyers Book Store, First and Broad Streets
Bell Book and Stationery Co., 914 E. Main Street

## Virginia Association Opposed to Woman's Suffrage

# HIDDEN FROM HISTORY

*We have sent you many hundreds like this*
*Anti-Suffrage Association*

As one of your constituents, I wish to express my disapproval of a woman suffrage Federal Amendment.

The platform of your party has declared in favor of STATE ACTION, and the voters of your State gave a majority of 194,984 against woman suffrage in November, 1915.

POPULATION TABLE (Men and Women)

| | |
|---|---|
| Male suffrage states | 78,144,206 |
| Woman suffrage states | 8,198,469 |
| Illinois (partial suffrage, granted by legislators, not by the vote of the people) | 5,638,591 |
| **States recently defeating suffrage at the polls** | **40,464,391** |

In the face of these figures the voters, having no vote on an amendment to the Constitution of the United States, might justly resent having Congress take the decision out of their hands and consider such action a deliberate attempt to circumvent majority rule.

SIGNATURE *Hugh R. Hughes*
*Schuyler N.Y.*

# HIDDEN FROM HISTORY

THE women who favor universal suffrage for women are intensely in earnest, and, at present, very active. It seems desirable that those who hold opposite views should be heard from at this time. If the so-called privilege is granted, a very heavy addition of work and responsibility will be forced upon every woman of intelligence and principle. The votes of ignorant and weak women will be controlled by unprincipled men, and countless and serious derangements of domestic life are sure to ensue. The great objection is fundamental. The "accident of sex" is not an accident. It defines and fixes the conditions and limits of human society. It does not imply a subordination of one sex to the other, but points out that all the duties in life of one cannot well be performed by the other. The petitioners (for suffrage) urge that "women are not responsible for having been born females." This is true; but, if certain duties appertain by nature to their sex, and certain duties to the other sex, each is responsible for the performance of its own. Suppose this question should be considered in the light of "duties," instead of the light of rights, will it not appear that there are natural duties, ordained of God, inconsistent and incompatible with the "rights" now claimed for women? If the duties and functions of public life, participation in public affairs, and eligibility to public office, are antagonistic to the duties of woman in the family, which are we to choose for her, the order of nature or the opposite?

You are requested to sign the petition of remonstrance.

# HIDDEN FROM HISTORY

## Argument Against Women's Suffrage, 1911
**Prepared by J. B. Sanford, Chairmen of Democratic Caucus**

ARGUMENT AGAINST SENATE CONSTITUTIONAL AMENDMENT NO. 8

Suffrage is not a right. It is a privilege that may or may not be granted. Politics is no place for a women consequently the privilege should not be granted to her.

The mother's influence is needed in the home. She can do little good by gadding the streets and neglecting her children. Let her teach her daughters that modesty, patience, and gentleness are the charms of a women. Let her teach her sons that an honest conscience is every man's first political law; that no splendor can rob him nor no force justify the surrender of the simplest right of a free and independent citizen. The mothers of this country can shape the destinies of the nation by keeping in their places and attending to those duties that God Almighty intended for them. The kindly, gentle influence of the mother in the home and the dignified influence of the teacher in the school will far outweigh all the influence of all the mannish female politicians on earth.

The courageous, chivalrous, and manly men and the womanly women, the real mothers and home builders of the country, are opposed to this innovation in American political life. There was a bill (the Sanford bill) before the last legislature which proposed to leave the equal suffrage question to women to decide first before the men should vote on it. This bill was defeated by the suffragettes because they knew that the women would vote down the amendment by a vote of ten to one.

The men are able to run the government and take care of the women. Do women have to vote in order to receive the protection of man? Why, men have gone to war, endured every privation and death itself in defense of woman. To man, woman is the dearest creature on earth, and there is no extreme to which he would not go for his mother or sister. By keeping woman in her exalted position man can be induced to do more for her than he could by having her mix up in affairs that will cause him to lose respect and regard for her. Woman does not have to vote to secure her rights. Man will go to any extreme to protect and elevate her now. As long as woman is woman and keeps her place she will get more protection and more consideration than man gets. When she abdicates her throne she throws down the scepter of her power and loses her influence.

Woman suffrage has been proven a failure in states that have tried it. It is wrong. California should profit by the mistakes of other states. Not one reform has equal suffrage effected. On the contrary, statistics go to show that in most equal suffrage states, Colorado particularly, that divorces have greatly increased since the adoption of the equal suffrage amendment, showing that it has been a home destroyer. Crime has also increased due to lack of the mothers in the home.

Woman is woman. She can not unsex herself or change her sphere. Let her be content with her lot and perform those high duties intended for her by the Great Creator, and she will accomplish far more in governmental affairs that she can ever accomplish by mixing up in the dirty pool of politics. Keep the home pure and all will be well with the Republic. Let not the sanctity of the home be invaded by every little politician that may be running up and down the highway for office. Let the manly men and the womanly women defeat this amendment and keep woman where she belongs in order that she may retain the respect of all mankind.

J. B. Sanford, Senator
4th District.

*Received by Secretary of State Frank Jordan on June 26th, 1911, for publication as part of a voters' information manual. Document is currently filed in the California State Archives under: Secretary of State Elections Papers, 1911 Special Election.*

# ARGUMENT

OF

## Hon. GEORGE G. CROCKER,

AT THE HEARING BEFORE THE COMMITTEE ON WOMAN SUFFRAGE, JANUARY 29, 1884.

# ADDRESS OF HON. GEORGE G. CROCKER.

Mr. Chairman and Gentlemen of the Committee: —

I appear here before you to-day to state in this building, as on several occasions heretofore, my convictions upon the question of woman suffrage, and I am impelled hereto not only by a sense of duty, but also by the earnest request of many ladies.

Of course, in the short time that is to be allowed to each speaker in one morning devoted to this subject, it is impossible to treat of it in any but a partial manner.

It is claimed by the woman suffragists that the right of suffrage is a natural and inalienable right, and if that claim is a correct one, then their case needs no further argument. What is the meaning of a natural and inalienable right? If you will look in the dictionary, you will find that a natural right is one which is fixed or determined by nature; one which pertains to the constitution of mankind; which is essential, and is not assumed, put on, or acquired. If the right of suffrage is a natural right, then it pertains to every man and woman, without regard to sex, without regard to age, without regard to educational qualifications, without regard to any fixed term of residence, and without regard to any requirements of naturalization. If the right of suffrage is a natural right, then every one of the limitations which we have imposed upon it are infringements of the right, and should be swept away at once. The mere statement of such a proposition proves its absurdity. Fortunately, the question as to whether the right of suffrage is a natural right has been brought before the Supreme Court in Maryland, in the case of Anderson *vs.* Baker (23 Md. Reports, p. 531), and before the Supreme Court of the United States, in the case of Minor *vs.* Happersett (21 Wallace, p. 162). In the latter case Chief-Justice Waite delivered the opinion, and it was held that from the foundation of the government citizenship had extended to women as well as to men, but that suffrage was not, and never had been, one of the necessary rights of citizenship.

Our Bill of Rights says that "Government is instituted for the common good; for the protection, safety, prosperity, and happiness of the people;" and the Preamble to the Constitution says, "The body politic is formed by a voluntary association of individuals; it is a social compact, by which the whole people covenants with each citizen, and each citizen with the whole people, that all shall be governed by certain laws for the common good." "The common good," therefore, is the end and the aim of government; and what we are seeking here to-day is to find out whether the extension of the right of suffrage to women will promote that "common good." I trust that there is no woman here who would say that she wants the right, in spite of the fact that she believes that the extension of suffrage would on the whole not conduce to the "common good." We are all questioning this, simply — what will promote the "common good?" If woman suffrage will promote that, then it ought to be granted.

One of the war-cries of our forefathers was, "Taxation without representation is tyranny." The colonies at that time were taxed by the English government without representation in Parliament. They were not only taxed without representation of their community, but also special taxes were imposed upon them which were not laid upon the people of England. They said, and said truly, "This is unjust; this is more than we can bear. Such taxation, without our being represented at all, without our interests and our needs being presented in Parliament, — such taxation is tyranny." That war-cry is invoked to prove that women ought not to be taxed without the extension of the suffrage to them. Our forefathers objected to the taxation because it was unjust. Is there anybody who can state to your Committee in what way the laws in regard to taxation in this State are unjust to women? The fact is that the property of women is taxed exactly in the same way as the property of men, with this single exception, — an exception and an exemption in favor of women, — the law providing that the property of widows and unmarried women, to the amount of $500, shall be exempt from taxation. The laws are more than just to women, they are generous.

Let us consider the question of taxation in another light. At the present time the complaint of the tax-payers is that those who own the property and who have to pay the largest amount of taxes do not have control of the expenditures and of the method of taxation, but that the control is in the hands of a large number of people, who, having no property subject to taxation, do not feel the burdens of taxation directly, and that therefore they are not as conservative in their expenditures or as wise in their legislation as they would be if they were voting away their own property as well as the property of others. Now, if we extend the right of suffrage to women, what will be the result? The proportion of women who are possessors of taxable property is smaller than that of men, and the consequence will be that the complaint, the danger, the evil to which I have alluded, will be aggravated. It is a fact, Mr. Chairman, I think, that thoughtful women in this Commonwealth who are owners of property will not be found advocating the extension of the right of suffrage to women. The change would only increase the danger of inconsiderate, unwise, and burdensome taxation.

Wherein will the extension of suffrage tend to promote the common good? In no way can we form a better estimate of the probable value of woman in the administration of public affairs than by considering what her success has been in the conduct of private business. Take a simple case. Women are liable to represent their property in corporations; but, in spite of the fact that they have that power, a lady seldom attends a meeting of a corporation; she almost always places her proxy in the hand of some man to vote for her. And why does she do it? Because she feels that man knows more about the affairs of the corporation than she does. The legal profession is open to women, but they do not rush into it as if it was a natural outlet to their pent-up energy.

Women go into the medical profession in greater numbers than into any other, but their success there is lamentably marred by a large percentage of humbug and immorality.

The ministry is open to woman. There has been no legal impediment in the way. It must be admitted that of all the occupations of men none requires less masculine force, none is more appropriate to the "higher moral character of women," than the ministry, and yet in that field the woman laborers are few and their harvest is small.

We all know that women as a rule do not go into business, and yet there is no legal impediment in the way. The wives of these members of the Committee are not members of business partnerships. Why do they not go into a business firm with men? Why do not the members of this Committee take women, married or single, into business partnerships with them? The question answers itself when it is asked. Nay, more, why do not ladies, when they wish their property to be taken care of for them, get other ladies to take care of it? Why, when they are appointing executors of their wills, or trustees, or agents to manage their estates, do they not appoint ladies? The answer is that they believe that their property will be better managed by men than it will be by women. Now there is no reason to suppose that women will be any more successful in politics than they have been in business. The fact is that the elements which have interfered with their success in private business will to a much greater extent interfere with their success in public affairs. Should we not hate to see our wives and our daughters taking that part in politics which we men are obliged to take, going round so freely as we are obliged to, in order that we may gain that knowledge of the questions at stake which will give us the groundwork upon which we can form a just decision? The management of a city or of a town is the management of a great business corporation. Do any of you gentlemen think that the "common good" will be promoted, that the affairs of a city or town will be better administered, by a majority of women rather than by men alone? I say "a majority of women" because it is to be supposed, if women are equally fitted, and are in a majority in the Commonwealth, that there would be a majority of women in the city and town governments. But I will not state it so. Do any of you gentlemen suppose that the affairs of a city or town would be better administered if there was a mingling of women and men in the government? Think what the duties of the city and town governments are. There is the educational department, and in respect of that we have given women the right of suffrage, because it has been argued that that is their especial province, and that they know more about that than men do. There is the charitable department, which comes the nearest to the educational; but when you strike out those two, you come to the question of taxation, and the affairs of the water department, of the sewer department, of the fire department, of the street department, of the police department, and of public buildings. Can any one claim that the affairs of those departments can be administered as well by an admixture of women? If it is so, why have business men not discovered it and taken women into their partnerships?

We are asked to try the experiment. The trying of the experiment is a very serious thing, Mr. Chairman. We ought not to try that experiment unless we are convinced, beyond the possibility of a doubt, that it will promote the public good, because that experiment will involve us in a great many changes, intricacies, and complications, some of which we can readily see and others of which we cannot well foretell. Among the first difficulties to be met and expenses to be incurred are those which will grow out of the necessity of furnishing in cities and towns accommodations for more than double the present number of voters. This would necessitate, in many cases, a change from a town to a city government. Let us now look at the question in another aspect. The family relation is the natural relation. Upon the perfection of that family relation depends the perfection of our society, of our State, and of our nation. In all our legislation the sacredness of the interests of that relation must ever have the most prominent position, and our laws must be general laws. We cannot make laws to suit exceptional cases. It is a common law principle, that the duty of protecting and supporting the wife and children devolves upon the husband. This is the common law, but it is also the law of nature. It can never be repealed; it can never be changed; it will stand forever, because it is the edict of the Almighty. If the husband is responsible for the protection and support of his wife and family, then the methods of securing that protection and support should be under his control. Persons cannot be held responsible for that which they cannot control. The degree of responsibility is dependent on the extent of control. If we hold a man responsible for the support and the protection of his family, we should leave in his hands not only the control of his business, but also the control of the administration of public affairs, because upon the wisdom of such administration depends not only his business prosperity, but the safety of his home. Suppose that men and women are mentally and morally equal. Upon any important question with reference to the financial or business interests of the town, the State, or the nation, by whose decision is it safest to proceed, — by the votes of men alone, who have spent their lives in the practical solution of questions of business and of finance, or by adding to their votes the votes of women, the prime of whose lives, as a rule, must be spent in the equally important duties of wife and motherhood?

I believe, then, that the extension of the suffrage to women will do harm; I believe that it is not for the "common good;" I believe that it is a wrong, and not a right; and, furthermore, I believe that nine tenths of the mothers in this State know that it is wrong in principle, and will prove injurious in its effects. Let man attend to his province, and perform his work as well as he can. Let woman attend to hers, and be as perfect in it as she may. Let each carry out the Creator's plan of the economy of nature, and, cheerfully assuming their division of the labor, do it to the best of their ability. But when man trenches on the province of woman, or when woman trenches on the province of man, the man becomes womanly, or the woman becomes manly, and, in either case, they lose the influence which they might otherwise have.

# AN ARGUMENT AGAINST WOMAN SUFFRAGE.

By MRS. KATE GANNETT WELLS.

### DELIVERED BEFORE A SPECIAL LEGISLATIVE COMMITTEE.

I have not come here with any hope of refuting in ten minutes all the arguments of our pro-suffrage friends, nor is it necessary that I should even try to do so, for repeated discussion of the subject has made us all familiar with our own convictions and those of our contrary-minded neighbors. Still less have I come in any unfriendly spirit to the pro-suffragists, for I know many of them too well not to acknowledge that they are working, heart and soul, for what they believe is one of the necessary, if not the most necessary, factors in human progress.

The anti-suffrage women are women so busy in their own homes, so occupied in charities and plans for the poor and ignorant, that they never have had time, more than that, they never have had the wish to come before the public, even in this Green Room. More than that, they do not think it is woman's place to argue or to refute statements in the arena of politics. For years they were silent, passive; their convictions strengthening all the while, they expressing them only as social intercourse demanded. But a year or two ago reproaches were heaped upon them for their passivity, which was called cowardice. They are not cowards, but they are women, and as such they prefer to stay at home and do their part through their home. There are but few of us trained to the public work of addressing you. Those few the distance of many miles keeps from us, but there are thousands of women who feel that if their silence is attributed to fear or to small numbers, they must summon courage to speak, and therefore have they asked me to come and speak as best I may for them.

I stand here because we anti-suffragists believe that the time has come for us to declare that our intellectual judgments, our moral convictions, and our belief in right expediency as one of the grounds on which governmental and constitutional changes should be made, are entirely opposed to the doctrine of female suffrage.

It is said that the casting of a vote is a slight duty, quickly performed. If it were that simple mechanical act, we might not object to such action, but to cast a vote ought to mean to cast it intelligently and honestly; and how can we gain that accurate intelligence except by attending caucuses, primaries, nominating conventions, and supplementing general knowledge as far as possible by personal acquaintance with candidates? Even if some women have time and ability for such work, most of us have not; and even if we all had the time, is it desirable that the presence and co-work of un-intelligent and depraved women should be added to the already jarring factions of political life? Every woman knows that all women cannot purify politics; and if a good woman can vote, so can a bad woman! Therefore, gentlemen, we say that to permit us to vote is to permit us to do many impossible things, which, nevertheless, we ought to do as patriotic women. The point in question is a vexed one between the pro and anti-suffragists. They say we have no right to prevent their doing what they consider to be right, and also that we need not vote because they do. We say that their demand for extension of the suffrage does involve us, and therefore we are put on the defensive against them. Party questions and reform measures of all kinds will arise; we may hold convictions different from theirs, and as we also care as much for our country's welfare as they do, when we see some measure we deem unwise likely to succeed, then, to save our country or State, we must vote; therefore do we beseech you not to grant female suffrage. And if it is replied that women will only vote and legislate rightly, I answer that I utterly disagree with such a statement. Women, as a rule, will vote on the side of pure moral issues, but they will also vote for illogical, inexpedient measures to secure some narrow, present good, which should be outweighed by the larger issues of legal stability, validity of order, constitutional and States' rights, which are also involved in the immediate settlement of any question.

What, then, is our general position?

1. That suffrage is not a *natural* right; if it were, no restriction of age, property, or education could be put upon it such as now exists.

2. That the essence of republicanism does not depend upon *every one's* voting, independent of qualification, but that it is the sovereign people, and not a monarchical power, who shall decide what persons may vote and under what restrictions.

3. That to be deprived of a vote is not to be deprived of one's personality; we are persons whether we are voters or not, and as persons should demand and receive careful legislation in all that concerns our interests.

4. Our opponents have rendered it useless for us to reaffirm that an intelligent woman is as capable of casting an intelligent vote as an intelligent man, or that some form of restricted suffrage might perhaps be desirable, for they demand unrestricted, universal female suffrage. They claim that suffrage is an educating power. We "anti" women grant that it may be, but we add that as the country is already so heavily weighted with an ignorant population, and that as our naturalization laws admit foreigners to vote before they have become Americanized, therefore we, as true patriots, will not burden our country with a great class of women to be educated.

We anti-suffragists will not yield one iota to the pro-suffragists in our belief in woman's capacity for advancement in every direction; in her right to receive the highest education, to demand equal wages with men, to work as physician, lawyer, minister, lecturer, or in any occupation she wishes. We also demand of our legislature that they erase from the statutes laws which discriminate unjustly against woman. We also believe that she should serve on school committees, on State boards of charities, and on all kindred institutions, so that we wish to effect no curtailment of a woman's sphere except in the direction of suffrage.

And why do we wish that she should not enter upon that? Because most women are not fitted for it. We do not say that they never will be, but that they are not now, and will not be for some generations to come. Because I am a woman, because I care for woman's advancement, because I believe that though a large number of women are already fitted to vote, an infinitely greater number of women are not fitted for it, do I — do we — implore you not to give to all what at least most of us are not able to use rightly. You cannot give us suffrage without letting loose influences akin to those which have already debased politics and given rise to words of doubtful morality like wire-pulling, bribery, log-rolling, etc. If you give suffrage to all, you will speedily find that women are adepts in political measures, and will no more shrink at trying all means to secure their ends than do men; though on the other hand many men do, and many women would, employ only honorable means.

It is not necessary that women should vote in order to have the laws more favorable for them. The changes that have already taken place in them are due to the great progress of modern civilization within the last fifty years, and have had nothing to do with suffrage.

There is an opinion in some minds that the State should more and more assume a paternal relation to its population; that it should provide whatever is asked, and that by the making of laws, oppression and poverty will cease. It is also supposed that women can legislate best for themselves. Gentlemen, those who assume either of these opinions are asking the State and the power of suffrage to do the work of personal righteousness. If women can best legislate for themselves, why should not minors, both girls and boys, ask to have themselves qualified before the present legal age? And why should not one class of women legislate for themselves, and still another class for themselves? That there are still unfair and degrading laws is granted, but if we ask for woman suffrage in order to rectify them, we open the way for increased private, class, and personal legislation of all kinds. Is woman suffrage going to cure the evils that come from one's own misdoings? Will a brutal, an intemperate husband be any less brutal or intemperate because his wife has the power to vote? Will trustees cease to speculate with their clients' money because those clients can vote? Again, it is personal righteousness that must do the work which so often is expected from legislation and suffrage.

It is woman's ignorance more than man's wickedness, or the law's injustice, which brings about the evils for which our sympathy is craved. Suffrage is not needed to beget self-respect, or a knowledge of contracts, investments, and the workings of the law, which if carefully studied before action is begun, would save later needless misery. Lastly, it is argued against us that for various reasons we need not fear that the unintelligent will vote. This must remain a matter of opinion between us and those who differ from us. I can only say that my experience has led me to the contrary conclusion. I had occasion one winter to be connected with some work at the North End. The women were too careless and wretched in their lives and in their dress to be here described. They talked with each other in little groups; many a one spoke of the time when she could vote, as the only vengeance left her to exercise upon the wealthy classes. Woman suffrage, they said, would give the unskilled workwomen more ample wages, for they could vote themselves what they needed. Again, I was in a house where workingmen came for their daily dinner. The men were also talking of this subject, and said that the women must vote, "for we want the eight-hour law, and can get it THROUGH the women. They must make the State give us work. The women must see to it that we have work, and only work for eight hours." These are but two instances, though I think they could be multiplied a hundred-fold; yet are they not indications of the way in which woman suffrage may be urged to forward some special party measure? Once let the great mass of uneducated women be added to the great mass of already uneducated men voters, and the State will slowly but surely be shaken under the varying demands made upon it for bread, work, money, leisure, and all kinds of laws to favor all kinds of persons. When those times come, there will be more bitter animosities of women against women, of secret warfare, of despicable wire-pulling, and of exercise of the power of personal charms as a weapon of persuasion, than now exists among men.

One word more. Even if in itself suffrage may be based upon the fundamental principle of justice, it does not follow that it should be applied when great injustice must be done. No wise government deals in abstract justice without considering the expediency of the steps necessary to remove justice from an abstract principle into a concrete action. Therefore, if in close argument I should be forced (which I could not be) to surrender all my assumed positions against woman suffrage, I could never be driven from this position, that in the present constitution of events, of facts,— physiological, social, financial, moral, and political, — it is inexpedient for government to grant universal female suffrage.

Inexpedient! Yes, forever inexpedient, until the highest type of morality and the clearest sense of justice and the widest reaches of law in its theoretical and practical applications are reached by all women. Women now do generous, wise, and lofty deeds, and women now do mean, foolish, despicable actions, — oh, how mean! how bad!

So finally we beseech you, gentlemen, to rectify all unjust laws against women; to strengthen the hands of good women all over the land in raising the fallen, in teaching self-respect and self-support to the ignorant, in bringing more happiness into every one's life; and to withhold from us the duty, necessity, right of suffrage, whichever it may be called, until you can have only *noble, honest* women for your voters and legislators.

*Printed by the Massachusetts Association opposed to the Extension of Suffrage to Women.*

Pamphlets and leaflets may be obtained from the Secretary of the Association, MRS. ROBERT W. LORD,
P. O. Box 2262, Boston.

# ARGUMENT

OF

# ARTHUR LORD

BEFORE THE LEGISLATIVE COMMITTEE ON WOMAN SUFFRAGE, 1889

IN BEHALF OF THE

# REMONSTRANTS

AGAINST MUNICIPAL SUFFRAGE FOR WOMEN

BOSTON
GEO. H. ELLIS, PUBLISHER, 141 FRANKLIN STREET
1889

# ARGUMENT.

Mr. Chairman:

Remonstrants and petitioners alike come here seeking the same object, animated by a common purpose: each asks for such legislation as in its judgment will conduce to the order and well-being of society and the prosperity of the State, and insure for its people happy and contented homes. It is of slight service to treat the question presented other than carefully, considerately, and seriously. The day for ridicule has gone. The question is of too much importance, and its decision involves consequences too serious and far-reaching to be considered lightly or indifferently.

Here are two millions of people, the constituents of a Commonwealth which has neither superior nor equal, we are glad to believe, among sister States or foreign nations, in virtue and education, in intelligence and prosperity, who, except in this room, and in hearings like this, we are always told and we know, are governed by just, humane, and wise laws, divided into cities and towns for the orderly administration of their local affairs, and united for that common legislation which affects all. It is proposed by a single law to more than double the number of voters upon whom rest the duties and responsibilities of the suffrage, and that half million voters whom the law proposed would place on the list, it is admitted, are as a class not especially fitted by their education, training, experience, and temperament for the consideration and determination of those practical questions in the very practical affairs of life which compose ninety-nine out of every hundred questions submitted to the voters of Massachusetts. "Not often in the history of the world has a body of voters deliberately opened its ranks to admit a re-enforcement larger than itself," writes Colonel Higginson, than whom there is no abler advocate of woman suffrage, in his "Unsolved Problems of Woman Suffrage."

We object first to the manner in which the end is sought to be accomplished. If it is to come, let it come after due deliberation, attended by such safeguards as the Constitution wisely requires before making any change in the organic law. It is of vastly more importance than the abolition of the poll-tax; yet, to do that, we are required to submit the question to two successive legislatures, and secure for its adoption two-thirds of the House and a majority of the Senate, and then it is submitted to the decision of the people before it becomes a law. Yet this measure they seek to pass by the majority of a single legislature, in the election of whose members it has not found an issue, and in its favor neither party has expressly declared.

When this agitation for the extension of the suffrage first began, it proceeded on broad lines, and involved the suffrage in the affairs of the State as well as in the affairs of every municipality. It continued so until the special champion of woman suffrage, the *Woman's Journal*, recognizing that wherever this change has been submitted to the people it has been overwhelmingly defeated, cried a halt, and directed "that every State legislature be asked to grant women by statute every form of suffrage not expressly prohibited by its State Constitution."

Now, while it is true that municipal suffrage may be granted to women by legislative enactment, it is no less true that such a plan was never thought of by the framers of the Constitution, and was only discovered and brought to light when these agitators found that there were almost "insuperable obstacles," as they were pleased to term them, against any change in the organic law when the matter was as deliberately considered as its importance demanded. I can well understand that a prudent and conservative legislator, whatever his views on this question of extending the suffrage may be, would hesitate to take the responsibility of permitting by his single vote a change admitted by its advocates to be so doubtful in its immediate effect, and by all to be attended by consequences which even the wisest cannot foresee. And for that reason I ask you, gentlemen of the committee, although I was assured by more than one speaker the other day in the course of his or her argument that they knew they had your sympathy and your vote, to pause here and say to these petitioners, The plan you propose is too important to be decided in this way: it is an organic change, and should be decided in the way provided by the Constitution for a change so important. We can vote to amend the Constitution, but we cannot take the responsibility of putting this change into effect without first submitting it to the people.

But, sir, if that cannot be, I submit that upon the merits of the proposed legislation your verdict should be, Inexpedient to legislate, and that the petitioners should have leave to withdraw.

### SUFFRAGE NOT A RIGHT.

They base their argument for the extension of the suffrage, first, upon the proposition that suffrage is their natural right, and appeal for support to the compact of the "Mayflower" and the Constitution.

The eloquent persons to whom we listened the other day were full of assertion that the municipal suffrage for which they labor was theirs by right, and that a grave injustice was done them by denying and continuing to deny it. Declarations and phrases are taken from their context, and perverted from the meaning which their authors contemplated, in order to prove an argument that this suffrage which they so fondly crave was a right secured to them by the founders of the republic and the builders of the nation, and is inherent in manhood and womanhood itself.

But this government was instituted by its founders, as they declare in the Bill of Rights, for the "common good," for the safety, prosperity, and happiness of the people. And that legislation which will best promote those objects is the legislation which is most in accord with the spirit of the Constitution, and the test which alone can be applied to it is whether it tends to subserve that fundamental and primary purpose of government.

We turn in vain to the history of this people for support for their doctrine of natural right. When the petitioners point to the compact of the "Mayflower" in support of their contention, I accept the test. The verdict of history is far different from what they seek.

The compact of the "Mayflower" was signed by the male members of the Pilgrim company only. And the persons of the colony intrusted solely with the management of its affairs were at first the signers of that compact and such persons as might be "joined thereto by a majority vote." Finally, it was provided, in 1671, that freemen must be twenty-one years of age, of sober and peaceable conversation, orthodox in the fundamentals of religion, and possessed of twenty pounds of ratable estate.

Suffrage was a duty which those who were permitted to exercise were required by law to discharge. And for default in appearance at the election of governor, assistants, and constables, without due excuse, such delinquent was amerced in three shillings sterling.

Suffrage was restricted under the colonial law, under the provincial law, and under the Constitution; and it has been reserved for the men and women of a later generation to discover that this restriction was an unwarrantable invasion of right.

The thoughtful men who framed the earlier laws never admitted for a moment that there was any right to vote inherent in any citizen, and limited the duty of suffrage to such classes of men, and such only, as, from time to time, they determined would wisely legislate for the protection, safety, happiness, and prosperity of the people. These glittering generalities about the unrestricted right of suffrage are the teachings of the school of the French Revolution, and not the simpler, purer, wiser school of the "Mayflower."

Why will the petitioners turn for argument to the constitution of State or nation, and distort fragmentary sentences into a meaning of which their authors never dreamed? The facts of history, the contemporary construction of constitutional provisions, the decisions of the court, are all opposed to their empty assertion. When the Federal Constitution was adopted, all the States, with the exceptions of Rhode Island and Connecticut, had constitutions of their own, and in no State were all the citizens permitted to vote. At the time of the adoption of the Federal Constitution, in all the States except New Jersey, the right of suffrage was conferred upon men alone, and not upon all of them. In New Jersey, there was a property qualification of fifty pounds; and, while it is true that women were allowed to vote having that qualification, the privilege of suffrage was taken away from them in 1806 in that State.

And the Supreme Court of the United States has unanimously decided, in Minor v. Happersett, 21 Wallace, that the Constitution of the United States does not confer the right of suffrage upon any one.

I refer to these constitutions and laws, not to argue that the limitations imposed therein upon the suffrage are wise and expedient to-day, but simply to enforce a proposition which seems entirely forgotten by these petitioners,— that a primary principle of every State and of the nation itself is the right to admit to and refuse the exercise of suffrage to such male citizens as they judge not desirable to include among the voters; and that, if any lesson can be drawn from the fundamental provisions from the compact of the "Mayflower" to the Federal Constitution, it is this,— that the whole policy and theory and scheme of our government is that the right or privilege or duty of suffrage, as you may be pleased to term it, may be granted or denied to such citizens, male or female, as in the opinion of the fathers would conduce to the well-being of the State.

And, when this claim as of right is made and the facts of history are appealed to for support, it is well to observe how baseless the claim and how contrary to the principles and policy of the founders of great States.

So much, sir, for the question of the right of suffrage, and the support which the Constitution and policy of this government in the past gives to the position of the petitioners to-day. If the object of the government is the common weal, and the greatest good of the greatest number is the end in view, as I believe, then the proposition for woman suffrage resolves itself into a question of expediency.

### WOMAN SUFFRAGE NOT EXPEDIENT.

If the dangers which everywhere threaten a republican government can be more easily met, if the evils which seem ever present in the administration of great cities can be more readily avoided, by the change proposed in the laws; if the peace and happiness and prosperity of the people can be more surely attained by an extension of the suffrage in the way proposed, then, sir, we welcome its coming. But we want to be very sure that we are on the right track, and that the good to be secured far outweighs the evils which may come, before we give to the measure our assent and co-operation.

The burden of proof is on those asking that change to prove by reasonable arguments that they are right and the remonstrants wrong, before so great a change in the existing order of things should be indorsed by committee or legislature. Assertions cannot be substituted for the facts of experience, and *a priori* reasonings must yield to common sense.

"Upon the manner of regulating the suffrage depends the destruction or salvation of States," says Montesquieu. What are the two great dangers which threaten our form of government in State or city? Are they not the indifference and the ignorance of the voters?

When the suffrage was given to women in school matters, that field was taken for the trial of suffrage extension which woman was believed, and rightly believed, to have the most interest in and the most knowledge of, the education of children. Governor Long, in his message of 1880, gave as a reason for not recommending a constitutional amendment giving full suffrage to women, that the Act of 1879, giving women a right to vote for school committees, furnished a practical test of the whole question.

Senator Knowlton, who strongly urged the passage of the Act, said, on the floor of the Senate in the final debate, "If they [women] will not vote on school matters, it settles it for any other form of suffrage." The *Woman's Journal* and other advocates of the measure burst into songs of thanksgiving at the great victory they had won, and lost no time in urging that every step be taken to secure the women of the State voting on this important measure. I will not weary you by citations, there is no dispute about it: the advocates of that measure rested their case for fuller suffrage upon the use which women would make of this new privilege, and urged its adoption upon the ground that it would furnish a satisfactory test for some of the objections to female suffrage.

### STATISTICS OF VOTES.

I have here House Document No. 175 of 1888, which gives the returns of the number of registered female voters for school committee from 1881 to 1887 inclusive, and the returns of the number who exercised the privilege. Remembering that this was the test proposed and agreed upon, let us turn to its pages:—

| Counties. | No. of towns in which Women never registered. | No. of towns in which Women never voted. |
|---|---|---|
| Barnstable | 7 | 7 |
| Berkshire | 25 | 27 |
| Bristol | 8 | 9 |
| Dukes | 5 | 5 |
| Essex | 19 | 21 |
| Franklin | 19 | 20 |
| Hampden | 13 | 13 |
| Hampshire | 16 | 18 |
| Middlesex | 15 | 19 |
| Norfolk | 8 | 11 |
| Plymouth | 10 | 17 |
| Suffolk (Winthrop) | | 1 |
| Worcester | 22 | 29 |

Of the 349 towns and cities in the State, there are 167 in which no woman ever registered and 197 in which no woman ever voted.

Of the 14 counties into which the State is divided, there are 9 in which not a hundred women, of all their great population, voted in any year for school committee, and the total female vote in 1881 was but 1,571 in the entire State, with its population of 1,783,000; and in 1887, although the population had increased to 1,942,141, the female vote had only increased to 1,912, a gain of 341.

And a comparison of the tables shows that the vote of Suffolk in each year was from one-third to two-thirds of the entire female vote.

Now, when we recall that this was to be the test of the interest of women in the suffrage, and that in 1879 the believers were content to base their claim for further extension of the suffrage upon this practical test, it is idle to explain this indifference by saying that the requirements are too onerous, when we find in many towns that even those who were registered did not take the trouble of voting; and in no town did the number who voted approach the number who were registered. But I hear it said, The returns for 1888 are an answer to all that. Then the women came out in battalions, and the vote of Suffolk jumped from 1,000 to 20,000. A little analysis of the vote of last December, in the minds of many thoughtful men and women, themselves believers in the right of woman suffrage, has furnished a better argument against a further extension of the suffrage than the indifference of the preceding seven years. Look at the facts: the duty and responsibility which suffrage puts on every voter failed to arouse the women from their indifference; the usual questions of school management, control, and discipline failed to influence them; it was reserved for a sectarian cry, unwise and unreasonable, to summon them from their retirement.

When last December you heard the alarm bells, and Faneuil Hall echoed, the platform sounded, and the pulpit rang with bitter appeals to sectarian zeal, it almost seemed as if they really believed that the "Armada" was in the offing, and Alva and his soldiers were at the city's gates.

Members of the committee, who for years had devoted themselves to the cause of education, who were fitted by experience and training for the duties they had wisely met, were summarily dismissed; the cry was, No popery, No Catholics on the School Board, No Catholic teachers in the school, Preserve the common schools! I take this from the printed circular widely distributed, entitled "An Appeal to Voters, from the Christian Women of Massachusetts."

Preserve the schools from what? A historical text-book contained a paragraph which was claimed to be untrue and offensive to a large number of citizens whose children throng the schools. Many Protestant scholars believed the criticism well founded. The text-book and explanation were certainly open to two constructions; and the school committee, Protestant and Catholic, voted to change the book and the master. From that small beginning, the agitation and excitement started.

If you want to jeopardize the public schools, if you want to furnish an excuse for the existence of parochial schools, can you devise a surer way than to insist upon sectarian qualifications for members of the school committee and for teachers? I submit the result of the election was only to confirm the impression where it existed, that the wishes and beliefs of a large number of citizens who deprecate religious strife and sectarian teaching in the public schools were to be disregarded, and that there was a strong determination among the women of Boston that a religious test should be applied to every school committee man and master.

There is a better cry than "No popery" to summon the women of Boston to the polls; and that is, No bigotry. Keep the schools free from religion and politics. Let your books be neither Protestant nor Catholic. As you said, Mr. Chairman, on Monday, when you stopped my examination of Professor Townsend, we should not ask whether the candidate for school committee was Protestant or Catholic, but simply whether he was a friend of the public schools. The point I sought to enforce was that your petitioners sought to make another and a far different test. It is an alarming sign when the good women of Boston can only be aroused from their indifference and driven to exercise their long-desired right of voting in school matters by heated appeals to prejudice and bigotry and sectarianism.

Said a prominent Democratic politician to me the other day in the State House, speaking of that December election, "We only cared to elect our mayor and the city government, and we were content not to make a special contest on the school committee this year; but if this ostracism is repeated, then when the pendulum swings back and Boston is again Democratic, we will call on our sodalities and church societies, and bring our Catholic women to the polls to defeat such a manifest subversion of the public school system."

When the women of Boston go to the polls because they are Protestants or Catholics, influenced by religious or sectarian zeal, and not because they are Americans seeking only the highest interests of the schools, it will be a spectacle more fraught with dangers to free institutions and free schools than Boston has ever seen; and some of the evils which the remonstrants and some of the petitioners in years past have feared will be brought to our very doors. And here let me remark, in passing, that that very desirable object, the election of women to the school boards in the towns of the Commonwealth, these returns, when compared with the reports of the Board of Education, show has not been aided by the school suffrage, and that those towns where the women take little or no interest in voting have been more likely to elect women to their school boards than even Boston, where their interest in the subject has been manifested the most.

The minority report of this committee in 1885 called attention to the fact that, of the 100 women on the school boards, 47 were in towns in which there was not a single woman voter; and in 1887 it was shown to the committee that in 72 towns and cities in this State there were women on the school committee, though in 36 of these towns no woman had ever voted, and in 16 less than 10 women have voted.

## PRECEDENTS FOR WOMAN SUFFRAGE.

And now what precedents have we to guide us in the determination of this question of municipal suffrage? When Mrs. Howe, a week ago, appealed to those women who are willing to copy English forms and precedents in other respects to copy the English law and practice of permitting women to exercise municipal suffrage, and finely quoted the lines of Byron,—

> "You have the Pyrrhic dance as yet.
> Where is the Pyrrhic phalanx gone?
> Of two such lessons, why forget
> The nobler and the manlier one?"

she seemed to forget that the Pyrrhic phalanx which she sought was, under the English law, composed only of spinsters and widows, with certain property qualifications. She does not ask for such a phalanx here. The limitations therein imposed are extremely at variance with the spirit of our institutions, and no petitioner to-day seeks any suffrage for women other than the freest and most untrammelled. As a precedent, England affords slight assistance for the course you suggest to-day. No instance of municipal suffrage abroad is brought to your notice where there are not certain restrictions and limitations also which defeat its value as a precedent for the change in our law which these petitioners propose.

## KANSAS.

The only State in this country where municipal suffrage exists, which has been brought to the attention of the committee, is the State of Kansas; and in that State their own witness frankly says that it came mainly from the desire to enforce the prohibitory amendment, which hitherto had proved a failure, and then the women were called in to vote for municipal officers who are charged with the enforcement of that law. And, even there, less than 30,000 women out of the total population of 1,268,000 voted the first year, and a still less number the second. Yet Kansas' vote for governor in 1886 was 273,000, exceeding by 30,000 the total vote for governor in Massachusetts that year. Tell me what was the explanation of that shrinking indifference, when full suffrage was given and no obstacle interfered? There is a little help, I submit, to be derived in our effort to arrive at a correct solution of this question from the experience of those municipalities in which women have been exercising the right of suffrage. In that long list of States and Territories which Mr. Blackwell gave us when he opened this debate, other than Kansas, there are only two where unrestricted municipal suffrage is granted; and those are the Territories of Wyoming and Utah. We have never heard much of the value of Utah as a precedent, even from the petitioners, except to count it in the column, and I admit there are peculiar reasons why Utah will not furnish to Massachusetts much help in the solution of the problem; and, if your petitioners insist upon leaving it out, I will gratify them by not dragging it in.

### WYOMING.

But, ever since this agitation began, Wyoming has furnished the stock argument for the petitioners. Occasionally, a visitor has been caught, as he was flying back to Wyoming, and brought into the State House to testify as to the great benefit which woman suffrage has been to Wyoming. I had the curiosity, therefore, to look up Wyoming; and I find, sir, that this suffrage was granted to woman in Wyoming in 1869, and in 1870 the United States took a census. In that year, the total population was 9,118, and the number of females of all ages from the first childhood to the second was less than 2,000, and they were scattered over a territory of about 98,000 square miles, or one female, whether in infancy or old age, to every fifty square miles of territory! Now, sir, isn't it nonsense to seriously cite Wyoming as a precedent for Massachusetts?

### POWERS AND OBJECTS OF A MUNICIPALITY.

If we consider what a municipality is, and what its powers and objects are, and then consider some facts which are patent to everybody's experience, I think we shall derive some light on our inquiry. A municipality is but a corporation intrusted with certain powers, charged with certain duties, the limits to its action as clearly defined by law as in any other business corporation which receives its charter from the State. It may incur debts, and raise money by taxation; it must elect certain officers, whose duty is that of administration merely; it holds real estate and personal property, and may make contracts; it builds highways, constructs systems of pipes for water and sewerage, regulates electric wires, establishes fire and police departments; its citizens assemble in town meeting or elect representatives to the city council; it provides for the schools and the poor; and, in brief, is limited to purely business matters pertaining to its own order and usefulness. Now we are asked to intrust these business details to the care and management of women voters, largely in excess of the male voters; and if the demand is placed on the ground of expediency, on which alone it can stand, it is because these affairs are now poorly managed, and, if intrusted to women, would be better managed.

We have a right to ask, What special experience, training, or temperament do they have which will make it probable that these purely business matters will be better conducted than now?

One of the eloquent speakers who addressed you the other day seemed to lay a good deal of stress on the "God-given insight of women on moral questions." Well, assume for the sake of the argument that God has given women a far clearer insight into moral questions than man, and that her intuition is worth all his reason, as they are pleased to claim. But the business details of the administration of either a great city or a small town are not moral questions: they are intensely practical, and call for business experience and training for their best solution. The business occupations of man furnish the special experience and training which enable him to decide them. The doors of every occupation, business, and profession stand wide open to-day, and no law prevents any woman from entering where she will. Take the profession of the law, which offers many opportunities for woman's work, and to which I know of no one who would interpose the slightest obstacle to her entrance; yet, so far as I am advised, but one woman throughout the length and breadth of the Commonwealth is actively engaged in the practice of that profession.

Take the profession of medicine, where there seems to be a special field for the honorable usefulness of woman, and certain special attributes of character and touch would seem to precisely fit her for it: outside of the few scholarly, skilful, educated women physicians in our large cities, there are but few female physicians, educated and trusted, from Berkshire to the sea. There is no legal impediment, and little or no prejudice now, to a woman's engaging in any business; but you may pass through the streets of Boston, and how rarely you find a single store or factory or establishment controlled or managed by a woman. There are no women in our banking offices, nor are our railroads intrusted to their control or management; no factory or great mercantile establishment finds them at its head; no market or shop obeys their orders. The great business operations of the city or the lesser ones of the town are not conducted to any appreciable extent by woman's hand or head. When you find an exception to the rule, it is so noteworthy that it is a matter of interested comment in the press of the day. When the Boston *Herald*, the other day, found one woman in the world at the head of a horse railroad company, it gave her two columns and a picture, so great was the wonder.

As a rule, then, our business affairs are intrusted to and controlled by men. How many corporation meetings did you ever attend, and find any woman taking any part, or even present? A railroad or a bank or a manufacturing business falls into difficulty, and no woman among its stockholders raises her hand to note the evil or point the way of safety and success. You may engage in any business enterprise you please, Mr. Chairman, with women as partners or associates: did you ever know it to be done? The care and management of her own property, as a rule, she intrusts to another; and husband, father, son, or brother carries on her affairs as he does his own. This may all be wrong in theory and inconsistent with the proper position of woman in the body politic; but, nevertheless, it is a fact, and the special agencies which fit man for the management of business details from choice she does not assume. I went, the other day, through a great factory employing hundreds of men and women, and the answer which was made me when I asked of the manager why the heads of the departments were all men was that the employment of women there was largely temporary in its nature: they came only to meet some present necessity, and, as soon as the exigency was lifted, they sought other employment in their own homes. If they married, they ceased working there, as a rule, and turned to the engrossing cares and duties of home life.

Now, if that is the case, we see one reason why the special training is lacking which fits them for the business management of those other business corporations, the town or the city.

Is it reasonable to suppose that those women will wisely manage the affairs of Boston or Brookline who gladly turn the management of their own business affairs into other hands, that they may devote themselves more closely to the no less important and far more exacting duties of wife and mother? It does not weaken the argument to point to this exception or that to the general rule. The fact that the captain's wife sailed the vessel safely to port when all the crew were stricken down with disease does not prove that women are designed to sail the ship in less trying times. Her special duty over, she gladly put aside the responsibility which necessity, not choice, had compelled her to assume.

How many cases do you recall where the business management of a great estate was placed in the hands of a woman, designedly and deliberately, by any woman? When Francis Jackson, the philanthropist of Boston, died, he named as trustees under his will some of the petitioners whom we see here to-day. But their trust was a peculiar one,— to expend the income of the property without responsibility to any one, in such time, amount, and place as they thought desirable, to promote the cause of woman's rights. And, although this bequest was declared invalid, yet Francis Jackson's daughter carried out her father's wishes by leaving her estate to the two most prominent woman suffrage advocates, and laid upon them the special obligation of using the money for the promotion of the cause of woman's rights. Am I wrong, Mr. Blackwell, in assuming that some of the annual interest in this suffrage legislation is due to the sagacious disposition of what was once Francis Jackson's estate, and that some of its advocates appear here not only from their interest in the cause, but also in the discharge of that moral obligation imposed upon them by the will of Francis Jackson and Mrs. Eddy?

With this exception, I do not recall at this moment another instance of the business management of a large property being intrusted to women in Massachusetts; and even the oppressor, man, was joined with them, under Mr. Jackson's will. Why, then, impose on women the burden of the care of municipal affairs, in which they have little interest and less experience? Their duties and occupations lie in other and more congenial fields. Will it not be time enough to intrust the management of these public corporations to them when they have shown some interest and desire to manage any one of the thousands of private corporations in which they have an interest and part, but which to-day they uniformly leave to other hands?

There is another suggestion in the management of certain departments of these towns and cities. In their churches and their schools, much has been done and much yet remains to be done by the influence and presence and labor of woman. In each community there are some few women who have the time, the inclination, and the experience necessary to do that work wisely and well. The tendency each day is growing stronger to intrust to these women a part of the management of these departments of public usefulness. She does not need the ballot to reach those fields of labor. It is possible that the fact that she has no political ends to serve enlarges her usefulness and influence in those positions. I am much impressed with the wise suggestions of Mrs. Leonard, whose valuable services upon the State Board of Lunacy and Charity have made her name everywhere known and honored in Massachusetts:—

It is the opinion of many of us that woman's power is greater without the ballot or possibility of office-holding for gain, when, standing outside of politics, she discusses great questions upon their merit. Much has been achieved by women in the anti-slavery cause, the temperance cause, the improvement of public and private charities, the reformation of criminals,— all by intelligent discussion and influence upon men. Our legislators have been ready to listen to women, and carry out their plans when well framed. Women can do much useful public service upon boards of education, school committees, and public charities, and are beginning to do such work. It is of vital importance to the integrity of our charitable and educational administration that it be kept out of politics. Is it not well that we should have one sex who have no political ends to serve who can fill responsible positions of public trust? Voting alone can easily be performed by women without rude contact, but to attain any political power women must affiliate themselves with men; because women will differ on public questions, must attend primary meetings and caucuses, will inevitably hold public office, and strive for it,— in short, women must enter the political arena. This result will be repulsive to a large portion of the sex, and would tend to make women unfeminine and combative, which would be a detriment to society.

### PUBLIC SENTIMENT.

But we are told that this great cause is moving forward with gigantic strides, and we are implored not to stand as rocks in the waves of progress and be overwhelmed by its rising flood. It is not the question whether the triumph of their cause is speedily coming, but rather whether it is wise for it to come. But, as these experienced agitators each year reiterate the statement and evidently attach some considerable weight to it as an argument for their cause, let us examine it in the cold light of facts.

In 1866, the first petition for woman suffrage was presented to Congress. In 1868, not long after the death of Francis Jackson, you notice, the New England Woman Suffrage Association was formed. In 1870, two ladies, Mrs. Livermore and Lucy Stone, were admitted as delegates to the Republican State Convention, and the following year woman suffrage was indorsed by the Republican State Convention and incorporated into the platform,— the first and the last time,— nearly twenty years ago.

In 1873, the movement reached high-water mark in the legislature. Eighty-three votes were recorded in favor of an amendment to the Constitution granting suffrage to women. Then the vote fell off each year till it reached 1880, when it was only 59, and for the last time the question in that form was submitted to the legislature.

Since that time, the vote has been taken on the question of municipal suffrage.

In 1881, the vote on that question was 76 in favor; and from that year the vote has fallen until it reached low-water mark, last year (1888) only 36 votes being recorded in its favor, not counting pairs. These figures show that the assertion that the public sentiment is enlisted on their side is not supported by the facts, and that for sixteen years woman suffrage has made no practical gain, and that a decade ago, even, the public sentiment as evidenced by legislative votes — a better test of public sentiment certainly than a file of petitions — was more strongly in their favor than now.

Look beyond Massachusetts. Two years ago, Dakota passed a suffrage law, and it was vetoed by the governor. This last legislature badly defeated such a law. Vermont has just defeated the measure by an overwhelming majority, — 192 to 37. Two years ago, it passed the House. New Hampshire gives the petitioners leave to withdraw; and the president of the Woman Suffrage Convention in Maine frankly admits to the committee that the majority of women are opposed to the measure.

Now, I submit that this public sentiment to which they appeal, on which they rely, and which they claim is strongly with them, and therefore their prayer should be granted, is, in fact, drifting away from them; that the younger generation, for some reason or other, and they may explain it as they please, is less favorable to them than its predecessor was; and that the public sentiment, which is better shown by legislative action for a number of years than by any number of petitions, is in reality voiced by the remonstrants, and not by the petitioners.

### REASONS GIVEN FOR EXTENSION OF SUFFRAGE.

It is interesting to note the reasons given by these petitioners for the extension of the suffrage. The debate was not confined to the narrow field of municipal suffrage alone, but covered every form of suffrage. The president of the Woman's Christian Temperance Union appeared here to voice the wishes of that honorable and useful organization, although even there it appears there is disaffection with the effort to yoke it to the wheels of the suffrage car, that many of the local societies have publicly protested against this union of temperance with suffrage; and it is openly stated in a letter to the *Congregationalist* of last week that there are "but six partisan unions in the State." And from this lady we are given some information as to why woman seeks the ballot, and what reforms she would institute if the ballot were given to her sex.

And first, in order to enforce the liquor legislation of the State more severely, she says woman would take away the right of appeal. The argument is, I suppose, that juries fail to convict, therefore the right of appeal to a jury trial should be denied to the accused. But this form of trial in criminal cases has been used from time immemorial among English-speaking nations, and seems to have been coeval with our government. More than once insisted upon in Magna Charta itself as the principal bulwark of our liberties, it is secured to the people in terms by the Constitution. A change so radical, so contrary to the spirit of our Constitution, fails to commend itself to your judgment, gentlemen of the committee; and, if it is for such legislation that she and the believers whom she represents seek the ballot, we may well question the expediency of extending the suffrage in the direction she seeks. In spite of her severe criticisms upon the legislature, to which I listened the other day, I still am not surprised that the legislature should sometimes pause and hesitate, and decline to follow everywhere that Miss Tobey points the way.

Another lady, in an interesting argument bristling with statistics, points out how the native population of the Commonwealth is fast disappearing, and the foreign population rapidly gaining control of the State. She would give the ballot to women, who would join with the native-born citizens, in order to check this swelling tide of foreign invasion. But, even on her figures and her theory, the day she fears would not be long postponed, since, on the plan she proposes, the ballot would be given as well to the foreign-born citizen as to the native New Englander; and she presents no evidence or argument to show that the institutions and the influences she seeks to save have any less to fear from the vote of the foreign-born female than of that of the foreign-born male.

I make these suggestions, gentlemen, simply because they meet some of the arguments on which the petitioners seem to rely and which they deem of sufficient importance to present to you.

### THE LEGISLATION OF MASSACHUSETTS.

Another line of arguments which these petitioners present, and which have been heard so often that I have no doubt they must have fallen here or elsewhere on willing ears until from their very repetition they are honestly believed to be true, are the arguments they seek to draw from the legislation of Massachusetts, which they claim falls more harshly on woman than on man, and that the ballot is the necessary and the only method of relieving woman from her oppression and her oppressors.

First, who are these oppressors? They are your husbands and fathers, sons and brothers, ladies; not aliens, but of your own households.

Second, name here and now the laws which oppress and unjustly bear so heavily upon you, and which, if we gave you the ballot, you would strike from the statute book. In the two years I served in this House on committees to which these grievances, if they existed, would naturally be brought for redress, I recall no instance where that redress was denied or desired. Every profession and business you are at liberty to engage in to-day: no legal barrier stands in your way. Fifteen years ago, married women were authorized to make contracts and convey property as freely as if they were *sole*. If a husband deserts his wife or fails to support her, or if she lives apart from him for justifiable cause, he can impose no restraint upon her. And the disposition of the children is to be determined by the Supreme Judicial Court, under the statute that the rights of the parents shall, in the absence of misconduct, be held to be equal, and the happiness and the welfare of the children shall determine their custody and possession. Would you have it otherwise?

The law establishes a special reformatory prison for women, gives a female superintendent, female attendant physicians in the lunatic hospital, and female agents for the care of discharged female convicts furnish assistance to such convicts; and we have a statute providing matrons for police stations.

If a husband assaults his wife, in addition to the penalty he must give bonds to keep the peace for two years. If he deserts her or fails to support her, she may rightfully leave him, and he may be compelled to comfortably provide for her by law, and may be punished by fine and imprisonment for refusing to do so; while no corresponding obligation is imposed upon the wife.

The humane limitation of the hours of labor in factories and mechanical establishments is imposed only for women and children. No statute regulation as yet determines the hours of labor for men. To guard the health of females employed in manufacturing, mechanical, and mercantile establishments, the laws require that seats should be provided for them when not actively employed.

A wife is not liable for the debts of her husband; but a husband is liable for such debts of his wife as she may incur, if he fails to support her in a style suited to her condition and circumstances. While he lives, he must provide for her; and, dying, he cannot deprive her of her share of his estate.

It is not necessary to go through the long list. I submit, sir, not without fear of contradiction, but without fear of contradictory proof, that the laws are more favorable to women than to men; that there have been thrown around her barriers and protections which as yet men have denied to their own sex; and that, instead of the laws of Massachusetts being oppressive and burdensome, they are liberal, just, and generous to her sex. There is no man who does not rejoice that it is so. I only present it in order to show that the argument that she needed the ballot to protect her from unjust and burdensome laws has no foundation in fact to-day.

Do not understand me to say that I believe the lot of woman is easier than that of man, or that the duties and responsibilities of wife and mother are less arduous and exacting than those of the husband and father. But I do say, if her burden is heavier than his, and observation and experience lead me to the conclusion that such is the case, it is the result of no *human* law. I am reluctant to add to those burdens and responsibilities another and a heavier one, of which the simple act of depositing the paper ballot is but a trivial part. It is the doing of that act wisely that calls for care and thought and effort.

You may state individual instances, of which there are very many, I am glad to believe, where the exercise of the suffrage by women would be of service to the State. It does not prove your case.

We legislate for the class, and not for the individual; for the many, and not for the few. You should hesitate to impose these new duties on the many at the request of the eager few.

Apply the test of your own experience: how many of your own household, of your own circle of friends and acquaintances, have sought this suffrage, have asked you to vote for it?

I do not like to seem to be doing an ungracious act in urging you to deny this thing they crave so much.

I have too much respect for her sex, both for the living, whose friendship I esteem, and for the dead, whose memory I cherish, to oppose the prayer of these petitioners, if I had not the sure conviction, confirmed by this hearing even, that to grant their prayer would be neither a service to woman nor to the commonwealth of which she forms an honored part.

There are fields of honorable usefulness wide open before her, waiting her hand to-day.

If no home ties bind her and the care of her own children impose no restraints on her time and thought and effort, there are other homes which need her aid, and there are other children who call for all her interest and care.

The great causes of temperance and charity and education need her best powers here and now.

Nature has intrusted to her love and care — a love and care which none but she can give — the coming generation. Can she better serve the State she loves so well than by helping to make that generation wiser, purer, nobler than the last?

# ARGUMENT

OF

# ARTHUR LORD

Before the Legislative Committee on Woman Suffrage, 1890

In Behalf of the

# REMONSTRANTS

Against Municipal Suffrage for Women

BOSTON
GEO. H. ELLIS, PUBLISHER, 141 FRANKLIN STREET
1890

## ARGUMENT.

Mr. Chairman:

Once more the petitioners for an extension of the Suffrage to Women have presented their case to a Committee of the Legislature of Massachusetts. They ask this year simply for municipal suffrage. They have asked in other years for fundamental changes in the Constitution which would grant the right of suffrage to every person without distinction of sex. They have asked for limited suffrage one year to school matters, another year to the voting on the question of granting licenses in municipalities. With a single exception, more than a decade ago, limited only to the voting upon the election of members of the school committee, their requests have been carefully considered, courteously heard, and always refused. For a quarter of a century this question has been pressed upon the attention of legislatures; and yet the President of the Woman's Suffrage Convention, in her address at the opening session of the 22d Annual Convention at Washington, looking back over a lifetime of persistent and devoted effort, was compelled mournfully to say, as a summary of these years of effort that, "though this movement was inaugurated by some of the most cultured men and women of the nation, and carried on with rare ability and heroism, yet the great truths proclaimed have been received with profound indifference by the vast majority."

If such is the fact,— and upon that question Mrs. Stanton should be an undisputed authority,— it must be that there are some reasons based upon the experience of men and women why this cause fails of success. It is no longer because of prejudice, it is not because man is naturally a tyrant and an oppressor as they are pleased to call them, it is not because their claims have failed of able championship or lacked opportunities for a presentation as full and as fair as its most zealous advocates could ask, that the cause has taken no longer stride forward. Forty years ago, in an address to the people of Massachusetts which in the years that followed has had no superior in ability and dignity and force, the rights of women to the ballot were presented to the people of Massachusetts. Forty years ago the foremost orator whom Massachusetts has yet produced urged the principles of that address upon a wider audience than those merely who were gathered in the hall, in an argument which covered the ground more eloquently than any which has followed; and yet their triumph is no nearer than when the echoes of the eloquence of Phillips had just died away. It does not seem to me, sir, that the consummation of their wishes is so likely to be speedily fulfilled as it seemed to their eloquent champion that day. The strong argument which he presented, that the suffrage was necessary to woman to relieve her from the grievous burdens and hardships of existing law, in view of the broad extension of all rights which man enjoys to woman also, has lost its force and its significance. When these petitioners come here this year, as in the years gone by, it is the right of this committee, and of the legislature which it serves, to ask them what new light the experience of the past year has thrown upon this question, what new reasons are to be presented in support of their claims which other committees and other legislatures have not attentively heard and fairly considered. It would be well, it seems to me, to let this annual agitation rest for a year or two.

It is possible, as Governor Long intimated in his speech at the last convention of the Suffrage Association, that familiarity might possibly have dulled the full force of the argument in behalf of Woman's Suffrage. I do not know, sir, that the record of victory or defeat is an argument for or against the cause; but, wherever there is assembled an association who ask this change, I find they always point with pride, to use their expression, to the success which the year preceding has brought. It is possible, however, that there are those elsewhere who justify their support of the cause upon prophecy, and not upon argument. I have heard it said within these halls that because it was sure to come in the future, therefore, the suffrage bill should receive their vote here and to-day. To those whom the predictions of future success influence and persuade, and those whom the record of present triumphs convinces or alarms, I submit the history of the agitation in this country the past year. I noticed in the annual address of the Massachusetts Convention what appeared to be a long list of sincere congratulations for the favors received. I turn in vain to the reports of the proceedings of the various legislatures which have considered this question from Maine across the continent to California for any result that can be cited in support of their propositions.

### SUFFRAGE IN OTHER STATES.

If the conclusions of the legislatures of sister States have any influence upon our own in the consideration of this question, if the experience of a Territory furnishes any lamp which may guide the feet of a State, then I submit that, so far as the past year is concerned, the weight of testimony is wholly in favor of the remonstrants. Maine, Vermont, Connecticut, and New Hampshire in our own New England, the great States of New York and Pennsylvania, that other Massachusetts on the banks of the Ohio, with Michigan and Wisconsin and California, considered, debated, and defeated in their respective legislatures every proposition for a further extension of the suffrage to woman. In the Territories which were just to assume the duties and responsibilities of a State the result of the agitation was the same. I beg to refer the committee to the action of the new State of Washington, for the Territory of Washington had long furnished an argument for your petitioners; for under its Territorial government the duty of suffrage was borne by women as well as by men, in its delights both had shared, its results had been watched and considered by all, but, when that convention met to frame a constitution, only eight delegates out of the whole number voting supported the motion to strike out the word "male."

The question of woman's suffrage was submitted in the form of a separate article at the same time with the new constitution to the voters of Washington, and was defeated by a vote of nearly two to one. If the fact that in Washington the women exercised the privilege of voting in common with men has furnished an argument in former years for an extension of the suffrage in Massachusetts,— and that argument has been repeatedly urged in this hall upon the attention of the committees,— will you not give to-day weight to the conclusions of that same Washington out of an abundant experience which led the people of the State to refuse in the years to come to the women of Washington the exercise of the suffrage and the power of the ballot? In Wyoming it has been claimed by these petitioners that there has been an emphatic indorsement of woman's suffrage; but in view of the fact that the total population of Wyoming at the time of the passage of the suffrage act of 1869 was but 9,000, and the number of females of all ages from the first childhood to the second was less than 2,000, and that they were scattered over a territory of about 98,000 square miles, or one female, whether in infancy or old age, to every 50 square miles of territory, it seems absurd to cite the Territory of Wyoming to control the action of the Commonwealth of Massachusetts.

These petitioners congratulate themselves upon the success of their cause in Dakota; but, sir, turn to the record of North Dakota, on which they rely; and there the convention adopted an amendment requiring ratification by the vote of the people for any act of the legislature on conferring suffrage upon women.

If such a provision were incorporated in the law of Massachusetts, the remonstrants would not be concerned over the possible action of a single legislature.

The fact is — and it cannot be concealed elsewhere than in a suffrage convention — that the great weight of the testimony of the past year is overwhelming against their claims and their desires.

Take New Jersey, which Mr. Blackwell referred to at the

last hearing in support of some of his propositions. I took occasion to look up the record of New Jersey.

It is true that at one time women in New Jersey had the right to vote. The act of 1793 gave it to them, and the act of 1807 took it away; and the reasons which led to the change I commend to the careful consideration of Mr. Blackwell.

## KANSAS.

Take Kansas, which furnishes the argument upon which they place their sure reliance. One difficulty in making an investigation there is found in the fact that "there is no provision in Kansas by which official returns are made to any central authority at the capital for compilation for public information." But I find in a little book which is largely circulated by these suffragists that 28,000 women voted in Kansas in 1887, and a less number in 1888. I do not suppose, Mr. Chairman, they underestimate the female vote. In view of the fact that Kansas cast 334,000 votes in the last presidential election to Massachusetts' 344,000, there does not seem any wide-spread interest in the matter. The suffrage law was passed in 1887, and, as appears from the testimony of one of their witnesses at the hearing last year, not so much to secure to woman her rights as to secure the enforcement of the prohibitory law. And, when we recall the fact that Kansas has only two counties with as large a population as Barnstable, and only two cities as large as Brockton, and that its population is widely scattered over a territory more than ten times as large as Massachusetts, some of the conditions and difficulties which confront us here seem there to be lacking; and Kansas loses largely its value as a precedent, and her experience, after all, furnishes to us little assistance.

I submit now, as I had the honor to submit to your predecessors a year ago, that, when it is proposed that a body of voters shall deliberately open their ranks, and admit a re-enforcement larger than itself, as Colonel Higginson states it, a change so revolutionary, so far reaching in its consequences, should not be the action of a single legislature, but attended with all the requirements which the constitution has provided for a change in the organic law.

No party in Massachusetts is committed to it in its platform, or has been committed since 1871. No member found it a controlling question in his own election. Without preparation, save from the lessons of his own experience, the representative of 1890 will consider it; and from his conclusions there lies no appeal.

What fair objection can be made to the position that any member of this committee may take who shall say to these petitioners, We cannot consent to a change so fundamental by our vote alone, there is no evidence of any general desire for the change you propose, there is no reason to believe that the sentiment of the people of Massachusetts has undergone any change since its representatives defeated your bill last year, following in the line of a continued series of precedents?

If this change is to come, let it be after a full discussion before the people, in the manner provided for a change in the constitution after the concurrent action of two legislatures, and with an expressed consent of a majority of the voters in Massachusetts.

It has always seemed to me that prudence would dictate that course, and her dictates may still be heeded to advantage even here.

### STATISTICS OF VOTES.

If you seek to know what the interest of the women of Massachusetts is in this question of suffrage, the evidence from a partial test is on file at the State House. The act of 1879, which gave women the right to vote for school committees, was urged upon the consideration of the legislature as a practical test of the whole question. "If the women will not vote for school matters," it was said on the floor of the Senate, "it settles it for any other form of suffrage." By agreement of all parties, the further extension of the suffrage was to rest on the use which the women of Massachusetts made of this privilege, and in its operation was to be found the test of the validity of some of the objections to female suffrage. We have tried it for ten years in Massachusetts. Your experience shows that it has resulted not only in not encouraging the election of women to the school committees, but often in partially preventing such elections in many towns; and yet the service of women on such committees would be largely productive of good to the committees and the schools.

If you are interested to read the instructive lesson of the practical operation of the law, turn to House Document No. 175 of 1888. I will not weary you with reading at length from its pages. Let me call your attention to a few of the conclusions.

Out of 349 towns and cities in this State there are 167 in which no woman ever registered during all the period covered by the report,— namely, from 1881 to 1887 inclusive; and during the same period 197 in which no woman ever voted. In 1881 the total female vote was but 1,571 in the whole State out of a population of 1,783,000; and in 1887 the female vote was only 1,912, although the population had increased to 1,942,000.

I have here, Mr. Chairman, the returns from 1881 to 1888; and I may pause here to say that the petitioners have ceased to ask for the publication of these returns.

I find that in your district, Mr. Chairman, only eight women voted in 1887, and less than a baker's dozen in 1888.

Your colleague from the Cape District represents three counties, and in them all only twenty-one women voted in 1888. Whatever his individual impressions may be, it is quite clear that his constituents, who have no superior for intelligence, industry, and sobriety, have neither interest in the cause nor confidence in its benefit.

Take the towns of Becket, Seekonk, Wayland, Winchendon, and Framingham, which are represented at your table. In Framingham no woman has registered or voted since 1884, and in the others no woman has ever registered or voted since the law was passed in 1879.

What interest do your female constituents show in this matter? And yet this was the petitioners' test.

Is there a greater peril to the suffrage than the indifference of the voter?

Is it wise to further extend it to a class which the experience of the past has shown to be utterly indifferent to its exercise? This indifference is due in no sense to a lack of interest on the part of the women of Massachusetts either in the prosperity of the schools or the welfare of the children, but may be attributed mainly to the sure conviction on the part of most women that the important questions of school management and control may still be wisely intrusted to the husbands and fathers of Massachusetts. It is an indifference to the suffrage which these returns show. If the women will leave the education of their children, as their reason and experience teach them they may safely do, to be regulated and provided for by the men, may it not be urged with still greater force that they will not be more eager and desirous to care for their streets and their sewers, to provide for their poor, to maintain their fire and police departments, and even to incur debts and to lay taxes, which seems to be the *summum bonum* in the minds of some of the enthusiastic advocates of these proposed changes?

There is another danger which some of the remonstrants fear might result from the extension of the suffrage, and which the experience of a single city in the Commonwealth shows to be not wholly imaginary; and the lesson of the returns in 1888 from the city of Boston, of the votes for school committee, is that the emotional vote may be more of a peril to the State than the indifferent vote. In that year, the vote of Suffolk County jumped from 1,000 to 20,000 under the bitter appeals to prejudice and bigotry and sectarianism.

The most Jesuitical of Jesuits could find no weapon fashioned to his use more effective in defence of the parochial school system than the intemperate appeals of excited women to the female voters of Boston. The "Appeal to Voters from the Christian Women of Massachusetts," which was widely circulated in the streets, with its demands for "No popery, no Catholics on the School Board, no Catholic teachers in the schools," was productive of a state of feeling which had no precedent since the burning of the Ursuline Convent, and has no place in the wiser councils of the present time. The church bells which summoned the women of Boston to the polls gave to the thoughtful ear a note of warning and alarm far different from that which fell on the eager throngs that day.

The policy of proscription which they countenanced and sought would do more to subvert the common school system than years of patient effort can restore; and in the emotionalism of the voters of that day may be found a new warning against the extension of the suffrage to a class which could only be aroused from indifference by appeals which have no place in a State where the freedom of the individual in the exercise of his religion has ever been guaranteed, and where the common school loses much of its usefulness if Catholic and Protestant do not alike share in its advantages, and fit themselves for the duties of citizenship in a State which makes no distinction by reason of difference of religious opinion in its children.

I pass now to the consideration of the three arguments which have been urged from the beginning of this agitation, and are still urged, in support of the extension of the suffrage to women.

They may be briefly distinguished as the argument of necessity, of right, and of expediency.

### ARGUMENT OF NECESSITY.

We were told that it was necessary to grant the suffrage to woman to enable her to protect herself against arbitrary, unjust, and oppressive laws.

You find this argument now largely among those in whose distorted imaginations man appears as the tyrant and the oppressor and woman as the subject and the slave.

The teachings of experience, the record of the years of ever-widening legislation, the mere statement of the present laws of Massachusetts furnish the conclusive answer to this argument.

The humanity and liberality of the laws relating to woman, which have ever broadened with the passage of the years, are ample witness that she does not need to have the making of the law to relieve herself from burdensome restrictions or protect herself against unjust enactments. If it were true that the laws pressed more heavily upon woman than upon man when this agitation began, half a century ago, it is not true in any sense to-day.

It would be difficult to name any law which in terms bears unequally upon woman. It would be impossible to name a law which in fact leaves her at a disadvantage, while the statute book contains many a humane provision which men have given to women alone.

I need not refer you to the limitation of the hours of labor in factories and manufacturing establishments, which apply to women and not to men, and to the special regulations for those establishments designed to promote her comfort and guard her health and her safety.

The broadest freedom is given her in all the business relations of life: whether married or single, she has the right to make contracts and convey property, and engage in every business and trade and profession. In the care and custody of her children, the law knows no difference in the rights of the parent; and the welfare of the children in case of separation is the paramount consideration controlling the action of the court. So far as the marital relation is considered under law, it may be said, without contradiction, that the wife is given special privileges and advantages which the husband does not share. He is liable for her debts incurred in providing her with a comfortable support, if he fails to support her in a style suited to their condition and circumstances. She is never liable for his.

From the home which he purchased, if the title stands in her name, she may exclude him without liability for his support elsewhere, either in sickness or poverty; but the obligation for her support always rests upon him, and he cannot lay it aside.

The legislature has enacted in the past, and will still continue to enact, laws specially designed for her protection and comfort, and leave to individual effort and private contract to secure a like gain to him. So far as the provisions of statute law are concerned, the legislature of Massachusetts offers no argument in support of the proposition that the ballot is necessary to her protection.

The wives and daughters throughout the Commonwealth may still trust the husbands and fathers to preserve to them all the privileges which the law gives them to-day; and, if there is any protection which the law can give which is not already secured, it needs but to be proved to be adopted.

The only suggestion that has been made at this hearing of any legislation which, if woman had the ballot, she would secure, and which has been denied her, was in the fervid appeal of Miss Tobey, in which she criticised the present legislature somewhat severely for not passing an act to secure scientific temperance instruction in the schools.

One reason, perhaps, why the House wisely refused to accede to her request may be found in the fact that five years ago the legislature passed such an act, and substantially in the form which she asks for this year.

If the law is not enforced, the remedy, I may be permitted to suggest, can be found in the election of a school committee by women voters, who will see to its enforcement. If some of these ladies would spend a portion of the time which they now devote to securing new laws in enforcing existing laws, some valuable time would be saved.

## SUFFRAGE AS A RIGHT.

So much, then, for the argument for the suffrage based upon necessity; but the argument for its extension rests more often upon the proposition that woman is entitled to the ballot as her natural right, and that its refusal is a wrong for which the State ought not to be responsible. It is easier to find assertions of this doctrine of natural rights than arguments to prove its existence. History, either here or abroad, from the earliest past to the immediate present, furnishes little evidence in support of that proposition. It is a generality which lies at the base of the argument, not a conclusion supported by the teachings of the past or the facts of the present. Everywhere there have been limitations on this so-called natural right,— limitations which vary with the age and the State, but which are ever found to exist in all communities of men. The foundation of this government was based, in fact, upon the principle of the right of exclusion from suffrage of males, as well as females, whose participation in it would not conduce, in the judgment of the body of the voters, to the welfare of the State. Nowhere was that exclusion more rigorously practised than in that community and by that company of Pilgrims who laid the corner-stone of the free institutions of America. The doctrine of natural right is of modern invention; but, if it were a principle, as it is claimed, universal in its application, inherent and inborn, it would have been limited to no age or clime. Every declaration of principles put forth by these petitioners assumes the existence of the right, but does not prove it. Granting the premise, it is easy to draw the conclusion that its denial is a wrong. Occasionally, we find it urged that this right is secured in terms by the Declaration of Independence and the provisions of the Constitution; but, as the committee of the national House put it, "the great misfortune of those who thus believe is that the Supreme Court holds just the contrary opinion." I need not refer the committee to the decision of the Supreme Court in the case of Minor v. Happersett, 21 Wallace, that the Constitution of the United States does not confer the right of suffrage upon women.

If suffrage is a natural right and, as one radical claimed, "inherent in every sentient being," distinctions of age or sex may not vary it, limitations of residence and citizenship and education ought not to control it: it is common to every race and universal in its application. This doctrine of natural right may perhaps be tested by an application of the principle in the direction where the irresistible force of logic must lead its supporters.

It is no less a right in Georgia than in Massachusetts. It

knows no distinction of color or race, if inherent in humanity.

If these petitioners are logical, they must insist upon the application of their principle to the ignorant negro woman of Georgia as well as to the intelligent and cultured woman of Massachusetts.

Because it is a natural right, these petitioners have told the National Committee elsewhere that to refuse the suffrage to woman is done at our peril, when we remember that God is still just. Does the fact that God is just make it necessary to extend the suffrage to every woman, whether she desires or is fitted for its intelligent exercise? I don't mean to suggest, of course, that because no one would insist, who had any conception of the problem which confronts the South to-day, that the suffrage should be extended to every woman south of Mason and Dixon's line, therefore it should be refused to the women of Massachusetts, but only that the argument upon which they rest their claim to secure it, if pressed to its logical results, leads to conclusions which no thoughtful man can contemplate without denial of the proposition.

The speculations of the philosopher must yield to the facts of experience. This hasty generalization respecting natural right has led to more confusion in the discussion of this question than any other consideration. We have always recognized in Massachusetts, we recognize still, limitations upon the exercise of the suffrage, which even these petitions would not change, which cannot be justified for a moment if we admit the principle of natural right, but which lead to but one conclusion, that the policy which shapes the destinies of States is not fanciful theories, but practical conclusions justified in the light of experience, and resting upon the principle that the greatest good of the greatest number shall shape the policy of well-ordered commonwealths. In the application of that doctrine, men may differ: in the recognition of the principle, there is no distinction of parties. It is difficult to show an instance of natural right in the affairs of the government. Even the rights of life, liberty, and property are recognized by the State and by the people generally as subject to certain limitations made necessary for the good of society. The life may be taken, the liberty destroyed, the property of the citizen appropriated for the well-being of society, and where it is necessary for its protection or progress.

These petitioners must leave these speculations about natural rights in the graves of the philosophers, long since forgotten, who evolved them from the inner consciousness, and not from the experience of mankind. They are glittering generalities of the school of the French Revolution, and find little support in the sober thought of New England. For fifty years they have pressed this proposition, that the suffrage is a right and its denial a wrong; but it has found slight credence, and furnishes no incentive to the legislation which they seek. In the history of legislation, each advance has been made, each change secured, each new law adopted, solely upon the assertion of or the proof of the proposition that the proposed modifications in the law conduce to the well-being of society and the safety of the State. Even the emancipation proclamation and the amendment to the Constitution were made necessary by the stern realities of war and the exigencies of the time, and were obtained not so much upon the ground of right as upon the ground of an imperative public policy. This extension of the suffrage which they seek will come, not because its denial is a wrong, but because its adoption is necessary to the cause of good government, State as well as municipal; and this extension of the suffrage rests entirely, in my judgment, upon the argument of expediency.

## THE ARGUMENT OF EXPEDIENCY.

When your petitioners show that the rights of the individual will be better secured, the welfare and integrity of the home more certainly protected, the happiness and prosperity of the community made more certain, the safety of the State be better assured, the advance of civilization aided and stimulated and the well-being of all the people protected and promoted, then, sir, the day for the adoption of a change so fundamental has come in Massachusetts; but even its supporters to-day make no effort to prove that proposition. There is a concurrence of testimony that the change proposed would be revolutionary in its character. Mr. Phillips boldly maintained that the immediate results might be disastrous, but was willing to trust to the future to correct the necessary evils attendant upon a change so momentous. His primary proposition was that the "law is always wrong." Admitting that proposition, he found no difficulty in urging any change which his fancy or his sympathy suggested. We are not here to-day to inquire whether in some future, distant or near as the case may be, the cause of good government may not be promoted by the fullest extension of the suffrage to woman. These are speculations not useful in dealing with the question to-day. Have the petitioners shown by facts or argument that here and now by this present legislature the law they seek should be adopted? Does the experience which you gain in your own home, in the community which you represent, lead you to the conclusion that there is a demand universal and widespread among the women of Massachusetts that you grant to them the ballot to-day? I am aware, sir, that there are long petitions on file in aid of this proposition; but it is difficult to suggest a change in the law which could not be supported by long lists of names. The marvel to me is, in view of the activity and persistency of some of these agitators, that the demand for a change in the law in this respect is so limited and confined. It seems to the remonstrants that there is less interest this year in Massachusetts than has been the case for many a year in the past. Is it possible that the attention of the leaders in this movement has been turned to more hopeful fields beyond the Mississippi, and that the money which Francis Jackson left to promote the cause of Woman's Suffrage has been spent in far-off Dakota, and that none remains to quicken the agitation here in Massachusetts? Even the question of license suffrage, which last year we were told was necessary to the salvation of the State, and in support of which this room echoed with the impassioned appeals of many a voice familiar in the Green-room, has been permitted without discussion and with the consent even of its petitioners to be buried in Massachusetts for this year at least. I can only account, sir, for this marvellous change in the condition of affairs that the interest in these measures on the part of ninety-nine one-hundredths of the people is more imaginary than real, and that, when the trustees of Francis Jackson's bounty turned their attention to other States, the interest in the cause appears to fade away here in Massachusetts. But, sir, we have been told that it is not expedient to exclude a class from the responsibilities of the government. For the sake of the argument, I might be willing to accept the proposition. Professor Goldwin Smith, who with John Bright was once in sympathy with the movement, and who with Bright changed his mind and has become a powerful opponent of female suffrage, tells us that "women are not a class, but a sex." This is the gist of the matter; and along the lines of thought which that suggestion makes may be found some arguments against the extension which are patent to every member of this committee, and which, if not stated here, still present considerations of special weight. "Sex is a fact,— no act of Parliament can eliminate it,— and woman as woman must be a power for good or evil over man," writes a distinguished lady in an English review, in an appeal against Female Suffrage.

The interests of the sexes, of the husband and wife, are in their nature identical, as Mrs. Thorp claimed the other day; not divided, but united; not separate, but the same. And the representation now afforded is the representation of both in the way which experience shows can be most effectively made, and with the least injury to the family or the State.

If the result or the tendency of the legislation proposed would be to weaken the "potent moral influence" which is exerted by woman to-day, to the great benefit of human society, then I submit the legislation is unwise and not to be desired.

And that is the danger which thoughtful men and women who oppose this movement fear, and have heard no reasons presented which tend to quiet that alarm.

Mrs. Leonard, whose services to the State upon the State Board of Lunacy and Charity give to her conclusions special weight and entitle her to long and grateful remembrance, writes in a letter which has often been quoted: —

"It is the opinion of many of us that woman's power is greater without the ballot or possibility of office-holding for gain, when, standing outside of politics, she discusses great questions upon their merit. Much has been achieved by women in the anti-slavery cause, the temperance cause, the improvement of public and private charities, the reformation of criminals,— all by intelligent discussion and influence upon men. Our legislators have been ready to listen to women, and carry out their plans when well framed. Women can do much useful public service upon boards of education, school committees, and public charities, and are beginning to do such work. It is of vital importance to the integrity of our charitable and educational administration that it be kept out of politics. Is it not well that we should have one sex who have no political ends to serve who can fill responsible positions of public trust? Voting alone can easily be performed by women without rude contact; but to attain any political power women must affiliate themselves with men, because women will differ on public questions, must attend primary meetings and caucuses, will inevitably hold public office and strive for it,— in short, women must enter the political arena. This result will be repulsive to a large portion of the sex, and would tend to make women unfeminine and combative, which would be a detriment to society."

The drift of legislation has been, of later years at least, to emphasize the importance of the individual, and to omit the consideration of effect of the legislation upon the family and the home. Some of the evils which threaten society have alarmingly increased, as a result of that tendency. The unit of the State for much of its legislation should be the family, and not the individual; and that wider legislation which treats questions broadly, and is not concerned about exceptions to general rules, will recognize that under the existing arrangement the family is represented at the ballot box.

Some of the results of this movement for industrial liberty for women tend constantly to the disintegration of family ties. The influence of the home is weakening everywhere in the struggle for industrial employment by both sexes. A thoughtful writer has pointed out that it is not so much womanhood as property which is the impelling force of much of this movement for equal rights. The desire to secure employment on the one hand, and the desire to secure cheaper service on the other, are driving women into the factory and the shop, and into places which have been filled by men, and then compel the employment of children in the place of both.

The position of the family in modern society has been too long unheeded, the disintegrating influences which environ it have been unwatched in the struggle of the individual; the problems of marriage and divorce, the preservation of the home, are not considered in this struggle, which knows no distinction of sex, and would give to the individual, as an individual merely, the privilege of voting, and leave to the future to determine the result of the "experiment of woman suffrage."

Is it not the duty of the wiser political thought to hesitate before urging or even yielding to the demand for the enfranchisement of woman until it has studied more closely the political relations of the family?

What is the occasion for this undue precipitancy? The mere form of voting in and by itself contains little that may eagerly be sought, except in its effect upon the policy of the State. The delights of voting are not in themselves so alluring that for the pleasure of its exercise women should hasten to throw down the barriers.

What would they do, if they had the ballot, which men are not now doing or willing to do, if they point out the way, for the improvement of society and the welfare of the family?

I do not find that there is any agreement of opinion even among the advocates of the suffrage as to the changes which, if they had the ballot, they would seek to effect.

There is no barrier to-day which remains to be removed which keeps them from any employment of man.

When the agitation began which sought to give to women the right to practise law in the courts, it was urged that it was unreasonable to close to her that avenue of usefulness and profit.

We welcomed her into the "gladsome light of jurisprudence"; and I can think of only one Portia who has assumed the robes of the advocate and seeks to persuade juries and convince courts.

The Epistle of Saint Paul, and not the Blue Books of Massachusetts, contains the only injunctions against women preaching in the churches. And yet, for some reason, they do not flock in any numbers to assume pastoral duties and influence society for good from the pulpit.

The profession of medicine has long been open to them, and there they are welcomed to a sphere of usefulness which seems especially appropriate in some of its departments, at least, to their nature and their hand. All would wish that every town in Massachusetts enjoyed the advantage of having in its midst at least one educated and skilful female physician; and yet, outside of a few cities, you will not find them actively engaged in the practice of that useful and honored profession.

I recall but one woman banker in the history of Massachusetts, and her career served more as a warning than as an example.

You may look in vain through all the great office buildings in Boston to find in any department of human activity her hand directing and guiding its affairs. Her money is invested in railroads: she does not concern herself with their management or even attend their meetings. Her name appears on the list of stockholders of most of the great business corporations of Massachusetts, and yet you never find her name on the list of their directors.

You can hardly mention any field of human labor where you will find she takes an active part where her position would involve the control of or the responsibility for other workers. Yet it is in such employments that is acquired that special fitness for the discharge of the duties of citizenship. Municipal affairs are practical affairs: the less of sentiment and the more of business management you can infuse into them, the less will be the burden which will rest upon the people.

You may find certain employments in which she enters freely, like teaching music, painting, or the arts; yet she preferably treats them as accomplishments, and not occupations, and they are the least in touch with the details of busy, practical, every-day life.

## OCCUPATIONS OF WOMEN.

At the last hearing, Mr. Blackwell presented an array of figures from the Report of the Bureau of Statistics of Labor, which he claimed tended to show how largely the women of this State were employed in gainful occupations, as an argument for the extension of the suffrage.

I have obtained since that hearing, by the kindness of Mr. Wadlin, Chief of that Bureau, some carefully prepared tables, showing the occupations of females in Massachusetts, arranged by age periods, and classified according to the class of occupation.

From these tables, it appears that there are in round numbers 162,000 women above the age of nineteen employed for wages in Massachusetts. Of that number, 139,000 are employed in domestic and personal service and in the factories of the State, not occupations either of them peculiarly fitted to qualify for the suffrage.

Of the remaining 24,000 wage-earners, 13,000, more than half, are employed as teachers, and of the remainder about 8,000 are employed in stores and trade, leaving in all the other pursuits and occupations less than 2,000 women actively engaged therein for wages out of all the women in Massachusetts.

Now there is another significant fact to be found in these returns; and that is that out of the 162,000 employed as above 95,000 are between the ages of twenty and thirty, and 33,000 are in the next age period, between thirty and forty.

The marked decrease in the number employed in these two age periods, when we remember that the average age at which women marry in Massachusetts is about twenty-five years and six months, as given by Mr. Wadlin, goes far, it seems to me, to establish the proposition which is made by the remonstrants, that such employment and occupation is largely regarded as and is, in fact, temporary in its character, the result of some exigency, which, when removed by marriage or otherwise, takes the women from the class of wage-earners, and substitutes therefor the duties and responsibilities of the family in the new home or the old.

It is the condition of the large majority, and not of the small minority, which shapes the policy of the State.

Reasoning from general principles, which exceptions do not affect, except to prove the rule, there is little reason to impose upon her the ballot, which the great majority of her sex do not seek, simply because it is asked for by the few who are led by glittering generalities to demand as a right the extension of the suffrage, which has never yet been granted in a free State until it was shown to be desirable as a measure of wise political expediency.

Perhaps it is the more eagerly prized because denied. If the interests of the family are to be encouraged and protected by every influence which wise legislation can throw around it, the fact that there are some women whom no home duties occupy and no home cares detain furnishes no reason why the ballot should be granted to all. If in England to a limited extent certain spinsters and widows enjoy or bear the duties of suffrage, that furnishes no precedent which can have weight in Massachusetts for a bill as broad and universal in its application as this.

### PAYMENT OF TAXES NOT THE TEST.

It was left to the ingenuity of to-day to apply the phrase that "taxation without representation is tyranny" as an argument for universal suffrage without distinction of sex. The property qualification perhaps would be a wise one in some conditions of society, but it has no place as a decisive test in the frame of government of Massachusetts. To argue that the woman should vote simply because she is a tax-payer would involve us in a train of reasoning which could lead but to one conclusion; and that is that the railroad, the factory, or every other great business corporation, should be represented at the City Hall and the State House because it bore its part of the taxes. It is interested in the question of streets, of fire and police, of sewers and water-works. The expenditures which the outlays in these several departments involve perhaps fall more heavily upon the corporations than upon the great body of the voters who meet at the town meeting and vote away their money. It may be that no share of its stock is owned by a single voter within the limits of the municipality. If you are to base the suffrage upon the payment of a tax, why not admit these corporations to a representation in the government? This principle has been recognized elsewhere, but it has yet found no place in the policy of this Commonwealth. But, if the proposition is true that women must vote because they pay taxes, it is no less true that the payment of a tax should permit the representation of other tax-payers simply for that reason. Press the principle because there is taxation therefore there should be representation still further, and you are led to the conclusion that the individual who pays the larger tax should have the larger share and influence in the disposition of the public money which is raised by such taxation. This plan is recognized in the city of Berlin, but it does not commend itself to the minds of most legislators as a correct principle to apply to the city of Boston. By far the larger number of women are represented to-day, and fully and fairly represented, by husbands, fathers, and brothers; and the overwhelming majority of these women, if the returns from the towns and cities of the Commonwealth prove anything, are wisely content to trust the management of the practical affairs of cities and towns to those to whom they daily trust the practical affairs of their every-day life. They trust their business affairs to them now, with full confidence in their considerate action and watchful care. Is there any difference which is worthy of special legislation in the expenditure of that small sum which they pay as taxes? There are special cases, perhaps, which can be brought to the attention of the committee, or have occurred in your own experience, which seem to be outside the rule; but legislation for special cases is usually unwise, and always to be avoided when it involves the imposition of an additional duty and responsibility upon a great majority who do not ask for it, simply that it may reach the special case. If husband and wife are each to have a vote and both to participate in public affairs, so long as they agree as to what the true policy of the municipality is,—and perhaps in the large majority of cases they would agree,—the result of the election is not changed, though the total vote may be increased by their joint participation and no different legislation results from this imposition of new burdens. When they disagree as to the duty of the hour, each neutralizes the vote of the other, and the harmony and peace and contentment of the home suffer in proportion to the bitterness of party strife and the intensity of their personal interests. You may not change the result, but you impose an unsought duty without any compensating advantage.

We were told last year by a gentleman whose zeal for every extension of human rights had led him into the support of this cause, although he admitted that the immediate results would be disastrous if the suffrage were extended to woman, that she needs the ballot for self-protection and self-respect. I have sought to show that for her protection no further legislation is needed; and no one has pointed out in what respect she suffers in the enjoyment of life, liberty, and property by the denial of the ballot. I will leave to the members of this committee the decision of the question upon the facts of their personal experience whether she needs the ballot to insure her self-respect. Is your wife or sister or mother, Mr. Chairman, less self-respecting or respected than yourself? What distinction of superiority can you point out between the husband and wife in the orderly homes of Massachusetts? Their duties and responsibilities may be different; but there is no difference in their dignity and importance to her disadvantage, whatever there may be in the weight of the burden which these duties and responsibilities bring. The home is of more importance still than the shop or the office or the factory. The husband's place may be filled by another in the rounds of his daily task, and there is neither shock nor loss; but the mother's place in the home can never be supplied. You will legislate wisely if you legislate for the home, and not for the individual. You will hesitate long, I think, before you experiment with the suffrage on the mere assertion of the petitioners that the family ties and the home influences are neither invaded nor weakened by a change so fundamental in the established order of society, and which would blot out forever any distinction of sex in the body politic of this Commonwealth. The change, once effected, may bring in its train complications which will prevent a return to the old order of things. The wiles of the demagogue will be more persuasive than the reasonings of the statesman, and new perils will threaten the existence of the State. These problems may well be left for solution to the future. The change, by evolution, if it comes, is far less dangerous than by revolution; and time will give the answer which the future legislature may wisely make to these demands. It was said by one of their champions the other day in Music Hall that the change must come, not as a revolution, but as "the unfolding of a beautiful flower." I do not know that I understand the full meaning of that somewhat mystic utterance, but I infer that he, too, thought that the time was not yet ripe for the change proposed. If this be the meaning, then, the remonstrants are fully inclined to agree with that eloquent speaker. In words less flowery perhaps, but no less significant, you will approve the conclusions of both, when you report on these petitions that "the petitioners have leave to withdraw."

# MUNICIPAL WOMAN SUFFRAGE.

## ARGUMENT

— OF —

## Clement K. Fay, Esq.

— FOR —

## REMONSTRANTS.

BROOKLINE:
The Chronicle Press: C. A. W. Spencer.
1887.

# MUNICIPAL WOMAN SUFFRAGE.

## I.

### *What does Municipal Suffrage for Women Mean?*

Municipal Suffrage for Women means that women may vote in all city and town elections; that high and low, rich and poor, good and bad, may swarm to the caucuses, the primaries, and the polls. It proposes to drag women down from a position of security and influence into the arena of city and town elections, and make them, if they do their duty, unwilling or unnecessary participants in those exciting contests. Municipal Woman Suffrage is a broad theme. It is treated by its advocates as a simple or elementary branch of suffrage in the abstract, but it is something which is much more vast than that. It would usher in a train of evils, especially in cities, which, it is no exaggeration to say, would multiply the political ills from which we suffer now, instead of lessening them.

We have not yet learned how to govern our larger cities. Boston is today struggling with this question. Philadelphia has recently adopted a new form of city charter. New York has done the same; Chicago stands aghast at the corruption in her high places; Brooklyn is about to be investigated by a legislative committee; and a number of other instances might be cited, to show that we are still wrestling with the momentous problem of honest city government on a large scale. Will that problem be solved by adding the female vote? In Boston there are 20,000 more women than men. To attempt to renovate and purify its government by opening the polls indiscriminately to women, in addition to men, is like trying to relieve an overloaded ship in distress by more than doubling its cargo.

Dr. Strong, in his remarkable book, "Our Country," says: "The city is the nerve center of our civilization. It is also the storm center." If Municipal Suffrage is extended to women, *it must include all alike.* Not the wise, the good, the pure only, but, shoulder to shoulder with them, the ignorant, the bad and the abandoned. Which of these classes would be the more likely to enter actively into the dirty work of city politics? Because Municipal Woman Suffrage might do no harm in a well-ordered town, where, also, it would do no good, will anyone seriously argue that it would work equally well in Boston?

## II.

### *Public Sentiment in Massachusetts Opposed to Municipal Suffrage for Women.*

*It is unwise to legislate against public sentiment.* That is an axiom in legislation. History proves it; wise men admit it. Laws made in defiance of it are inoperative, and react against their authors and even the government itself. The large preponderance of public sentiment in this Commonwealth is distinctly and emphatically opposed to Municipal Suffrage for women. In the terse and appropriate language of Lucy Stone (as she prefers to be styled), "*An ounce of fact is worth a pound of theory.*" In order to refresh the memories of those who already know the facts, and to enlighten those who do not, let me briefly call attention to the legislative history of this Woman Suffrage movement in Massachusetts since the year 1872. In the earlier days of its existence attempts were made to obtain Woman Suffrage by appeals to the General Court for an Amendment to the Constitution. A Resolve was introduced in the Legislature, for several years in succession, ending in 1880, "to amend the Constitution so as to secure the elective franchise to women." It met with defeat year after year, so there was a change of tactics. The Suffragists then fell back on the question, pure and simple, whether or not women should have the right "to vote in all Municipal and Town elections."

What progress have they made in the General Court during the last fifteen years? Here are the official figures showing the legislative votes, annually, from 1872 to 1887.

VOTES UPON THE PROPOSED AMENDMENT TO THE CONSTITUTION.

| YEAR. | YEAS. | NAYS. |
| --- | --- | --- |
| 1873 (H. of R.) | 83 | 141 |
| 1874 (S.) | 14 | 19 |
| 1875 (H. of R.) | 75 | 120 |
| 1876 (H. of R.) | 77 | 127 |
| 1877 (S.) [Defeated in the H. of R.] | 18 | 13 |
| 1878 (S.) | 16 | 19 |
| 1879 (H. of R.) | 82 | 85 |
| 1880 (H. of R.) | 59 | 137 |

VOTES UPON MUNICIPAL SUFFRAGE FOR WOMEN.

| YEAR. | YEAS. | NAYS. |
| --- | --- | --- |
| 1875 (S.) | 10 | 27 |
| 1876 (S.) | 11 | 19 |
| 1877 (H. of R.) | 83 | 122 |
| 1878 (H. of R.) | 92 | 128 |
| 1879. Municipal suffrage not asked for. | | |
| 1880. Leave to withdraw. | | |
| 1881 (H. of R.) | 76 | 122 |
| 1882 (S.) | 12 | 21 |
| 1883 (H. of R.) | 60 | 127 |
| 1884 (H. of R.) | 50 | 144 |
| 1885 (H. of R.) | 61 | 130 |
| 1886 (H. of R.) | 59 | 114 |

These figures show — and we must remember that "*an ounce of fact is worth a pound of theory*" — that in the Legislature, Municipal Suffrage for women has made no practical gain whatever, for the last fifteen years. Although the Suffragists have been to the State House, year after year, with able and eloquent speakers and witnesses, yet, with all their agitation and discussion of this subject, they have never been able to induce the legislative branch of the government to favor it; but, on the contrary, the votes five or ten years ago were more favorable to their cause than they have been of late years. This result shows, conclusively, that public sentiment is opposed to Municipal Woman Suffrage; and it also illustrates the sterling good sense of our legislators in recognizing that fact.

## III.

### *Municipal Woman Suffrage a Parasitic Movement.*

There can be no question that a large majority of the Suffragists are strong advocates of Temperance; and they labor under the delusion that, by pushing Municipal Suffrage for women, they will best advance the Temperance cause. As a matter of fact, the movement for Municipal Woman Suffrage has become *parasitic* in its nature. It has a fictitious strength. Take from the ranks of those who nominally favor Municipal Woman Suffrage those of them who are laboring for Temperance, or some other worthy cause, and the number who actually want Municipal Woman Suffrage, for its own sake, is reduced to a mere handful. In other words, a small but active nucleus of Municipal Woman Suffragists has reached out and clung desperately to Temperance, and other strong and vital public measures, hoping to ride on to victory with the aid of that *public sentiment* which they have tried, in vain, to win upon the merits of their own cause, but which they expect to secure in this vicarious way. The Temperance movement has been growing stronger every year for the last fifteen years, and has enlisted in its ranks thousands of us who believe in it; and I must enter my protest, as a thorough advocate of that noble work, against having it any longer weighed down by this incubus of Municipal Woman Suffrage, which does not commend itself to the sound judgment of one citizen in a thousand; whereas, not one self-respecting citizen in ten thousand is opposed to Temperance. There is this difference between the two measures: Municipal Woman Suffrage *invades* our homes; Temperance *protects* them. The bitterness of political contests is well known. Under a new system, which would allow and even compel women to mix with men at the caucus, in the town meeting, and at the polls, a difference of sentiment between the members of a household upon some political question or candidate, would prove as potent a factor in destroying the happiness of that household as the entrance of the fiend Intemperance itself.

Surely, it is time for the friends of Temperance to unclasp and free themselves from the drowning embrace of Municipal Woman Suffrage, and leave it to sink or swim by itself. But it is not Temperance alone which is the object of this unbidden and devitalizing partnership with Municipal Woman Suffragists. Overtures have been made by them, with equal fervor, to the Knights of Labor, the Pope of Rome, and Mr. Gladstone. Everywhere we see the same restless, feverish eagerness to engraft their unpopular measure upon something, or somebody, through which, or by means of whom, they fondly hope to win that public favor which has been, and in Massachusetts will continue to be, withheld. As long as the vast majority of men and women distrust Municipal Suffrage, with all that that term implies, that movement has no chance of success. Any public measure which depends for victory upon an act of domestic disloyalty on the part of a majority of the people's sworn representatives, will never win in the Bay State.

## IV.

### *School Suffrage for Women a Failure.*

Again we must resort to our "ounce of fact" to show the worthlessness of the Suffragist's "pound of theory" as demonstrated by the failure of the female School Suffrage law. The official statistics upon this subject are invaluable, and are conclusive against the Suffragists. Before the year 1879 they had agitated the question of allowing women to vote throughout the State for members of School Committees. At length in that year the Legislature passed the so-called School Suffrage law, granting women that privilege. And certainly, *as they then claimed*, there can be no higher and better use of the ballot by the mothers and sisters of Massachusetts than to wield it for the best welfare of children and their teachers, and the strengthening and perfecting of our public school system. The passage of the School Suffrage law was hailed with joy by the Suffragists. An editorial signed "L. S.," in the *Woman's Journal* of April 12, 1879, says, "*It is with profound thankfulness* that we record the fact that the bill to secure School Suffrage for women in Massachusetts, which passed the Senate by 24 ayes to 11 noes, has, on Thursday of this week, April 10, passed the House by 129 ayes to 69 noes. This is a great gain, *and the Senators and Representatives who eloquently and well supported this measure, will be held in grateful remembrance, forever, by all who love justice and who care for the best welfare of the schools.*" And again on April 19, 1879, the *Woman's Journal* says, editorially, "*The new law* just passed by the Massachusetts Legislature, *which secures to the women of this State the right to vote for members of the School Committee, will be hailed with rejoicing and thankfulness far outside of Massachusetts.* . . . Now that women can vote *upon this important matter* of the School Committee, no time must be lost in finding out and publishing the exact steps to take, *so that no votes shall be lost for lack of preliminary care.*" Thus the School Suffrage law was launched in 1879, amid the enthusiastic plaudits of the Suffragists. How has it fared? I quote from the official records in the office of the Secretary of State, from 1881 to 1885, inclusive:

```
1881, No. of women who registered in Mass. . . . . . . . . . . . . 3,349
  "      "    "    "      voted        "       . . . . . . . . . . . . 1,571
                                                                     _____
  "      "    "    "   neglected to vote . . . . . . . . . . . . 1,778
```

Thus nearly 1800 women, or considerably more than half of those who registered, failed to vote in 1881.

```
1882 . . . . . . . . . . . . . . . 2,951 women registered and 1,346 voted.
1883 . . . . . . . . . . . . . . . 3,138    "          "       "  1,469   "
1884 . . . . . . . . . . . . . . . 3,778    "          "       "  1,896   "
1885 . . . . . . . . . . . . . . . 5,260    "          "       "  3,227   "
```

Apparently there was a marked gain in the votes of 1884–5; but, unfortunately, when analyzed these figures present a suggestive and fatal argument against the Suffragists. *The apparent gain was made almost wholly in Boston.* If we deduct from the number who voted throughout the State, in 1885, the number who voted in Boston in that year, we have the following result:

```
1885, No. of women who voted in Mass . . . . . . . . . . . . 3,227
  "      "    "    "    "    "  Boston . . . . . . . . . . . . 2,062
                                                                _____
  "      "    "    "    "    "  outside of Boston . . . . . . . . 1,165
```

Now let us deduct from the number of those who voted in Massachusetts in 1881, the number of those who voted in Boston in that year:

| | |
|---|---:|
| 1881, No. of women who voted in Mass. | 1,571 |
| "     "     "     "     "     " Boston | 640 |
| "     "     "     "     " outside Boston | 931 |

Thus it appears that:

| | |
|---|---:|
| 1885, No. of women who voted outside Boston | 1,165 |
| 1881,   "     "     "     "     "     " | 931 |
| Gain in female vote, outside Boston | 234 |

From 1880 to 1885 the population of the State increased from 1,783,085 to 1,942,141, and yet *the female vote increased* (from 1881 to 1885) *by only 234!* Now let us look at Boston:

| | |
|---|---:|
| 1885, No. of women who voted in Boston | 2,062 |
| 1881,   "     "     "     "     " | 640 |
| Gain in Boston from 1881 to 1885 | 1,422 |

So that Boston, from 1881 to 1885, inclusive, gained 1,422 female voters while all the rest of the State was gaining only 234. Now place by the side of this showing the ominous fact that since 1882, when the female vote began to increase in Boston, not a single woman has been elected a member of the School Committee, although every year there have been female candidates for that office. In other words, Female School Suffrage has apparently driven women off the School Board in Boston. That women themselves realize this unpleasant truth may partly explain the fact that only 878 voted in that city in 1886,—a falling off from the vote of 1885 of 1,188 votes; and the registration in Boston in 1886 was 1,145 less than in the year 1885. There are 20,000 more women than men in Boston. May it not be the fact that some of the women themselves in Boston have voted against female candidates for the School Committee?

*In 170 towns* out of the 347 towns and cities in Massachusetts in 1885, *not one woman has ever registered or voted. In 200 towns not a woman has ever voted*, although in 30 of those towns a few have occasionally registered. I might multiply official statistics to show the practical collapse of the School Suffrage law for women. The Suffragists say, in extenuation of women's indifference in this matter, that "it is too trivial and unimportant a subject to bring out women's votes." How do they reconcile that explanation with the arguments and appeals which they made for the passage of the law; or their apparently heartfelt thanks when the law was passed, in 1879; or their conscientious views, then and now, as to the grave responsibilities of voting? It would seem, from the practical working of this important branch of suffrage, that either the vast majority of women do not want to vote, or that when they have a chance to do so they will neglect it more than men themselves do (to the shame of the latter be it said). *Ex uno disce omnes.* In the final debate on the School Suffrage bill in 1879, Senator Knowlton, who strongly urged its passage, said, "*If they* (women) *will not vote on schools, it settles it for any other suffrage.*" In the *Woman's Journal* of April 19, 1879, appears this editorial:

### THEY WILL NOT VOTE.

"Women will not vote if they have the right" has been the constant assertion of the opponents of woman suffrage. But an ounce of fact is worth a pound of theory. Here it is. In Concord, N. H., three meetings were held to choose members of the School Committee. The *Independent Statesman*, reporting the fact, says:

It will be noticed that the number of ladies participating in the balloting has rapidly increased since the first session of the meeting. On the first evening, about 150 voted; at the second, 299, and last Saturday, 662. The proportionate attendance of women has also increased.

Comment is unnecessary. L. S.

Feeling some curiosity to know how the School Suffrage law has worked in Concord, New Hampshire, since that time I recently wrote to the City Clerk for information and have received from the Clerk of the Union School District the following reply: "We have no women on our School Committee or Board of Education, but they have been eligible to that office with a right to vote in district affairs since 1879. We have in our Union School District about 6,000 voters, about half of each sex. *Usually but very few women come to our school meetings; since the first meeting, when possibly six to eight hundred came out, it has not averaged 25 voters of that sex."*

It would appear from the foregoing that the "ounce of fact" is worth more than the Suffragist's "pound of theory" in New Hampshire, as well as in Massachusetts.

## V.

### *Fictitious Value of Woman Suffrage Petitions.*

The Suffragists have circulated copies of a petition in aid of their cause, signed by eminent political leaders in the Republican party, and a duplicate petition signed by an equal, or greater, number of eminent political leaders in the Democratic party. This reminds me of a story told about a colonel of one of our regiments in the late war. One day a clergyman applied to him for leave to baptize some of his men. The colonel curtly refused. "Well, Colonel," said the clergyman, "I'm sorry. Colonel Blank, of the regiment camped next to you, here, let me baptize fifteen of his men, yesterday." The Colonel sprang to his feet, and shouted to one of his officers, "Captain X, detail *twenty-five* men to be baptized! *I don't propose to let Colonel Blank get ahead of me, if I know it!*"

Nothing is more apt to be misleading than a petition. Many sign because others have signed. Others are afraid to refuse; others think it will help them, politically, to sign; and, alas, a great many sign to get rid of the applicant. For twenty years or more the Suffragists have thoroughly canvassed the State, for signatures to aid their cause, until they claim to have some 50,000 names. I think the number is exaggerated, for I suspect some have signed more than once; but assuming it to be true, what percentage of the population of the State does it represent? The population of Massachusetts is nearly 2,000,000. Therefore, after twenty years of effort, the Suffragists have secured $2\frac{1}{2}$ per cent of it. If *public sentiment* favored their cause, they could get five, or ten, or twenty times as many names, in less than a year. Suppose, for example, that the Federal Government should pass a law withholding the appropriation for Post Offices in this State. If we sought redress by petition, does anyone doubt that we could get 500,000 genuine signatures in a few weeks, or months? And yet, such an act of oppression is not, according to the Suffragists, half as glaring as it is for us to deprive them of their (alleged) right to vote. Petitions, to be of value, and to secure ready and willing signers, must represent some great good to be gained, or some great wrong to be righted.

An amusing feature of the eminently respectable petitions first above referred to is that they were signed (I am told) by several of those Republican and Democratic leaders some years ago, when the movement was stronger than it is now, and have been made to do service ever since, during the periodic disturbances of Woman Suffrage agitation.

## VI.

### *Many who oppose Municipal Woman Suffrage advocate Woman's Rights.*

As we have noted the sturdy opposition of our legislators to Municipal Woman Suffrage for the past fifteen years, let us see what has been done *for the practical good* of women during that period.

In 72 towns and cities in this State there are women on the School Committee. In 36 of those towns no woman has ever voted, and in 16 towns less than 10 have voted. Even in the remaining 20 towns and cities it cannot be claimed that the female vote has elected, or even perceptibly aided in electing, the women members of the School Committee. For this recognition of their fitness women are chiefly indebted to men in private life, who will yield to no one in their loyal advocacy of Woman's Rights, but who draw the line at Municipal Woman Suffrage.

One of the rallying cries of the Suffragists is that they are "without representation in the Legislature." True, there are no female Senators and Representatives, but the records show that there, also, women have been ably and generously represented by men,—even those men who have never allowed their common sense to be dominated by the Utopian dreams of the Suffragists, or the yearnings of political ambition. Let us remember that the good works which they have done for women have been, *not on account of*, *but in spite of* the agitation for Municipal Woman Suffrage.

Look at this record of legislation in behalf of women, for the past fifteen years, enacted with the aid of Senators and Representatives who, during that time, were setting the seal of their condemnation, annually, upon Municipal Woman Suffrage:

### *1873.*

Chap. 58. AN ACT CONCERNING THE WAIVER BY WIDOWS OF THE PROVISIONS MADE FOR THEM IN WILLS.

This Act provides as follows: " When any legal proceeding is instituted wherein the validity or effect of any will which has been proved and allowed is drawn in question, the Probate Court may, within six months after the probate of such will, on petition of the testator's widow, and after such notice as the Court shall order, authorize such widow to file in the probate office, within six months after the final determination of said legal proceedings, her waiver of the provisions of the will, and such waiver, so filed, shall have the same legal effect as if filed within six months after the probate of the will."

### *1874.*

Chap. 184. AN ACT IN RELATION TO THE RIGHTS OF HUSBAND AND WIFE.

This Act allows married women to lease and convey their property and make contracts, with the right to sue and to act in a fiduciary capacity, as if they were sole; thus materially enlarging the scope of the common law.

Chap. 205. AN ACT RELATING TO THE RIGHTS OF HUSBANDS AND WIVES, AND FOR THE PROTECTION OF MINOR CHILDREN.

This Act prohibits a husband who has deserted his wife, or who fails to support her, or from whom she is living apart for justifiable cause, from imposing any restraint on her personal liberty. It also allows a Justice of the Supreme Judicial Court to decide which parent shall support and which shall have the custody of any minor children.

Chap. 221. AN ACT TO REGULATE THE HOURS OF LABOR IN MANUFACTURING ESTABLISHMENTS.

This is the famous Ten-Hour law, so called, by which the laboring hours of women and minors in mills were limited to ten a day.

Chap. 274. AN ACT FOR THE MORE EFFICIENT RELIEF OF THE POOR.

This Act, in section two, reduces the period within which women may gain a settlement from ten years to five. Men, in addition to the requirements for women, have to pay taxes for three years.

Chap. 385. AN ACT TO ESTABLISH A REFORMATORY PRISON FOR WOMEN.

For this deserving object the Legislature appropriated $300,000, and the institution, which is wonderfully well managed by its female Superintendent, has been liberally cared for every year by the General Court.

Chap. 389. AN ACT MAKING WOMEN ELIGIBLE TO SERVE AS MEMBERS OF SCHOOL COMMITTEES.

This is self-explanatory.

## 1876.

Chap. 118. AN ACT RELATIVE TO NIGHT-WALKERS.

This Act makes male night-walkers liable to the same punishment as common night-walkers.

## 1877.

Chap. 128. AN ACT TO AUTHORIZE MOTHERS TO APPOINT BY WILL GUARDIANS OF THEIR MINOR CHILDREN.

This is self-explanatory.

## 1878.

Chap. 199. AN ACT CONCERNING MARRIED WOMEN WHO ARE INSANE.

This Act provides that when an insane woman is deserted, and not supported by her husband, or has left her husband for cause and subsequently become insane, her guardian may obtain from the Supreme Judicial Court an order for her support, with the right, if necessary to attach her husband's property, to enforce the order.

## 1879.

Chap. 31. AN ACT TO AMEND CHAPTER TWO HUNDRED AND FIVE OF THE ACTS OF THE YEAR EIGHTEEN HUNDRED AND SEVENTY-FOUR, ENTITLED "AN ACT RELATING TO THE RIGHTS OF HUSBANDS AND WIVES, AND FOR THE PROTECTION ON MINOR CHILDREN."

This Act amends Sts. 1874, chap. 205, *supra*, so as to allow the wife to enforce her rights by attachment of her husband's property.

Chap. 42. AN ACT FOR THE PROTECTION OF MARRIED WOMEN.

This Act gives the courts power to compel any husband, who has assaulted his wife, to give bonds to keep the peace for two years, if necessary, in addition to the penalty inflicted on him for the offence.

Chap. 86. AN ACT CONCERNING LETTERS OF ATTORNEY FOR THE CONVEYANCE OF THE REAL ESTATE OF MARRIED WOMEN.

This Act relieves a wife from the necessity of executing a joint power of attorney with her husband when constituting an attorney to act in her behalf.

Chap. 133. AN ACT CONCERNING GIFTS TO MARRIED WOMEN FROM THEIR HUSBANDS.

This Act makes the wearing apparel and articles of personal ornament of a married woman, and articles necessary for her personal use, acquired by gift from her husband, not exceeding $2,000 in value, her sole and separate property. This is a more liberal provision than that which the law has made for men.

Chap. 223. AN ACT TO GIVE WOMEN THE RIGHT TO VOTE FOR MEMBERS OF SCHOOL COMMITTEES.

This is the School Suffrage law hereinbefore mentioned.

## 1880.

Chap. 64. AN ACT GIVING THE PROBATE COURTS JURISDICTION OF RIGHTS OF HUSBANDS AND WIVES, AND FOR THE PROTECTION OF MINOR CHILDREN.

This Act transfers the jurisdiction of the cases named in Sts. 1874, chap. 205, *supra*, from the Supreme Judicial to the Probate Court, thus making it much easier for women to confer directly with the Court, and thereby save themselves expense and delay.

Chap. 151. AN ACT TO PROVIDE FOR BINDING OUT FEMALE PRISONERS FROM COUNTY PRISONS.

This is self-explanatory.

Chap. 194. AN ACT TO AMEND "AN ACT TO REGULATE THE HOURS OF LABOR IN MANUFACTURING ESTABLISHMENTS."

This Act amends the Ten-Hour law (Sts. 1874, chap. 221) by requiring notices to be posted in each room where help are employed, giving the number of hours work required of each woman, and of minors under eighteen years. It also increases the original penalty for violation of the Ten-Hour law.

## *1881.*

Chap. 33. AN ACT TO AMEND CHAPTER 64 OF THE ACTS OF 1880.

This amendment facilitates the operation of Sts. 1874, chap. 205, and Sts. 1880, chap. 64, *ubi supra*.

Chap. 90. AN ACT IN RELATION TO THE RELEASE OF PRISONERS FROM THE REFORMATORY PRISON FOR WOMEN.

This Act authorizes the release of female prisoners on the ticket-of-leave system by the Commissioners of Prisons, upon certain conditions.

Chap. 179. AN ACT TO PROVIDE FOR THE ASSISTANCE OF DISCHARGED FEMALE CONVICTS.

This Act authorizes the Commissioners of Prisons to employ a female agent for the purpose named in the title of the Act, at a salary of not more than $700 a year, with the right to give the discharged convicts pecuniary aid to an amount not exceeding, with the salary, $3,000 a year.

Chap. 191. AN ACT RELATIVE TO THE RIGHT OF WOMEN TO VOTE FOR SCHOOL COMMITTEES.

This Act amends Sts. 1879, chap. 223, (the original School Suffrage law), with the intent to facilitate women's voting. An important feature of this Act is that in Section 3 it provides that the names of all women who have complied with the law, may be placed on a separate list and kept there as long as they continue to reside in any town or city, and to pay any State or County, city or town tax that has been assessed on them, or their trustees, in any such city or town in the Commonwealth, within two years previous to any voting day. (This explains the fact that so many women have apparently registered, annually, since 1881. To illustrate, in the case of Brookline: In 1881 the number of women who actually registered in that town was 17. In 1882, '83, '84, '85 and '86, the number fell to 16, as registered. But the vote which was 14 in 1881, dropped to 8 in 1882, 7 in 1883, 4 in 1884, and 1 in 1885 and 1886. Sixteen of the 17 names, originally registered in 1881, have been kept on the list ever since that year.)

### 1882.

Chap. 139. AN ACT TO PERMIT WOMEN TO PRACTISE AS ATTORNEYS AT LAW.

This explains itself.

Chap. 141. AN ACT RELATING TO THE DISTRIBUTION OF THE PERSONAL ESTATE OF MARRIED WOMEN.

This Act provides that when a married woman dies, leaving issue, her personal estate, not lawfully disposed of by will, shall be distributed, one-half to her husband, and the other half to her heirs.

Chap. 150. AN ACT FOR THE PRESERVATION OF THE HEALTH OF FEMALES EMPLOYED IN MANUFACTURING, MECHANICAL AND MERCANTILE ESTABLISHMENTS.

This humane law requires seats to be provided for female employes when not engaged in active duties.

### 1883.

Chap. 157. AN ACT RELATING TO THE EMPLOYMENT OF MINORS AND WOMEN.

This Act extended the provisions of the Ten-Hour law to "Mechanical or Mercantile" establishments.

Chap. 252. AN ACT TO AUTHORIZE THE GOVERNOR TO APPOINT WOMEN, WHO ARE ATTORNEYS AT LAW, SPECIAL COMMISSIONERS TO ADMINISTER OATHS, AND TO TAKE DEPOSITIONS AND THE ACKNOWLEDGMENT OF DEEDS.

This is self-explanatory.

### 1884.

Chap. 116. AN ACT PROVIDING FOR THE APPOINTMENT OF FEMALE ASSISTANT PHYSICIANS IN STATE LUNATIC HOSPITALS.

This is self-explanatory.

Chap. 275. AN ACT RELATING TO THE EMPLOYMENT OF MINORS IN MERCANTILE ESTABLISHMENTS.

In this noticeable Act no mention is made of "women," but Section 4 reads as follows: "Section 4 of Chapter 74 of the Public Statutes (which is Sts. 1874, chap. 221), as amended by Chapter 157 of the Acts of the year 1883, *shall not apply to mercantile establishments.*" By this ingenious amendment women in shops and other mercantile establishments were deprived of the protection of the Ten-Hour law, which was amended for their benefit in 1883. A prominent Woman Suffragist is said to have conceived and carried through this scheme.

Chap. 301. AN ACT RELATING TO THE POWERS OF MARRIED WOMEN IN THE DISPOSAL OF THEIR SEPARATE ESTATE BY WILL OR DEED.

This Act amends Public Statutes, Chapter 147, Section 6, (which allows women to make their wills, subject to certain restrictions), and introduces the following radical but just change in the law: " A married woman deserted by, or living apart from her husband for a justifiable cause, when the proper court having the jurisdiction of the parties shall have entered a decree, establishing the fact of such desertion by, or living apart from her husband for justifiable cause, may make a will in the same manner and with the same effect as if she were sole, and may by such will, or, under such circumstances, by deed, without her husband's written consent, dispose of all her real and personal estate."

*1885.*

Chap. 7. AN ACT EMPOWERING WOMEN TO HOLD THE OFFICE OF ASSISTANT REGISTER OF DEEDS.

This is self-explanatory.

Chap. 176. AN ACT IN RELATION TO THE BETTER PROTECTION OF WIVES AND CHILDREN.

This Act provides as follows: " Whoever unreasonably neglects to provide for the support of his wife or minor child, shall be *punished* by a fine not exceeding twenty dollars, or by imprisonment in the House of Correction not exceeding six months. All fines imposed under this section may, in the discretion of the Court, be paid, in whole or in part, to the town, city, corporation, society or person actually supporting such wife or minor child at the time of making the complaint." Thus it is made *a criminal offence* for a man to neglect, unreasonably, the support of his wife and minor children.

Chap. 255. AN ACT RELATING TO THE POWERS OF MARRIED WOMEN IN THE DISPOSAL OF THEIR SEPARATE ESTATE BY WILL OR DEED.

This Act enlarges still further the powers conferred on women by Sts. 1884, chap. 301, *supra*.

## 1886.

Chap. 68. AN ACT IN RELATION TO THE ASSESSMENT AND REGISTRATION OF WOMEN AS VOTERS.

This Act, which was intended to facilitate the working of the School Suffrage law for women, is as follows: "In the months of May and June of each year, the assessors or assistant assessors of taxes shall visit each dwelling house or building in their respective cities or towns, and make a true list of all male persons, twenty years of age and upwards, liable to be assessed for a poll tax, returned to them by the owners or occupants of such dwelling houses or buildings as residing therein, *and of all women* who personally, or in writing, express to an assessor or assistant assessor a desire to be assessed for a poll tax, together with their occupation and age, as near as may be, and residence on the first day of May of the preceding year; and shall also furnish the original list, or a certified copy thereof, to the registrars of voters of their respective cities and towns, from time to time, before the fifteenth day of July ensuing; and all assessors and collectors of taxes shall furnish any information in their possession, necessary to aid the registrars and assistant registrars in the discharge of their respective duties." (*Vide* Sts. 1884, chap. 298, § 28.)

Chap. 104. AN ACT TO AMEND THE CHARTER OF THE TEMPORARY ASYLUM FOR DISCHARGED FEMALE PRISONERS.

This Act enlarges the powers of the beneficent and useful institution at Dedham, by allowing it "to afford shelter, instruction and employment to women charged with crime, whose cases are disposed of without sentence," and secures pecuniary aid from the State for that purpose, as in the case of " discharged female prisoners."

Chap. 150.  AN ACT TO DECLARE WOMEN ELIGIBLE TO SERVE AS OVERSEERS OF THE POOR.

This is self-explanatory.

Chap. 177.  AN ACT TO PROVIDE FOR THE ASSISTANCE OF WOMEN CHARGED WITH CRIME, WHOSE CASES ARE DISPOSED OF WITHOUT SENTENCE.

This Act supplements and makes effective Chapter 104, preceding.

I wish I might add to the foregoing, " An Act to provide Matrons for Police Stations."

It is but just to state that Woman Suffragists have, themselves, done valiant service in furthering this legislation. Their energy and persistency in this worthy direction have not only enlisted the support and approval of those who distrust Municipal Woman Suffrage, but have secured a more patient consideration of that measure than would otherwise have been accorded it. Think what a powerful influence for good the Suffragists might wield, if they would but drop the agitation of their hopeless hobby! Such a change of base would bring them into friendly alliance with thousands who now stand aloof, because they cannot and will not indorse that unwise movement. In whatever tends to protect and elevate woman, to secure her " rights," in the best sense of that word, to open before her new avenues of useful employment, " to comfort and help the weak-hearted, and to raise up those who fall," all true-hearted men and women should join. In such work there should be no difference of purpose; but, if it is to be treated by some as a politic means to an impolitic end; if its results are to be vaunted as arguments for Municipal Woman Suffrage, then must the majority continue, regretfully, to stand apart, to the detriment of noble and useful work for woman. The Municipal Woman Suffragist retards, more than she hastens, the good of her sex.

## VII.

### *The Welfare of the State of greater importance than Municipal Woman Suffrage.*

It is a mere truism to say that no general law should be enacted which does not benefit the entire State — the city as well as the town. Special legislation is unwise, but legislation which may prove useless, and perhaps injurious, is worse. If, as in the case of Municipal Woman Suffrage, it is called for by an undeniable minority of the people, such legislation would be not only special in its character but useless and injurious as well. The burden of proof is clearly on the Suffragists to show wherein Municipal Woman Suffrage will benefit the citizens of the Commonwealth (or even the small number of them which they themselves represent). It is not enough for them to ask us of the majority to look Eastward three thousand miles and view the restricted system of Female Suffrage in England, where it is confined by limitations which are absolutely impracticable in this State. Nor does it strengthen their position to bid us turn our eyes three thousand miles Westward and view the example of one or two Territories where the relative proportion of the sexes is more than reversed, and the magnitude of area, the sparseness of population, and the nature of the industries are in such striking contrast to our own. I cannot bring myself to admit that Massachusetts must take lessons in civilization from Washington Territory or Wyoming. The most that can be claimed for Municipal Woman Suffrage in those vast, remote and scantily populated regions, is that it appears to work well there. The same thing might, perhaps, be said of "Lynch law," but ought we therefore to adopt it?

*Our Commonwealth should continue to be a teacher, not a pupil, in the school of civilization.* Shall we deliberately ignore the fact that public sentiment in Massachusetts is overwhelmingly against Municipal Woman Suffrage? Are the Suffragists determined to learn nothing from the long and unbroken record of their defeats, and the utter failure of their one practical demonstration of female voting? Can they shut their eyes to the mighty contest that is waging here and elsewhere between Capital and Labor, the judicious settlement of which demands the utmost care and patience and study from our legislators, and ask them to complicate still further a political system which we are even now testing?

It is often said, "*Why should not those women vote who own property and are taxed for it?*" The answer, if not satisfactory, is final,—*because our political system will not permit it.* They must take that system as it is, not as they would have it. If the Municipal Woman Suffragists think that our fathers were too visionary or precipitate in allowing *men* to vote without sufficient qualifications as to property or education, how can they consistently ask our law makers of to-day to repeat the mistake with *women?* Or, if they approve the present system, can they not tell us how to make it produce happier results in our densely populated cities? Legislation which enlarges the right of Suffrage differs essentially, in a Republic, from every other kind. Generally speaking, a bad or useless law passed by one Legislature may be easily repealed by a subsequent one; but it is not so with Suffrage. Once let that right become vested, and it is difficult, if not impossible, to uproot it. It will not do to experiment rashly with the foundation of any structure. Our political fabric rests upon the votes of the people. Any attempt to tamper with the base may cast that which it supports "out of plumb." But the shortest and most decisive argument against Municipal Woman Suffrage is, that *nine women out of ten do not want it.* When they do, they can have it for the asking. If each member of the Legislature will vote in accordance with the wishes of the women of his own household, Municipal Woman Suffrage will be crushingly defeated.

# WOMAN SUFFRAGE

## ARGUMENT

OF

### MRS. A. J. GEORGE
OF BROOKLINE, MASS.

BEFORE THE

## COMMITTEE ON WOMAN SUFFRAGE
## UNITED STATES SENATE

APRIL 19, 1913

ARGUMENT OF MRS. A. J. GEORGE, OF BROOKLINE, MASS., BEFORE THE COMMITTEE ON WOMAN SUFFRAGE, UNITED STATES SENATE, APRIL 19, 1913.

Mrs. GEORGE. Mr. Chairman and gentlemen of the committee, the National Association Opposed to Woman Suffrage appears before this committee, which is understood already to be committed to a favorable report, in order that it may place on record the principles which are held by what is undoubtedly the majority of the women of this country, in regard to the distribution of the duties of life among men and women. The vote is far from being the whole story in this dispute.

The question of recommending an amendment to the Constitution of the United States interferes with our State system of determining the electorate—a system which up to the present time has been shown to advantage; particularly where those most concerned are not able to vote upon the question it is desirable that the State should hesitate to confer the franchise upon an electorate the majority of which is acknowledged to be indifferent or opposed to the exercise of the franchise, and it is desirable that the State should wait until the actual balance of opinion is shown to be with those who demand the extension of the franchise before so extending it.

Since the days of the *Mayflower* compact to the time of the Arizona constitution we have been a people bound to obedience under what is undubtedly the will of the majority; that the majority of the women of this country do not desire the suffrage, and that in no selfish way, but do not look upon the ballot as the best means of contributing their social efficiency to the body politic is shown by the fact that when the question is submitted to women a very small percentage of women go on record as in favor of woman suffrage.

The figures of the National Suffrage Association show that a scant 8 per cent of the women of voting age in this country are enrolled as suffragists, and surely we can reasonably assume that if an American woman wants a thing she is quite likely to ask for it.

The only State which has had a poll of all the women of the State made possible is my own State of Massachusetts. In 1895 all persons who were eligible to vote for school committee were eligible to vote on the question submitted at the general election in November, Is it expedient that municipal suffrage should be granted to the women of Massachusetts?

Many people are in favor of municipal suffrage who do not advocate full suffrage for women. The suffragists had a splendid organization, 50 years old. They did everything they could during that summer of 1895 to bring out a large vote in favor of municipal suffrage for the women of Massachusetts.

## WOMAN SUFFRAGE.

Our association was organized only in May of that year. There was also a man suffrage association, with Hon. Eben S. Draper as president, which worked to bring out the men's vote against the question, but urged the women who were opposed not to go on record, but to let the stay-at-home votes show the indifference of the average woman of Massachusetts. What was the result? Four per cent of the women of Massachusetts cared enough about municipal suffrage to go to the polls and register in favor of it at that November election.

The majority given by the men was the largest majority ever given to any question submitted to the people of the State. Every county and every congressional, councillor, senatorial, and representative district in the Commonwealth cast a majority against the proposition. The majority against woman suffrage in Massachusetts was more than twice as great as that against either prohibition or biennial elections.

That was in 1895, and you may say the world has moved rapidly since those days and that we should have another vote of the women now. It is an extraordinary thing that wherever you suggest to the suffragists that this measure should be submitted to the women they make lively opposition. In other words, they say that woman must have the ballot on every other question save this one in which she is most vitally concerned; and they contend that an electorate of men can properly decide this question, although an electorate of women must be enfranchised in order to properly decide all other questions.

There is nothing that so frightens a suffragist as a suggestion that this question be submitted to a vote of the women. They remember our vote in Massachusetts of 1895, where only 4 per cent of the women went on record in favor of woman suffrage, and they also remember that the membership of the National Suffrage Association is a small percentage of the women of the country, and they know, too, that where women have the opportunity to vote, when the novelty of the thing is passed, we find a small proportion of women voting.

In my State women have had the right to vote for school committees since 1879. A woman need only tell her age, which is a difficult proposition sometimes to make to the woman. You may smile, but you must remember that the first legislation put through in Colorado and the first legislation put through in California after women were enfranchised was a bill that a woman need only declare that she is of voting age. That is not equal rights; that is special privilege. But in my State if a woman is brave enough to tell her age and is a citizen she can register and vote for school committee without paying any poll tax. She paid a poll tax from 1879 to 1884. In 1884 the prepayment of a poll tax by men as a qualification for voting was done away with. It is not necessary now for anyone to show a receipt of payment of poll tax. It is only necessary to show that the voter has been assessed a poll tax, and a woman does not have to pay any poll tax whatever. Yet in Massachusetts in the last 17 years we have had a registration of women amounting to 4.8 per cent throughout the State of all the women who could register and vote, and of those only 2.1 per cent, less than 50 per cent of those registered, got to the polls on election day.

In 1879 the suffragists, eager and zealous and sincere women, who looked upon the ballot as the best means of showing woman's social

WOMAN SUFFRAGE.

efficiency, said, "Evidently we can not hope for the full franchise at present, but give us the school vote and we will show you what we will do with it." And they have made a clear case for the anti-suffragists.

You may say that this is a peculiar situation, that men would not vote if they could vote only on school matters, but the women said, "Give it to us as a test of our interest, and we will show you what we will do."

In Boston last year, where the situation was very clear, we had a candidate of the machine and we had a woman candidate for the school board. We had not had a woman member of the school board for seven years. In passing it is interesting to note that we have had as strong women, if not stronger women, on our school boards in Massachusetts under the votes of men than we have had under the votes of men and women. But this year the issue was very clear. We had a machine candidate against a woman. The suffragists refused to indorse the woman because she would not indorse woman suffrage. She did not say she was opposed to woman suffrage, but she did not indorse woman suffrage. There was no question of her fitness; there was no question of her ability, because of her long training in educational work; but the suffragists refused to indorse her because she would not indorse the special means by which they proposed to better the conditions of our educational system.

Yet we found that under these conditions in this year 1913 fewer women went to the polls on election day than have gone any time since 1879, with two exceptions, and the votes of the men elected that woman.

We have never had so much agitation for woman suffrage in Boston and we have never had so little exercise of the suffrage which the women now hold.

The same holds true in Connecticut. From $2\frac{1}{2}$ to 3 per cent of the women who can register and vote do so. The very day before the Connecticut women went before the Legislature of Connecticut to ask for the full vote there was a school election in Hartford, Conn. Eighteen thousand women were entitled to register and vote at that election, and 95 women cast their vote on election day.

A current magazine widely circulated (The Outlook of Apr. 19, 1913, p. 839) cites the vote in the town of Dedham, Mass. Dedham is a fortunate town, and a particularly fair town to cite in evidence of woman's readiness to use the school suffrage. This magazine citation, however, does not take the actual number of votes cast, but does take the number of registered voters, and gives 49 as the number of the women voters in Dedham this year. As a matter of fact this was the number of women registered, for not a single woman has remembered it was election day for 11 years—for 11 years in the town of Dedham. I will leave with the clerk the figures furnished by the town clerk of Dedham:

WOMAN SUFFRAGE.

OFFICE OF THE TOWN CLERK.
Dedham, Mass., April 12, 1913.

*List of male and female voters in Dedham from the year 1879 to 1912, and also the number of men and women who voted between the years 1879 and 1912.*[1]

|  | Voters. | | Actually voted. | |  | Voters. | | Actually voted. | |
|---|---|---|---|---|---|---|---|---|---|
|  | Male. | Female. | Male. | Female. |  | Male. | Female. | Male. | Female. |
| 1889 | 1,264 | 154 | 756 | 154 | 1902 | 1,642 | 74 | 1,271 | 3 |
| 1890 | 1,350 | 180 | 766 | 58 | 1903 | 1,643 | 72 | 1,240 | 1 |
| 1891 | 1,367 | 91 | 916 | 34 | 1904 | 1,670 | 69 | 1,113 | 0 |
| 1892 | 1,505 | 74 | 1,001 | 10 | 1905 | 1,634 | 65 | 1,326 | 0 |
| 1893 | 1,534 | 41 | 1,078 | 32 | 1906 | 1,687 | 65 | 1,422 | 0 |
| 1894 | 1,536 | 116 | 1,264 | 19 | 1907 | 1,687 | 63 | 1,340 | 0 |
| 1895 | 1,573 | 116 | 1,201 | 2 | 1908 | 1,719 | 60 | 1,354 | 0 |
| 1896 | 1,665 | 101 | 1,311 | 37 | 1909 | 1,681 | 56 | 1,260 | 0 |
| 1897 | 1,423 | 102 | 1,306 | 43 | 1910 | 1,793 | 55 | 1,439 | 0 |
| 1898 | 1,476 | 91 | 1,189 | 59 | 1911 | 1,803 | 55 | 1,540 | 0 |
| 1899 | 1,471 | 82 | 1,194 | 17 | 1912 | 1,884 | 49 | 1,587 | 0 |
| 1900 | 1,574 | 79 | 1,186 | 2 | 1913 | 1,948 | 49 | 1,469 | 0 |
| 1901 | 1,570 | 78 | 1,249 | 32 |  |  |  |  |  |

[1] 1879–1888, no record of number of voters or vote cast.

It is very difficult to give the figures in regard to the woman's vote in the suffrage States, because we are told by the secretaries of state of those States, that the votes of men and women are not segregated, they are not kept separate. I have it, however, on the authority of the commissioner of elections in San Francisco that "about two-thirds" of the registered women voted at the election of November 5, 1912. The commissioner reports that two-thirds of the registered women voters and two-thirds of the registered men voters voted. But he gives figures which show that only 39 per cent of the women registered. Therefore if only two-thirds of them got to the polls on November 5, only 26 per cent of the women of San Francisco availed themselves of the opportunity to vote for the first time in the history of their State for presidential electors on November 5, 1912.

Three years ago here in Washington you were told that there was to be a petition signed by a million women presented to Congress, and when that petition was presented it contained in round numbers the signatures of 160,000 women, of 122,000 men, and, according to suffrage reports, official reports, 119,000 unclassified. If they are not men or women I hardly know in what class we shall put that 119,000.

A Voice. Children.

Mrs. George. Some one suggests children. I have a photograph of the youngest member of the National Suffrage Association, and it is a baby 6 weeks of age. We saw in the parade last May babies wheeled up the street with the sign, "I wish mother could vote" on the perambulators. We also saw boys 12 years of age carrying banners, "I wish our schoolteacher could vote"; but, gentlemen, the matter of the extension of the suffrage to women is a more serious matter than questions of tariff or finance, and I fancy that the members of this committee would not give great weight to babies' arguments in regard to tariff or finance, or would not even take the experience of 12-year-old boys as a safe guide in a fundamental principle of government. [Applause.]

WOMAN SUFFRAGE.

In Ohio in September last there was a majority of 87,000 against woman suffrage, and that majority was rolled up not because the special interests were opposed to women suffrage, not because men wished to withhold from women something which the men had, but because the average voter in Ohio voted as he believed the women he knew wished him to vote, and only 19 out of 88 counties in Ohio voted "yes" on the constitutional amendment for woman suffrage.

In New Hampshire a vote of the constitutional convention of that State was taken on June 20, 1912. The measure to submit to the people a constitutional amendment for woman suffrage had gone through the constitutional convention 10 years before, and had been defeated at the polls. Last June a similar measure did not even get through the constitutional convention, but was there defeated by a vote of 208 to 149, and, largely, we believe, because of the organized opposition of the women of New Hampshire, who believe that woman can best do her work apart from party politics. In three weeks the women of New Hampshire who had been roused to the dangers of the woman-suffrage propaganda, in three weeks those women collected one-half as many names of women 21 years of age and over— that is, possible voters—opposed to woman suffrage as the suffragists had gathered of men, women, and minors in 40 years of agitation. They reported about 3,500 signatures collected in three weeks as against 7,000 signatures collected "with great effort" by the suffragists in 40 years.

In 1848 the first woman's rights convention was held in Seneca Falls, N. Y., and at that time a long list of grievances was drawn up, known as the "Declaration of sentiments." It forms interesting reading. I quote briefly:

> The history of mankind is a history of repeated injuries and usurpation on the part of man toward woman, having as the indirect object the establishment of an absolute tyranny over her. To prove this, let facts be submitted to a candid world.
>
> Man has endeavored in every way he could to destroy her confidence in her own powers, to lessen her self-respect, and to make her willing to lead a dependent and abject life.

And so the citation of "grievances" goes on, and always "her inalienable right to the elective franchise" is urged as the means to free women and girls from the yoke of men.

In 1848 there were many injustices and inequalities for women before the law still existing from the common law which we had inherited from England. It is a curious thing, however, that while all this agitation for woman suffrage has gone on, with the attempt to show that woman must have the ballot in order to be an equal with man, woman has had an increasing recognition of her legal and civil rights.

Since 1848 the civil and legal rights of women have been so fully recognized that in the movement for woman suffrage we forget that the procession has passed and woman does not need the ballot as a means of justice.

There is no need to call to the attention of this committee the various rights and exemptions which woman enjoys to-day before the law. We were told last February in an edition of a New York daily that a certain woman would march up Pennsylvania Avenue in the parade of March 3 with hands shackled to show the condition

WOMAN SUFFRAGE.

of the unenfranchised woman of this country. Curiously enough the same paper which gave us that information told us that a measure had been introduced in the Assembly of New York providing for a constitutional amendment which should forbid any distinction before the law on account of sex and should make inoperative on its passage all such existing laws.

Which is the true picture of the condition of unenfranchised woman in this country—the woman who chooses to have her hands tied with rope and represent the state of the unenfranchised woman in this country, or the splendid recognition of woman's service to the State, which she alone can perform, and because of which a great State like New York gives her special rights and exemptions in order that the motherhood of the race may be protected and that our citizens shall have the birthright and the inheritance of a strong and vigorous childhood? [Applause.]

I have met a few suffragists who say that this is all wrong and we should have equal rights, responsibilities, and duties for all, and special privileges to none.

Mr. Henry B. Blackwell said repeatedly before the Massachusetts Legislature that he believed women should have equal rights, responsibilities, and duties; and on one occasion he said, "And the wife should be equally responsible with the husband for the financial maintenance of the household." [Applause.]

They said back there in 1848, "Man has denied woman the facilities for obtaining a thorough education, all colleges being closed against her."

It is a curious thing that there are to-day more institutions which grant degrees to women in this country than there are institutions which grant degrees to men—largely because of the fact that the men's colleges grant degrees from their graduate departments to women, while I know of but one woman's college which has granted even an honorary degree to a man, and that was within the last four months.

A great many things in life are coincident which are not consequent one upon another as cause and effect.

Whatever part the agitation for woman suffrage has played in the opening of educational opportunities to women—and the work of the suffrage party has been for coeducation rather than for higher education—we must admit that the results have come, not by the use of the woman's vote, by which alone the early suffragists said they could accomplish these desirable results, but without the use of the ballot.

The foundation of Vassar, of Wellesley, of Smith, of Mount Holyoke, was in no way connected with the suffrage movement. The splendid pioneer work of Mary Lyon and Emily Willard and Catherine Beecher in showing what women could do found its logical result in the opening of the splendid colleges for women. If there were opportunity it would be worth while to consider the story of the opening of Harvard University examinations for women, and the opening of the graduate departments of Yale University to women. In both instances, by a curious coincidence, by a curious combination of circumstances, the men and women who worked for the opening of these educational opportunities for women in these

WOMAN SUFFRAGE.

two old, conservative universities have been antisuffragists, not a suffragist in the lot. [Applause.]

The same is true in England. Mrs. Snowden told us here in her wonderfully brilliant addresses on woman suffrage, that the time had come in England where if a man said he was opposed to woman suffrage he argued "either that he was not very intelligent or not very good." But Mrs. Snowden knew at that time that the president of the National League for Opposing Woman Suffrage was Earl Cromer, the maker of modern Egypt, and that the vice president was Earl Curzon, of Kedleston, former viceroy of India now the president of the league in England; Lord Curzon as regent of the great University of Oxford, has been foremost in urging that old conservative university to grant its degrees to women.

The connection between the agitation for woman suffrage and the higher education of woman is not apparent to those who read the history of the movement.

They said back there in 1848 that man had "monopolized nearly all the profitable employments." By the census returns of 1900 we are told that women are actually engaged in 295 out of the 303 occupations in which men are engaged. Women, it is true, are not soldiers, sailors, or marines; neither are they street-car drivers; neither are they foremen in fire departments, nor are they apprentices to roofers and slaters, nor are they helpers to steam boiler makers or brass workers; but they are actually engaged in every other of the 303 occupations in which men are engaged, and still they do not have a vote in the great majority of the States of the Union. This is a great change from the days when women were engaged only in such occupations as household service, spinning and weaving, teaching dame schools, setting type, and keeping taverns. Everyone welcomes the opportunity of woman to earn her livelihood, but we are just beginning to realize that the State can not afford to drive its women into industry if thereby the State must lose woman's distinctive contribution as a citizen. After two generations of more or less thoughtless exploitation of women as wage earners, we are beginning to see that the woman goes into industry to meet all the hardships, all the problems of the workingman, plus the handicap of her sex, of her lower physical and nervous vitality. And, therefore, if woman is to be in industry, we must protect her especially, because we must protect the potential motherhood of the race. [Applause.]

We are only beginning to find the truth of this, and we are beginning to see by our reports on the conditions of such a city as Fall River, in my State, the report of the vice committee in Chicago, by the reports of the minimum wage commission in Massachusetts, that the girl and woman in industry can not go in as an equal with man in industry, but that she must be there with special safeguards, because she is the mother of the future citizen.

I know it is a favorite argument of the suffragist to say that because of this fact, because of the entrance of woman into industry, we must give the industrial woman the ballot in order to protect herself. Protect herself against whom? we may ask. It is an extraordinary thing that the study of the body of remedial and protective legislation for working women shows that these against whom the working woman must be "protected"—these men—have

## WOMAN SUFFRAGE.

enacted laws more favorable to women in industry, more carefully safeguarding the child in industry in male-suffrage States than have been enacted in States where women vote. [Applause.]

This is not a charge against the working of woman suffrage, but it is a fair contention that where the industrial conditions have so developed as to show the waste to the State of employing women as men are employed we have the body of legislation best safeguarding the woman and the child.

To explain: Women do not vote in Massachusetts; women do not vote in Nebraska; women do not vote in Indiana; and yet in those three male-suffrage States, and only in those three male-suffrage States, have we a prohibition of night work for women in manufacturing and mechanical establishments, and a prohibition of night work for women is considered the foundation principle of the best standard law you can have for women in industry.

One day's rest in seven is not provided for in these suffrage States under laws made under an electorate of women. You have a provision for one day's rest in seven in California. The eight-hour law was passed there nine months before the women voted, but it is always claimed as a suffrage victory; I do not know just why. But the law there does provide for one day's rest in seven. It does not prohibit night work; neither does it apply to women who are at work in the canneries, and canning is one of the great industries in California.

Massachusetts has a 54-hour law for women. It has a minimum wage commission, the first in this country. It has a maternity act, the first in this country, and that maternity act was adopted by New York, a male suffrage State, last year. The minimum wage and the maternity acts were copied, not from woman suffrage States, for women have voted in four States in our Union at periods varying from 20 to 44 years, but those laws were copied from continental Europe, which had found that it was poor economy to recklessly use the womanhood of the State in industrial lines, because of the inevitable results to the race.

As to child-labor laws: The national child labor committee has done more to have legislation for the protection of the child in industry spread upon the statute books than all the votes of men and women together, and women and men have worked together in getting before the people the conditions which should arouse public sentiment, so that it should insist upon legislation which shall protect the child.

The best child-labor law, in 1912, Dr. McKelway tells us—and I believe he is a suffragist—was in Massachusetts. I hope that some other State will this year outstrip the law of Massachusetts, so we shall again be put on our mettle and recognize the inexcusable waste which comes with the entrance of children into industry. It is particularly to the credit of Massachusetts that she has a good child-labor law, because with her great textile industries she has a temptation to exploit the work of women and children; but on suffrage authority we are told that not in some suffrage State but in a male suffrage State we have the best child-labor law. Again I say that it is not because the woman suffrage has failed to bring this legislation about, but because under male suffrage the law is enacted when public opinion stirs the public conscience.

## WOMAN SUFFRAGE.

Another thing which they said back there in 1848 was that taxation without representation was tyranny. It is a familiar saying, and we have seen it on banners carried in political parades, and it has been overworked on political platforms. But when James Otis gave utterance to those words in the old statehouse he was speaking about taxation of a colony that had no voice in a government overseas. He was not dreaming of universal manhood suffrage, let alone woman suffrage, and the tying up of the tax and the vote is a return to our old system when we had a property qualification; the vote and the tax have gone further and further apart since colonial days; there is but one State in the Union, the smallest State in the Union, which still has a property qualification required of the voter.

The tax is the price which the resident and the nonresident, which the man and the woman, which the alien and the citizen, which the individual and the corporation pay for the maintenance of roads, for the maintenance of schools, for the protection of property, and for those various other enterprises which make life safe and which make the forward march of civilization and a clean life possible in any community. The citizens of the District of Columbia are taxed, but they have no vote.

While suffragists demand the ballot to cleanse society of the social evil, vice commissions in several States report the lack of proper home training as a chief cause of the downfall of our girls and our boys. If the ballot in woman's hands is to suppress this ancient evil, why does this dread thing flourish in States where women have voted from 20 to 44 years? Although these States do not possess the densely populated communities which offer the most perplexing problems of the evil, the votes of women have not shown, even in these sparsely populated areas, a way to reinforce the faltering weakness of human nature. These evils must be corrected along educational lines rather than by political propaganda. The Federal law, dealing with the white-slave traffic, known as the Mann law, was placed on the statute books June, 1910. Up to January, 1913, the Government had obtained 337 convictions, while there had been but 35 acquittals. Other laws must and will follow as the knowledge of the extent of the evil awakens the public conscience and the moral sense of the people is aroused.

There is a danger that women's political activities may hinder this work of education. This danger is revealed in the testimony of Dr. Helen L. Sumner in her book Equal Suffrage—The Results of an Investigation in Colorado Made for the Collegiate Equal Suffrage League of New York State, on page 84 of which we read:

> Prostitutes generally vote, and their vote is cast solidly for the party in control of the police force. * * * The vote of these women, to whom police protection is essential, is regarded as one of the perquisites of the party in power. * * * Whenever "repeating" is to be done their aid, naturally, is required. * * *

And again, on page 93, this trained investigator reports:

> * * * The red-light district is freely used by the party in power, and its women are compelled, not merely to vote, but often to repeat.

If, as a measure of justice, to protect woman—and we might ask again, Protect her against whom?—woman does not need to vote,

WOMAN SUFFRAGE.

ought woman to ask to vote in order to promote the general welfare? Now, in spite of the fact that here in Washington you were told the other day that all antisuffragists were hypocritical liars, in spite of the fact that we are quite accustomed to the kind of attack which you men find in politics, plus the venom of a scorned woman, in spite of all these things, suffragists and antisuffragists are about the same. The only difference is that the suffragist says, "It is through the vote you are going to moralize and reform society, and therefore give women the vote"; and the antisuffragist says that the vote is the least part of good government, and that matters of education, matters of forming and training a scientific public opinion are in the hands of women to an unusual degree, and that we need not an increased electorate, not a duplication by woman of man's methods, but what we need to-day is to be specialists in our line and not to be afraid of being specialists as women and working along the lines wherein I believe women have been somewhat successful in the last 19 centuries.

If men are doing so poorly that women must come in in order to help them out, what shall we say of the women who have trained men? [Applause.] If any mother feels that on election day she is handicapped when her son goes to the polls because she can not direct his vote, it is because she forgot to do what John Boyle O'Reilly used to tell us to do—"Catch him while he is young, because," he said, "you can do what you will with us men if you catch us while we are young."

If men are doing poorly—and I do not believe they are doing poorly when we realize the scale of the experiment of manhood suffrage which is being worked out here for the first time in the history of the world—but if men are doing poorly, is it not because the underlying principles of integrity and honor and righteousness have not been sufficiently insisted upon by the motherhood and by the educational force of this country? Eleven-twelfths of the teachers of secondary schools in my State are women. So it is no excuse for a woman to say, "I have not a boy to train." Will the daughters we have trained accomplish by the vote what the sons we have trained fail to accomplish?

Fortunately the average woman is worthily employed in very old-fashioned concerns. She has responsibility; she has opportunity, all she can use, and political responsibility and political opportunity offer no solution to her problems. The antisuffragist's objection to voting is not an objection to thinking, but we do believe that we are in a time when the specialized contribution of woman should be distinct and apart from the specialized contribution of man.

I have not forgotten, gentlemen, that I am addressing a committee a third of whom come from States where women form a part of the electorate. Even if you could prove that conditions in Utah, Idaho, Colorado, and Wyoming, or even in California and Washington, were bettered by the woman's vote, this would form no criterion for the whole of the country. [Applause.]

The great test of our democracy, of our form of government, comes in the cities, in the densely populated areas, and it is worth while to consider some of these conditions. The population of Colorado, Wyoming, Utah, Idaho, Washington, and California is, in round numbers, 5,160,000, according to the census of 1910. This is nearly

WOMAN SUFFRAGE.

4,000,000 less than the population of the single State of New York. It is 500,000 less than the population of the State of Illinois, and it is 2,500,000 less than the great industrial and mining State of Pennsylvania.

The population of the State of Colorado is equal to the population of the city of Boston plus the population of the city of Fall River, where we have a peculiar situation because of the alien population. The population of the whole State of Wyoming is about equal to that of the city of Worcester, Mass., and it is only twice the population of the city of Manchester, N. H. The population of Utah is not equal to the population of the District of Columbia, and the total population of Utah, Idaho, Wyoming, and Colorado is only 9,600 more than that of the Borough of Brooklyn.

There are some peculiar problems which the East and the Middle West have to meet with their density of population, with the presence of the alien vote, as there are problems which the South has to meet with its race question.

If the experiment of woman suffrage has worked ever so well in Colorado and Utah and Wyoming and Idaho, even in those States where women have voted only one or two years, as in Washington and California, yet we must ask that they try the experiment a little longer before we try it under conditions where a patriotic woman or man must hesitate before bringing in an increased electorate and double the difficulty of getting a question clearly before the voters. [Applause.]

A great menace—I might almost be warranted in saying the greatest menace we have to-day—is not the ignorant voter, so called, or the uninformed voter; it is the indifferent voter. If by admitting women to the electorate we are to increase the number of the indifferent voters, surely we must hesitate before we undertake this reform, which Mr. Gladstone called a "revolutionary" one. You will remember that Mr. Gladstone and America's good friend John Bright and Herbert Spencer had all been in favor of woman suffrage, but they reversed their opinion and came out strongly against the parliamentary franchise for women.

What do we find in the States of Colorado, Utah, Wyoming, Idaho, Washington, and California in the last presidential election? I will not read these figures. I will simply refer to them and ask that they be incorporated in my remarks.

The CHAIRMAN. You may do just as you please about that.

Mrs. GEORGE. These figures are taken from authoritative sources; where there has been a report available from the secretary of state, that has been used; where census reports have been available, they have been used; and in the other instances the best available authority has been used. Of course those are subject to the limitations of human fallibility.

The total vote cast in the six woman suffrage States for the Presidency—that is, where you have an electorate of men and women—in 1912 was 1,521,590. The relation of this vote to the actual number which might have voted, 3,200,152 men and women (exclusive of Japanese and Chinese), was 47.5 per cent.

Take neighboring or adjacent States, six of them, Kansas, Nebraska, Oregon (a male-suffrage State at that time), Nevada, South

## WOMAN SUFFRAGE.

Dakota, and Missouri, and you find a total vote cast of 1,587,984, out of a total male population, 21 years of age and over, leaving out in these cases Japanese and Chinese, of 2,295,119; which makes a percentage in the male-suffrage States of a possible vote cast of 69 per cent, as against a percentage in the woman's suffrage States of 47½ per cent.

If 69 per cent of the men voted in the woman-suffrage States, as they did in the nonwoman-suffrage States (we do not say that they did, probably they did not), but if the same percentage of men voted in the suffrage States as voted in the nonsuffrage States an analysis of the figures shows that only 17.8 per cent of the women voters in the suffrage States actually voted.

Here are the striking facts: In the six woman-suffrage States only 47¼ per cent of the total possible vote was cast. In the six nonsuffrage States near the suffrage States—a fair comparison, I submit—69 per cent of the total possible vote was cast, showing that woman suffrage, according to these statistics, secured from the secretaries of state of the various States and from the most accurate published figures available, tends to decrease the actual voting strength, rather than to increase healthy interest in politics.

*Figures showing the surprising weakness of the total vote of both males and females in the six suffrage States in the last presidential election, and the contrasting high percentage of the total vote in six adjoining nonsuffrage States.*

### WOMAN-SUFFRAGE STATES.

| | |
|---|---:|
| California (population 21 years of age or over, exclusive of Japanese and Chinese): | |
| Males | 890,794 |
| Females | 655,450 |
| Total possible vote | 1,556,244 |
| Actual vote for Presidency | 673,527 |
| Colorado: | |
| Males | 269,211 |
| Females | 213,340 |
| Total possible vote | 482,551 |
| Actual vote | 266,871 |
| Wyoming: | |
| Males | 61,519 |
| Females | 28,426 |
| Total possible vote | 89,945 |
| Actual vote | 42,296 |
| Washington: | |
| Males | 428,825 |
| Females | 276,429 |
| Total possible vote | 705,254 |
| Actual vote | 322,799 |
| Idaho: | |
| Males | 108,847 |
| Females | 69,761 |
| Total possible vote | 178,608 |
| Actual vote for Presidency | 104,203 |

## WOMAN SUFFRAGE.

Utah:
- Males ... 101,902
- Females ... 85,648

Total possible vote ... 187,550
Actual vote for Presidency ... 111,894

Total population of men and women 21 years or more of age, exclusive of Japanese and Chinese, in six suffrage States, and therefore the approximate total possible vote in those six States ... 3,200,152
Total vote actually cast in those six States for the Presidency in 1912 ... 1,521,590
The per cent which voted ... 47½

### NONWOMAN-SUFFRAGE STATES.

Kansas:
- Males 21 years of age or over, exclusive of Japanese and Chinese ... 508,425
- Votes cast ... 365,442

Nebraska:
- Male votes possible ... 352,995
- Votes cast ... 249,871

Oregon:
- Male votes possible ... 244,719
- Votes cast ... 137,040

Nevada:
- Male votes possible ... 38,443
- Votes cast ... 20,744

South Dakota:
- Male votes possible ... 178,054
- Votes cast ... 116,325

Missouri:
- Male votes possible ... 972,483
- Votes cast ... 698,562

Total men 21 years or over in six nonsuffrage States ... 2,295,119
Total vote in the six nonsuffrage States for President ... 1,587,984
Percentage of possible vote cast in six nonsuffrage States ... 69

If this is so, then the woman's vote will add another problem to the problems which already confront the man who is in politics, to the man who knows that the danger to-day lies in the indifferent and stay-at-home voter, and not so much in that vote which can be brought out, no matter what the weather conditions may be. We have "summer soldiers and sunshine patriots" enough under present conditions.

A position of a remonstrant is a very difficult one under any conditions. It is particularly difficult when a woman opposes what other women most sincerely want. It is particularly difficult when one speaks in regard to conditions in States where woman suffrage obtains. But it is fair to ask that those States which to-day have adopted woman suffrage should wait to work out the problem before the other States assume the burden which would come with this change.

If you are only to double the outlay in election expenses, if you are only to double the number of voters, if you are only to double the time and money and energy which must go into political organization and into political work, is it not unsound and uneconomic to have two people do what one person can do? Unless your average woman voter is going to be a better voter, a more intelligent voter, a more safe voter, a more trained voter—shall I say a less emotional voter—than the average man, the extension of suffrage to women will not bring about a condition which will warrant the turning off of

WOMAN SUFFRAGE.

woman's activities from channels in which women are already worthily employed into political activities. [Applause.]

There is reason that we should consider the situation which would arise in a community where those who made the laws had ceased to be those who could enforce the laws. Woman suffrage has never yet been brought to the test of a national crisis, when political feeling is at the greatest tension, yet only under such conditions could its value as a practice of government be fully tested. To-day in California we have a hint of woman's responsibility in a possible international complication when we have a legislature elected by the votes of women and men enacting legislation in regard to the holding of land by aliens, which has grave possibilities for the other States of the Union.

Thomas Jefferson said that a democracy ceased to be such when those who made the laws ceased to be those who could enforce the laws.

There are three portents of the times which are looming large in this suffrage movement. We have a great many middle-of-the-road suffragists who say, "Oh, let the women vote if they want to"; and those others who say, "I want to vote, and if I want to vote I should be allowed to vote, although I am the only woman in the United States who votes," as Mrs. Catt has said. But there are three portents in relation to woman suffrage, and I am no alarmist if I cite them. One is the very evident alliance with the socialistic propaganda. Those who have the intellectual honesty to follow the suffrage premises to their logical conclusion are more often than not socialists. I do not mean by this the "brotherhood of man," in which we all believe, but I mean that Socialist Party which cast its vote for Eugene V. Debs for President of the United States at the election of November 5, 1912. If you doubt this, if it seems the word of an alarmist, I would call attention to the fact that in the parade which moved down Pennsylvania Avenue on March 3 the socialistic contingent carried this banner, which is shown on this photograph, which I would like to have incorporated in the record.

(The photograph referred to shows a portion of the suffrage parade on Pennsylvania Avenue, with the following banner being carried by some of the marchers: "One million Socialists work and vote for woman suffrage.")

[Applause.]

We evidently have some Socialist sympathizers here, and they have the intellectual honesty to follow their premises to their logical conclusion and to agree with certain officers of the National Suffrage Association that the era of the home as the unit of society has passed and we are coming to a "splendid" era when the individual shall be the unit of society.

Mrs. Ida Husted Harper said over her signature:

Woman has not attempted one advance step which has not been blocked by these two words, "wifehood" and "motherhood."

Mrs. Catt, then president of the National Suffrage Association, said in Collier's Weekly in 1901:

Women will sink out of existence in the body politic and will rise again as citizens.

"If a women possesses ability, great or small, talent, genius, noble purpose, lofty ideals," Mrs. Catt continues, "shall she contribute these directly to the

## WOMAN SUFFRAGE.

welfare of the world or through the doubtful channels of influence on husband and children?"

If the influence on husband and children is a doubtful one to any woman, the ballot box is not going to give her certainty. [Applause.]

A suffrage speaker in Boston recently said:

> Woman, waiting on her husband and children, forbids the economic independence, which is the basis of sex morality, and so retards her own development.

[Applause.]

Rev. Dr. Anna Shaw, the president of the National Woman's Suffrage Association, says:

> I would make motherhood a governmental institution.

[Laughter and applause.]

She is consistent.

> I would pension all mothers and have them provided for first to last by the State. I believe that motherhood should be independent of man.

[Continued laughter.]

I do not find it amusing. There are a few women who may make these extraordinary statements, but the menace lies in the fact that there are thousands of women in this country of ours who follow these leaders and who come here and ask for woman suffrage and then devise these schemes in order to make the woman's vote operative.

It is not necessary for some one to stand up and say, "I come from Colorado" or "I come from California, and the home there is not neglected and the babies are not neglected." If a woman's vote is going to be worth anything it is going to fall differently from the vote of the man of the same class, or else it simply doubles the return on election day.

Those who look to woman suffrage for the so-called emancipation of the sex are forced to devise these schemes by which the State shall care for the children. But it is a curious thing that at the very moment when experts have found that the child is better off in a poor home than in a good institution these women come along and say: "Let us have these institutions." At the very moment when these advanced suffragists say, "We will take the child from the amateur mother, who is the real mother, and give her to the expert mother," we are told by the highest authority on infantile diseases that the breast-fed baby has ten times the chance to survive that the bottle-fed baby has. That is not interesting, perhaps; you may say it has nothing to do with the woman-suffrage propaganda. It has, because when the president of the National Woman's Suffrage Association makes utterances such as this she is devising a scheme by which woman shall be able "to sink," as Mrs. Catt tells us, "sink out of existence in the body politic and rise again as citizens."

The secretary of the National Suffrage Association says progressive people are agreed that the wife should be economically independent, and so she devises a five-hour shift by which the mother shall be in the home five hours and shall be gainfully employed five hours, and the father shall go back into the home for five hours and care for the children, and then he shall be gainfully employed five hours. [Laughter.]

WOMAN SUFFRAGE.

Those things are not amusing; they are alarming as a menace that carries out the tenet of socialism, that we are to have a kind of economic independence, which has very well been called by no less authority than Col. Roosevelt "a glorified State free-lunch counter and State foundling asylum."

The other menace, the second menace, the second portent, is the menace of feminism bound up with the menace of socialism. We find that the brilliant young woman who led the suffrage parade down Pennsylvania Avenue writes as follows:

> This pressure toward a constantly growing freedom and power on the part of the sex means that in the long run the institutions most certain to be changed are the institutions in which the sex as a sex is most peculiarly and vitally interested, and these institutions, it is hardly necessary to point out, are the home and marriage itself.

A writer who is indorsed by the suffragists and dedicates her book to Mrs. Pankhurst and her daughters, an American woman, says:

> Two words were burned upon my brain—

She had been to a suffrage lecture—

> laws made by men for women that must be unmade by women for women.

She says:

> We must stop talking and act—fight.

She says:

> Throw stones; do anything; it does not matter what, so long as we get the vote and can legislate in our own protection and the protection of the children.

But you may say that is an isolated illustration not fair to use. When the National Suffrage Association cabled, less than two weeks ago, to Mr. Asquith asking him to put an end to the intolerable conditions in England and to introduce a franchise bill into the present Parliament, they practically indorsed Mrs. Pankhurst, as they had given already a vote of sympathy to Mrs. Pankhurst.

An officer of a New York suffrage association has written this week in an open letter to the New York Times—and, lest you think I speak in parables, it is Mrs. John Brennan, a daughter of Charles A. Dana:

> It is quite possible that if the Eastern States continue to deny enfranchisement to the women while the Western States continue to grant it the women thus discriminated against would find the political anomaly of their position so impossible to bear that even militancy would seem to them justifiable.

Miss Milholland, in speaking with me at Philadelphia, said:

> Acid throwing and bomb throwing have their places under certain conditions.

We who oppose the extension of suffrage to women ask that not too great weight be attached to the argument of rights which suffragists put forward, who at the same time do not observe the rights of property belonging to noncombatants, who indorse the lawlessness of women over-seas, who by their lawlessness seek to show a more excellent way in government.

The third menace, then, is militancy. The indorsement of militancy by leading suffragists, the indorsement of militancy by the National Suffrage Association—that is, militancy on the part of the English women—is significant of the temper of those women who say the end justifies the means.

WOMAN SUFFRAGE.

The only flag displayed over the entrance to the congressional headquarters of the National American Woman's Suffrage Association here on F Street is the purple, green, and white emblem of the Women's Social and Political Union of England, of which Mrs. Emmeline Pankhurst is president.

There was a great woman in England who did work second to none in the housing of the poor and the care of the children, the establishment of playgrounds, and so on. Her name was Octavia Hill. At the end of a long life she said:

> I had hoped to be kept out of this suffrage contention, but I feel that after all these years I must say that it is important that one-half of the workers should be outside of party politics. This service is far more valuable than any voting power could possibly be.

That is where we antisuffragists contend that women can do their work best. The average woman is worthily employed already. To give her political responsibilities will not help out the situation unless she does something far more important than merely casting a ballot on election day. She has got to be a more informed voter than the average man of to-day if her vote is to be effective.

In passing, let me ask our suffrage friends to compare like with like. A favorite cartoon of the suffragists depicts a woman scrubbing, and a drunken man sitting at the table with his head bowed over, and the legend beneath the picture reads: "He can vote, she can not." Society is not made up of scrubbing wives and drunken husbands. Unfortunately both types exist, but, in all fairness, let us compare like with like, and until we are sure we are going to get a better state with the woman's vote than without it, we should hesitate before we hinder the best service women can do by putting them into political activities.

The ballot is the least part of good government, and those who advocate this instant doubling of the present electorate are behind the times. They emphasize the ballot as "the greatest of all modern reforms," and even urge that those who are to-day contributing to other reforms should withdraw or curtail their contributions to other causes until the ballot for woman is secured. (See appeal of M. Carey Thomas, February, 1913, for funds for National American Woman's Suffrage Association.)

If I may be permitted to say it here, the lady from Massachusetts, Mrs. William Lowell Putnam, exemplified in an extraordinary way what women can do without the ballot. She is chairman of the department of public health of the Women's Municipal League and she is also chairman of the executive committee of the Massachusetts Milk Consumers' Association, an association which has done more for the cause of a pure milk supply in the State of Massachusetts than the votes of men or of men and women could possibly bring about.

These women in this country of ours are doing an increasing amount of public work, but it is no sophistry to ask you to distinguish between a few women in public work, well equipped, full of knowledge to match their zeal, and all women in political life. Where you find a woman doing a distinctive work, where you find that it is constructive, you will find that it gains its quality and it gains its distinction because the woman is working not as a Republican or a Democrat or a Socialist or a Progressive, but she is working as

WOMAN SUFFRAGE.

a woman who is informed, who is ready to direct public opinion, and who has no personal political motive to serve. [Applause.] She works as a disinterested, nonpartisan factor for the public good, and there is no reason that she should take the retrogressive step which should make her work identical with man's. It is not a question of right, it is not a question of woman's inferiority or her superiority; it is a question of what is expedient for the State, and the antisuffragists believe that it is expedient for the State that the motherhood of the State should not be drafted off into political channels. I thank you. [Applause.]

## ARGUMENTS FOR WOMAN SUFFRAGE CONSIDERED.

It is proposed to consider in this paper certain assertions made by suffragists, with a view to the refutation of the conclusions drawn from them.

1st. Women who used to work at home now work more and more in factories and shops. Here they work under the same conditions as men. The number of women doing this is now very large, and it is continually increasing. Therefore, the suffragists assert, they should have the vote.

2d. The courts are taking a new attitude toward women, treating them not as wards and children, but as complete citizens, not giving effect to special legislation in their favor, but treating them as part of a whole community. Therefore they should vote as does the male citizen.

3d. The word "politics" should be used to cover the whole field of activities in which the public is or might be interested. Women are, therefore, as factory inspectors, as members of school boards, trades unions, etc., already in politics, and should as a matter of course obtain what they want through the ballot as men do.

4th. The object of general suffrage is to bring all classes under equal protection; to secure to all classes equal consideration, and to unite all classes for the common welfare. Women should therefore be represented as a class.

5th. The ballot will correct the evil conditions in working women's lives.

6th. The ballot is an educational power.

I. As to the first statement, it is to be admitted that it is partially true. Great numbers of women, and doubtless constantly increasing numbers, are engaging freely in all sorts of occupation away from the home. To be sure, it should be remembered that in the majority of such cases, the occupation is regarded by the women themselves as temporary, and not as a life work. That under such circumstances so large a movement should take place, and with such ease and rapidity, indicates what the fact is, namely, that no obstacles, legal or other, are placed in the path by men, and that the conditions must all be favorable, or at least not hostile. It is evident, therefore, that woman does not need the suffrage to facilitate her entrance into wider fields of industrial occupation; but it is at least a very serious question whether such increased entrance into industry is not a social danger. The ideal community is one where women can devote themselves to the most important duty of rearing and training the family. No society can long endure in safety if great numbers of its children must be left to grow up uncared-for and untrained, as must be the case when both father and mother devote themselves to the exacting pursuit of gaining a livelihood. The increasing density of population, and the growing difficulty of maintaining a family, may compel such a condition; but it is a most unfortunate social situation, full of dangers, and sure to precipitate the most serious social problems. It is an evil to be warded off as long as possible, and with all the means at hand, by the true social reformer. Less than this cannot be said by any one who looks into the future to find the dangers to be guarded against.

II. The second proposition is that the laws and courts are extending the rights and privileges of women.

This, too, is true. In fact, so far has this tendency been carried, that now in almost all our States women have all the legal rights and privileges that men have, and many protections and safeguards that men have not. Without the suffrage they have been put in most States in a distinctly better position than men. This is believed to be right; but it certainly has taken place without female suffrage. It has been demonstrated that women could secure greater protection from our laws without suffrage than men get with it. Surely no one can claim that the facts stated in this second proposition demonstrate, or tend to demonstrate, that women need the suffrage for their protection in these respects. Devotion to a preconceived theory must be carried very far not to see that chivalry has given, and is giving far more to women than suffrage could ever do, in all the respects under consideration. And so doubtless will it ever be as long as human nature remains what it is, and as long as sex is permitted to remain what it is.

III. We come now to the third point.

As before stated, this is a definition of "politics" that includes almost every form of human activity; at least so far as industrial pursuit is concerned. In the definition is included all associations of men or women in corporations, syndicates, trusts, etc., and all the infinite variety of labor associations, male or female.

This is a wholly new definition of "politics." As truly it may be said to be a wholly incorrect definition. You might as well lump all these varied human activities, and call them religion, art, or science, as politics. There is no justification for such hazy thought or statement. As it has usually been assumed that all political questions are properly settled by votes, the only object of this definition would appear to be to persuade that these questions, which are so interesting to all people, are political questions. If, therefore, the coiners of this definition could satisfy every one that all questions of vital interest to every individual could only be properly settled by votes, they could perhaps convince more people that every one should have a share in the voting. But in any rational consideration nothing would seem to be gained by such inaccurate thought or definition.

IV. The fourth proposition is that general suffrage is to be desired as a means to bring all classes under equal protection; to secure to all classes equal consideration, and to unite all classes for the common welfare. It follows, the suffragists claim, that women as a class should be represented.

When it is said that classes, by organization of various kinds, secure advantages from time to time, that is certainly correct. When it is intimated that sometimes such advantages are secured by legislation, that is also correct. Now if it were claimed that all this tended to prove the benefits of *organization*, no one would take issue with such a conclusion.

It is now generally believed by the laboring classes that they owe in large measure the progress they have made to their unions and societies, and associations of various kinds. No one would deny the right of women to associate similarly; in fact they do so already, and in many instances in union with the men. It may be that they should do so more largely, and it is probable that they will if the present movement on the part of women towards industrial pursuits should continue or increase.

It is a safe prediction that the previous experience of women will be repeated; that, just as they have secured more privileges and protection on the whole than men in the same community, so they will secure more privileges and better conditions than men in their industrial pursuits, and under the influence of the same causes.

Everything that the suffragists claim as to the benefits of

organization among all classes, may be admitted, at least for the sake of argument. But the fallacy that lies at the bottom of their conception is that the division of human beings into males and females is in any true sense a "class" division.

Nature scouts such an idea. It takes the male and female to make one class. The great, fundamental fact is that the males and females in any class of society are in full sympathy in most of their feelings and emotions, and opinions. The world would be a hell if this were not true. You might as well say that a man's right hand belonged to one class, and his left to another. The males and females of the race that we call human have no hostility to each other any more than have the males and females of other species that we see and know. In fact all nature demonstrates just the contrary. You cannot separate the interests of males and females and thus get "class interests" in any true sense.

It is true that there is a difference of function; but it is absurd to say that this makes a "class" difference, or that the function of one is any more important and honorable than that of the other. It is not in any just sense a badge of woman's inferiority to man to say that he votes and she does not; any more than it is a badge of man's inferiority to woman to say that she bears children and he does not.

The only question is, and always must be, what under all the circumstances is the proper and suitable division of function between the male and female. This should always be determined by many considerations.

V. The suffragists claim that the ballot will alleviate the condition of working women.

Sympathetic and emotional minds and hearts, when contemplating the evils of life, and the sufferings, hardships, and miseries of human beings, are very apt to long for, and finally to think they have discovered, some direct remedy for what seems unbearable. In fact a great part of the nonsense, and most of the crude nostrums of the world have this kindly origin. Earnest souls see evils of various kinds, enumerate them sympathetically and convincingly, and carry themselves and their listeners along, so that when with confidence a single remedy is announced for the admitted evil, it seems just the needed panacea. Unfortunately in the real world the case is not so simple.

The silver crank of to-day exploits free coinage as the sovereign remedy for evils vividly portrayed, and readily believed. But his remedy would aggravate the case. The suffrage enthusiast offers his nostrum, and he too would probably aggravate all the evils he so clearly sees. Nature's methods of cure take time and patience. She knows no short cuts. The world with its slow evolution in the right direction shows us that only patient pursuit by right methods promises any real relief in all our social problems.

One hears sympathetic narrations of the evils found among working women, — what one of their most ardent friends describes as "a feeling that they are shut up to a life in which only the meanest personal interests are matters of consideration;" "a blind and stupid selfishness that does not and cannot see the wrong of base, political strife;" "a feeling that they and their interests are not sufficiently considered;" "a growing feeling of antagonism towards that vague personification known as the State."

To all this the reply is that it could almost identically be said of the men in the same class; and that with the density of our population, and the increased difficulty of support of the family, it is being felt more and more by both the men and women in their class; and that female suffrage will not remedy it, as male suffrage has not.

But is it safe to double the number of ignorant, discontented, and dangerous voters, and to do it *because* they are discontented, ignorant, and dangerous?

Some such question is often asked; but so much is hoped from the educating influence of the ballot, that its advocates are willing to take the risk.

VI. The educational power of the ballot. The suffragists exaggerate the educating influence of the ballot; they also underestimate the dangers attending so overwhelming an increase of the suffrage; and they seem strangely unaware of the fact that the very same feelings and sentiments found among the women, exist, and have increased, among the men of the same class, notwithstanding the possession of the suffrage.

Suffrage of any kind is not an end, but a means to an end; a contrivance to secure the best government, the greatest security, the best protection for our lives and property, — a contrivance, it may be added, to afford that stable and orderly condition under which our rights shall be most secure, and under which all the forces of civilization shall have the best opportunity to work out the best results. It is not in itself a right of nature, any more than the privilege of holding office is a natural right.

Many just and good governments have existed and worthily performed their functions without providing for the exercise of the privilege of suffrage. The privilege should be exercised everywhere, and at any time, so far, and only so far as it will conduce to the end which alone justifies its existence, and which has been already defined; in a word, in so far only as it will continue to give the best government.

The denial of this privilege is not the denial of a right. Its granting or extension is to be determined simply by its political wisdom.

We have extended this privilege of suffrage in this country very far: so that it now practically includes all males of the age of twenty-one and upwards, whether native or foreign; for the residence required of a foreigner is only five years.

If the question could now be considered an open one there are many things that could now be said against so sweeping and indiscriminate an extension. But the chief vice of an extension is that it is under our system of government practically irrevocable.

Shall we *now* extend the suffrage to the other half of the community? No.

It may be well to state that the reason for saying "No" is not that women are in any way inferior to men. They do have different functions; and these do seem to point the way to an arrangement that shall assign to each different duties and responsibilities. The world has not hitherto been wrong in generally agreeing that the man shall as a rule support the family, carry on the contests of the world, fight its battles when war becomes necessary, sit on juries, and exercise the correlative privilege of voting; and that to the woman shall be assigned other and by no means less important duties and privileges.

Shall we double our suffrage now?

Certainly we all agree that we should not unless we feel absolutely certain of its wisdom. No mere balance of probabilities in our minds; no mere groping after education; nothing, in short, but absolute conviction of its wisdom can justify any one in favoring it. The awful extent of the change, its absolute irrevocability, demands the utmost certainty before any reasonable being can favor it.

It is foolhardy for any one to say he has such certainty. Political changes should never be so sweeping; government should never be so rashly experimented with. It is only an experimental science at best, and the experiments should be moderate.

This is the whole science of political wisdom.

It is believed that enough has been said in this paper to show that extension of suffrage is not an appropriate remedy for the existing industrial evils, or for any of the existing miseries of mankind. What a mistake to draw off the intelligent thought and effort that should be directed to the cure of the countless social evils that beset us in our times, by consideration of this quack remedy, whose only effect would be the intensification of all the disorders it was supposed to cure! A thousand times better to accurately diagnose our diseases, correct all the loose and false notions with regard to this supposed remedy, and clear the field for an honest, and above all patient effort to better our condition.

Let us stop talking and thinking as if we regarded suffrage of any kind as a God-given right — to be deprived of which by any human creature would be an act of oppression — and as a panacea for all social ills, and let us apply ourselves to real remedies.

There are many objections to female suffrage that will readily suggest themselves to most people, on the social or family side of the subject. That field is now only entered by way of suggestion, in passing.

It seems impossible to exaggerate the objection to the extension of suffrage to women, that comes from a consideration of the present conditions and tendencies of the industrial and social state in this country. The increasing density of our population; the vast and rapid expansion that all our industries have had; the growing difficulty of sustaining and properly rearing the family; the bad effect on the future generation of being deprived of sufficient home training, because of the increasing necessity that the mother as well as the father shall work; all these and many other conditions work together to divide our people into real classes, with much jealousy of each other, subject to many discomforts and sufferings which to them seem unjust. Those philanthropists in whom emotion predominates over intellect are always preaching to such people dangerous doctrines.

The notion that comfort — or such comfort as is obtainable — and success come primarily from the practice of the old-fashioned virtues of temperance, frugality, and self-restraint, is not encouraged. In place of these a new gospel is inculcated. They hear that somebody besides themselves is at fault; that the world owes every one comfort; and soon all get to feel that if they are not as comfortable as in their opinion they should be, some one or some class is at fault.

The homely virtues are lost sight of, and every one must

be a statesman. The ballot is held up as the great instrument of getting from one, giving to another. So this class feeling is being fed more and more, and the thought and activity of one class is more and more directed to getting in some way from another class. The most serious danger to our civilization now comes from the struggle of these classes.

The forces of order are hard pressed in the battle now. If they are overborne it will be in this way. It is to be feared that the hostility between classes may increase, as an increasing population makes the conditions of life in this country increasingly difficult. The men and women of the same class have — as has been said before in another connection — the same feelings and aspirations, the same antipathies and prejudices.

The women of our ignorant classes have the same sense of injuries and wrongs as the men; the same crude notions of what the world owes them; the same fierce desire to get in some way, if in need, from those who have. If now you double the voting power of all these dangerous ideas you quadruple the danger, you give to them at once such a terrible preponderance that the stoutest heart may well quail, the firmest courage feel unequal, to the contest.

In our mad confidence in ourselves do not let us try to shoot this political Niagara.

*Printed by the Massachusetts Association opposed to Extension of Woman Suffrage.*
Pamphlets and leaflets may be obtained from the Secretary of the Association,                       MRS. ROBERT W. LORD,
P. O. Box 2262, Boston, Mass.

# As to Suffrage in New York State.

To the Editor of the Sun:—*Sir:* Is it expedient to grant suffrage to women in New York State? Will it be for the best interests of the State? Will it be for woman's best interest?

These are the questions that the people of New York State have had forced upon them since the Constitutional Convention assembled in 1894, when the women desirous of suffrage for their sex asked that the word "male" be stricken from the Constitution, and the women who were opposed to the extension of suffrage woke up from their seeming lethargy and demanded that they should not be forced into the political arena.

The reasons advanced by the "opponents" and "anti-suffragists," together with the common sense of the great majority of the men who formed the Committee on Revision, led to the defeat of the suffragists. They worked like beavers. They promised to bring the names of 1,000,000 women, over 21 years of age, signed to petitions asking for suffrage; but they failed to get one-half the number, even though they gave their own figures as to results; even though they paid for the collection of names; even though they claimed the vote of large corporations through the signature of one man; even though they cajoled men and boys into signing, and even though they forgot the age limit and let everyone sign who could wield a pen.

It was hoped that the action of the Constitutional Convention would settle the matter for twenty-five years, and that the women who had been forced into work that was distasteful might now return in quiet to their round of home duties and divest themselves of the publicity and notoriety thrust upon them.

But the suffragists continued the fight. Last winter, coached by an astute politician, whose name has been recorded on the "anti's" books for overwhelming defeat if they are ever forced to vote, they, the suffragists, worked cautiously and quietly, and, by buttonholing, flower-giving, and lobbying, succeeded in carrying through both

Houses a concurrent resolution which is to give the people of the State a right to vote upon the question of suffrage for women.

That the men of both Houses realized the objectionable methods of work is made apparent by their passing a regulation which they are enforcing this winter, that no women shall be permitted on the floor of either House without a card of admission.

There was an error in the wording of the resolution, and the result is that it will still have to pass two consecutive Legislatures, and the work of last winter is null and void.

Why did it pass both Houses last winter? In answer I give the replies of many of the men in both Houses—that, though objecting to woman suffrage, they felt that to relieve themselves from the constant annoyance of the women lobbyists it would be well to let it go to the people and be settled at once for all time. But they did not realize what would be the action of the suffragists even though the people gave an overwhelming defeat to their project, as they did last fall in Massachusetts. What was the result there? They are forcing their claim upon the Legislature again this winter; and when they were denied a hearing by a committee appointed on woman suffrage, they immediately declared their intention of forcing a hearing by three other committees. And that would be the result in New York State if the concurrent resolution were passed and an overwhelming defeat met with at the polls. And so we come back to our original questions, which should be the only ones to influence our legislators.

It is said above that the suffragists of New York State claim to have about half a million names to their petition. At the annual suffrage convention in Washington, held last month, a paper was read on the relative amount of suffrage organization in the different States and the statement was made that there were only 1,600 enrolled suffragists in New York State. In the city of Albany, alone, in one month, there were enrolled upon the anti-suffrage lists more than five times that number.

No reason has ever been advanced showing positively that woman or the State would be benefited by the vote of women. Wyoming and Utah are held up as patterns for New York! The history of woman suffrage in Wyoming does not give one a great longing to see it in force in New York. And if Wyoming, with a territory twice as large as the State of New York, with a population scattered over it of about 60,000, less than that of one of the smallest of New York's second-class cities, is what it is to-day through twenty-five years of woman suffrage, New York, with more than 6,000,000 inhabitants, has done well not to follow in the wake of this baby State. As for Utah—well, we all know what Utah was under woman suffrage, or from 1869 to 1886, when the women were disfranchised. What it will be now is only a question of time, but as it has a white population of only about 200,000, it can scarcely, under any circumstances, be set up as a pattern for New York State.

The legislators of New York should not inflict upon the women of the State the unpleasant duty of entering the field in opposition to suffrage, which a vote to allow it to pass to the people for final action would entail. Neither should any legislator who believes that it would not be for the best interest of woman or the State to grant suffrage to women lend his influence by voting to pass it to the people. And it would not release us from suffrage clamor.

The *Woman's Journal* says editorially:—"More than one hundred petitions for woman suffrage have already been forwarded to members of the Massachusetts Legislature. Others are coming in daily."

As there are only 1,600 enrolled suffragists in New York State, and as these are only in part women, should not the desire of the silent majority—a majority of many millions of women—influence our legislators to give an overwhelming defeat to the concurrent resolution when it is again brought up? Until it can be shown by sworn statements that a majority of the women of the State demand suffrage, no Legislature has the right to submit the question to the male vote. And any one familiar with the abuse of the male suffrage will not deem it wise or prudent to more than double the atrocities that are now being perpetrated under the guise of political emergencies. Let the suffragists enforce the laws already made. That will keep them busy and be helpful to the State.

ALBANY, *February 22*.  A. P. P.

# FROM THE SEATTLE DAILY TIMES,

February 14th, 1898.

## AS TO WOMEN.

The Idaho Register of Idaho Falls, commenting upon an address given at that place during the suffrage campaign by Mrs. Catt, gave the following personal testimony regarding Wyoming:

"It seems that she has allowed some enthusiast in Wyoming to fill her mind with wonderful stories about the results of equal suffrage in that State, and she, taking them as true statements, tells them as such. From some of them one is led to believe that Wyoming is a paradise.

"She demonstrated that the compulsory education law was responsible for the small per cent of criminals in the penitentiary, and of idiocy in the state, and then claimed that this was the fruit of female suffrage.

"One who was not better informed would imagine that the juries and political conventions were mostly composed of women."

"The writer was a resident of Wyoming from 1870 to 1880, and during that time attended every territorial convention, both Republican and Democratic, and every county convention in the two western counties that were held during that time, and no woman ever sat as delegate in any one of them; and it was usually only by urging and stating that others had voted, and their vote was wanted to offset it, that a large portion of the women could be induced to vote."

# Ask Suffragists to Explain This

*FROM THE NEW YORK STATE ASSOCIATION OPPOSED TO WOMAN SUFFRAGE 37 WEST 39TH STREET NEW YORK CITY*

The following questions were addressed to the suffrage speakers who closed the "whirlwind campaign week" by four meetings at the Philadelphia City Hall Plaza, Saturday, October 24, 1914. Mrs. Horace Brock, president, and Mrs. J. Gardner Cassatt, vice-president, of the Pennsylvania Association Opposed to Woman Suffrage, who asked these questions, said they believed that the public deserved a straight answer, and suggested that the newspapers, as non-partisans, secure them from the suffragists.

A copy of these questions was forwarded to each of the Philadelphia newspapers, and five official copies for speakers' use were sent to the Suffrage Headquarters five hours before the addresses began. Although asked by the representatives of at least three morning and one evening newspaper, the suffragists declined to answer these questions, in one case claiming they had not been sent "officially," but in another admitting they had been received, but "could be answered by each voter for himself," as they had not time to take them up. Persons who were present at the meetings say that they do not recall any references having been made to these questions by the suffrage speakers. One advocate of the cause claimed that the franchise question was "beyond argument," which is probably *true,* in view of the anti-suffrage victories at all the debates last year at Yale, Harvard and Princeton, and the present suffrage neglect to answer salient questions. One Philadelphia evening newspaper, noted for fairness, published two installments of these questions—without answers—though the city editor was especially requested to secure answers if possible.

### Headquarters, Pennsylvania Suffrage Association:

In fairness to the public, and in order to extend an accurate knowledge of just what woman suffrage may be expected to do in view of its past record, the Pennsylvania Association Opposed to Woman Suffrage invites your speakers this afternoon to answer the following questions, and to give a clear explanation of the following facts and figures:

1. Why is it that after 65 years of constant agitation the woman suffrage cause is opposed by women themselves more vigorously than ever?

2. Why is woman suffrage the only movement among women that has excited against itself an organized national and state opposition from other women?

3. As the census report on occupations issued June 20, 1914, shows only 8,075,772 feminine workers over *ten* years of age in the United States, why do suffragists claim that "eight million *women* workers demand the ballot?"

4. The National American Woman Suffrage Association claimed a membership of "about 650,000" in June, 1914. The Congressional Union for Woman Suffrage, the National's rival, claimed 4000 members about the same time. This makes 654,000 suffragists in America, which is less than *one-twelfth* the 8,000,000 feminine workers, less than one-half the total number of women enfranchised in the nine full suffrage States (1,998,163, according to the census), and only 2.7 per cent. of the women over 21 in America. Why have 97 women out of every 100 rejected woman suffrage for 65 years, and why do less than half the enfranchised women approve their own "emancipation" and less than one-twelfth the women workers believe in "votes for women"?

5. Since the census figures show 4,338,337 of the feminine workers are employed in agricultural pursuits and domestic service—on farms and in homes—and that of the 24,555,754 women over 21 in America, 20,518,833 are, or have been, married, and are obviously "making homes" for the 20,255,555 families who live in the 17,805,845 dwellings in the United States, how do you prove that "woman's work has gone out of the home and into store, factory and shop?"

6. Woman suffrage, you claim, will bring better labor conditions. Colorado has had woman suffrage 21 years. Why, then, is Colorado the only State in the Union that has called for Federal aid in suppressing anarchy and riot twice in ten years—in 1904 and 1914?

7. Woman suffrage will do away with child labor, you assert. Abovementioned census report (pp. 73, 442 and 512) shows the same percentage of children from 10 to 13 at work in Colorado as in Pennsylvania. BUT in Colorado the highest number of such children work out as farm laborers, whereas in Pennsylvania the highest number are employed on the home farm. Nearly twice as many children work out on farms in Colorado as are employed by their own parents. In Pennsylvania the situation is so reversed that nearly three times as many children work for their own parents as for others. Does "votes for women" force more children to leave home and work for others?

8. Woman suffrage will bring "economic independence," you declare. Why, then, does the census show nearly THREE times as many *women laborers on farms* in Colorado and Wyoming, *after 21 and 45 years of woman suffrage*, as are similarly employed in Nebraska and Nevada, where women do not vote? Why, too, are there over EIGHT times as many INDEPENDENT women farmers in the two male suffrage States as in the two States where they have votes? These are all neighboring States of equal density of population.

9. If votes will raise wages, as suffrage agitators promise women workers, why do men in the same industries depend on labor unions rather than on votes to get higher pay?

10. If woman suffrage will help the woman worker, explain the following testimony, after three years of suffrage in California, before the Federal Industrial Relations Commission, at Los Angeles, September 10, 1914. Mrs. Katherine P. Edson, member of the California Industrial Welfare Commission, declared:

"No doubt a large part of our social trouble, such as the *children in the street*, is due to men working for an inadequate wage and women being forced to go out and work. It seems to me a hopeless situation. My opinion is that there are more women working outside their homes here than there should be. Some large dry goods stores, I understand, are contemplating refusing to employ married women because of the numerous complaints from unmarried women workers."

Why does a woman call the condition of labor "hopeless" where women vote?

11. Various department stores in Philadelphia allow their employes all day off Saturdays during the summer. Where have women secured Saturday holidays with "a piece of paper in a ballot box"?

12. Woman suffrage will rout rum, you allege. Then why has no State ever gone "dry" with "votes for women," although ELEVEN have done so by the moral influence of woman on the votes of MEN ONLY.

13. Where were the women voters of Colorado on November 5, 1912, when that State defeated prohibition by a majority of 40,897 votes, 116,774 ballots being cast for the saloons? As there are 213,425 women over 21 in Colorado (p. 118, Census Abstract), it would have taken only 58 per cent. of them to make the State "dry" by a majority of 6012, without a single male vote to help them. Does this not prove that most of the women who WILL vote are against the very temperance that all women desire and have secured under male suffrage?

14. Wyoming got woman suffrage in 1869. It has remained the forty-seventh Commonwealth in the Union to this day, according to the census. If women seek "emancipation," why has the colonization of Wyoming been so sadly neglected for 45 years, and why are there only 100 women to every 168 men in that State, which is the second lowest proportionate feminine population in the United States? Why women avoid Wyoming wants explanation.

15. Suffragists say women should vote because they pay taxes. On this plea the foreign corporation or individual or non-resident who pays taxes should vote. The majority of women are not taxpayers, however, and their addition to the electorate would only increase the number of voters who do not pay taxes. Do suffragists advocate further extension of irresponsibility?

16. Suffragists are indorsed by all the unstable elements in our population—the Socialists, the I. W. W. and the Feminists. Do suffragists, in turn, indorse socialism, sabotage and communism? If not, why do they accept the support of Socialists and Feminists and run standing appeals for such support by officially advertising for it in revolutionary magazines given over to the defense of convicted rioters and the glorification of masculine and feminine rebellion? (See a copy of the *Masses*.) Note standing advertisement of National American Woman Suffrage Association.

17. If women are competent to vote on every question, why not allow them to vote on their own enfranchisement?

18. In view of the fact that woman suffrage proposes another duty to women, an unnecessary duty inconsistent with her highest natural duties and functions, and, furthermore, involves great risk and additional expense to the State, we have a right to ask what it can do to improve civic conditions, and where it has done so. If suffragists cannot prove "votes for women" are worth while, how can they show any reason why woman suffrage should not be rejected?

19. An electorate, like a standing army, is a governmental instrument to carry out the will of the people. Its extension can only be advocated as a necessity or a service to the common good. Where and when have women proved their supreme moral influence as the mothers, wives, daughters, sisters and teachers of men as "inferior" to the ballots and bullets that men must sometimes use? What reason can suffragists give for asking women to use the weapons of men in a vain attempt to exercise political power, when the wishes of women and the wisdom of the centuries teach us to rely on the moral might that women wield in the church, the school and the home, where our citizens are made and molded —by women?

(Signed)    Mrs. Horace Brock,
*President.*

(Signed)    Mrs. J. Gardner Cassatt.
*Vice-President.*

---

### BOOKS RECOMMENDED FOR READING

The Ladies' Battle ($1.00) ................................................. Molly Elliott Seawell
The Business of Being a Woman ($1.50) ................................................. Ida Tarbell
Votes for Men (50c) ................................................. A Book for Men by a Man
Unrest of Women ($1.00) ................................................. E. S. Martin
Woman Adrift (English) ($1.50) ................................................. Harold Owen

Subscribe to "The Protest" ($1.00)

---

ISSUED BY

### THE PENNSYLVANIA ASSOCIATION OPPOSED TO WOMAN SUFFRAGE

261 S. FIFTEENTH STREET, PHILADHLPHIA

# BEWARE!

MEN OF THE SOUTH: Heed not the song of the suffrage siren! Seal your ears against her vocal wiles. For, no matter how sweetly she may proclaim the advantages of female franchise,—

REMEMBER, that *Woman Suffrage* means a reopening of the entire *Negro Suffrage* question; loss of State rights; and another period of reconstruction horrors, which will introduce a set of female carpet-baggers as bad as their male prototypes of the sixties.

DO NOT JEOPARDIZE the present prosperity of your sovereign States, which was so dearly bought by the blood of your fathers and the tears of your mothers, by again raising an issue which has already been adjusted at so great a cost.

NOTHING can be gained by woman suffrage and much may be lost

---

(*Extracts from The Messenger*)

# THE NEGRO
## AND THE
# NEW SOCIAL ORDER

A Reconstruction Program, Prepared by Chandler Owen and A. Philip Randolph (negroes),
Editors of *The Messenger*, March 10th, 1919

### THE MESSENGER PUBLISHING CO.
2305 SEVENTH AVENUE          NEW YORK CITY

---

### POLITICAL PROGRAM

Page 6—Political action must go hand in hand with industrial action. A class of people without the vote or the privilege of determining the kind of government under which they live, has neither security of life nor property from which liberty proceeds.

In view of the foregoing WE DEMAND the rigid enforcement of the 13th, 14th and 15th Amendments to the Constitution, which were primarily framed to give protection to negroes.

WE DEMAND the reduction of representation in the South upon the basis of actual voting population. The negro is not allowed to vote, which is in criminal violation of the Federal Constitution.

We condemn all property and educational tests for suffrage.

WE DEMAND *universal suffrage without regard to race, color, sex, creed or nationality.*

### WOMAN SUFFRAGE

We favor the adoption of the Susan B. Anthony amendment to the Constitution, granting suffrage to women—both white and colored.

("*Suffrage democracy knows no bias of race, color, creed or sex.*"—*Mrs. Carrie Chapman Catt.*)

### SOCIAL EQUALITY

Page 9—*We favor "social equality" in every sense of the phrase.* WE DEMAND a new order based upon a society of equals. Evasions, pretexts and excuses cannot explain away the fact that no genuine brotherhood can exist so long as the issue of social equality is not squarely met.

SOCIAL EQUALITY has grown out of the two cardinal and corollary principles of *identity of treatment* and *free interchangeability*.

### INTERMARRIAGE

We now approach the American bugaboo—the question upon which the negroes and whites alike set up false theories in flagrant violation of the most fundamental principles of social evolution. *We refer to intermarriage between the whites and negroes.* WE FAVOR THE INTERMARRIAGE between any sane, grown persons who desire to marry—whatever their race or color. WE FAVOR THE INTERMARRIAGE OF WHITE MEN WITH COLORED WOMEN AS WELL AS COLORED MEN WITH WHITE WOMEN, because there is no natural or instinctive aversion.

Race purity is both a myth and without any value.

WE THEREFORE DEMAND THE REPEAL OF ALL LAWS AGAINST INTERMARRIAGE AS BEING INIMICAL TO THE INTERESTS OF BOTH RACES. We further call attention to the fact that there is no desire to check the associations of white men with colored women, colored women with white men, nor to serve serve any interests of negro men. And inasmuch as no law requires any woman under any circumstances to marry a man whom she does not will or want to marry, *these laws narrow themselves down to the prevention of* WHITE WOMEN MARRYING COLORED MEN *whom they desire to marry.*

WE DEMAND as much intercourse—economic, political, and social, *as is possible between the races.*

---

"Women and negroes, being seven-twelfths of the people, are a majority; and, according to our republican theory, the rightful rulers of the Nation." *Official History Woman Suffrage, Vol. 1, page 281.*

"We will see that Negro women in the south shall vote." *Ida Husted Harper, Editorial Chairman of the National American Woman Suffrage Association, in the New York Globe, November 4, 1918.*

# BISHOP SEYMOUR ON THE NEW WOMAN.

## God Created Man and Woman Somewhat Differently—The Difference cannot Be Obliterated.

The Right Rev. Geo. F. Seymour, D. D., while conversing with a Times reporter said: "God created male and female in the image of God. The image of God unites them and the hand of God differentiates them in making them two halves of a whole. Each has its place, and the woman has, if one pleases, the better place, as she is the 'better half.'

"Having said this, I wish to add that God, in making woman, implied her place in her physical constitution, organic functions, and practical duties. These lines are drawn by the divine hand. Human hands may seek to obliterate these lines and succeed in obscuring them, but they cannot destroy them.

"Man may apparently suspend for a time the laws of God by his presumption and folly, but he cannot repeal them, and human genius and ability cannot create a new man, much less a new woman. They may seem to do so in a wretched counterfeit and distortion, which may seem for a time to be a success, and gratify, and perchance amuse those who covet novelties, but in the end it will be, and must be a failure.

"The blessed gospel of our Lord and Savior Jesus Christ, has steadily emancipated woman from the thraldom under which the brutality and lust of man had brought her, and restored her to the place which God originally assigned her.

"As a son, as a brother, as a husband, I bless God for the place which he gave women in creation, and to which he restored her in the person of Jesus Christ in the blessed gospel. As a woman, as God made her and as Christ dignified her she is all glorious within, and protected by the reverence and affection of the civilized world. As the new woman, she will be divorced from the home, from her children, from her brothers, from her husband, and from her former self, and become a creature indescribable."

The officers of the Anti-Suffrage society of Third Judicial District, State of New York, are

    Mrs. J. V. L. Pruyn, - - *President.*
    Mrs. William J. Wallace, *1st Vice-President.*
    Mrs. Wm. Bayard Van Rensselaer,
        - - - - *Secretary.*
    Mrs. Joseph Gavit, - - *Treasurer.*

    *Executive Committee.*

    Mrs. W. Winslow Crannell, *Chairman.*
    Mrs. Erastus Corning,
    Mrs. William Cassidy,
    Mrs. J. Howard King,
    Mrs. Joel R. Reed,
    Mrs. Wm. O. Stillman,
    Mrs. Frederick Townsend,
    Miss Lucy A. Plympton,

Apply for more papers to Anti-Suffrage Association, 13 Elk Street, Albany.

# *Can Anybody Terrorize Tennessee Manhood?*

## *The Susan B. Anthony Amendment Will Never Be Ratified If Tennessee Representatives Do Their Duty NOW*

### Because the People Do Not Want It

ANY state that wants Woman Suffrage can adopt it for itself by popular vote, without changing a word in the FEDERAL CONSTITUTION. In fifteen states woman suffrage was thus adopted in the course of the last fifty years WITHOUT AFFECTING OTHER STATES. The ONLY REASON why anybody asks FEDERAL WOMAN SUFFRAGE is because in twenty-one STATE ELECTIONS SINCE 1912, woman suffrage was DEFEATED AT THE POLLS by 1,387,344 majority—FOUR TIMES the total majority FOR woman suffrage in the fifteen states which adopted it. They now want to put it in the Federal Constitution, where thirteen states can prevent its REPEAL, however unsatisfactory or even ruinous it may prove.

NO state constitution can be amended without the consent of the PEOPLE. A STATE amendment must be submitted to POPULAR VOTE, and can be CHANGED or REPEALED any time THE PEOPLE VOTE to do so. A FEDERAL AMENDMENT CANNOT BE SUBMITTED TO POPULAR VOTE. It is decided ONLY by LEGISLATURES, which may or may not represent PUBLIC OPINION. If some 4,000 members of THIRTY-SIX LEGISLATURES vote for a Federal amendment, it goes into the United States Constitution BY FEDERAL BLANKET LAW OVER THE HEADS OF THE 110,000,000 PEOPLE of the FORTY-EIGHT SOVEREIGN States. The Federal Constitution NEVER WAS INTENDED to be used to BETRAY the will of the American people, but it can be ABUSED for that purpose, and driven over the rights of the people, just as an automobile can be driven over a child by anybody wicked enough to do so.

### The Present Situation

THIRTY-FIVE LEGISLATURES have passed resolutions purporting to ratify the Susan B. Anthony Amendment. The legality of two of these alleged ratifications (Missouri and West Virginia) is being appealed to the United States Supreme Court, as well as the validity of the amendment itself. Another ratification would NOT necessarily complete the adoption of the Amendment, but it would throw the coming presidential election into the courts and create another Hayes-Tilden conest. EIGHT LEGISLATURES—Alabama, Georgia, Virginia, South Carolina, Maryland, Mississippi, Delaware and Louisiana—HAVE REJECTED THE AMENDMENT, three of them, Alabama, Maryland and Louisiana, DENYING THE VALIDITY of the amendment, and calling on their sister states to REJECT IT.

### Only Five States Yet to Act

TENNESSEE, North Carolina, Florida, Connecticut and Vermont are the ONLY states yet to act. North Carolina IS NOW IN SESSION and will REJECT. Florida, Connecticut and Vermont legislatures WILL NOT MEET UNTIL 1921. ALL THREE STATES ARE AGAINST THE FEDERAL AMENDMENT, and will be more against it after the PRESENT ELECTION, because those states WILL ELECT NEW LEGISLATURES ON THIS ISSUE, and their people are now fully AROUSED.

### Tennessee's Opportunity

ELIHU ROOT says: "If you enable some sections of the country to coerce other sections by use of national power you will ultimately break up the Union. . . . That is precisely what this Federal Suffrage Amendment undertakes to do."

BUT TENNESSEE CAN SAVE THE STATES!

Not only are the alleged ratifications of West Virginia and Missouri being appealed to the Supreme Court, but POLITICAL CAMPAIGNS a· already under way to RESCIND ratification in other states—Texas, West Virginia, Maine, Wisconsin, etc.

The Federal Suffrage "Drive" is Dead if Tennessee will answer the call of her own constitution, her own people, and that of her sister Southern states.

In Texas, with women voting in the primaries, former Senator Joseph Weldon Bailey, who spoke against woman suffrage in every address, has just been nominated for governor with the suffragists, as well as state and national party machinery, against him. His election means that Texas, which defeated woman suffrage in 1919 at the polls, and was betrayed three weeks later by a card-indexed legislature, can RESCIND that action if Tennessee will give her the chance.

### Federal Suffrage Not "Inevitable"

NO Federal amendment HAS EVER BEEN RATIFIED after its rejection in EIGHT STATES. Tennessee and North Carolina will make TEN, and THIRTEEN REJECTIONS will nail down the coffin of the Susan V. Anthony Amendment. People who say it is "bound to come" are either uninformed or trying to mislead you. Some persons said Germany was "bound to win," and a suffrage leader (Mrs. Lucretia Blankenburg) said "the anti-suffragists are just like little Belgium." Perhaps they are. It was at the hardest period of the war, with Ludendorff almost at the gates of Paris, that Clemenceau of France said:

> "In all wars he is a conqueror who can believe, a quarter of an hour longer than his adversary, that he is not beaten. We shall continue the war to the last quarter of an hour, for the last quarter of an hour will be ours."

That is the spirit that broke all the machine-made calculations of the great German "drive" of 1918, as Ludendorff himself admits in his book.

### The "Card Index" Pressure System

ADVOCATES of FEDERALIZED suffrage, in addition to the parrot-talk of "bound to come" by which THEY HOPE TO WEAKEN YOUR MORALE, employ a CARD-INDEX PRESSURE SYSTEM OF POLITICAL BLACKMAIL ("More extreme than men ever dreamed of."—New York Times) to control the people's sworn representatives.

The character, religion, politics, record, relatives and FINANCIAL BACKERS of legislators are put down on a series of TWENTY-TWO CARDS FOR EACH MAN. This SECRET CARD-INDEX SYSTEM is then used either to CONTROL THE MAN'S VOTE, or to get "men higher up" to control OTHER MEN'S VOTES. We have absolute and convincing PROOF of the existence of this system, and the SIGNED CONFESSIONS of suffrage leaders ADMITTING IT.

This is what Gov. Clement meant when he said, "I refuse to indorse political blackmail in any form."—(New York Times, July 18, 1920.)

### A Peril to the South

FEDERAL Suffrage, which gives Congress complete power (under the 14th, 15th and 19th amendments) of ENFORCEMENT, means control of state elections by FEDERAL FORCE BILLS. This issue concerns REPUBLICANS as well as DEMOCRATS, for what would it profit the REPUBLICANS to double a vote within their ranks that would TURN OVER THEIR OWN PARTY, in many sections of the South, to the control of another race? Northern FEDERALISTS, it seems, don't care WHO controls the Republican party in the South—so long as it votes the National ticket—but good Southern Republicans KNOW that their party must remain in control of Anglo-Saxons here for the sake of LOCAL conditions that politically ambitious FEDERALISTS never seem to consider. Some Republicans in Oregon or Maine may favor another Southern reconstruction, but NOT the real men of the Republican party in the South.

### The Constitution vs. Platform

IN 1916, both the Democratic and Republican parties indorsed and recognized "the right of each state to settle this question for itself." That right is a CONSTITUTIONAL right, hitherto guarded in both Federal and State Constitutions. A CONSTITUTIONAL RIGHT reserved to the states or the people cannot be abolished by the say-so of any committee, convention or party that happens to change its mind. If it was a right in 1916 it must still be a right in 1920. No party can command a man to violate a constitution he has sworn to support or to betray fundamental principles of the American people's government. When a party, under the influence it may be of one or two men on a Resolutions Committee, goes beyond its legitimate authority as a party, and declares in effect that it is now "expedient" to rob the people of rights they have reserved since 1776, it merely cancels its claim upon those who hold the American form of government unalterable by such methods. If there were such things as State Rights, Majority Rule or Local Self-Government in America in 1916, they were beyond the power of any party to change by self-contradiction in four years!

VICTORY is mostly a question of MANHOOD and MORALE. The Federal Suffrage "Drive" is a PROOF that the PEOPLE are against woman suffrage, for wherever the people WANT woman suffrage they can have it WITHOUT FEDERAL AMENDMENT. This desperate drive to FORCE FEDERALIZE SUFFRAGE on states and people because they do not want it deserves the answer that Clemenceau gave Ludendorff and that Gov. Clement gave the suffragists. You can stop ANYTHING but death and taxes if enough REAL MEN say "it shall not pass."

### The Acid Test of Experience

BLACKMAILERS always work by inspiring FEAR. No person can be blackmailed who is unafraid. The suffragists have never defeated ANYBODY who had the COURAGE to face their "blacklist."

In 1914 they "blacklisted" eighteen members of Congress. Every one was re-elected, Senator Undeı wood, one of the blacklisted, going to the Senate.

In 1916 they blacklisted President Wilson, toured the country against him, and he carried TEN out of ELEVEN suffrage states against Judge Hughes, who said, "I want the support of the women of the country"—and lost both the women's vote and the election.

In 1918 Gov. Whitman of New York, the "suffrage governor," with women voting and with the active support of Mrs. Catt & Company, lost the election to a man who had voted, spoken and worked against woman suffrage, and polled 15,000 FEWER VOTES in New York City, with women voting and suffrage "support" than he received from the MEN ALONE in 1916.

In 1918 EVERY NEW YORK CONGRESSMAN who had voted AGAINST Federal suffrage was re-elected by an INCREASED majority, Representative Gould, anti-suffragist, polling the largest congressional majority ever given in New York.

In 1918 Senator Borah of Idaho, blacklisted by suffragists because he opposed FEDERALIZED suffrage, won by 30,000 majority with women voting.

In 1919 Speaker Sweet of New York, blacklisted by the suffragists, who ran a WOMAN candidate against him, polled the largest majority ever given a legislator in New York.

In 1920 Senator Overman of North Carolina, opposed by a Federal suffragist, (Brooks) won by 90,000 majority.

In the same state, Cameron Morrison, on an anti-ratication platform, has won the Democratic nomination for governor by 9,000 majority over Lieutenant-Governor Gardner, who advocated ratification.

IN WEST VIRGINIA, EVERY MAN WHO VOTED FOR RATIFICATION in March, who ran for re-election, WAS DEFEATED IN THE PRIMARIES IN MAY. (See Pittsburg Dispatch and Charleston Mail, June 1, 1920.)

IN MAINE, F. J. Parkhurst, anti-suffragist, has overwhelmingly defeated Gov. Milliken, Federal suffrage advocate, in the primaries.

IN IOWA, men who OPPOSED Federal suffrage have led the field.

IN NEW YORK, the headquarters of Federal suffrage agitation, Senator Wadsworth, who has been attacked constantly by the suffragists, was nominated in convention two weeks ago by 988 to 97 scattering votes. In the suffrage leader's district (Westchester county) there were 48 votes—and ALL went to WADSWORTH.

A man CANNOT LOSE by sticking to his own conscience and the solemn convictions of the AMERICAN PEOPLE on this issue. Gov. Clement of Vermont has won the admiration and applause of the whole country for his MANLINESS in refusing to "tear up the Constitution" for Mrs. Catt & Company.

So will it be in Tennessee. The men who vote FOR RATIFICATION will find it a LOSS, rather than a GAIN to them, for the American people are not going to have MEASURES they oppose put over by men they elect to represent them, without showing their deep and just resentment at the polls. The people cannot vote on a Federal amendment, but they can ALWAYS VOTE against the man who betrays them.

The men who vote AGAINST RATIFICATION will go down in American history as the SAVIORS OF OUR FORM OF GOVERNMENT, and the true DEFENDERS of Womanhood, Motherhood, the Family and the State.

*This is the opening argument in a great campaign to save the States from destruction.*

*If YOU believe in the right of the people of each State to control their own elections, we ask your active support*

**SOUTHERN WOMEN'S LEAGUE FOR REJECTION OF THE SUSAN B. ANTHONY AMENDMENT**

Headquarters and Exhibition, Mezzanine Floor, Hermitage Hotel

| | | |
|---|---|---|
| **Don't Fail to Visit the Exhibition** | **—Come and See— "The Woman's Bible"** | **Have You Seen the Three Force Bills?** |

# Can Anybody Terrorize Tennessee Manhood?

### The Susan B. Anthony Amendment Will Never Be Ratified If Tennessee Representatives Do Their Duty NOW

## Because the People Do Not Want It

ANY state that wants Woman Suffrage can adopt it for itself by popular vote, without changing a word in the FEDERAL CONSTITUTION. In fifteen states woman suffrage was thus adopted in the course of the last fifty years WITHOUT AFFECTING OTHER STATES. The ONLY REASON why anybody asks FEDERAL WOMAN SUFFRAGE is because in twenty-one STATE ELECTIONS SINCE 1912, woman suffrage was DEFEATED AT THE POLLS by 1,387,344 majority.—FOUR TIMES the total majority FOR woman suffrage in the fifteen states which adopted it. They now want to put it in the Federal Constitution, where thirteen states can prevent its REPEAL, however unsatisfactory or even ruinous it may prove.

NO state constitution can be amended without the consent of the PEOPLE. A STATE amendment must be submitted to POPULAR VOTE, and can be CHANGED or REPEALED any time THE PEOPLE VOTE to do so. A FEDERAL AMENDMENT CANNOT BE SUBMITTED TO POPULAR VOTE. It is decided ONLY by LEGISLATURES, which may or may not represent PUBLIC OPINION. If some 4,000 members of THIRTY-SIX LEGISLATURES vote for a Federal amendment, it goes into the United States Constitution BY FEDERAL BLANKET LAW OVER THE HEADS OF THE 110,000,000 PEOPLE of the FORTY-EIGHT SOVEREIGN States. The Federal Constitution NEVER WAS INTENDED to be used to BETRAY the will of the American people, but it can be ABUSED for that purpose, and driven over the rights of the people, just as an automobile can be driven over a child by anybody wicked enough to do so.

## The Present Situation

THIRTY-FIVE LEGISLATURES have passed resolutions purporting to ratify the Susan B. Anthony Amendment. The legality of two of these alleged ratifications (Missouri and West Virginia) is being appealed to the United States Supreme Court, as well as the validity of the amendment itself. Another ratification would NOT necessarily complete the adoption of the Amendment, but it would throw the coming presidential election into the courts and create another Hayes-Tilden contest. EIGHT LEGISLATURES—Alabama, Georgia, Virginia, South Carolina, Maryland, Mississippi, Delaware and Louisiana—HAVE REJECTED THE AMENDMENT, three of them, Alabama, Maryland and Louisiana, DENYING THE VALIDITY of the amendment, and calling on their sister states to REJECT IT.

## Only Five States Yet to Act

## Federal Suffrage Not "Inevitable"

NO Federal amendment HAS EVER BEEN RATIFIED after its rejection in EIGHT STATES. Tennessee and North Carolina will make TEN, and THIRTEEN REJECTIONS will nail down the coffin of the Susan V. Anthony Amendment. People who say it is "bound to come" are either uninformed or trying to mislead you. Some persons said (Mrs. Lucretia Blankenburg) said "the anti-suffragists are just like little Belgium." Perhaps they are. It was at the hardest period of the war, with Ludendorff almost at the gates of Paris, that Clemenceau of France said:

"In all wars he is a conqueror who can believe, a quarter of an hour longer than his adversary, that he is not beaten. We shall continue the war to the last quarter of an hour, for the last quarter of an hour will be ours."

That is the spirit that broke all the machine-made calculations of the great German "drive" of 1918, as Ludendorff himself admits in his book.

## The "Card Index" Pressure System

ADVOCATES of FEDERALIZED suffrage, in addition to the parrot-talk of "bound to come" by which THEY HOPE TO WEAKEN YOUR MORALE, employ a CARD-INDEX PRESSURE SYSTEM OF POLITICAL BLACKMAIL ("More extreme than men ever dreamed of."—New York Times) to control the people's sworn representatives. The character, religion, politics, record, relatives and FINANCIAL BACKERS of legislators are put down on a series of TWENTY-TWO CARDS FOR EACH MAN. This SECRET CARD-INDEX SYSTEM is then used either to CONTROL THE MAN'S VOTE, or to get "men higher up" to control OTHER MEN'S VOTES. We have absolute and convincing PROOF of the existence of this system, and the SIGNED CONFESSIONS of suffrage leaders ADMITTING IT.

This is what Gov. Clement meant when he said, "I refuse to indorse political blackmail in any form."—(New York Times, July 18, 1920.)

## A Peril to the South

FEDERAL Suffrage, which gives Congress complete power (under the 14th, 15th and 19th amendments) of ENFORCEMENT, means control of state elections by FEDERAL FORCE BILLS. This issue concerns REPUBLICANS as well as DEMOCRATS, for what would it profit the REPUBLICANS to double a vote within their ranks that would TURN

VICTORY is mostly a question of MANHOOD and MORALE. The Federal Suffrage "Drive" is a PROOF that the PEOPLE are against woman suffrage, for wherever the people WANT woman suffrage they can have it WITHOUT FEDERAL AMENDMENT. This desperate drive to FORCE FEDERALIZE SUFFRAGE on states and people because they do not want it deserves the answer that Clemenceau gave Ludendorff and that Gov. Clement gave the suffragists. You can stop ANYTHING but death and taxes if enough REAL MEN say "it shall not pass."

## The Acid Test of Experience

BLACKMAILERS always work by inspiring FEAR. No person can be blackmailed who is unafraid. The suffragists have never defeated ANYBODY who had the COURAGE to face their "blacklist."

In 1914 they "blacklisted" eighteen members of Congress. Every one was re-elected, Senator Underwood, one of the blacklisted, going to the Senate.

In 1916 they blacklisted President Wilson, toured the country against him, and he carried TEN out of ELEVEN suffrage states against Judge Hughes, who said, "I want the support of the women of the country"—and lost both the women's vote and the election.

In 1918 Gov. Whitman of New York, the "suffrage governor," with women voting and with the active support of Mrs. Catt & Company, lost the election to a man who had voted, spoken and worked against woman suffrage, and polled 15,000 FEWER VOTES in New York City, with women voting and suffrage "support" than he received from the MEN ALONE in 1916.

In 1918 EVERY NEW YORK CONGRESSMAN who had voted AGAINST Federal suffrage was re-elected by an INCREASED majority. Representative Gould, anti-suffragist, polling the largest congressional majority ever given in New York.

In 1918 Senator Borah of Idaho, blacklisted by suffragists because he opposed FEDERALIZED suffrage, won by 30,000 majority with women voting.

In 1919 Speaker Sweet of New York, blacklisted by the suffragists, who ran a WOMAN candidate against him, polled the largest majority ever given a legislator in New York.

In 1920 Senator Overman of North Carolina, opposed by a Federal suffragist, (Brock,) won by 20,000 majority.

In the same state, Cameron Morrison, on an anti-ratification platform, has won the Democratic nomination for governor by 9,000 majority over Lieutenant-Governor Gardner, who advocated ratification.

IN WEST VIRGINIA EVERY MAN WHO VOTED FOR

# HIDDEN FROM HISTORY

The legality of two of these alleged ratifications (Missouri and West Virginia) is being appealed to the United States Supreme Court, as well as the validity of the amendment itself. Another ratification would NOT necessarily complete the adoption of the Amendment, but it would throw the coming presidential election into the courts and create another Hayes-Tilden contest. EIGHT LEGISLATURES—Alabama, Georgia, Virginia, South Carolina, Maryland, Mississippi, Delaware and Louisiana—HAVE REJECTED THE AMENDMENT, three of them, Alabama, Maryland and Louisiana, DENYING THE VALIDITY of the amendment, and calling on their sister states to REJECT IT.

## Only Five States Yet to Act

TENNESSEE, North Carolina, Florida, Connecticut and Vermont are the ONLY states yet to act. North Carolina IS NOW IN SESSION and will REJECT. Florida, Connecticut and Vermont legislatures WILL NOT MEET UNTIL 1921. ALL THREE STATES ARE AGAINST THE FEDERAL AMENDMENT, and will be more against it after the PRESENT ELECTION, because those states WILL ELECT NEW LEGISLATURES ON THIS ISSUE, and their people are now fully AROUSED.

## Tennessee's Opportunity

ELIHU ROOT says: "If you enable some sections of the country to coerce other sections by use of national power you will ultimately break up the Union. . . . That is precisely what this Federal Suffrage Amendment undertakes to do."

BUT TENNESSEE CAN SAVE THE STATES!

Not only are the alleged ratifications of West Virginia and Missouri being appealed to the Supreme Court, but POLITICAL CAMPAIGNS a . already under way to RESCIND ratification in other states—Texas, West Virginia, Maine, Wisconsin, etc. The Federal Suffrage "Drive" is Dead if Tennessee will answer the call of her own constitution, her own people, and that of her sister Southern states.

In Texas, with women voting in the primaries, former Senator Joseph Weldon Bailey, who spoke against woman suffrage in every address, has just been nominated for governor with the suffragists, as well as state and national party machinery, against him. His election means that Texas, which defeated woman suffrage in 1919 at the polls, and was betrayed three weeks later by a card-indexed legislature, can RESCIND that action if Tennessee will give her the chance.

MEN'S VOTES. We have absolute and convincing PROOF of the existence of this system, and the SIGNED CONFESSIONS of suffrage leaders ADMITTING IT.

This is what Gov. Clement meant when he said, "I refuse to indorse political blackmail in any form."—(New York Times, July 18, 1920.)

## A Peril to the South

FEDERAL Suffrage, which gives Congress complete power (under the 14th, 15th and 19th amendments) of ENFORCEMENT, means control of state elections by FEDERAL FORCE BILLS. This issue concerns REPUBLICANS as well as DEMOCRATS, for what would it profit the REPUBLICANS to double a vote within their ranks that would TURN OVER THEIR OWN PARTY, in many sections of the South, to the control of another race? Northern FEDERALISTS, it seems, don't care WHO controls the Republican party in the South—so long as it votes the National ticket—but good Southern Republicans KNOW that their party must remain in control of Anglo-Saxons here for the sake of LOCAL conditions that politically ambitious FEDERALISTS never seem to consider. Some Republicans in Oregon or Maine may favor another Southern reconstruction, but NOT the real men of the Republican party in the South.

## The Constitution vs. Platform

IN 1916, both the Democratic and Republican parties indorsed and recognized "the right of each state to settle this question for itself." That right is a CONSTITUTIONAL right, hitherto guarded in both Federal and State Constitutions. A CONSTITUTIONAL RIGHT reserved to the states or the people cannot be abolished by the say-so of any committee, convention or party that happens to change its mind. If it was a right in 1916 it must still be a right in 1920. No party can command a man to violate a constitution he has sworn to support or to betray fundamental principles of the American people's government. When a party, under the influence it may be of one or two men on a Resolutions Committee, goes beyond its legitimate authority as a party, and declares in effect that it is now "expedient" to rob the people of rights they have reserved since 1776, it merely cancels its claim upon those who hold the American form of government unalterable by such methods. If there were such things as State Rights, Majority Rule or Local Self-Government in America in 1916, they were beyond the power of any party to change by self-contradiction in four years!

polling the largest congressional majority ever given in New York.

In 1918 Senator Borah of Idaho, blacklisted by suffragists because he opposed FEDERALIZED suffrage, won by 30,000 majority with women voting.

In 1919 Speaker Sweet of New York, blacklisted by the suffragists, who ran a WOMAN candidate against him, polled the largest majority ever given a legislator in New York.

In 1920 Senator Overman of North Carolina, opposed by a Federal suffragist, (Brooks) won by 90,000 majority.

In the same state, Cameron Morrison, on an anti-ratification platform, has won the Democratic nomination for governor by 9,000 majority over Lieutenant-Governor Gardner, who advocated ratification.

IN WEST VIRGINIA, EVERY MAN WHO VOTED FOR RATIFICATION in March, who ran for re-election, WAS DEFEATED IN THE PRIMARIES IN MAY. (See Pittsburg Dispatch and Charleston Mail, June 1, 1920.)

IN MAINE, F. J. Parkhurst, anti-suffragist, has overwhelmingly defeated Gov. Milliken, Federal suffrage advocate, in the primaries.

IN IOWA, men who OPPOSED Federal suffrage have led the field.

IN NEW YORK, the headquarters of Federal suffrage agitation, Senator Wadsworth, who has been attacked constantly by the suffragists, was nominated in convention two weeks ago by 968 to 97 scattering votes. In the suffrage leader's district (Westchester county) there were 48 votes—and ALL went to WADSWORTH.

A man CANNOT LOSE by sticking to his own conscience and the solemn convictions of the AMERICAN PEOPLE on this issue. Gov. Clement of Vermont has won the admiration and applause of the whole country for his MANLINESS in refusing to "tear up the Constitution" for Mrs. Catt & Company.

So will it be in Tennessee. The men who vote FOR RATIFICATION will find it a LOSS, rather than a GAIN to them, for the American people are not going to have MEASURES they oppose put over by men they elect to represent them, without showing their deep and just resentment at the polls. The people cannot vote on a Federal amendment, but they can ALWAYS VOTE against the man who betrays them.

The men who vote AGAINST RATIFICATION will go down in American history as the SAVIORS OF OUR FORM OF GOVERNMENT, and the true DEFENDERS of Womanhood, Motherhood, the Family and the State.

---

*This is the opening argument in a great campaign to save the States from destruction.*

*If YOU believe in the right of the people of each State to control their own elections, we ask your active support*

## SOUTHERN WOMEN'S LEAGUE FOR REJECTION OF THE SUSAN B. ANTHONY AMENDMENT

Headquarters and Exhibition, Mezzanine Floor, Hermitage Hotel

---

| Don't Fail to Visit the Exhibition | Come and See "The Woman's Bible" | Have You Seen the Three Force Bills? |

# HIDDEN FROM HISTORY

CARDINAL GIBBONS SAYS WOMEN
 SHOULD KEEP FROM THE POLLS

# HIDDEN FROM HISTORY

## CARDINAL GIBBONS SAYS WOMEN SHOULD KEEP FROM THE POLLS

Prince of the Church Declares Descent Into Politics Would Rob the Home of Its Best Uplifting Influence.

### ALWAYS HAS OPPOSED SUFFRAGE; ALWAYS WILL

(From a Staff Correspondent.)

BALTIMORE, June 22.—"* * * Woman suffrage?" questioned the cardinal, in response to a request that he explain his opposition to that propaganda. "I am surprised that any one should ask the question. I have but one answer to such a question, and that is that I am unalterably opposed to woman's suffrage, always have been, and always will be.

### WHAT IS BEST.

"This is not a new subject with me. I have preached against it, talked against it and written about it for years. Naturally I have not reached my conclusions without study of the most serious kind—study from the standpoint of what is best for woman herself; what is best for her husband and what is best for her children. The answer is that woman should not be given the right to vote."

"Why should not a woman have the right to vote?" the cardinal was asked.

"Approach the subject in another way," answered the distinguished prelate. "Why should a woman lower herself to sordid politics? Why should a woman leave her home and go into the street to play the game of politics? Why should she long to come into contact with men at the polling places? Why should she long to rub elbows with men who are her inferiors intellectually and morally? Why should a woman long to go into the streets and leave behind her a happy home, her children, a husband, and everything that goes to make up the ideal domestic life? Answer these questions for me, and then we may proceed with a discussion of the subject, but I think the average man and woman will admit that it will be difficult to find reasonable answers to them.

"I am hostile to woman's suffrage, always have been, and will continue to be. Some one is always asking me why I oppose woman's suffrage. I am always wondering why they ask me that question. I have written about the subject for years; I have preached about it, and I will continue to urge that nothing be done which will take woman out of her proper sphere.

### WOMAN GAINS NOTHING.

"When a woman enters the political arena she goes outside the sphere for which she was intended. She gains nothing by that journey. On the other hand, she loses that exclusiveness, respect, and dignity to which she is entitled in her home.

"Who wants to see a woman standing around the polling places; speaking to a crowd on the street corner; pleading with those in attendance at a political meeting? Certainly such a sight would not be relished by her husband, or by her children. Must the child, returning from school, go to the polls to find his mother? Must the husband, returning from work, go to the polls to find his wife, soliciting the votes for this man or that, for this woman or that? It would seem to me that the questions answer themselves.

"I am not unaware of the cry among women for 'equal rights.' It seems to me, however, as I have pointed out in one of my essays on the subject, that the women of this and other countries confuse 'equal rights' with 'similar rights'.

"As a result of this cry for 'equal rights' it is quite ordinary to hear of ladies, gentlewomen, daughters of some of our country's best men, mounting the rostrum to harangue their audiences. Is it any wonder that a feeling of sadness creeps over one that such things should be? . . . .

### APOSTLES BY PRAYER

"Women, it is true, are debarred from the exercise of the public ministry and the celebration of the sacred mysteries, for they are commanded by the apostle to 'keep silence in the churches.' But if they are not apostles by preaching, they are apostles by prayer, by charity, and by good example. If they cannot offer up the sacrifice of the mass, they are priests in the broader sense of the term, for they offer up, in the sanctuary of their own homes and on the altar of their hearts, the acceptable sacrifice of supplication, praise and thanksgiving to God. Viewing, then, woman's dignity and her work in the cause of Christ, well may we apply to her these words of the Prince of Apostles: 'You are a chosen generation, a royal priesthood, a holy nation, a purchased people.'

"The noblest work given to woman is to take care of her children. Let Christian mothers recognize their sublime mission. Let them bear in mind that to them is confided the most tender portion of the flock of Christ, which on that account should be watched with the greater care. On them devolves the duty of directing the susceptible and the pliant minds of their children and of instilling into their youthful hearts the principle of piety. It is theirs to plant the seed of the word of God in the virgin soil, and when a more experienced hand is required to cultivate it the ministers of God will not be wanting in developing its growth.

"I would exhort mothers in the name of the holy religion they profess; in the name of their country, which expects them to rear, not the scourges of society, but honorable and law-abiding members, in the name of God, who requires them to have their offspring fed with the nourishment of sound doctrine, in the name of their own eternal salvation and that of the souls committed to their charge, to provide for their children at home a healthy, moral, and religious education.

"Woman is queen," said the cardinal, in bringing the interview to a close, "but her kingdom is the domestic kingdom."—*New York Globe* (N. Y.), June 22, 1911.

# HIDDEN FROM HISTORY

## EXTRACT FROM A MESSAGE

FROM HIS EMINENCE

## JAMES, CARDINAL GIBBONS

To the National Association Opposed to Woman Suffrage

Read by

### THE RIGHT REVEREND WILLIAM T. RUSSELL

Bishop of Charleston, S. C.

at

### NATIONAL ANTI-SUFFRAGE CONVENTION

Washington, D. C.

(December 7, 1916)

"* * * When I deprecate female suffrage I am pleading for the dignity of woman; I am contending for her honor; I am striving to perpetuate those peerless prerogatives inherent in her sex, those charms and graces which exalt womankind and make her the ornament and coveted companion of man. Woman is queen indeed, but her empire is the domestic kingdom. The greatest political triumphs she would achieve in public life fade into insignificance compared with the serene glory which radiates from the domestic shrine and which she illumines and warms by her conjugal and motherly virtues. If she is ambitious of the dual empire of public and private life, then, like the fabled dog beholding his image in the water, she will lose both; she will fall from the lofty pedestal where nature and Christianity have placed her and will fail to grasp the scepter of political authority from the strong hand of her male competitor.

"* * * I regard 'woman's rights' women and the leaders of the new school of female progress as the worst enemies of the female sex. I wish I could impress on American women the dangers that would attach to such innovations. I wish I could show them the ultimate result of participating in public life. It has but one end—the abandonment, or at least the neglect, of the home.

"The most precious undeveloped asset of any nation is its children. An all-wise God through the law of nature has committed this precious treasure in a special manner to the mother. Any occupations, however alluring in its specious pretence, which draws woman's attention from her most exalted duties of motherhood, will result in detriment to the nation and the race. Women cannot vote intelligently unless they give time to an intelligent study of political questions, and all such time taken from the household will be injurious to the future generation, by robbing it of its natural right, a mother's care, without giving to the present generation any appreciable benefit in the purifying of the ballot. * * * "

JAMES, CARDINAL GIBBONS.

## EXTRACT FROM LETTER OF CARDINAL GIBBONS

To the Maryland Association Opposed to Woman Suffrage, April 22, 1913.

"* * * Equal rights do not imply that both sexes should engage promiscuously in the same pursuits, but rather that each sex should discharge those duties which are adapted to its physical constitution and are sanctioned by the canons of society. To debar woman from certain pursuits is not to degrade her. To restrict her field of action to the gentler avocations of life is not to fetter her aspirations after the higher and the better. * * *

"The insistence on a right of participation in active political life is undoubtedly calculated to rob woman of all that is amiable and gentle, tender and attractive; to rob her of her innate grace of character and give her nothing in return but masculine boldness and effrontery. Its advocates are habitually preaching about woman's rights and prerogatives and have not a word to say about her duties and responsibilities.

"They withdraw her from those obligations which properly belong to her sex and fill her with ambition to usurp positions for which neither God nor nature ever intended her. Under the influence of such teachers we find women, especially in higher circles, neglecting her household duties, never at peace unless she is in perpetual motion or unless she is in a state of morbid excitement. She never feels at home unless she is abroad. When she is home, the home is irksome to her. She chafes and frets under the restraints and responsibilities of domestic life. Her heart is abroad. Her afflicted husband comes home to find it empty or occupied by a woman whose heart is empty of affection for him. She is ill at ease. Hence arise disputes, quarrels, recriminations, or the last act of the drama so often, divorce. * * *"

# HIDDEN FROM HISTORY

## CARDINAL GIBBONS MISQUOTED BY SUFFRAGISTS

In a suffrage edition of the "Boston American," issued April 17, 1915, Cardinal Gibbons was quoted by the suffragists as having said in an interview that he thought Woman Suffrage inevitable.

Mrs. Robert Garrett, of Baltimore, wrote the Cardinal, inquiring about the alleged interview, and has received the following reply:

"Dear Mrs. Garrett:

"About the quotation attributed to Cardinal Gibbons, that suffrage for women must come, his eminence says he has no recollection of having said those words. FURTHER, THAT HE HAS ALWAYS HOPED THAT THE GOOD SENSE OF AMERICAN WOMEN WOULD PREVENT SUCH A CALAMITY."

(Signed) Louis O'Donovan, Sec'y.
May 7, 1915.

## THE VOICE OF COMMON SENSE

"The indirect influence of women which in a well-ordered state makes for the moral order, would suffer severe injury by political equality. The opposition expressed by many women to the introduction of woman suffrage as, for instance, the New York Association Opposed to Woman Suffrage, should be regarded by Catholics, as at least the voice of common sense."—(From the Catholic Encyclopaedia, Vol. 15, p. 694, published under the imprimatur of Archbishop, later Cardinal, Farley of New York.)

## CARDINAL O'CONNELL'S MESSAGE TO CATHOLIC WOMEN

### SCORES GOSPEL OF "UNSEXED"

Cardinal O'Connell Says "New Woman" Is Not a Real Woman at All

Sends Message to Catholic League

Cardinal O'Connell in a message sent to the League of Catholic Women at the opening of their three days' bazaar at Symphony Hall yesterday, declared that: "The Christian woman, just because she is profoundly responsive to Christian law and Christian ideals, better than all others meets the most modern needs and duties of life —as a woman.

"The tendency of non-Christian and anti-Christian modern movements is to destroy these ideals, to override them, to defy them; and so we hear much of the new woman—who is not a real woman at all."

### CARDINAL'S MESSAGE.

The Cardinal's message states that: "The League of Catholic Women represents an organized movement for unity among all women of the faith, with the purpose of conserving true Christian ideals and of defending them against attacks now so persistently launched by the neo-pagan influences of our day." The message continues:

"Christ came to teach us the laws of life. They are as clear, as efficacious, as applicable now as they were twenty centuries ago. As truth is ever the same, the Christian ideals never change. They are as vital and as satisfying now as ever before.

"Environment changes, but human nature remains fundamentally the same, so does the family, so does society, so does womanhood. This, however, does not mean unadaptability under certain definite conditions and restrictions.

"The consequences of this gospel of the unsexed, are already visible around us. They affect the family, marriage, progeny, and mostly woman herself.

"Woman has her place, her capabilities, her aspirations, her duties. None of these are new. They are founded on the very nature of woman and her place in the plan of life, and are sanctified and confirmed by Christian law and custom and ideals.

### SACRED DUTY OF WOMAN.

"It is the sacred duty of woman to see that her inheritance is not squandered, her dignity not debased, her value not dissipated.

"That is what precisely is meant by this league, and that is what, by God's help, our league sets itself to achieve. Nothing that is really of womanhood is alien to it. No good work is outside its scope . . ."—(*Boston Herald*, April 28, 1920.)

### ISSUED BY

## NATIONAL ASSOCIATION OPPOSED TO WOMAN SUFFRAGE

Headquarters, 268 Madison Avenue, New York, N. Y.
Branch Office, 726 14th St., N. W., Washington, D. C.

March 11th, 1920

# HIDDEN FROM HISTORY

*Reprint from New York World, March 9, 1920*

## "SINISTER FEMINISM" IS DUE TO THE ABDICATION OF MAN, SAYS CARDINAL O'CONNELL.

Women Are Becoming Masculine and Men Effeminate, and This Is Disorder, He Declares—Father of a Family Should Not Let His Girls Run Rampant—Warns Against Tendency to "Perpetual Strikes."

*Reprint from New York World, March 9, 1920*

# "SINISTER FEMINISM" IS DUE TO THE ABDICATION OF MAN, SAYS CARDINAL O'CONNELL.

### Women Are Becoming Masculine and Men Effeminate, and This Is Disorder, He Declares—Father of a Family Should Not Let His Girls Run Rampant—Warns Against Tendency to "Perpetual Strikes."

(Special to The World.)

BOSTON, March 8. — Cardinal O'Connell made a vigorous protest against what he termed "sinister feminism" at the closing exercises of the mission for men in the Holy Cross Cathedral yesterday. He urged men to exert their rightful authority in the home against certain tendencies of the times, and also spoke of the prevailing unrest and warned against the tendency toward "perpetual strikes." Seventeen hundred men heard him.

"The one thing that will preserve proper order in your house is the Christian authority of the Christian father of a family," says the Cardinal. "There is no doubt that one of the main causes of this sinister feminism, of which we read so much and see quite enough, is what would appear to be a growing weakness on the part of the manhood of the Nation.

"The very fact that women are so often clamoring to take all power and authority into their hands is certainly no compliment to the manhood of the Nation. And really we must admit that there are signs of decadence or lack of proper authority and self-respect in fathers of families.

"After all, women, the wife and the children, expect a father to have and to exercise the rightful authority due to his position. But if he abdicates that position, if he has no love for his home, if he is away from it whenever he can be, if he takes no interest in the children, except merely to give enough money to support them—well, no one can be surprised if, little by little, women learn to do without the authority of man and begin to usurp a great deal of it themselves.

"That leads to a false feminism which certainly, unless it is curbed in time, will have disastrous results for humanity, because it is unnatural. I am not talking now about the proper sphere of woman. I am talking of the lack of authority in the household and the Nation on the part of man which is giving an undue prominence to the feminine side.

"The women are becoming masculine, if you please, and the men are becoming effeminate. This is disorder. The remedy is the proper exercise of authority by man in his own place, and especially as the father of a family. Not domination, not tyranny, but rightful, legitimate, kindly authority.

"How can he look on and see his children, especially the girls, running rampant, without any consideration for the modesty, the beautiful womanly virtues, which they ought to inculcate in their manners, in their habits of life? You say they won't listen to you, but there must be something wrong in you if they do not listen to your authority.

"Now, my dear, good Catholic men, you have no right to abdicate the position you occupy by the grace of God as the Christian head of the house. You must be kind, of course, and considerate, but there must be order, and the man, by every natural and divine right, is the head of the family. That headship means that he ought to look after the morals of the whole family."

# CHICAGO CHRONICLE, JULY 10, 1896.

## OPPOSE WOMAN SUFFRAGE.

### MRS. CRANNELL ENDORSED.

Mrs. W. Winslow Crannell, who spoke against the granting of suffrage to women before the committee on resolutions, was criticised by her opponents for saying she spoke for twelve different States. Since then she has received the following letters:

Cleveland, O.—I heard recently that your Anti-suffrage association is to be represented at the democratic convention in Chicago, and I should like to say that my name may be mentioned as one in sympathy with your movement. As far as I know the women of my State, many of them at least, would also be glad to be known on your side.

MARY H. POMEROY.

From Oakland, Cal., comes the following:

I know there are a great many women, and it seems to me the best class, opposed to political equality, but the Misses Anthony and Shaw have been here a long time and are making a terrible fight for it here. * * * There is an anti-suffrage league in San Francisco. * * * I wish you would include the protest of many California women in your request to the democratic convention. * * * Yours with success and gratitude for the preservation of our woman's birthright.

EMMA C. PERCY.

The following was received from Colorado:

Thank God that there is one woman in this land brave enough to enter her voice in protest against this great wrong sought to be enforced upon woman. I live in Colorado, where I know what woman suffrage means. To-day, if the question arose, it would be defeated by an overwhelming majority, but they tell us we can do nothing to relieve ourselves of this added burden and responsibility. Cannot you suggest a means of escape from this slavery, and show us how to regain our liberty, our freedom? We would be only too glad to follow so brave a leader as you, but to be known would mean the political ostracism of every member of one's household, and so, while we hope you will enter a protest in the name of many thousand of women of Colorado, for the sake of their sisters in other States, I am too much a coward to have my name used. You, with your brave heart, will scorn me from this, but I am sure you will realize what it would mean to me, a woman who finds all her pleasures in her home and family, and who has never even dared to pray in public, to place myself in a position where my name would be tossed from paper to paper, as well as from mouth to mouth, in derision, and to be attacked, as I would be, by the women suffragists. May the God who made us women keep you well and strong to battle for us.

Many telegrams were received by Mrs. Crannell, among them the following:

"The loyal women of Connecticut thank and congratulate our Portia."

"Always true as steel. That is your record of old, and Delaware women thank you."

"You should have for your motto: 'Veni, Vidi, Vici.' Accept the New Jersey women's thanks."

A message from Albany, N. Y., tenders thanks for the work done.

# THE CONSENT OF THE GOVERNED [1]

MUNROE SMITH

Professor of Jurisprudence, Columbia University

THE question whether women shall vote appears to me to be a question of social and political expediency. It is not, I think, to be settled by the citation of any such aphorism as that which bases the powers of government on the consent of the governed. Political aphorisms, even when they are formulated in the interest of progress, are always based upon preceding developments. Like legal maxims, they are always broader than the range of cases they were first framed to cover, and their application to new and different cases is always disputable. To say that they have come to represent social and political " ideals " is to beg the question whether their application should be extended.

I

" The consent of the governed " has meant, historically, the consent of those who were actually or potentially fighting units. Voting was invented, in early communities, to find out whether the rank and file of fighting men would or would not support action proposed by their leaders. That was the whole significance of the weapon-clash in the early Teutonic assembly and also of the more elaborate voting by tablets in the assemblies of the ancient Mediterranean city-states. Whether the modern referendum means anything more is at least a debatable question.

These early assemblies consisted of the active army and the veterans. As soon as a young man was armed he became a voter. In the Teutonic assembly and in the earliest Roman assembly the voters appeared with arms in their hands. In the Roman assembly they voted by companies of horse and foot. In a later organization of the Roman assembly, the

[1] Discussion of woman suffrage at the meeting of the Academy of Political Science, November 20, 1914.

citizens voted by local districts or wards; but so long as all free Romans were held to military duty, they all voted. When the Roman armies became mercenary forces, their commander and paymaster became lord of the Roman world and voting disappeared.

In the medieval and modern history of Europe, the proportion of the population whose consent must be obtained in the operation of government has broadened or narrowed with the right and duty of exercising armed force to protect the frontier, to maintain internal peace, and to secure submission to the law. In the eighth and ninth centuries of the Christian era, when the tribal armies of Western Europe, fighting on foot, were unable to resist the Moorish horsemen and it became necessary to meet this light cavalry with a superior heavy cavalry, knight service became the basis of political power. Those who furnished bodies of knights were the only persons whose consent was important. When at a later period a new and efficient infantry was developed, first in the shape of pikemen, and then, after the invention of gunpowder, in the shape of musketeers, the cities which could equip such forces began to count politically; and when, as in many of the cities, the duty of defending the walls as well as that of maintaining the internal peace was imposed upon all able-bodied male citizens, democratic government reappeared. When, at the close of the middle ages, some of the kings and princes, by taking money in lieu of feudal services and by developing other fiscal rights of the crown, were able to hire and equip bodies of soldiers which replaced the feudal and city troops, they were in a position to dispense with the express consent of any of their subjects. In the nineteenth century, when the hired armies were replaced, first by volunteer armies, then by drafted armies, and finally by armies based on universal military training, the manhood suffrage of the early tribe reappeared in Western and Central Europe.

In England the line of political development was somewhat different. Here the monarchy was never able to break the power of the feudal aristocracy so completely as on the continent; and the great landed estates, although freed from feudal

(83)

duties, retained the power they had formerly earned by service. Naturally, under these circumstances, the theory developed that the parliamentary franchise existed to protect property; it was even asserted that the state was based on property; and the gradual widening of the suffrage in the nineteenth century was based on the claim of other economic interests to their share of political power. These English theories we inherited or borrowed, and they were largely invoked in the early part of the last century by those who supported property qualifications and opposed the demand for universal manhood suffrage in the United States.

To-day, however, alike in England and in the United States, suffrage may be regarded as resting, in principle, on the historic basis of armed service that may be exacted; not alone upon the duty of service in foreign or civil war, but also on the duty to maintain the peace and to aid in the enforcement of the law. Under our national and state laws every male citizen within certain age limits may be called upon for such service. This duty is a more defensible basis of suffrage than the protection-of-interest theory. This latter theory assumes that, in some mysterious way, general social interests will be realized through the clash of conflicting class interests. It seems certain, on the contrary, that social interests are effectively secured only through the subordination of class interests to the general good.

## II

It must be conceded that the antiquity of any social or political arrangement affords no conclusive proof of its continued necessity. In course of time all such arrangements are sure to be superseded or modified. At any given time, however, there is at least a presumption in favor of the existing system. As far as we can judge from history, social progress demands, at any given time, the modification of only a relatively small part of the entire social order. Even in such periods as the late Roman Empire and the old régime in France, the great majority of the existing institutions, laws and customs were well adapted to contemporary conditions; and what was swept

(84)

away in the Teutonic conquests of the fifth and sixth centuries and in the revolutions of the eighteenth and nineteenth centuries was far less important than what persisted. The perennial belief of the radical reformer that the greater part of the social order needs to be changed, and that there is a presumption against any existing institution in proportion to its antiquity, springs from the concentration of his attention upon the things which he dislikes. This very concentration causes him to overlook the far more numerous things with which even he is content.

The presumption in favor of an ancient institution is nevertheless one that may be overthrown by evidence; and it is always legitimate to inquire whether it is not now antiquated. The historical argument in favor of manhood suffrage is commonly met by the assertion that conditions have changed. In the middle of the last century it was claimed that human society had passed from the militant to the industrial type of organization. During the last fifty years, however, the civilized portion of the world has been more militant than during the preceding fifty years. At present it is claimed, more vaguely, that we have at least emerged from the period when the state should be viewed as the organized force of the community and law should be regarded as an enforceable system of order.

This claim rests, unfortunately, rather on aspirations than on facts. There is really no evidence that the nature of the state or that of law has materially changed. I do not assert that the state has ever been based on force alone. On the contrary, I emphatically repudiate any such theory. Even in the earliest stages of political organization, economic interests and what we may fairly call ethical forces have played an important part. It is nevertheless true that until the physical force of the community is brought under central control there is no state; and whenever this central control ceases to exist the state is in abeyance. That is to-day the condition of Mexico. When in November, 1914, President Gutierrez announced that the agreement between the leaders of the warring factions at Aguas Calientes had re-established " the government of the

(85)

people," he of course meant government by the consent of those people whose consent counted; and we must admit that, if the agreement had been generally and loyally observed, it would have gone far to re-establish the Mexican state.

It is still true, moreover, that force is the characteristic and proper implement of the state—the means by which the state realizes its purposes. That the state requires this implement in its international relations, and will probably require it for an indefinite future period, need hardly be argued to-day. Visions of universal peace appear only after long periods of peace. And it is quite clear, as Mr. Roosevelt has recently said, that if international war is ever to disappear, it will be suppressed through international federation and the development of an efficient international police. Even in the world state armed force will be required.

In the internal operation of government, also, force is still the characteristic and proper tool of the state. So far from being true of early forms of state alone, this becomes increasingly true in proportion as society grows more civilized and the state attains its highest development. An imperfectly developed state permits physical coercion by groups and associations within its territory. The fully developed state restricts the use of physical force, except by individuals in self-defense, to its official agencies: it asserts complete monopoly of force.

In our conception of law, again, the potential support of physical force cannot be disregarded. I do not assert that the substance of legal rules has at any period been determined by physical force; might has never made right. I maintain, however, that the rule that cannot be supported by physical force is not law, and is not any more like law to-day than in the earliest stages of legal development. A proposal to make a law involves two considerations: first, is the proposed rule desirable? second, shall it be supported by physical force? The first question is usually determined before voting begins. It is settled by all those complex processes through which public opinion is formed. In the formation of public opinion women have always played an important part. It is only in answering the second question that they have no voice.

From these points of view, it seems wholly reasonable that the determination of state policy and the making of law, directly or through chosen representatives, should be left to that part of the community which may be called upon to support the policy or to enforce the law with arms. Broadly—and all social arrangements are necessarily made on broad lines—this means that such matters should be left to the adult males.

### III

So long as force plays any part in the determination of policy, in the operation of government and in the maintenance of the legal order, there is possible and even probable danger in the inclusion of women in the electorate. We are accustomed to think that when we have voted, the defeated party must necessarily accept the result. The earliest method of counting votes was probably by division. The division was probably, at the outset, a line-up for a fight, and the submission of the shorter to the longer line was due to ocular demonstration that resistance would be hopeless. To-day we come nearest to such a demonstration when we hold a referendum, submitting a proposal to the direct vote of a masculine electorate. But under the representative system it is not always certain that the victorious party is really a majority. And when, as sometimes happens, the struggle is one in which important sectional or class interests are at stake and party feeling rises to passion, if the defeated party does not believe that the victorious party really possesses superior physical force, there is serious risk that it will resort to the wager of battle. In our own country, in 1860, Lincoln had a majority in the electoral college. The Southerners knew, however, that he was a minority president, and they declined to accept the result. In England, in 1913, an Irish home-rule bill was passed by a considerable parliamentary majority. The men of Ulster and the Unionists asserted that this majority in Parliament did not represent the majority of the men in Great Britain. A referendum was suggested to test the point, but it proved impossible to carry such a proposal through Parliament. James Russell Lowell once said that voting was counting heads in place of breaking them. Here was a case where the count could not be made and the breaking was imminent. It seems highly probable that civil war was averted only by the outbreak of the European war.

We are accustomed to think, again, that laws and judgments of courts are practically self-executing. This impression is in part due to the fact that the more perfect our administrative machinery becomes, and the more certain it is that force will be used if it be needed, the less often is it necessary to use force. But when class interests are involved and class feeling runs high, obedience to the law is by no means assured. In some of our states the struggle between employers and employed is so keen as to amount to continuous latent war; and not infrequently it comes to open war. A similar situation exists in some of our states in consequence of race hostility.

When the results of an election are peacefully accepted by the defeated party, and when laws and judgments appear to be self-executing, it seems highly probable that acquiescence still depends to some extent upon the conviction that resistance is hopeless. If now we inject into the electorate that portion of the adult population which does not represent fighting force —which was taken off the fighting line when men advanced from savagery to barbarism—what will be the effect upon the men who have been defeated in elections or who object to the enforcement of particular laws? Their disposition to acquiesce will certainly not be increased. How far it will be lessened depends on two further questions. The first of these questions is whether, in any given case, these men are likely to believe that the election was carried or the law established by the votes of women rather than by those of men. Where this is not ascertainable, they may choose to believe whatever they wish to believe. The second and more fundamental question is, how far the most civilized nations of the present day have emerged from barbarism and become wholly and sweetly reasonable. It is not until this last evolution is completed that men will always and unhesitatingly accept a vote as an expression of the social will, ceasing to ask or to care how much force there is behind the will.

(88)

# DECLARATION OF PRINCIPLES

## OF THE SOUTHERN WOMEN'S LEAGUE FOR THE REJECTION OF THE PROPOSED SUSAN B. ANTHONY AMENDMENT TO THE CONSTITUTION OF THE UNITED STATES.

1. We believe in the political principle of Local Self Government and that **State Sovereignty is essential** to the Liberty, Happiness, True Progress, and Welfare of the American People.

2. **WE ARE UNALTERABLY OPPOSED TO THE ADOPTION OF THE SUSAN B. ANTHONY AMENDMENT TO THE CONSTITUTION OF THE UNITED STATES,** which Amendment will force the unrestricted ballot upon unwilling majorities in Southern States, and will place the control of the electorate outside the Sovereign State.

3. We deny the Justice of the Compulsory Regulation of the Electorate of our States by a **combination** of other States, who have no sympathetic understanding of our peculiar Social and Racial problems.

4. We oppose any measure that threatens the continuation of **Anglo-Saxon** domination of Social and Political affairs in each and evey State of the Union without strife and bloodshed which would inevitably follow an attempt to overthow it.

5. We oppose **SOCIALISM, BOLESHVISM, RADICALISM** and all the Social disorders that are now disturbing the world and are rapidly encroaching upon our own Republic, and believe that these disorders will be aided and multiplied and more effectually forced upon the Conservative States such as we represent, through the adoption of the Susan B. Anthony Amendment.

6. We declare that the REJECTION of the Susan B. Anthony Amendment to the Constitution of the United States, in **NO** way affects the rights of the several individual States, **TO SO AMEND THEIR CONSTITUTIONS,** as to enfranchise the women of those States, where a **majority** so elect; and to throw safeguards and limitations upon electoral qualifications as local conditions demand.

7. We believe that in its present form, we live under the fairest and most liberal Government in the world, and desire to see it perpetuated in order that generations coming after us may enjoy the same Liberty in the Pursuit of Happiness we have enjoyed; and to that end we pledge our most earnest and continued efforts in behalf of the **Rejection of the Susan B. Anthony Amendment to the Constitution of the United States,** and call upon **all true Americans** to join us in this fight.

# HIDDEN FROM HISTORY

## DEFEAT OF WOMAN'S SUFFRAGE IN STATE OF WASHINGTON.

From Portland "Oregonian," of 12th Nov., 1898.

The woman suffrage amendment was buried in the same grave with the single-tax proposition by the voters of Washington on Tuesday. Political suffrage for woman is a slowly dying cause, and it is dying because it is without excuse for further existence. The real wrongs of women which existed when Lucy Stone began her agitation in 1847 have mostly been redressed by legislation. To-day every political principle advocated at the outset is enjoyed by women, save full suffrage, and every legal right sought by Lucy Stone has been granted to women. They are even treated with partiality by the laws, compared with men. Their individuality is not lost in marriage, as it was when Mrs. Stanton, who is now over 80, was a young girl. Every avenue of activity is open to them : they are as free as men to earn their living in any lawful way they please. The conjugal, parental and property rights of women have been recognized and established by the political action of men without the aid of woman suffrage, simply because the vast mass of influential women and public opinion thought that the best way. The present situation is totally different from that of forty years ago, when "woman's rights" was a genuine cause, because there were genuine woman's wrongs to be righted and legal disabilities to be removed. The agitation and the organized effort begun more than fifty years ago had much to do with the recognition and redress of these wrongs, legal disabilities and inequalities; but with the accomplishment of these reforms the cause of woman suffrage has made no real progress. Its modern revival in Kansas, Colorado and Idaho was but the out-growth of the temporary socialistic spirit that prevails in those States.

The lack of the ballot surely robs a woman of no rights of life, liberty or property. The reason why woman suffrage is not favored by the mass of women or the mass of men is because it is a barren ideality. It rights no wrongs, it corrects no disability. Women to-day have without the ballot all the civil and social rights exercised by men. As a natural right, suffrage belongs to neither man nor woman, for the ballot is only the child of an artificial social order to be granted or withheld as a matter of social and political expediency. The mere wish of a few women to vote is of no more consequence to the State than the mere wish of a few women to enlist in the regular army. That Moll Pitcher served her wounded husband's gun at Monmouth is not an argument for the expediency of enlisting women as artillerymen.

# HIDDEN FROM HISTORY

## Diagram of Official New York Vote, Proving Woman Suffrage Carried by N.Y. City Converts to Socialism and that Majority of Democrats and Republicans, in City & State, Voted Against Suffrage

> *"Every Socialist is a Suffragist"*
> —OFFICIAL SOCIALIST PARTY BANNER BORNE IN WOMAN SUFFRAGE PARADES.

> *"1,000,000 Socialists Vote and Work for Woman Suffrage"*
> —OFFICIAL SOCIALIST PARTY BANNER USED IN SUFFRAGE PARADES AND CONVENTIONS OF NATIONAL AMERICAN WOMAN SUFFRAGE ASSOCIATION.

> *"We Welcome Every Socialist Vote"*
> —DR. ANNA HOWARD SHAW, HONORARY PRESIDENT NATIONAL AMERICAN WOMAN SUFFRAGE ASSOCIATION.

SCALE, 1/25 INCH = 1,000

### New York City (Five Boroughs: Manhattan, Brooklyn, Bronx, Queens and Richmond)

**1915** — VOTE FOR WOMAN SUFFRAGE BY DEMOCRATS AND REPUBLICANS — 206,311
MANHATTAN 76,873 | BROOKLYN 77,182 | BRONX 27,312 | QUEENS 19,040 | Rich. 6,904
BY SOCIALISTS — 31,787: M. 12,013 | BN. 10,220 | BX. 6,995 | Queens 2,355 | Richmond 204
TOTAL 238,098
SOCIALIST GAIN (CONVERTS) — 113,545
SUFFRAGE GAIN (CONVERTS) — 115,568

**1917** — VOTE FOR WOMAN SUFFRAGE BY DEMOCRATS AND REPUBLICANS — 208,334
MANHATTAN 78,236 | BROOKLYN 80,721 | BRONX 22,286 | QUEENS 20,648 | Rich. 6,443
BY SOCIALISTS — 145,332 — 41%
MANHATTAN 51,176 — 40% | BROOKLYN 49,880 — 38% | BRONX 30,374 — 58% | QN 13,477 — 39% | Richmond 1,425 — 16%
TOTAL 353,666
SUFFRAGE MAJORITY — 103,863

**1917** — VOTE AGAINST WOMAN SUFFRAGE BY DEMOCRATS AND REPUBLICANS — 249,803
MANHATTAN 89,124 | BROOKLYN 92,315 | BRONX 36,346 | QUEENS 26,794 | Rich. 5,224
TOTAL 249,803

NOTE: In 1915, the Anti-Suffragists Won New York City by 82,755 Majority and the State by 194,984 Majority. In 1917, the Anti-Suffragists won the State Down to the City Line.

SCALE, 1/50 INCH = 1,000

### New York State (Including New York City as Indicated)

**1915** — VOTE FOR WOMAN SUFFRAGE BY DEMOCRATS AND REPUBLICANS — 507,404
NEW YORK CITY — 206,311 | "UP STATE" — 301,093
By Socialists: 46,944 — State 15,157 | N.Y.C. 31,787
TOTAL 553,348
SOCIALIST GAIN — 149,293
SUFFRAGE GAIN — 149,781

**1917** — VOTE FOR WOMAN SUFFRAGE BY DEMOCRATS AND REPUBLICANS — 507,892
NEW YORK CITY — 208,334 | "UP STATE" — 299,558
BY SOCIALISTS — 195,237 — 28%
NEW YORK CITY — 145,332 | "UP STATE" — 49,905
TOTAL 703,129
Anti-Suffrage Majority of Democrats and Repubs. — 92,884 — 6 to 5
SUFFRAGE MAJORITY — 102,353

**1917** — VOTE AGAINST WOMAN SUFFRAGE BY DEMOCRATS AND REPUBLICANS — 600,776
NEW YORK CITY — 249,803 | "UP STATE" — 350,973
TOTAL 600,776

---

> "Socialism and suffrage, inseparable companions in revolutionary political thought and action, have triumphed in the election in New York City and state."
> —The New York Call, Official Socialist Organ.

> "We have secured the vote to the women of the State. Now that the returns, the subject has ceased to be one of speculation and has become a matter of mathematical demonstration. The 150,000 votes which we gained in the State of New York turned the defeat of two years ago into a decisive victory this year, and these votes have come in decisive numbers and nowhere from precisely the same districts which have given us the heaviest socialist pluralities." —Morris Hillquit, Socialist Candidate for Mayor of N.Y. City.

> "Since the election of Mayor in 1913, the socialist vote in New York has increased by 10,000. It is, therefore, clear that the victory for suffrage in this election is largely due to the socialist vote, since this vote in New York City alone would have been enough to swing the majority to the side of suffrage."
> —The Suffragist, Official Organ of National Woman's Party.

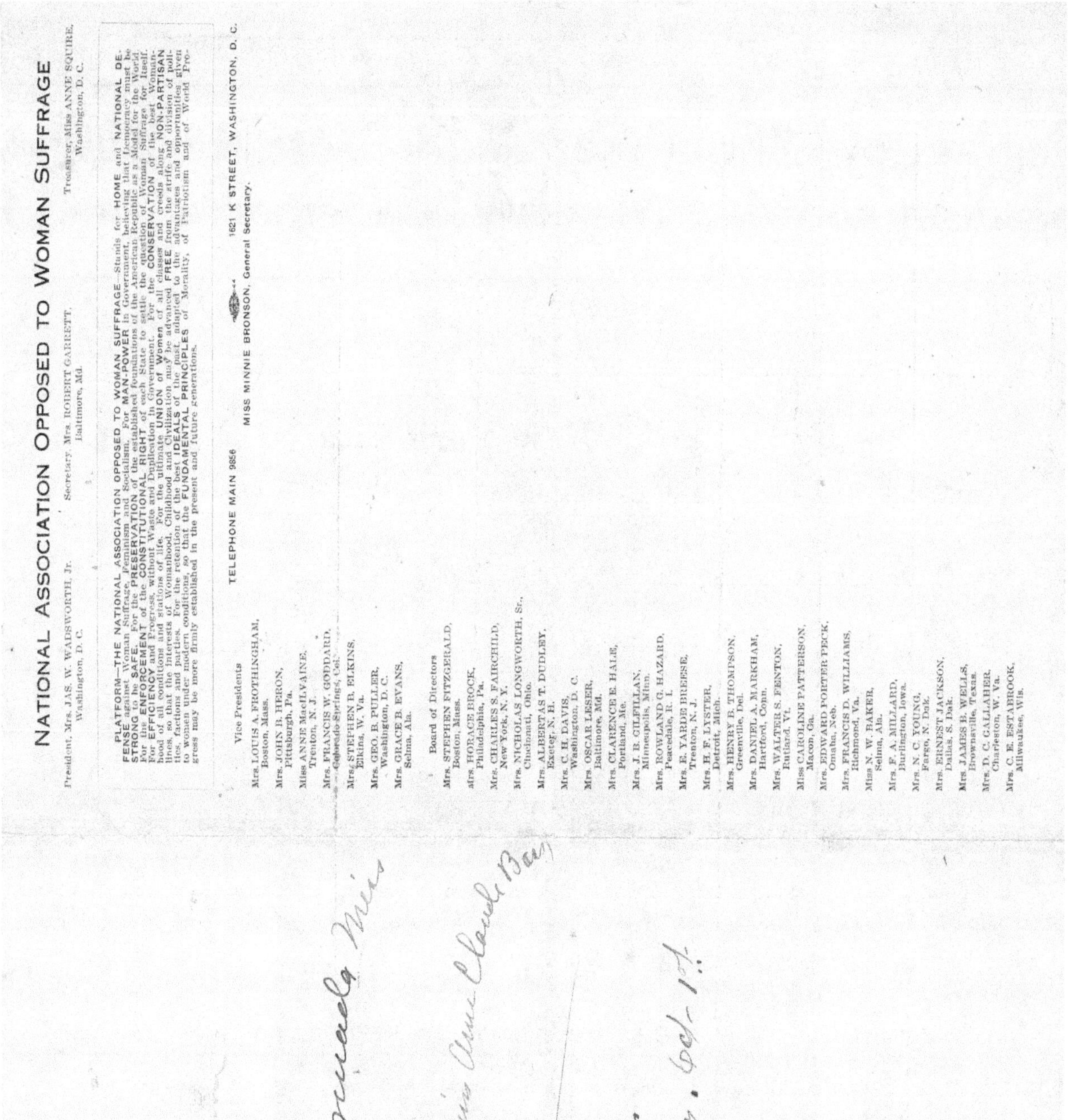

## NATIONAL ASSOCIATION OPPOSED TO WOMAN SUFFRAGE

President, Mrs. JAS. W. WADSWORTH, Jr., Washington, D.C.
Secretary, Mrs. ROBERT GARRETT, Baltimore, Md.
Treasurer, Miss ANNE SQUIRE, Washington, D.C.

**PLATFORM**—THE NATIONAL ASSOCIATION OPPOSED TO WOMAN SUFFRAGE—Stands for HOME and NATIONAL DEFENSE against Woman Suffrage, Feminism and Socialism. For MAN-POWER in Government, believing that Democracy must be STRONG to be SAFE. For the PRESERVATION of the established foundations of the American Republic as a Model for the World. For ENFORCEMENT of the CONSTITUTIONAL RIGHT of each State to settle the question of Woman Suffrage for itself. For EFFICIENCY and Progress, without Waste and Duplication in Government. For the CONSERVATION of the best Womanhood of all conditions and stations of life. For the ultimate UNION of Women of all classes and creeds along NON-PARTISAN lines, so that the interests of Womanhood, Childhood and Civilization may be advanced FREE from the strife and division of political factions and parties. For the retention of the best IDEALS of the past, adapted to the advantages and opportunities given to women under modern conditions, so that the FUNDAMENTAL PRINCIPLES of Morality, of Patriotism and of World Progress may be more firmly established in the present and future generations.

TELEPHONE MAIN 9856  MISS MINNIE BRONSON, General Secretary.  1621 K STREET, WASHINGTON, D. C.

**Vice Presidents**

Mrs. LOUIS A. FROTHINGHAM, Boston, Mass.
Mrs. JOHN B. HERON, Pittsburgh, Pa.
Miss ANNIE MacILVAINE, Trenton, N. J.
Mrs. FRANCIS W. GODDARD, Colorado Springs, Col.
Mrs. STEPHEN B. ELKINS, Elkins, W. Va.
Mrs. GEO. B. PULLER, Washington, D. C.
Mrs. GRACE B. EVANS, Selma, Ala.

**Board of Directors**

Mrs. STEPHEN FITZGERALD, Boston, Mass.
Mrs. HORACE BROCK, Philadelphia, Pa.
Mrs. CHARLES S. FAIRCHILD, New York, N. Y.
Mrs. NICHOLAS LONGWORTH, Sr., Cincinnati, Ohio.
Mrs. ALBERTA S. T. DUDLEY, Exeter, N. H.
Mrs. C. H. DAVIS, Washington, D. C.
Mrs. OSCAR LESER, Baltimore, Md.
Mrs. CLARENCE E. HALE, Portland, Me.
Mrs. J. B. GILFILLAN, Minneapolis, Minn.
Mrs. ROWLAND G. HAZARD, Peacedale, R. I.
Mrs. E. YARDE BREESE, Trenton, N. J.
Mrs. H. F. LYSTER, Detroit, Mich.
Mrs. HENRY B. THOMPSON, Greenville, Del.
Mrs. DANIEL A. MARKHAM, Hartford, Conn.
Mrs. WALTER S. FENTON, Rutland, Vt.
Miss CAROLINE PATTERSON, Macon, Ga.
Mrs. EDWARD PORTER PECK, Omaha, Neb.
Mrs. FRANCIS D. WILLIAMS, Richmond, Va.
Miss N. W. BAKER, Selma, Ala.
Mrs. F. A. MILLARD, Burlington, Iowa.
Mrs. N. C. YOUNG, Fargo, N. Dak.
Mrs. ERNEST JACKSON, Dallas, S. Dak.
Mrs. JAMES B. WELLS, Brownsville, Texas.
Mrs. D. C. GALLAHER, Charleston, W. Va.
Mrs. C. E. ESTABROOK, Milwaukee, Wis.

---

*[Handwritten notes:]*

Mrs J A Taylor
521 Oates St
Chattanooga, Tenn

Judge W L McKee, Yazoo Miss

Mr. H. C. Bass (Miss Ann Claude Bass)
Brundidge, Ala.

Tell Mrs Westerfield to come to Mrs Taylor Saturday morning, Oct. 1st.

## Diagram of Official New York Vote, Proving Wo[man Suffrage is] Socialism and that Majority of Democrats and Rep[ublicans...]

> "*Every Socialist is a Suffragist*"
> —OFFICIAL SOCIALIST PARTY BANNER BORNE IN WOMAN SUFFRAGE PARADES.

> "*1,000,000 Socialists Vote and W[ork for Suffrage]*"
> —OFFICIAL SOCIALIST PARTY BANNER U[SED AT] CONVENTIONS OF NATIONAL AMERICAN [...]

### New York City (Five Boroughs: Manhat[tan, Brooklyn, Bronx, Queens, Richmond])

**1915** — VOTE FOR WOMAN SUFFRAGE BY DEMOCRATS AND REPUBLICANS—206,311
- MANHATTAN—76,873
- BROOKLYN—77,182
- BRONX—27,3[..]

**1917** — VOTE FOR WOMAN SUFFRAGE BY DEMOCRATS AND REPUBLICANS—208,334
- MANHATTAN—78,236
- BROOKLYN—80,721
- BRONX—22,286

**1917** — VOTE AGAINST WOMAN SUFFRAGE BY DEMOCRATS AND REPUBLICANS—249,803
- MANHATTAN—89,124
- BROOKLYN—92,315

NOTE: In 1915, the Anti-Suffragists Won New York City by 82,755 Majority and the St[ate...]

### New York State (Including New York C[ity])

**1915** — VOTE FOR WOMAN SUFFRAGE BY DEMOCRATS AND REPUBLICANS—507,404
- "UP STATE"—301,093

**1917** — VOTE FOR WOMAN SUFFRAGE BY DEMOCRATS AND REPUBLICANS—507,892
- "UP STATE"—299,558

**1917** — VOTE AGAINST WOMAN SUFFRAGE BY DEMOCRATS AND REPUBLICANS—600,776
- "UP STATE"—350,973

> "Socialism and suffrage, inseparable companions in revolutionary political thought and action, have triumphed in the election in New York City and state."
> —The New York Call, Official Socialist Organ.

> "We have secured the vote to the women of the Sta[te...] returns, the subject has ceased to be one of speculation [...] matical demonstration. The 150,000 votes which we gain[ed turned] the defeat of two years ago into a decisive victory this [...] decisive numbers and heaviest from precisely the same [...] heaviest socialist pluralities."—Morris Hillquit, Socialist

# HIDDEN FROM HISTORY

## Woman Suffrage Carried by N. Y. City Converts to Republicans, in City & State, Voted Against Suffrage

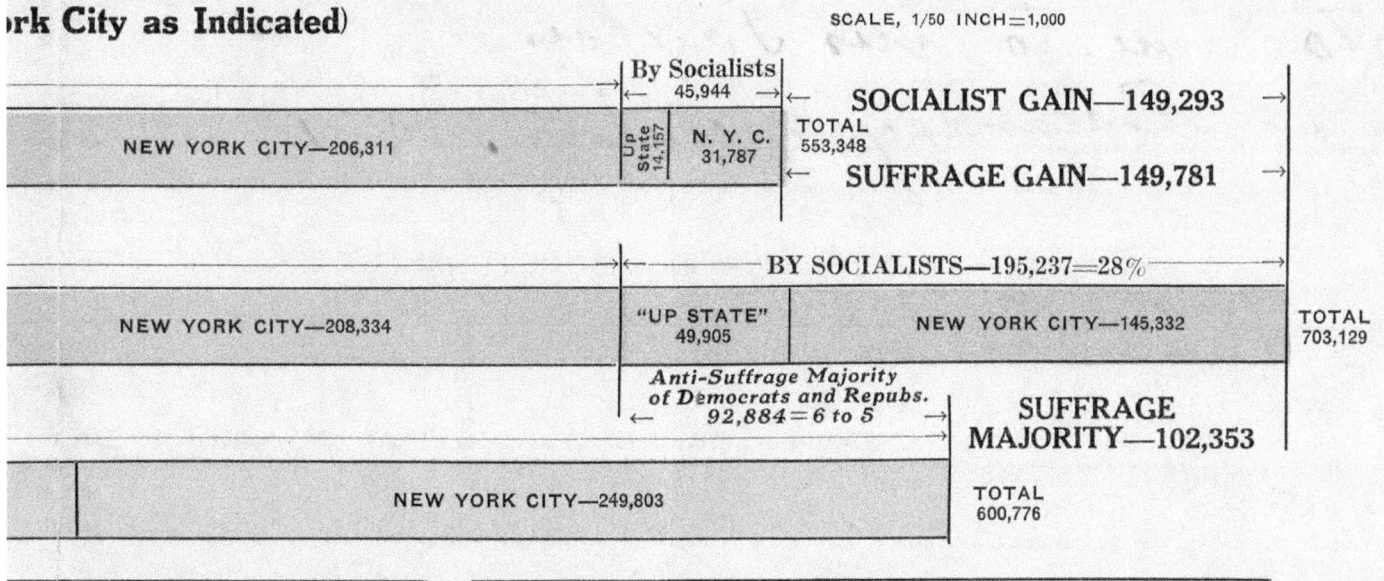

Mrs H*** ***
321 Elm St
Chattanooga, ***

Judge W C McLean  Granada Miss

Mr F.C. Bass (Miss Anne Claude Bass)
Brundidge, Ala.

Tell Mrs Westerfield
to come to Mrs Taylor
Saturday morning, Oct 1st

## NATIONAL ASSOCIATION OPPOSED TO WOMAN SUFFRAGE

President, Mrs. JAS. W. WADSWORTH, Jr.
Washington, D. C.

Secretary, Mrs. ROBERT GARRETT,
Baltimore, Md.

Treasurer, Miss ANNE SQUIRE,
Washington, D. C.

---

PLATFORM—THE NATIONAL ASSOCIATION OPPOSED TO WOMAN SUFFRAGE—Stands for HOME and NATIONAL DEFENSE against Woman Suffrage, Feminism and Socialism. For MAN-POWER in Government, believing that Democracy must be STRONG to be SAFE. For the PRESERVATION of the established foundations of the American Republic as a Model for the World. For the ENFORCEMENT of the CONSTITUTIONAL RIGHT of each State to settle the question of Woman Suffrage for Itself. For EFFICIENCY and Progress, without Waste and Duplication in Government. For the CONSERVATION of the best Womanhood of all conditions and stations of life. For the ultimate UNION of Women of all classes and creeds along NON-PARTISAN lines, so that the interests of Womanhood, Childhood and Civilization may be advanced FREE from the strife and division of politics, factions and parties. For the retention of the best IDEALS of the past, adapted to the advantages and opportunities given to women under modern conditions, so that the FUNDAMENTAL PRINCIPLES of Morality, of Patriotism and of World Progress may be more firmly established in the present and future generations.

---

TELEPHONE MAIN 9856

1621 K STREET, WASHINGTON, D. C.

MISS MINNIE BRONSON, General Secretary.

Vice Presidents

Mrs. LOUIS A. FROTHINGHAM,
Boston, Mass.

Mrs. JOHN B. HERON,
Pittsburgh, Pa.

Miss ANNE MacILVAINE,
Trenton, N. J.

Mrs. FRANCIS W. GODDARD,
Colorado Springs, Col.

Mrs. STEPHEN B. ELKINS,
Elkins, W. Va.

Mrs. GEO. B. PULLER,
Washington, D. C.

Mrs. GRACE B. EVANS,
Selma, Ala.

Board of Directors

Mrs. STEPHEN FITZGERALD,
Boston, Mass.

Mrs. HORACE BROCK,
Philadelphia, Pa.

Mrs. CHARLES S. FAIRCHILD,
New York, N. Y.

Mrs. NICHOLAS LONGWORTH, Sr.,
Cincinnati, Ohio.

Mrs. ALBERTAS T. DUDLEY,
Exeter, N. H.

Mrs. C. H. DAVIS,
Washington, D. C.

Mrs. OSCAR LESER,
Baltimore, Md.

Mrs. CLARENCE E. HALE,
Portland, Me.

Mrs. J. B. GILFILLAN,
Minneapolis, Minn.

Mrs. ROWLAND G. HAZARD,
Peacedale, R. I.

Mrs. E. YARDE BREESE,
Trenton, N. J.

Mrs. H. F. LYSTER,
Detroit, Mich.

Mrs. HENRY B. THOMPSON,
Greenville, Del.

Mrs. DANIEL A. MARKHAM,
Hartford, Conn.

Mrs. WALTER S. FENTON,
Rutland, Vt.

Miss CAROLINE PATTERSON,
Macon, Ga.

Mrs. EDWARD PORTER PECK,
Omaha, Neb.

Mrs. FRANCIS D. WILLIAMS,
Richmond, Va.

Miss N. W. BAKER,
Selma, Ala.

Mrs. F. A. MILLARD,
Burlington, Iowa.

Mrs. N. C. YOUNG,
Fargo, N. Dak.

Mrs. ERNEST JACKSON,
Dallas, S. Dak.

Mrs. JAMES B. WELLS,
Brownsville, Texas.

Mrs. D. C. GALLAHER,
Charleston, W. Va.

Mrs. C. E. ESTABROOK,
Milwaukee, Wis.

BULLETIN No. 11

# DIGNITY OF WOMANHOOD

## ILLINOIS ASSOCIATION
OPPOSED TO WOMAN SUFFRAGE

CHICAGO

---

OFFICERS

Mrs. Caroline F. Corbin, *President*

*Vice Presidents,*

Mrs. S. M. Nickerson      Mrs. James M. Walker
Mrs. R. J. Oglesby      Mrs. T. B. Blackstone
Miss J. C. Fairfield - *Secretary and Treasurer*
1523 Dearborn Avenue

## THE DIGNITY OF WOMANHOOD

Perhaps the most insistent question before the world at the present time concerns the true worth and dignity of woman. Put concretely, it resolves itself into this: Is the old assumption of the existence of the race in two sexes, one having mainly to do with the outer world and the other with domestic life, true in its inception and evolution, or has the world hitherto been mistaken in its estimate of this duality? Are mankind and womankind,—for it seems that Nature itself has made such a distinction inevitable,—essentially different in character, and the continuance of the race by means of the two sexes a matter of capital importance. or is it only a casual incident? Are the two halves of the sexes, for all purposes of progress and aggrandizement one and the same, and the moral welfare of the race, a thing quite apart from their co-operation, or has this co-operation its own necessary intent and purpose? That is, have love and morals anything to do with each other? We used to think they had, but at the present day it seems doubtful. And over this very simple question, the whole world seems to be going crazy.

In contributing our mite to this discussion, we confess at once that we rank ourselves on the side of woman; not only the vital necessity of the world to make the most of her, but also the advisability of the masculine half of it, for its own sake and glory, to see that such contribution as she may make to the welfare of the race, shall be the best of which she is capable. If the world is to have a woman at all, and it always has had, let it, we contend, be that sort of woman who will contribute most to its welfare and happiness. And first let us ask, for what was the woman ordained? We may well say of her as Isaac Walton said of the strawberry, "Doubtless God might have made a better woman but doubtless God never did." Just as she is now, she has been in her essential nature, from the beginning. The whole original process of making her, her physical capacity, her mental constitution, her spiritual culture, seem to have been, as proclaimed at the outset, that she should be the wife of man, the mother of the race. So universally true is this that whenever we speak of feminine things, we mean womanly things. Taken at the best, she has always been called the best thing that the world affords; diverted to any lower use, mankind has always declared her to be the most mischievous thing that exists.

It therefore seems, that for the enhancement of the destiny of the race, the world needs, not so much a new and undersized kind of man, as a better woman. Not a letting down of the woman to the man's estate, but a lifting up of the man to the higher moral and spiritual ideals of woman. The question then arises: ought this to be done so far as the work of the woman is concerned by setting her to perform the work which has always been hitherto assigned to him, or by stimulating her to a higher and nobler use of those womanly powers which were given to her in the beginning. Should she improve the work of man by doing it for him, or do her own work of motherhood so much better, as to make a nobler and more useful man of him.

We contend that women in striving to make the world better by improving the laws are beginning at the wrong end of the business. It is as a child that man is put helpless in her hand, given over by nature herself for forming and education, especially in morals in its first and most helpless stages, to the woman who bore him. In the first five years of woman's work he has gained his primary lessons in obedience, in the distinction of right and wrong, in purity and the doing by others as he would have them to do by him, which is simply perfect politeness. At ten years of age, the whole decalogue should be stamped upon his forming mind, in characters never to be forgotten. Long before he has reached the age when the State declares that he should be properly qualified for voting he has been fitted, often mainly by his mother, with an education which should make of him an honest and good citizen. If he has been properly reared by well intentioned parents, it will be difficult to make of him, after that time, a selfish, vicious, evil-minded voter. The home that would produce so imperfectly educated a son as this, could hardly be expected to turn out a daughter better fitted to serve the world as a law-maker. How the world would be benefited by doubling the number of ill-trained, ill-brought up voters by turning loose the daughters as well as the sons, of these neglected homes upon our electorate, we cannot see. If the legitimate voters had been properly brought up, they would not need the help of their sisters.

Is not prevalence of loose and commercialized morals in the present generation the result, at least in part, of the selfish and aspiring nature of those women who have learned to scoff at marriage as a serious, religious rite, and have come to regard it only as a civil or social incident, who change their love mates at their pleasure, and avoid children as a nuisance, a drawback to their personal convenience or pleasure. It is well known that many, if not most of these women, and their ranks are seriously increasing, are found among those whose secret thought if not their open cry, is for "votes for women," and that their views sympathize with and are gained from a class of people who ignore the spiritual life altogether, and look upon the increase of the race if they regard it seriously at all, as a matter to be left wholly to chance, or to the carelessness of the general public, untrained as it must be under such circumstances in all spiritual welfare and conditions. That the above is not an exaggeration of the effect of neglected homes upon the generation some of whose women are now seeking for an extension of the ballot, let us cite the fact that one of the first pronounced successes of the women of California as voters was in the defeat of a prohibition bill which they voted against ostensibly "because the men wanted them to." This is a State in which they had voted for less than a year. In Colorado, where Woman Suffrage had prevailed for fifteen years, for a similar reason, all the four women sitting in the legislature of 1910-11 actually voted for a most vile race-track gambling bill, by their votes and example greatly aiding its passage by the legislature. The folly, not to say the wickedness of their action was fortunately retrieved by the prompt veto of Gov. Shafroth—a "mere man," by the way—who administered a scathing rebuke to these women in his veto message, saying that "if this bill became a law, the finger of scorn and ridicule would ever after be pointed at the influence of women's franchise in State affairs." (See the Boston Remonstrance, January, 1912.)

But let us not be discouraged, even when so distinguished a socialist and suffragist as Prof. Charles Zueblin, declares, as he did in a recently published address in Philadelphia, that "no woman can stay at home and be a good mother. The old-fashioned mother is not only out of place in the world today, she is immoral." To which very advanced theory the New York World truthfully replies:

"The old-fashioned mother did leave her fireside, at least long enough to cultivate her relatives and friends, do shopping, attend church, work in a sewing or missionary society, and perform in a real, direct and businesslike way, the neighborly tasks which sociologists perform less effectively in the settlements now. But her first care was for her children, and well she looked after them."

And well do her children look after her! The women who in this generation have been leaders in the home tasks of studying the welfare of children outside their home and deserted by parents, male or female who have given up their personal tasks and gone out into the world after the vain lure of freedom and emancipation, are the direct descendents of those early old-fashioned mothers who learned so well the lesson of child necessities in their own homes a generation ago.

It is not easy to make them believe in the socialistic idea put forward by Karl Marx and his associates, who were the leaders of Socialists in their time, and among the first and strongest Woman Suffragists known to history. These men advocated that love, that is, the relation of the sexes, is merely a sensual matter having no spiritual duties, and that no sexual relation should last longer than this merely sensual attraction lasts. The fate of the two daughters of Karl Marx, both radical followers of their father and his party, should prove a sufficient answer to the theory. That of Eleanor Marx is related by one who knew her story well, in a publication of this Association. The fate of the other was settled in a brief paragraph which went the rounds of the newspapers at the time of its occurrence.

Paul La Fargue and his so-called wife Laura, daughter of Karl Marx, committed suicide on November 26th, 1911. La Fargue was for many years one of the most active of the revolutionary Socialists of France. His last words were, "Long live Communism; long live Socialism." In a letter to his nephew he added this information, that the double suicide was caused by the fact that he felt old age coming on and did not care to meet its loneliness and trials. Such is the effect in two conspicuous instances of the hopeless and godless philosophy preached by Socialism; a theory always accompanied with the doctrine of Woman Suffrage and the impersonal care and responsibility for children.

Chicago, March, 1912.

# Do not want the Ballot.

A Correspondent Who is Opposed to Making Them Voters.

*To the Editor of the New York Tribune:*

One of the arguments of the anti-suffragist is that if women be allowed to vote, the corrupt or purchasable vote of women — which even a suffrage fanatic would not be so unwise as to imply would not exist—would be used as the purchasable male vote is now used—to further selfish ends and promote unwise and corrupt legislation.

This is often meet by the statement that the women in the country districts will overbalance any preponderance of ignorant and vicious votes that may obtain in our city wards. The fallacy of this argument shows plainly upon the face of it. If the male vote of the country can not counteract or overwhelm the corrupt male vote of the cities, how will the condition of things be bettered by doubling, not only the vote of the country, but that of the city?

But what will the ballot mean to the women in the country? Nothing at all, except physical discomfort. In the first place, it will necessitate their registering, on one of two days, at the place of registry, which, in many instances, will be at least five miles from their homes. The variation of weather, which to-day is one of the elements of political uncertainty, will be a strong factor in the polling of the female ballot, particularly in the country.

If the day of registration be fair, it is just possible that husband, wife, sons and daughters, with the "hired help," male and female, and the baby, and the small children, who cannot be left at home alone, will drive to the village tavern, where the registration is usually held, and register; and that, on the coming "election day," they will all be bundled together again in the farmer's wagon and be driven to the same tavern to cast their ballots.

But what will they do if it rains, or snows, or the baby is ill, or one of the members of the family is an invalid? Will the men drive to the polls and back, and then send the women to register, and again to vote? And what will those women do whose fathers or husbands have no horses, and there are many of those in the little villages in country towns? Even the men often have to beg rides to and from the polling place.

But for the sake of the argument, suppose all the women in the country register and vote, what will be the result? After having talked with scores of country women on the subject, I am willing to affirm that each woman would vote as her father or husband voted, and that the result obtained would be only a double number of Democratic and a double number of Republican votes cast, and these would be expected to offset a doubled ignorant and corrupt vote in the city!

Would not the condition of things to-day obtain in greater force? The intelligent women of the country who have not been bitten by the tarantula of Unrest do not want the ballot, and would not use it if they had it; and this assertion I make advisedly and upon authority.

ALBANY, *March 22, 1896*.                                       E. S. C.

## DO WE WANT IT IN MASSACHUSETTS?

JAMES T. GARDINER, an eminent scientific and business man, says in regard to what he has observed in his constant visits to Kansas as to the results of woman suffrage :—

"The first year or two, women took little interest in municipal elections. Then one party put up a man of questionable reputation as mayor, the other party nominated a man of spotless character. Soon the latter's friends found that the other party were enlisting women to their cause by sympathy and by bribes. We then saw that all would be lost if we could not arouse our wives and sisters to their duty as enfranchised women to vote for pure elections. They at first demurred, but we showed them what a disastrous effect upon the city it would be in every way should the other candidate be elected. Soon they became interested and began canvassing amongst their neighbors. Constantly they increased in enthusiasm and numbers, until finally people who had been friends and neighbors for years would not speak, and the whole history of each candidate, with that of his ancestors and followers, was discussed in every household, even before its youngest members. Women caught the fever of politics and it raged high and furiously. For over a month before election day, the whole dirty stream of politics flowed over my hearthstone, washing away all the quiet happiness and peace which had reigned there before. And, as a climax, on election day we saw our wives and daughters driving through the city, picking up women of the lowest possible class and morality, and then walking with their arm around them to the polls to see that they voted rightly. Every means of intimidation, bribery and cajolery which had been used by men was employed unhesitatingly by women on election day, and yet when the votes were counted, the result was no different than if they had remained quietly at home, without the ballot."

The election above described was in Leavenworth. After several years' experience of municipal suffrage for women in Kansas, the voters of Kansas in 1894 rejected by 34,000 majority a constitutional amendment extending full suffrage to women.

ISSUED BY MASSACHUSETTS MAN SUFFRAGE ASSOCIATION, 7A PARK ST., BOSTON.

# DO WOMEN WANT THE VOTE?

By WILLIAM M. BRAY

[Reprinted from The Atlantic Monthly for April, 1916]

**William M. Bray** ('Do Women want the Vote?'), after graduating from Northwestern University and Harvard College, engaged in the lumber business in Wisconsin. Always interested in politics, **Mr. Bray** has of recent years played an active part in his State Legislature, serving as a member of the Assembly in 1908 and subsequent years, and since 1914 representing his native city of Oshkosh in the State Senate. The significant investigation into the political desires of the women of his senatorial district is in this article set forth accurately, and the *Atlantic* has in its possession a sworn statement of the figures. Since this constituency is not untypical of a very large portion of the Middle West, the figures cited seem of importance. The discussion which rages about the question whether women want the vote is commonly subjective in its value, expressing with more emphasis than information the wishes of the several disputants. The facts given in this article seem to invite very profitable speculation.

ISSUED BY THE
MAN-SUFFRAGE ASSOCIATION OPPOSED TO
POLITICAL SUFFRAGE FOR WOMEN
52 BROADWAY
NEW YORK

# THE ATLANTIC MONTHLY

*APRIL, 1916*

## DO WOMEN WANT THE VOTE?

### BY WILLIAM M. BRAY

I

When the honest voters of his district elected him to represent them in the state senate, he had some idea of what might be expected of him. He had served in the legislature before. When he announced his candidacy and published his platform, however, he had not anticipated that woman suffrage would be an issue. The equal-suffrage advocates had been overwhelmingly defeated two years before when the suffrage question had been submitted to the voters of the state by means of a referendum. He knew that most suffragists were determined, persistent women who thoroughly believed in their cause and meant to win. He should have known that they would keep the suffrage question an issue until they did win. Had he been wiser, he would have realized that women's 'rights' were becoming more and more important politically, and were already a most vital issue. Not only in many states, but in Congress as well, suffragists were playing a most prominent part. Sooner or later practically every legislator in every state, every member of Congress, and almost every voter in the United States would be called upon to take a stand on the equal suffrage question.

Our legislator soon discovered his mistake. Nowadays a candidate for political office has no chance to remain deceived on the suffrage question. Our embryo statesman meant to do what was right. He did not like to oppose women. He had always believed that if a majority of women wanted the ballot they should have it; but he did not know that a majority of them did want it. How could he find out? Practically all women who said anything to him about suffrage wanted to vote. They told him so in no uncertain terms. Probably a majority of the voters in his district were opposed to equal suffrage, however. Two years before they had voted against suffrage very decisively. Perhaps public sentiment on the suffrage question had changed since then, but presumably there had been no change, if no evidence were brought to prove it. He saw very plainly that the suffrage problem would be a difficult one for him. What was he to do?

He did not have to be told the easiest course for him to pursue. That would be to vote on this question as a majority of his constituents had voted. But should he take the 'easiest way'? He knew that when questions of right and wrong were involved, strong men did not suppress their convictions — even to please their constituents. Perhaps he was not a strong man, but he did not want to be a weak one. He had always believed it to be the duty of a legislator to keep in close touch with his constituents, to seek the help of their advice and the benefit of their judgment, and to give their interests preference over his own. He also believed just as firmly, however, that it was a legislator's duty to realize that he was elected to make laws, not only for his own district, but for the whole state as well; and to remember too that he owed it to all for whom he must so legislate, to use his best judgment for their welfare and to be something more than a mere reflector of opinions — even of the opinions of those to whom he might owe the position which made his judgment important.

The next legislature would be asked to submit another suffrage referendum to the people. Legislators would be judged to be for, or against, equal suffrage, as they voted on this proposed referendum. Its passage would be demanded, not because there were more or better arguments in favor of equal suffrage now than there had been two years before, and not that there were any indications that the result of another popular vote would be different; but simply because suffragists wanted the vote and proposed to keep up an untiring and never-ceasing agitation in favor of what they wanted until they got it. If they could not convince the opposition, they meant to tire it out.

Without regard to the merits of equal suffrage, he could not help feeling that the legislature should not permit the state to be subjected to the annoyance and uncertainty of these proposed repeated referendums, without first being shown at least some substantial evidence to warrant the belief that public sentiment had materially changed since the previous election. The suffragists had no right to ask the coöperation of the legislature in attempts to win a suffrage victory by coercion and agitation. Surely continual agitation was not in and of itself fair argument. Suffrage should win on its merits or not at all.

Our would-be statesman had often been warned that equal suffrage would win eventually, and that therefore, as a matter of policy, it would be well for him to give it his support. He thought that that consideration should have no bearing in helping him to determine his duty, however. Certainly he could not support a cause any more conscientiously simply because he thought it would win.

While a member of the legislature before, he had known several suffrage lobbyists. They had given members a great deal of attention. He remembered their persistent ways. Some had been very emphatic in expressing their opinions. Many had been quite intolerant of any ideas entertained by those who differed with them. He knew that most suffragists were good, earnest, conscientious, public-spirited women, who wanted to vote only because of the greater opportunities for doing good that they thought the ballot would give them. He wished all of them could be more charitable toward the opinions of those who did not always agree with them.

Our law-maker had met female-suffrage advocates who could see no good in any man opposed to equal suffrage, and who apparently looked upon man as woman's natural enemy — unsympathetic to her interests, unfair to her in matters of legislation, and woefully lacking in all humanitarian instincts. Such women seemed to feel antagonistic toward men as a class, and no doubt would consider any suffrage gain a victory over men. He did not admire this type of woman very much, but he realized fully that allowances should be made for them and that he should not allow their prejudices to influence him to be unfair toward them or their cause.

His mother was a suffragist. She was not the shy, timid, modest, retiring kind either. Fortunately, however, she was one of that rarer variety who do not take even their own opinions too seriously. He was very fond of his mother and very proud of her. He knew that her ideas were generally sound and well worth listening to. She often said that her women friends needed something worth while to do more than they needed the ballot. She doubted if woman suffrage would result in better government. She did not want to vote. In her opinion, however, all mature people, without regard to sex or color, education or intelligence, taxation or property rights, or any other qualification than that of citizenship, who contributed to support government and gave up part of their personal liberty to conform to government rules and regulations, were entitled to an equal share in the management of government business. She firmly believed that, as a matter of simple justice, women should be given the ballot on an equality with men. She maintained that suffrage was a 'right' to which every woman was entitled, and that those women who wanted suffrage were justified in demanding their 'rights.' Whether or not other women wanted suffrage — or 'rights' — had no bearing on the question.

Our friend had great respect for his mother's opinions, but would have preferred not to discuss them with her. Experience had taught him that the suffrage question was an extremely difficult subject for men and women to discuss together. In all such discussions, sooner or later the relative merits of the two sexes were almost invariably brought up for debate, and disagreeable comparisons generally followed. He had learned that suffrage arguments between men and women were to be avoided, if possible.

II

But, try as hard as he might, our well-meaning state senator could not always avoid suffrage arguments with women. Believing as he did that women should not have the ballot until a majority of them wanted it, the question that interested him particularly was whether or not most women really did want it. He found that very few equal suffrage advocates were interested in this question, however. In his discussions with them, they generally argued that suffragists should be given the ballot even if most women were opposed to it.

To present his point of view, he often tried to question those who differed with him:—

'Are suffragists in the majority?'

'Don't you think women who are opposed to equal suffrage have "rights"?'

'Is not suffrage a duty and a responsibility as well as a "right"?'

'Are you fair in trying to force duties and responsibilities upon all women, without regard to whether or not they want them, in order to secure "rights" for suffragists?'

'Don't you think the "rights" of all women should be considered in the determination of so important a question as their enfranchisement? or do you think anti-suffragists should be disfranchised on the question of enfranchisement?'

'If women are well enough informed to exercise the right of suffrage, are they not sufficiently intelligent to decide for themselves whether or not they want suffrage?'

Our inquiring young legislator liked to ask questions of others, but one day one of his mother's friends asked him a question.

She said: 'The government of this country is the business of its citizens, each holding just one share of stock. I know I am counted a stockholder, for I am called upon to help pay the bills. The men of the country will not permit me and other women to vote our stock. They do not even allow us to vote by proxy as no one has more than one vote. You are a business man and a stockholder in this business. I don't think you or any other business man should say that I cannot vote my stock because I am a woman, or because many other women stockholders do not care enough about the business to vote their stock. How would you and your friends in the legislature like to be compelled to support a business run with such a lack of principle?'

Well, our legislator was staggered! He was flabbergasted!

Could all his fine theories be exploded by one plain simple question? Had not his mother's friend presented a strong case? Were not her premises correct? Was not her reasoning logical? Could there be more than one conclusion? He had to admit that he was quite overwhelmed. At first thought her question certainly seemed unanswerable, except in one way. He must take time and think it over. Perhaps he ought to state the hypothesis in his own way and see if he arrived at the same conclusion.

'We are all stockholders in a public business called "government," but we have never been equal stockholders so far as voting our stock is concerned. All stock is evenly divided into two kinds — common and preferred. You and other women have always owned all the preferred stock, and have had no opportunity to take part in the management of the business except in an advisory capacity. Other men and I have always owned all the common stock and managed the business for what we believed to be the best interests of all stockholders, preferred as well as common.

'In order to permit you women to take an active part in running the business, would it be right for us to force all women — very much against the wishes of a majority of them perhaps — to exchange their preferred stock for common stock and in that way be compelled either to become active themselves in the management of the business, or to intrust their interests partly to you?

'Would not we common stockholders be fairer to you preferred stockholders, if we said to you: "You may decide for yourselves whether you want to leave the business of running this government to us or prefer to take an active part in its management. We will abide by your decision. If most of you want the right to vote, all well and good, you may have it; but if a majority of you do not want a change in government management, we will not let a minority force it upon you.'

Our young friend felt relieved. He had discovered the flaw in the lady's argument. At first, her question had seemed fairly to represent the situation and to knock all his theories in the head. He now saw plainly, however, that in her hypothesis she had failed to consider the interests of those women who did not want to be forced to take an active part in public business in order to protect their own interests, and who also did not want to have their business managed, even in part, by other women.

Our representative finally decided that the only way he could determine for himself whether or not women should be given the ballot was to submit the question to the women themselves. He resolved to find out, if possible, what proportion of the women living in his own district wanted equal suffrage. He was sure his women constituents were no less intelligent and well informed on the suffrage question than were the women of any other district in the commonwealth. If there proved to have been a decided change of sentiment throughout his district in favor of suffrage since the referendum vote of two years before, there would probably have been a proportionate change throughout the state. If a majority of the women in his district desired equal suffrage, very likely a majority in the state would favor it. For fear the women of his district were more intelligent and well informed than the average, however, and therefore, that a poll of his district would not prove a fair test of suffrage sentiment elsewhere, he finally interested other members of the legislature and induced some of them to agree that, if he would take a poll of women in his district, they would do likewise in their respective districts located in different parts of the state.

How to make a fair test was another problem. Our legislator was determined that, above every other consideration, his poll should be fair. He realized that, because of the expense involved, he could not afford to poll all of his district. He finally decided to canvass half of it, selecting such parts of each city, village, and country town as he thought would be most representative. But, being puzzled to know just how to make his canvass, he sought advice. A variety of suggestions was received. Most of them were manifestly impractical, and few of them appeared unbiased.

One suffrage advocate advised him to poll only schoolteachers, librarians, and other educated women. It seemed to her that a general poll of women, including 'uninformed and indifferent working girls' and 'home-bodies,' would not be a fair test.

A very prominent suffragist living in a large city told him: 'The only fair method of taking a test vote would be to visit every house in the district selected, carefully explain to each woman the advantages of woman suffrage, and hand her a ballot with the request that she mark it, voting "yes" if not opposed, and "no," of course, if opposed.' The prominent suffragist said that she herself had taken many test votes in this manner and found results 'most satisfactory.'

What our inquisitive friend wanted, however, was a record of the equal-suffrage sentiment then prevailing throughout his whole district; not a selected test of such sentiment, or a test of general sentiment as it might be after arguments on one side had been presented. He made up his mind to have some ballots printed and to take his poll in his own way.

After he started his canvass, I did not see him for many days, but I heard of him frequently. One day I saw a young lady, who did not look as if she would hurt any one, approach our good old German housekeeper, who was busily hanging out the family washing, and offer her a slip of paper.

There was a short pause; then a mouth full of clothespins sputtered, 'Ach! Gott in Himmel! I got no time for such foolishness!'

I was puzzled, but finally guessed the reason for so much vehemence. The stranger was one of our legislator's suffrage canvassers. She looked tired, and graciously accepted my invitation to come in.

Her little ballots were plainly printed and read that members of the legislature wanted to know whether or not women wanted the vote. Women were asked to take the ballots somewhere where they could be alone, mark them with a cross (x) to indicate whether or not they were in favor of equal suffrage, fold them so that their vote could not be seen, and deposit them in the ballot bag carried by the collector.

The modest young canvasser said there were other ballots to be sent by mail to women of different nationalities living in the country districts. These ballots were worded in very much the same way, but printed in different colors — one color for each nationality. She thought her employer was curious to know if nationality made any difference in suffrage sentiment.

I asked her if she were a suffragist. She said she could not tell me. Neither could she discuss suffrage nor tell how the vote was going. She had been instructed to be very careful, in talking with women, not to give any advice or information that might influence a vote. Most of the ballots were folded before being handed back to her, and she seldom looked to see how they were marked. She was expected to visit every house in the districts assigned to her. Practically every woman she saw voted, almost always without hesitation. She understood that both men and women were employed as canvassers and that half of them had been selected because they favored equal suffrage and half because they were opposed to it. None of them were allowed to inform any one how they stood. She thought there were many canvassers. Most of them were employed calling from house to house in different cities and villages, while others were taking polls in factories, stores, offices, libraries, and schools. Her employer had said he intended to secure as many votes as possible before his canvass became advertised, so that he might get a fair, impartial vote before any one interested attempted to influence the voters.

I did not think that she looked either part, but the young canvasser thought that many people judged her to be either a 'suffragette,' or employed by the 'liquor interests.' A large number of women had told her they were interested in suffrage only because of the liquor question. Many wanted the ballot for just one reason — to close up saloons. It made no difference to her how women voted or why they voted one way or another. The man soliciting in the ward with her was an experienced canvasser. He had told her that he always put his foot in a front door as soon as it was opened, to prevent its being slammed in his face before he could explain his business. She would like to visit longer, but her employer expected her to work. Perhaps she had stayed too long. Some boys outside had followed her, calling her 'suffering cat.' She had been hoping they would go.

That same day the newspapers began to take notice of our legislator's canvass. News articles appeared, telling about 'mysterious strangers seen canvassing different parts of the city and many other places.' Because officers of the 'Equal Suffrage League' knew nothing about it, prominent suffragists were inclined to believe that 'interests inimical to the cause of suffrage, probably the liquor people,' were back of the poll.

Next day our law-maker was interviewed. He attempted to explain the mystery, but no explanation was satisfactory or acceptable. There must be something 'crooked' about the canvass, because leading suffragists had not been consulted. It was inconceivable that a fair poll could be taken by any one outside of equal-suffrage organizations. One suffragist said that she had stayed at home for three days (something she had never been known to do before) for fear the canvassers would miss her, but she had not been called upon. Another had 'called up fourteen prominent advocates of suffrage and not one of them had been asked to vote by the mysterious canvassers.' Others had told the canvassers at just what houses they should call to get suffragist votes, but many of these calls had not been made. Surely the liquor people were back of it. 'Mysterious strangers should not adopt dark, mysterious methods!'

III

I had not seen my friend the legislator for so long a time that I began to think he must be in hiding, when one day I met him coming out of a large office building. He seemed pleased to see me, and said he was 'glad to meet a friend.' He had been home for days counting ballots. There were thousands of them, and he had counted them all himself. His telephone had rung so incessantly that he was glad to leave home occasionally. His mail had grown enormously. The offices he had just visited had been canvassed twice, as sixty-one young women employed there had managed to vote eighty-two times in the first poll. He knew of no other instances, however, where the ballot-box had been 'stuffed.' He thought probably some one had been trying to play a 'practical' joke. At that particular place, a telephone exchange, he had been obliged to leave the ballots to be called for later on, after they had been marked. In every other case, his canvassers had passed the ballots around and then taken them up immediately. He was very much pleased with the success he had had in taking a fair poll. He felt sure no fairer test could be made of the sentiment of the women of his district on the suffrage question. Many thousand ballots had been cast. With very few exceptions, probably less than two per cent, every woman solicited had responded to the invitation to vote. The few women called upon who had seemed in doubt and undecided which way to vote had not been encouraged to vote at all; but there had been very few who were not ready to vote promptly.

His ballots had been distributed in his own ward first. Most of the women living in his ward were the wives of workingmen. They had voted against equal suffrage four to one.

Another workingmen's ward had voted the same way. Two others had opposed suffrage three to one.

He had next canvassed a ward where he thought the residents were more representative of all classes. In this ward homes ranged in value from two hundred dollars to as high as twenty thousand dollars and more. Two thirds of the vote in this ward had been 'no.'

A majority of the men living in the seventh ward had voted in favor of suffrage two years before. A careful canvass indicated that their women were now opposed to suffrage by a small majority.

In the thirteenth ward, the largest in the city, almost eight hundred workingmen's wives had marked ballots. Seven out of eight had not wanted women to vote.

He had polled in all six and one half of the thirteen wards in his city. Only one fourth of the three thousand women called upon in these wards had voted 'yes.'

At first he had thought that perhaps the result would be different when he polled the women whom his canvassers had not found at home — the working women in factories, stores, schools, and other places.

Most teachers, older scholars, librarians, nurses, and dressmakers had voted 'yes.' A large majority of bookkeepers, stenographers, clerks, factory girls, and hotel employees had voted 'no.'

In the other two cities in his district, the vote had been practically the same.

About seven women out of ten did not want the ballot.

There were two villages that had shown strong equal-suffrage sentiment two years before. The suffragists in these villages had almost won in his poll, but in each case a very small majority of women had been opposed.

Not a single ward, city, or village in his district had returned a majority for suffrage.

He had found the rural districts almost as strongly opposed to women voting as the cities had been. Thirteen out of sixteen country towns had voted 'no.'

In these country towns he had mailed different colored ballots to different nationalities. Three fourths of the German women answering had voted 'no.' The Irish had voted 'no.' A close majority of the Scandinavians and English and most of the Welsh had voted 'yes.'

In all he had polled almost eight thousand votes. The results indicated that fully two thirds of all the women in his district were opposed to suffrage. The referendum on suffrage two years before had shown almost exactly the same proportion of men opposed to giving women the ballot. Evidently there were no indications of a gain in suffrage sentiment in his district.

The other members of the legislature who had promised to poll their districts did not do so. He thought that they had refrained, either because they did not want to incur the expense, or did not want to agree to abide by the results. In the absence of any other test, he must assume the suffrage sentiment in his district to be a fair indication of suffrage strength throughout his state.

Just before the equal-suffrage measures introduced in the state legislature came up for consideration, our representative called upon me. He was in trouble. His mother had written him a letter asking him to support equal suffrage. She said it would settle the liquor problem. She was visiting in a western state where women had the ballot. He did not like to disappoint his mother. Her letter read: —

My Dear Boy: —
What an opportunity you now have as a state senator to make our state a cleaner and better home for its citizens.

Your first privilege will be to help women to secure the ballot. I am so sure of your absolute integrity and high sense of honor that I feel certain you will not deny women justice.

My western visit has made me a real 'votes for women' enthusiast. The ballot has already done wonders for women in the west, and these recently enfranchised western women are accomplishing so much in return.

Every western man I have met tells me he is glad to have women vote. Even those who were most opposed to equal suffrage have become converted. Men out here seem to believe in women, and the women are showing themselves to be worthy of this trust.

After fifty years of saloon politics under man rule in Oregon and Washington, the women of these states have stepped in with their new untried weapons, women's votes, and banished 'demon rum' from the country. Men in politics in the east are afraid to vote against saloons, but in these western suffrage states men no longer fear the liquor vote. They know that women's votes count more than saloon votes.

In civilization there is no room for the saloon. Women realize this more than men, perhaps, because women suffer more from the effects of liquor than do men, while their judgment is not prejudiced by a taste for it. Women know that absolute prohibition is the only permanent solution of the liquor problem.

I wish we could rid our state of saloons, but I am sure this can never be done until women are given the ballot. My faith in you is so great that I am sure you will vote for woman suffrage, for you must choose between the two, equal suffrage and saloons. I know my boy could not align himself with the saloon.

Your loving<br>
MOTHER.

I was interested to know how our state senator would answer his mother. He finally wrote her in part:—

You will not agree with me, mother, but I believe no one should support equal suffrage because of the liquor problem.

In our state, as well as in others, the equal-suffrage movement is linked with the prohibition movement. Most suffragists are opposed to saloons. Many are suffragists only because of saloons. They want women to have the ballot only to bring about prohibition.

In my opinion the liquor problem is of minor importance in comparison with the suffrage question. Whether or not women vote, it is generally admitted that the liquor problem will be permanently solved in the course of time by laws that will have public sentiment back of them to make them enforceable. On the other hand, equal suffrage is for all time. When suffrage for women is once granted, it is an irrevocable step. How unfortunate it would be to take an irrevocable step for a reason that will no longer exist after a comparatively short time.

Friends of good government should consider the advisability of equal suffrage entirely aside from any effect women's votes might have on the liquor business. If equal suffrage ought not to be granted for other reasons than because of its effect on the saloon business, then it ought not to be granted at all, for the saloon question will be taken care of without women's votes. Linking the two questions together only tends to prevent a fair, impartial judgment of each.

And, mother, if a majority of the men in our state really want saloons (as they seem to), bad as the saloon is, would we be better off to have it abolished by women? Would it be well to have most women voting against most men? Would equal suffrage bring about such a situation?

My conscientious friend opposed all equal-suffrage bills introduced in the state senate. One of these measures failed to pass by only one vote.

# Does Suffrage Work Pay?

The annual report of the New York State Woman Suffrage Association shows by the treasurer's report that the receipts for the year were $3,261.77; and the disbursements were $3,061.24; there were 132 membership fees and dues from 28 counties of $450.30. Chautauqua county leads with $79. Albany, the capital county, makes a poor showing with $7. The expenses were largely the salaries paid for organizing and legislative work. Miss Harriet M. Mills received $680; Miss Julia R. Jenny, $25; Miss Harriet A. Keyser, $81.28, and Miss Emma Taylor, $50.25, making an aggregate of $836.53 for organizing during the year. Mrs. Martha R. Almy received $455.75 for legislative work. Miss Anthony received $25, and Mrs. Greenleaf $50, and Mrs. Searing $33, while Miss Babcock was paid $90.89 for press work.

The report on organization is not particularly cheerful for the amount of time and money expended. The chairman organized four counties, eleven locals and four committees; and in answer to the question whether the work was permanent, acknowledges that "experience shows that it is impossible to insure the permanence of many of the new clubs." She speaks of "the apathy of the women," "the unwillingness of women to take office, and above all, the lack of conscience about answering letters."

The chairman of the legislative committee reports that on account of clerical error in the suffrage resolution passed last year, the "final submission" is "necessary postponed" until 1899. But she consoles her hearers with the statement that "in the minds of the committee the chances of carrying the measure at the polls will be better in 1899, or later, than next year."

The chairman of the press committee reports the expenses of her work as $109.30 She says that the articles sent out were received more readily than she had hoped, as the American Press Association thought, in answer to her request that they use suffrage articles, that there was no demand for them ; and the publishers of "patent insides" also refused to take articles for the same reason. She then tells of her personal efforts with editors, and she adds, "My plan has been to obtain men and women of prominence to write short articles upon the various phases of the woman question. With some editors the suffrage points must be cunningly disguised, but they are there just the same."

Altogether the report makes interesting reading, even to an Anti—*Albany Evening Journal, February 14, 1896.*

Second Edition—4th Thousand

BULLETIN No. 4

# Equality

BY

MRS. CAROLINE F. CORBIN

ILLINOIS ASSOCIATION
OPPOSED TO WOMAN SUFFRAGE
1523 DEARBORN AVENUE
CHICAGO

# EQUALITY

"I W-A-N-T to be equal with men," wailed Mrs. Cobden-Sanderson, the English Suffragette, in her address before the Chicago Woman's Club, during her mission to this Country; not once but many times.

But what reason has Mrs. Sanderson, or any other woman, to believe that the right to vote would make her, in any true sense, more nearly the equal of man than she is at present? Speaking for the sex as a whole, would it change for the better, her physical constitution, her mental processes, her spiritual capacities, or even the weight and worth of her influence in the mental or moral world? Would she be better fitted for the rough work of civilization; would her collective judgment of men and things be materially improved by the possession of the ballot? Would it make, or has it made any essential difference even in her power over legislation?

In the states where woman suffrage prevails, how many important offices have ever been held by women? In Colorado, during the first years after the ballot was obtained, a few women were elected to the legislature, but Louise Lee Hardin, then editor of the Business Woman's Magazine at Denver, said editorially, that every year after women were allowed to vote, fewer places were allotted to them on party tickets, till at last there was not a woman in either house of the legislature. A well-known woman of Utah adds to this testimony that "the nomination of a woman to an elective office is now considered by all parties as an element of weakness. It is no longer considered essential to recognize or cater to the woman vote at any convention by any political party." "Women," says Mrs. Hardin, and it must be remembered that she was a thorough suffragist, and had voted more than once in the earnest faith that the ballot in the hands of women would be an elevating influence, "have only followed where men led. It is true that they have caused the passage of some petty measures, but it was only as a little sop to keep them in line for something which men had promised a great corporation that they would put through."

Whatever good has been accomplished by women in any suffrage State, has been gained by influence quite as much as by votes, and the sum of it has not been greater than that which has been achieved in other States by the old-fashioned way. In no State has the ballot brought to woman an equal power or influence to that exercised by men.

Is such false and specious equality as that, an equality founded the mere dictum of law-makers without regard to the fundamental principles of power or character a real improvement upon the present status of women.

Every rational human being is a social integer of a certain power and value. It may be roughly said to be like an industrial factor of so many horse-power, 20, 40, 60, or perhaps no more than 10, or even a minus quantity, but like a steam-engine it may be put to various uses. A stone-crusher or a steam spinning-jenny may be of equal numerical power, yet they would be of far different qualities as industrial agents. One would be destructive, the other constructive. Or you might compare the electrical power which would shatter a mighty oak, with that which illuminates a vast auditorium. There might be a mechanical equality in the voltage employed in the two phenomena, but a very great disparity in the kind of benefit obtained. It is clear, therefore, that the true meaning of equality is not simple but complex; and we may safely argue that the voltage of power may be equal in men and women, while it is employed for very different purposes. Observation and reflection tend to show that the power of men in the intellectual and political world, is not greater than the power of woman in the social, moral, and spiritual life; but it may be very seriously questioned whether an interchange of the purposes and methods of the two sexes would result in good to either, or to civilization at large.

For light upon the important subject of equality between men and women, let us look to nature as interpreted by the master minds of modern science.

In primordial protoplasm we find the nearest approach to equality which living matter affords, but the moment that the spirit of progress moves upon the face of matter what a stirring is there among the primal cells. New forms, new functions of less or greater value begin to appear. The creeping things, the flying things, those that swim in the water, those that burrow in the earth or roam upon it, begin to separate themselves from each other, and there is no longer even an apparent equality among them. There is no dictum of biological science more universal nor more authoritative than that "Specialization of function is the first law of progress." Nature is extravagant to an almost incredible degree in the production of new forms, new species, new definitions. The thing she seems most to abhor is uniformity, sameness, equality. The fundamental idea of progress seems to express itself in change, unlikeness, variety of form and value.

But amid all these myriad variations from original conditions which seem at first view intended to be stable, one idea remains constant as the guiding, propelling force of evolution, and that is the principle of sex, the phenomena of parentage. It is the concensus of biologists of all schools that from sexual parentage all new variations from any established stock arise; that in the domain of fatherhood and motherhood whether of plants or animals, all upward steps in the path of progress are taken.

For proof of this statement, see not only the leading writers on biology, but such practical experimenters as Burbank and the professors in our agricultural schools. The better defined in any species are the differences of sex; the higher its rank in the scale of being the greater its chance for still further progress. The inequalities which spring from sex are the dynamic force of evolution. It is these inequalities which both socialist and suffragist are seeking to destroy.

The laws of nature are quiet but far-reaching in their action. Any fool may flaunt them in their faces with his foolish talk unrebuked, but when he invades their practical domain, attempts to carry his wild theories into action, he is likely to find himself in a stern grip which awakens a lively fear that they ante-date and may outlive him.

As for instance, Mr. Jack London in his War of the Classes, in the chapter entitled "A New Law of Development," thus prophesies concerning the era of the common man:

"When the common man's day shall have arrived, the new social institutions of that day will prevent the weeding out of weakness and inefficiency. All, the weak and the strong will have an equal chance for procreation, and the progeny of all, of the weak as well as the strong, will have an equal chance for survival. This being so, if no *new effective law of development be put into operation*—then progress must cease. And not only progress (sic) for deterioration would at once set in. It is a pregnant problem. What will be the nature of this new and most necessary law of development? Can the common man pause long enough from his undermining labors to answer? Since he is bent upon reconstructing society, can it be so reconstructed that a premium in some unguessed way will still be laid upon the strong and efficient, so that the human race will continue to develop? Can the common man, or the uncommon men who are allied with him, devise such a law, and when devised put it into execution?"

A Socialist of larger caliber than Mr. Jack London could hardly have stated the case more clearly, but being a protagonist, he would probably have taken counsel of his better judgment and not have stated it at all.

CHICAGO, June, 1910.

# HIDDEN FROM HISTORY

EXTRACT FROM AN ADDRESS ON

## TAXATION WITHOUT REPRESENTATION.

By Mrs. H. A. Foster, Des Moines, Iowa.

The phrase "taxation without representation" as applied to the question of the enfranchisement of women is not pertinent. In this country taxation has nothing whatever to do with representation, which is in no way based upon property. Men do not vote because they own property and pay taxes; property is merely incidental, as is the color of the eyes. It is possible that a property qualification, or an educational qualification, or some other qualification, might be better, but those limitations have not yet been placed upon suffrage.

Let us turn to the practical effects of present methods upon the men and women who really do pay the taxes, particularly to the tax-paying maiden or widow who is, as they say, "unrepresented." First, as we are dealing with the taxation question and nothing else, we will, for convenience, separate the voters into two classes, the tax-paying and non-tax-paying, or the responsible and the irresponsible. These terms are here used with the utmost respect and deference for the latter class, with a full recognition of their value to the people and the nation, and simply to distinguish them in the matter of taxation from those who really feel the burden. It is natural to account everything cheap and every luxury necessary that costs neither money nor effort, and very natural, therefore, that the irresponsible voter should favor, as he usually does, every new so-called improvement. His vote is regarded with dread by all property owners, male and female. The "unrepresented" tax-paying woman to-day is at least not subjected to the imposition of taxes voted upon her by the non-tax-paying woman. The property-owning male citizen, while often actuated doubtless by selfish motives, incidentally protects the "unrepresented" woman, — not as much as she would wish, perhaps, but in a far greater degree and more effective manner than her own vote could, if subjected, as it would be in this republic, to the nullifying effect of the vastly greater numerical strength of the non-tax-paying woman. If the statement be true that the larger the proportion of non-property-owning citizens the greater the danger of burdensome taxation, is it not apparent that the conditions to which tax-paying women object would be greatly intensified by the addition of the vote of the non-tax-paying woman, who would be as an hundred to one against her?

*Printed by the Massachusetts Association opposed to Extension of Woman Suffrage.*

Pamphlets and leaflets may be obtained from the Secretary of the Association,
Mrs. Robert W. Lord,
56 St. Stephen Street, Boston.

# HIDDEN FROM HISTORY

## Extracts from an Article by the Rev. J. M. Buckley,

―――ON―――

## The Wrongs and Perils of Woman Suffrage.

In an argument in favor of giving suffrage to women, a senator of Massachusetts brought forward as an example of intellectual and moral fitness for the franchise Mrs. Clara Leonard, whom he justly characterized as the highest living authority on private and public charities. Mrs. Leonard has recently thus expressed her wisdom on the value of the ballot to woman: "It is the opinion of many of us that woman's power is greater without the ballot or possibility of office holding for gain, when standing outside of politics she discusses great questions on their merits. Much has been achieved by woman for the anti-slavery cause, temperance, the improvement of public and private charities, the reformation of criminals and by intelligent discussion and influence upon man. Our legislators have been ready to listen to women and carry out their plans when well formed.

* * * * * *

To her name I add that of "the most useful and distinguished woman that America has produced", whose influence is felt throughout the world upon every sphere of philanthropy and is preserved in the laws of every civilized nation, Dorothea L. Dix. She saw the rise of the American Woman's Suffrage movement, studied it in its advocate's arguments, sentiments and tendencies, and rejected it. Her biographer states that she believed in " 'woman's keeping herself apart from anything savoring of ordinary political action. She must be the incarnation of a purely disinterested idea, appealing to universal humanity, irrespective of party or sect' ".

# HIDDEN FROM HISTORY

## Extracts from an Article by the Rev. J. M. Buckley,

———ON———

## The Wrongs and Perils of Woman Suffrage.

Woman suffrage cannot achieve what its advocates expect. They think that it will reform public morals, close the saloon and other places of evil resort, and realize absolute prudence, honesty and economy in management. Laws that do not carry the votes of a majority of the men in a community cannot be enacted. That under ordinary circumstances the instincts of women would be in favor of good laws there is no doubt : but how far their temperaments would affect the character of special enactments, and how far their personal prejudices and prepossessions would affect their political action are practical questions of moment. "Women will always vote against war, and thus put an end to it in the world. They will not send their husbands, fathers, brothers and friends to slaughter." Does history support this statement? Wherever there has been a war women have been as much interested as men. They have even encouraged their husbands, fathers, brothers and lovers to enlist, and would have despised them if they had not. In the last war in this country the women on both sides were more intense and irreconcilable than the men.

* * * * * * *

In England, when women first appeared upon the hustings, they were received with the old chivalry, but in recent elections, the contest being fierce, all respect has disappeared. Noted women were treated most disrespectfully in the very heart of London, and people of all parties agree that England has never seen so much participation of women or such rude treatment of them as in the last election. In Wales, Mrs. Cornwallis West tried to quell a disturbance, but was silenced by yells and hisses, and was finally compelled to retire from the platform.

* * * * * * *

Should the suffrage be extended to women, the grant can never be recalled. Experiments in legislating upon economic questions, even if unwise, need not be permanently harmful, for they may be repealed ; but in dealing with the suffrage or moral question, new laws, if bad, are exceedingly dangerous. They will develop a class lowered in tone or deriving personal, pecuniary or political advantages from the new environment, who will vehemently declare that the effect of the innovation is beneficial and resist all efforts to return to the former state. Should the duty of governing in the state be imposed upon women, all the members of society will suffer.

# EXTRACT FROM AN ADDRESS DELIVERED IN 1903 BEFORE THE MASSACHUSETTS FEDERATION OF WOMEN'S CLUBS

### BY MR. HORACE G. WADLIN

THE question most frequently asked with reference to the wages of women is, "Why are they not paid the same wage as men for doing the same work?" Nevertheless, it is becoming more and more the fact that, except in certain exceptional and transitional cases and in certain employments requiring special talent, professional skill, and extended education, women do not do the same work as men, if the adjective "same" is used in the sense of identical, as relating to the kind of work without regard to its quality, and one of the reasons that women do not in general receive so large wages as men is because they do not in general do the same work. In many industries women do better work than men and are preferable to men for various reasons. They gravitate towards certain employments for which they are, at present, better fitted. In these employments they drive out the men previously employed, and while this operation is going on, they compete with men for employment and undoubtedly for wages; but these are generally, under present conditions, employments requiring no particular skill nor extended training, and therefore large numbers of women seek them. The time is exceedingly short in any industry during which women perform the same work as men. The work best adapted to women becomes not worth the man's while; he goes into other employments. For the most part, therefore, women in industry do not compare with men, but with other women, and this is one of the leading causes of their lower wage level.

Again, the wages of women are affected by their lack of training and by the fact that the adult woman competes with the young woman. Experience, as a rule, brings no larger reward to the woman worker, for the work mainly open to her is mechanical and routine work. Besides this, the fact that women have not generally entered the higher positions of skill and trust operates adversely upon their wage status. The man in industry has hope of advancement; the woman, except to a very limited degree, cannot as yet look forward to such preferment: she mainly looks forward to marriage. Marriage generally takes her out of industry. Not so with men. Women workers, too, are largely unorganized, and are therefore unable to present the united front in opposition to attempts to reduce or prevent the advance of wages which to a greater or less extent is presented by unions among men.

There is another economic reason for the lower wage standard of women workers. As a rule, wages, which constitute the price paid for services, are fixed by the cost of production of such services, and the cost of living for women is lower than for men, because, notwithstanding numerous exceptional instances, they do not in general support others, and in many cases the young women constantly entering industry and taking the places of those who through marriage leave it, are partially supported by parents or relatives. More efficient training for the woman in industry will raise the wage level of women workers; the further advance of women into the higher pursuits, operating as an incentive, will also tend in the same direction, and the industrial organization of women workers will, in the future, do much to advance the sex industrially, as it will help to place them on an equality with men workers who are already organized.

Printed by the Massachusetts Association opposed to Further Extension of Woman Suffrage.

Pamphlets and leaflets may be obtained from the Secretary of the Association,

Mrs. Robert W. Lord, P. O. Box 2262, Boston.

EXTRACTS FROM AN ADDRESS ON CO-EDUCATION, BY ANDREW S. DRAPER, PRESIDENT OF THE UNIVERSITY OF ILLINOIS, BEFORE THE TWENTIETH CENTURY CLUB, BOSTON.

About the only right our foremothers had was the right to live and be our foremothers. Indeed, the law knew nothing of them beyond keeping their marriage within the control of the king, or the lord of the manor, until they took the step which conferred upon us the high privilege of being here. After that, if by any chance they had personal property, it became the husband's absolutely. So with real estate; he could alienate it by deed or will. Man and wife were in no sense equal before the law. Their lives were legally merged in one, but the one was not a new creation: the one remained the life of the man. And the law made him about as troublesome to her after he was dead as when he was alive. If he left any property when he died, she could claim the income of one third of it, and no more, during the ordinarily brief time while she remained his widow. If she had brought the property to him when she married him, or if they had accumulated it together, it made no difference. If he failed to sell it or give it away in his lifetime, or neglected to dispose of it by will, the law came in at his death, and considerately corrected his oversight in his interest. She could not make a will at all. He could give or will her property to his relatives. Her services and earnings were his. She had no right of control over the children, except in subordination to him; the income of their labor, as well as of their mother's, was his. He had the right to chastise not only them, but their mother as well. Often the man was so sane that he did not think of going to the limits of this insane law: and sometimes the woman was so strong that he considerately waived his technical right for considerations which were both obvious and conclusive.

So long as all this could persist, no one, not even woman

herself, could think of the education of woman. And it did persist until democracy, without chart or plan or understanding of what the end would be, merely obeying the conscience and using the force of the mass, bore down the unbroken traditions of a thousand years. Our often-deprecated much legislation is entitled to the credit of it. The statutes of our many States, a little here and a little there, copying and advancing upon one another, have made the legal rights of woman about the same as as those of man. Where not fully equal they will yet be made so.

No one can doubt the cause of this, for wherever democracy has had any development in the world, even under autocratic or aristocratic forms, there the rights of women have been enlarged. The opportunity has been so much larger and the advance so much stronger in America than in any other land that we have become conspicuous in a world movement. But the movement is on all over the world. It is one of the great strides to the high destiny of the race. Ill-advised selfishness was able to keep the mass in ignorance of natural right through long, long years, but the dawn of a glorious day came at last, and the sun of promise is now well up in the heavens.

Naturally there has been some illogical reasoning, some irrational misconceptions about it all. Confusion about personal rights and public duties has arisen. Because a woman has the right and should have the opportunity to make the most of herself, it does not follow that she should serve in the army or the jury box. It would be a brutal view that because she should have the same opportunities as men for moral and intellectual advancement, she should be made to stand while a man sits in a street car, or in any other way bear a man's part in public places. The opening of the advanced schools to woman has nothing to do with imposing the franchise upon her.

Woman is by her very nature fitted for certain functions and man for certain other functions in the social economy. Each class of functions and the inherent rights of each sex claim as a right the best that the schools can give. But it does not follow that each is to bear the same burden. The essence of government is protection. Voting, serving in the legislature, is sharing in government. It is a burden, not a right. When it comes to bearing burdens, man is to do what he can do best and woman what she can do best. Man is the natural protector, the natural voter. Physiological and social considerations come in. Because men do not always vote as safely as they ought, it does not follow that women would do it any better. There is some reason for fear that they might not do it as well. Because a few men and a few women want to change the political order of things, and what seems to me to be the natural order of things, it by no means follows that it should be done. When the majority of the most substantial women want to take up the burden of managing government, the majority of the men will doubtless be willing. It is a matter of expediency, and if that time ever comes the men will probably agree.

But natural rights are not to depend even upon majorities. They are to inhere in every one, and be enforceable by every one, regardless of sex. Participation in government is not necessary in order that woman may secure her rights. The sufficient proof of that is found in the fact that the widest range of civic and political rights conferred upon woman in all the world, or in all time, has been given in this country, not by princes, or by judges, but by the plain, common, blundering men. They do not always blunder. Acting in the mass, and after discussion, they do not often blunder. They have not blundered in this matter, for in the social economy woman must bear responsibilities quite as important to the common good, and claiming quite as high an order of moral and intellectual aptitude, as the burden of protection against the external and internal enemies of the social order which logically falls upon men.

---

*Printed by the Massachusetts Association, opposed to Extension of Woman Suffrage.*

Pamphlets and leaflets may be obtained from the Secretary of the Association,

Mrs. Robert W. Lord,
P. O. Box 2262, Boston.

# EXTRACTS FROM ADDRESSES

OF

## The Rt. Rev. Wm. Croswell Doane, D. D.,

BISHOP OF ALBANY,

To the classes graduated from St. Agnes' School, Albany,

June 6th, 1894 and June 6th 1895.

PUBLISHED BY THE ALBANY ANTI-SUFFRAGE ASSOCIATION.

1895.

# HIDDEN FROM HISTORY

## FROM THE ADDRESS OF 1894.

There must be individuality; the distinct character which differentiates man from man, or machine from machine. For each is "after its kind." And there is no waste of power so great, as when one loses sight of this and sets the day laborer to adjust the niceties of the chronometer, or puts the poet behind the plough. This is the critical question of all. The power of a "Reaper" to tie up sheaves with their own straw, with a delicacy of machinery alive almost to its finger ends, would not be proven, if it were set to break stones on the road. Nor would the capacity of the trip hammer be tested, if it were used to drive the needle of the sewing machine. What is it for? "What wilt thou have me to do?" Purpose as the test of power; object, intention, place and kind of work; this is what I mean by individuality. "What she could;" "what she had;" "what I can." I am sure that there never was a more important time in all the world, to emphasize, and drive home into the minds and consciences of women, this most important lesson. We are living in a period of reaction, and reaction always means a tendency to violent extremes. The slowly working leaven of Christianity for eighteen hundred years, has been lifting women up from the low level into which they fell in Eve, to the higher lines of life and service to which they rose in Mary. One by one, openings and opportunities for congenial and convenient service have been opened up to her. One by one, the bars of the cage have been let down, and the barriers of foolish custom have been taken away, which hindered and held her back from openings and opportunities of usefulness. And one by one, the *false* restraints and *unwise* discriminations have been done away; until to-day, by the common consent, by the Christianized instinct, by the chivalrous endeavor, of men, womanhood,—and nowhere more than in America,—stands fairly out upon that position of correlation and coequality with men, which really was the purpose of Almighty God in the double creation; which in no sense contradicts the divine intention of the primacy of the first created, and the subordination of the second; but which utterly destroys, and does away with, the false theory of superiority and sovereignty on the one side, as meaning inferiority and subjection on the other. And now the world is full of agitations, which would destroy, if they could be carried out, that exquisite balance which the revealed purpose of God, and the implanted and inherent differences between men and women, indicate as the wise and true relation between the two. Coequality, side-by-sideness, divided sovereignty, the *mutual* superiority and subordination of influence and control, the interdependence of the "man who is by the woman" and "the woman who is of the man;" these are not only truths and theories, but facts and realities; which can not be forgotten nor disregarded without serious injury and loss. Nobody who reads the record of the Revelation rightly, or studies history or examines the experience of his own life, can fail to feel that whatever distinctions and differences there may be between the *kind* of mind, of capacity, of character between the two sexes, there are no differences whatever in the degree. But it is the falsest kind of logic which argues, that, because the two sexes are equal in the sight of God, therefore, they are interchangeable. All that the man can do, the woman can not do. All that the woman can do, the man can not do. And, therefore, the talk to-day of "woman's rights," apart from the falseness of the application of the word,—for the rights of either man or woman are fewer and far less important than their duties,—has this inherent fallacy; that it presupposes that because their rights are *equal*, therefore they are the same. Surely, if one takes the other and the better word, it is plain to the blindest, that the duties of men and women are not the same; that the trend of their tastes and capabilities is different; and that if the women are to do the men's duties, their own duties must be left undone, or done by those who are unfitted for and incapable of their discharge. Nothing is wilder or stranger, than the misconceptions and the disproportionateness of all this theory. It is contradicted by the whole material world, in which we live; and in which, its own functions are given and its own duties assigned to every separate plant and tree and animal. Nor could a wilder confusion be produced than if, by some blind force, these unthinking and unreasoning things should set themselves to tasks, which have not been assigned them; and for which they are not intended by their creation. And *why*, the highest order of created things, to whom Almighty God has given not only the consciousness of their peculiar and different capacities, but the plain and evident ability of recognizing the fact and reasoning just why these lines of differences are drawn, should prove itself duller and more stupid than the inanimate creation, is difficult to see. Earnestly I beg that this lesson of the personal pronoun "I"—which never in any language changes sex because the equal individuality of both the sexes must be acknowledged as the fundamental principle of character,—may plant itself deeply in your conscience. You may turn into the feminine gender that great sentence, "I can do all that may become a *woman;* who dares do more is none." You can realize all this by the divinely implanted instincts of your nature, by the limitations or the enlargements of your capacity, by the opportunities and occasions of your providential place in life. And that will be the clue, which you may safely follow, as indicating the lines along which every faculty of your nature is to be set, with utmost intensity and directness of aim, to do "your duty in the state of life into which it shall please God to call you."

I am urging the recognition of such limitations as God has set, *first* in your sex, which are written in laws so plain and facts so irresistible that only the blindest can fail to read and see them. The utter misconception of equality of position, as though it meant sameness of duty, between men and women, is among the facile follies and the fatal fallacies of the age. Facing great evils, moved in some instances by high motives, women who used to be quiet and content to stand in their lot, are joining in the wretched unrest of the effort, which, until recently, was in the hands of wild and unwomanly fanatics, to unsex themselves and unsettle the peace of the household, and the prosperity of the world. I have a general dislike and distrust of the term *woman* in the abstract. And in the manner of its use it is most confusing. There are women *and* women, as there are men *and* men. And the fond imagination that the evils of unqualified suffrage given to men, which are the most dangerous element in our American political world to-day, can be cured by extending the evil to *unqualified women*, is the strangest delusion that ever possessed the human mind. If it should be permitted, which God forefend, the abstract *woman* may rejoice, but it will be in the spirit of the maniac who has laid waste the homes and marred the happiness and murdered the hopes of *women*. Privilege, courtesy, chivalry, respect, deference, consideration, will have melted away. And there will come instead unseemly contests, selfishness, the bitterness of partisanship, the dregs of strife and corruption, incrimination and the demoralization of the deepest and highest and dearest relations of society; while in its political effect it will only multiply corrupt and irresponsible ballots, not to equal, but to outweigh the intelligent suffrage of reputable women. Nothing will be altered in results. Nothing will be gained in the issues. And the irreclaimable mischief will have left its blight and scar on our social life. Two handed humanity (that is the figure of the man and the woman in the body politic) has a right hand and a left hand, each equal to the other, each needful to the other. But the hand that is nearest the heart, the woman, is not used, and is not meant to be used, to grasp the sword, the pen, the reins; nor to seize the rough difficulties, and wring out of them the stern successes, of the strife. They are both hands. They are equally hands. Each is imperfect without the other, but their functions are apart and different. Learn the divine, the human, the instinctive, the evident limitations of your sex. And when you have filled out with "all you *can*" the sphere of your allotted service, you will have no time, nor strength, nor desire to reach out for other work to do.

## FROM THE ADDRESS OF 1895.

One gets sick and tired of the way in which the talk of woman's vocation fills the air, not merely in the wild vagaries of its blatant assumptions, but in the parade and push of its claims for recognition of what are called "its rights." I have had occasion here, a year ago, to say what *wrong* to womanhood these women's *rights* would be. And I have no desire to recall a word, to shade down any statement, or to abate a jot of effort to protect the silent many from the noisy few. For the agitators are really in the minority. Numberless names on these modern "millenary petitions" mean only the thoughtless and good-natured yielding to persistent pursuit; just as legislative majority votes stand, in not a few instances, for a mistaken courtesy or an unmanly cowardice. I believe that God will yet save this State and Nation from the aggravated miseries of an enlarged, unqualified suffrage, which, in its universality of *male* voters, is our most threatening danger to-day. But if we are to be visited with this infliction, as a well-earned punishment for many national sins, then I believe that, when we have tasted its bitterness, we shall be brought back, perhaps through anarchy and revolution, to a democracy, which shall demand, for its existence, government by men, whom education and actual Americanism of vital interest in the Nation qualify to govern. Meanwhile, when a new Bible shall have been translated into a denial of the original record of creation—a really "reversed Scripture," as one once called "the revised version"—when Constitutions shall have been altered, to disturb the equipoise of the relation between man and woman; when motherhood shall be replaced by mannishness; when neglected homes shall furnish candidates for mismanaged offices; when money shall buy the votes of women, as it does now themselves; when the fires of political discord shall be lighted on the hearthstone of domestic peace; when the arrogant assertion of demanded rights shall have destroyed the instinctive chivalry of conceded courtesies; when "woman," as has been well said, "once the superior, has become the equal of man;" then the reaped whirlwind of some violent political reaction will be gathered "in tears," by those who are sowing the wind, in the mad "joy" of the Petroleuse of the French revolutions. The vocation of womanhood is the highest and the holiest in the world. Guard it, my dear children in your own selves, from the desecration that would drag it into the publicity and prostitutions of political strife. Year by year, as the centuries have gone on since the great Partheno-Genesis of humanity, its highness and its holiness have been more and more made clear. Apart from, and in spite of, all the violence of agitation, the duties, the opportunities and the privileges of women have opened out before them: service to the State, in the training of boys and the moulding of men; in influencing great reforms; in organizing charity; in elevating education; in the protected ministries of mercy to the sick, the poor, the fallen; in the adorning and sanctifying of homes. But the shoulder that is unfitted for the musket, and the hand that was not made to guide the plough mean, and mark off, by very physical distinctions, the vocation of women, from the rough and public stir and strife of men. If *equality* means *similarity* of rights and duties, then the harmony of nature and the balance of the world would be destroyed. The milch cow and the ploughing ox are not meant for the same service. The herb that ministers healing, and the flower that yields its fragrance to the summer air, have *equal* and yet most *different* duties to render to mankind, from the tall wheat which gives its life up for our sustenance, or the great tree which falls to float our commerce on the sea. There is no hive of bees, no field of growing things, no human household, no housing place of cattle, no machine of man's making, with its complex adaptation of each piece to its work, that does not cry out against the mad mistake of confusing and confounding, into likeness, the distinct and different functions, among which there is no unequalness that means inferiority. And never in any age of the world, nowhere in any land, and nowhere in America, so much as now in our own Empire State, was there such absolute unreason, for the clamour which seeks to distract women from the duties of "the vocation to which they are called," into the mad pursuit of the greatest wrong that can be done to their sex, their country and mankind. Forgive me if, all unwilling, I disturb the sacredness of this place and the sweetness of this scene, with such unwelcome thoughts. But the man who is set in public place to-day, to train *some* of the women of America for their vocation, may not, in times like these, withhold his voice of warning against the dangers and delusions of the hour.

It is what St. Paul calls a high calling; a calling upward, an Ἄνω Κλῆσις, my dear children, to which you are called by every inherent indication of your nature—physical, intellectual, moral, spiritual—to the womanhood of womanly service to God and man.

*OFFICERS OF THE ALBANY ANTI-SUFFRAGE ASSOCIATION.*

| | |
|---|---|
| Mrs. J. V. L. Pruyn, *President.* | Mrs. W. Winslow Crannell, *Chairman.* |
| Mrs. William J. Wallace, *1st Vice-President.* | Mrs. Erastus Corning, |
| | Mrs William Cassidy, |
| Mrs. William Bayard Van Rensselaer, *Secretary.* | Mrs. J. Howard King, |
| | Mrs. Joel R. Reed, |
| Mrs. Joseph Gavit, *Treasurer.* | Mrs. Wm. O. Stillman, |
| | Mrs. Frederick Townsend, *Executive Committee.* |

To any one of whom requests for leaflets may be sent.

Extracts from the remarks of Judge Edgar Aldrich, of Littleton, in the New Hampshire Constitutional Convention of 1902, upon the question of Woman Suffrage, in which he brought before that body certain paragraphs from an Address of the late venerable Harry Bingham

Mr. ALDRICH, of Littleton. Mr. Chairman, I deem it a very great misfortune to myself that I am drawn into the discussion of this question this afternoon. I deem it unfortunate for myself, being in opposition to this measure, to be obliged to state my position in five minutes, because if a man finds himself in opposition to the women, even in the little things of life, it requires more than five minutes to explain why he is there. [Laughter and applause.] But to be serious, the proposition is startling that a question which involves the overthrow of one of the pillars of our civic structure should slide through this Convention on grounds of chivalry with a five-minute limitation upon members desiring to state the reasons for their action upon so important a measure. If I am in opposition to the proposition to strike the word "male" from the Constitution it is not because I deem women as a class less intelligent than men, nor is it because I deem the sphere of woman less important than that of man. I accord to no man a higher appreciation of womanhood than I hold myself. My belief is that the sphere of woman in the world is just as important as that of man. The function of woman in working out the destinies of the home, the destinies of the state, and the destinies of the nation, is quite as important and more exalted than that of man. Man receives his inspiration from woman, and he governs his actions by the judgment of woman, as he finds it in the home. I doubt whether the function of woman would be as important in the affairs of life and the affairs of the nation if she were thrust into the tumultuous turmoils incident to the town meetings and the ward meetings. I doubt if the world would get along as well as it is doing now if the position of women in respect to the home and to voting were changed. Woman's sphere is not to walk elbow to elbow with man into the strife and the tumultuous turmoils of the town meetings and the wars! Man's inspiration, pride, and action largely depend upon his respect and appreciation of woman. I doubt very seriously whether man's chivalric appreciation of the inspiring and beautifying influence of womanhood will remain through many generations if woman shall relinquish her exalted position — her supreme point of vantage — and come down into the struggles of the country and city voting places. It will lower the woman and antagonize rather than elevate the man. It would disturb the serene security of motherhood, and no insistence upon the idea of the abstract right of women to vote can compensate for such a loss as that. It must be remembered that conferring the right to vote imposes the duty. If bad women exercise the right to vote, all women must, or the equilibrium in voting will be wholly lost.

I shall not say anything more upon this question, but I ask the attention of the Convention to a few paragraphs from the address of a very distinguished and a venerable man who sat in this hall for many years. He was one of the grandest men I ever knew, one of the most tolerant, one of the most learned and philosophical. I refer to the late lamented Harry Bingham. His respect for motherhood and the home was sublime.

I remember hearing him say that great nations were impossible without great men, and that great men are possible only where great and good mothers preside over the childhood and the home. The address to which I refer was delivered before the Grafton Bar Association a few years ago, and I ask the Secretary to read the paragraphs which I have marked, and I make them a part of my remarks upon this question.

(The Secretary read:—)

There are some things that without doubt will always remain for the men to do, while other things are left exclusively in the hands of the women. Women will never be called upon to carry the musket or to dig ditches; certainly not except in extraordinary exigencies. The household, the home, the family, are the proper dominion of the wife and mother. There she should be supreme. War, invention, discovery, the subjugation of the wilderness and fitting it for civilization are the business of the men. In a vast number of employments it is not likely that a definite line of demarcation will ever be drawn between what shall be done by one sex and what by the other. No doubt some occupations always will remain open to both sexes alike. No superiority of one sex over the other is implied because in some matters the services of one are preferred to the services of the other. The sex enabled by its peculiar powers to perform a given work better than the other sex can, is preferred and ought to be preferred.

There are questions more or less discussed at the present time about the ballot; whether or not that should be given to woman, and whether or not her participation in such business would be congenial to herself and tend to promote human progress. The class of women (to whom allusion has been made already as of no account) prancing along on the divisional line that society has fixed between the sexes as to manners and costume, putting on mannish airs, garments, and headgear, and exhibiting only faint traces of what would indicate the sex to which they belong, are extremely urgent and vociferous in their demands for the ballot. Although it must be admitted that there are some women and perhaps some men of character endowed with large intellectual powers, who sincerely believe that the whole domain of politics and government ought to be thrown open to women the same as it is to men, that women ought to have universal suffrage and be eligible to all the offices in all departments of the government, and to all positions in every branch of business; yet much the larger part of the sober-minded, sensible women do not regard it as their duty to seek such an extended opening for female action. On the contrary, they denounce the idea and say that it calls upon them to do what does not belong to them to do according to the natural and proper division of work between the sexes, and that they might just as well be called upon to carry the musket or dig ditches.

The propriety and rightfulness of thrusting upon women all the turmoil, uproar, and unseemly strife that the carrying out of such an idea would involve is certainly very doubtful. It would not enable her to use her natural and legitimate influence to any better advantage. On the contrary, it would place her in an unnatural position and where she would not feel at home, and thus she would be compelled to exercise her wholesome and necessary influence at a disadvantage. Her influence to be effective and useful must operate through the natural channels of female influence and in accordance with the laws of her being. The suggestion that we ought to wait until the human race is further advanced in light and civilization before we thrust upon woman the responsibility of the ballot fully extended, and of running the government in all its branches, is certainly reasonable. The intimate association of woman with children and youth, the deep interest she feels in their welfare, and her special responsibility for them, have caused everybody to agree that she ought to have a potential voice in their training and education. In accordance with this general popular assent, a movement was inaugurated some time ago by which women have been made competent voters in school meetings, and eligible to the offices which have the management and control of the schools.

Certain Rocky Mountain states and other Western states have imposed upon their women the responsibility of the ballot, and of taking an equal part with the men in administering the government in all its branches. This movement must be regarded as simply tentative and experimental. We shall do well if we watch it long enough to be satisfied as to its character. We shall then be able to draw inferences that may aid us in determining what we ought to do. It will no doubt be a good disposition of this question if we leave it to be determined by the next generation. We have shown already what that generation is expected to be. We have shown that in it and a part of it will be the sons and daughters of mothers who are now girls receiving training and discipline in our numerous institutions for the higher education of women. We have a right to expect for this reason that the next generation will have the capacity to judge in regard to this and all other questions more wisely than we of this generation can. Also, facts bearing on the question now unknown will then have come to light. The results of the experiments now going on in the Rocky Mountain and other Western states will then be known, and the evidence presented to the next generation may remove all doubt and make very plain the way this question ought to be decided. What gives the question importance is the effect that its determination either way may have upon human progress. Whenever it shall come to pass that the level-headed, sober-minded, sensible women substantially concur in the conclusion that woman never will have her normal position in organized society until she has the ballot and takes equal part with man in governmental affairs, and that the welfare and future progress of the race require her to assume those responsibilities, in the interest of harmony between the sexes which must be preserved, it will then be necessary to inaugurate and try the experiment without delay.

In settling this question and all other questions as to the position each sex ought to occupy in society, let it always be remembered that man and woman are partners in the business of maintaining and improving the human race; that their joint obligation to contribute to the progress of the race will continue until mankind have advanced in knowledge, virtue, and goodness as near to Divinity itself as the lot of humanity will permit.

\* \* \* \* \*

Mr. Aldrich, of Littleton. Mr. Chairman, I do not want to be outdone by the gallant gentleman from Bow [Mr. Baker] in chivalric devotion to the fair sex. [Laughter and applause.] I have a wife and a daughter, and they are both opposed to this proposition, and I am bound in making up my judgment to consider the sanctity of the home. Everybody is bound to do that. Now, in voting upon my judgment, I vote against the unqualified declaration to strike the word "male" from the Constitution, because, if the proposition prevails, the impression will go out to the world that this Convention, voting upon its judgment, has declared in favor of woman suffrage.

\* \* \* \* \*

*Printed by the Massachusetts Association opposed to further Extension of Suffrage to women.*

Pamphlets and leaflets may be obtained from the Secretary of the Association,

Mrs. Robert W. Lord,
P. O. Box 2262, Boston.

BULLETIN No. 7

# FACTS AND FALLACIES

ABOUT

# WOMAN SUFFRAGE

ILLINOIS ASSOCIATION
OPPOSED TO WOMAN SUFFRAGE
1523 DEARBORN AVENUE
CHICAGO

*The Association*

# The Illinois Association Opposed to Woman Suffrage

### OFFICERS

*President,*
Mrs. Caroline F. Corbin

*Vice Presidents,*

| | |
|---|---|
| Mrs. S. M. Nickerson | Mrs. James M. Walker |
| Mrs. R. J. Oglesby | Mrs. T. B. Blackstone |

Mrs. Geo. W. Kretzinger............................................*Recording Secretary*
Miss J. C. Fairfield.................................................................*Treasurer*

### EXECUTIVE COMMITTEE
The Officers and,

| | |
|---|---|
| Mrs. B. F. Ayer | Mrs. Francis Lackner |
| Mrs. John de Koven | Miss Larrabee |
| Miss Mary Pomeroy Green | Mrs. J. H. Roseboom |
| Miss M. D. Hutchison | Mrs. Orson Smith |
| Mrs. R. N. Isham | Mrs. John C. Willing |

### SECRETARY FOR LITERATURE
Miss J. C. Fairfield
1523 Dearborn Avenue, Chicago

# Facts and Fallacies About Woman Suffrage.

In a recent issue of a leading New York daily the Woman Suffrage platform is summed up as follows:

"We want to vote.
We ought to vote.
We will keep up this agitation till we are allowed to vote."

In this paper it is proposed to comment upon these affirmations, and cite opposing circumstances.

It is a mistake to suppose that the great majority of women want to vote. **They do not.** In proof of which we state the following facts, which can easily be verified. We mention first the Massachusetts referendum of 1895, in which the women of that state, which was one of the earliest and strongest advocates of suffrage for women, were invited to put themselves on record, by the same means that men do, and under the same conditions, as to whether or not they desired the ballot. Less than four per cent of all the women of the state, of voting age, expressed such a desire, and that in spite of the earnest efforts of the suffragist agitators to call out a large affirmative vote. The proposition was ingloriously defeated all over the state, from Cape Cod to the Berkshire Hills, no measure having ever met with so overwhelming an overthrow in the state. Very naturally a proposition for a similar referendum in New York state in 1910 was strongly opposed by the suffragists.

School suffrage, now granted in about half our states, has been a lamentable failure, the woman vote averaging scarcely 2 per cent in any state. In the state of Ohio the number of women responding to the privilege has been so small, and the expense of registering and counting it has been so relatively large, that it has been seriously proposed to withdraw it altogether.

In Chicago, in the election of November 8, 1910, where women are allowed to vote for University Trustees, in spite of the earnest efforts of the suffragists to bring out the full woman vote of the city, its population being counted by millions, 490 females registered, and of these but 243 voted.

Several years ago it was proposed to send a monster petition, signed by a million women, to the Congress of the United States. The changes upon this petition were continually rung in our ears, and the petition itself was circulated throughout the country, and women's names were sought, begged, entreated and cajoled in every possible way. During the last session of Congress (1910) the petition was carried to Washington, with great noise of trumpets and tooting of automobiles, but when the signatures were examined they were found to number less than half a million; to be exact, women 163,438, men 122,382, and 119,005 described by the presenters as "unclassified." We do not know exactly what this term implies, but it has been suggested that they may be babes and children, whose names were enrolled on the supposition that when they were grown up they would no doubt be suffragists. The population of the United States according to the census of 1910, is considerably more than 90,000,000. We decline to figure out the insignificant percentage of the number which the names signed to this petition, represent.

The Woman's Home Companion, a large and very popular woman's magazine, concludes a lengthy and impartial article on the subject of woman suffrage in its number for October 1st, 1910, by saying of New York City:

"It is a picturesque struggle, this daily and hourly fight of not more than two thousand women, to convert a city of four million souls, to a cause which the nation has thought for fifteen years dead," and it cautions the women to beware of "the dull thud of the American man's foot," which may be slow in coming down upon the fanatical schemes which women sometimes advocate, but which in the end is tolerably sure. We quote the paragraph for the statistics it contains. We believe they afford a generous estimate of the relative numbers of the women who desire to vote.

### Why Women Vote in Colorado.

But it is said that women vote in Colorado and the other States where the full vote is allowed, as freely as the men. To this we reply, that the rivalry of parties forces out many unwilling voters, on both sides, including women who vote at the solicitation of men anxious for the passage of certain measures, as well as the illiterate and immoral who are the prey of bosses and ringsters. We have testimony to this fact from both Suffrage and Anti-Suffrage sources. We cite first a long and impartial article in the Ladies' Home Journal of November 1st, 1910, a paper having a circulation of more than a million copies. It sent Mr. Richard Barry, a well known writer on Sociological topics to Colorado with instructions to prepare a full and accurate account of the results of woman suffrage in the suffrage States, and his statements we know to be confirmed by the testimony of many estimable women in Colorado, who state that they are not nearly as free in working for philanthropic measures as in the old days when their influence was unhampered by partisan responsibilities.

Mr. Barry's testimony on this as well as upon many other points is very strong, but too long to be transcribed entire. For our present purpose we prefer to quote from a book prepared by Dr. Helen L. Sumner, a woman suffragist, who spent two years in Colorado at the request of an Equal Suffrage Association in New York, to prepare a true and unbiased account of the effect of suffrage upon the individual and society. Her statement of facts coincides so generally with that of Mr. Barry, that if her individual theories and conclusions were cut out of it, the book might almost as well be used as Anti-Suffrage as Suffrage campaign literature.

Dr. Sumner says (page 258), speaking of the woman vote, "Its effect upon party politics has been slight." "In 1906 a woman sat through the sessions of one of the long tedious conventions in Denver with a nine-weeks-old baby in her arms. Neither she nor her husband believed in Woman Suffrage but her husband held a political position." She also quotes, with apparent approval, "Woman's sense of honor has been blunted," "Women have been made bolder and more self assertive." A county chairman over his own signature testified "In the last campaign women who sold their influence agreed to work for both parties for cash—the highest price paid $25, lowest $5. I myself bought one woman for $10 when the Democrats bought her for $15, and we have her endorsement on both checks." There are many pages in Dr. Sumner's book which strikingly confirm Mr. Barry's statements.

### Uplift in Morals Consequent Upon Woman Suffrage.

As regards the boasted improvement in morals consequent upon the woman's vote, in a table of statistics, gathered from public sources in Colorado, where women have voted since 1896, Mr. Barry shows conclusively that there has been a steady decline in the morals of the States of Idaho, Utah, Wyoming and Colorado in regard to marriage and divorce since they were admitted to suffrage. Illiteracy is much greater and the care of children much less, as indicated by the alarming increase in juvenile crime in a State where the Juvenile Court only recently established, takes rank over the mother and the home. All these are matters in which women might be supposed to be specially interested, but these States fall far behind in morals, the most advanced of the non-suffrage States. Every page of this article, which is in fact a report fortified by undeniable statistics, is so full of evidence of the demoralizing effect of Woman Suffrage, that it needs to be read to be appreciated.

### Taxation Without Representation.

But, say the suffragists, "tax-paying women certainly ought to vote." To which we reply that in this country great pains have been taken to make voting and tax-paying as unrelated as possible. Representation, which is all that the old war-cry ever demanded, is, and always has been a very different matter from voting. Women, as the record shows, have always, in this country at least, been represented with a growing sense of fairness and justice on the part of men; till now in many States, Ilinois among them, their right to property and the guardianship of children are more fully protected by law than those of men. The fathers of the Ameriacn Revolution felt that their women were, as much as themselves, in need of emancipation from the old and out-grown feudal rule; and one of the first things to which they turned their attention when the new government was established, was to ameliorate their legal condition, and make it correspond in its own way with the progress which they had won for themselves. And this was long before woman suffrage had a shadow of influence in the councils of the state. Men indeed reserved to themselves the right to make the laws of the state, but they emphatically testified that it was not as property owners that they voted, but simply as citizens, who could serve the state in governmental capacities, or be drafted into the army in time of war, both of which services from physical incapacity, women would be unable to render. That rich women should ever be entitled to vote when poor women were not, thus establishing a plutocratic aristocracy, was certainly opposed to their ideas of public polity. But that is precisely what a tax-paying vote for women would imply.

### Working Women.

"But surely," say the suffragists, "the working women ought to vote." We reply that the census of the United States shows that a very large percentage of female workers are quite below the voting age, and that the majority of these are married before they reach full maturity, giving way to another army of girls who are not yet considered by the state mature enough to vote. Miss Minnie Bronson, formerly a special agent of the United States Bureau of Labor, Washington, D. C., says, in a paper devoted to proving that the working woman is quite as well protected in non-suffrage, as in suffrage states, and that the possession of the ballot could not improve her condition: "In the great strike of the shirt-waist makers in New York in 1910, of these strikers 40 per cent were men, 60 per cent of the remainder were under twenty-one years of age, and 25 per cent of all the women voters of voting age had not been in the country long enough to gain a residence." So fallacious are the statements generally made in regard to the need of women workers for the ballot. It may be added, that as to the demand of unmarried women, educated or otherwise, many of whom have not reached maturity of age or experience, we fail to see that their opinions have a greater claim to recognition than the conclusions of women, who through marriage and motherhood have come to a practical understanding of what woman's work should be.

### Woman's True Work.

Which brings us to the second affirmative of the suffrage platform, as above quoted: "We ought to vote," which we answer by another question—If women "ought to vote" why have men, in this free country, been so ready to protect her in the rights she now enjoys, rather than to bestow upon her those political rights, which they have reserved to themselves? Why indeed, unless because they instinctively recognize that distinct specialization of sex, which is the first and most manifest distinction which nature bestows, not upon mankind alone, but upon all the sentient works of her hand.

Male and female are as distinctly specialized in the "prehistoric protozoa" as they are today in the human race. It is nature's way of setting apart a certain percentage of any generation for the specific duty of bearing and rearing the next generation, and so of continuing her work, and of laying the foundations of the higher or moral side of the world's life. It is not now as universally recognized as it undoubtedly will be as science advances from the consideration of material things to that of the moral phases of life, that the work of continuance and moral upbuilding, which has its foundation in the co-relation of male and female attributes, makes the natural sphere of women fully equal with that of the opposite sex. Woman does not need the ballot to make her equal with man. If she faithfully performs the duties which nature lays upon her, and upon her alone, she is not only his equal, but more than his equal. It is as the mother of men that she reigns supreme. To lower this attitude by claiming for her a material equality is to reduce her from a powerful and beneficent necessity, to a weak and lamentable copy of the original type from which she was so wisely and beneficently segregated.

As a proof that without the ballot women are to a good degree and increasingly, fulfilling this intention, we instance the progress which has been made during the last decade in the pursuits of the domestic arts and sciences, in the care and proper upbringing of children, in the regulation of the hygienic and moral conditions in our schools, and in bringing to light and commenting upon the evil and vicious social theories, which have so long hidden themselves from the public view, and many other needed and valuable reforms. In all these lines of progress women have been either the originators of public beneficence, or its faithful and untiring helpers.

The public part of this work has not been, could not have been done by the universal suffrage of all women, young and old, wise and foolish, indifferent and thoughtful, as it has been done by voluntary or appointed officials, chosen from the ranks of tried and experienced women, upon whose judgment and unselfishness the public has learned to rely, and the reason that as a rule they stand higher in the world's estimation than the average man, is that they do not represent the universal element of politics, but are in themselves a selected and specialized class, peculiarly fitted in the eyes of the public, for the duties to which they are appointed.

It remains to note the summing up of this very apt newspaper platform.

"We will keep up the agitation till we are allowed to vote."

That matter lies wholly in the hands of men. Will they, or will they not listen to the shallow and oftentimes misleading arguments of agitators, and renounce the distinctive manhood with which nature and civilization have crowned them; will they degrade the sphere to which nature has elevated their sisters, wives and mothers, and which promotes, as we truly believe, the moral uplift of the race; will they reverse all that wonderful machinery which nature has devised to ensure the ever increasing progress of the world in gentleness, peacefulness, and spiritual aspiration?

Chicago, March, 1911.

# FEMALE SUFFRAGE.

A LETTER

FROM

THE RIGHT HON. W. E. GLADSTONE, M.P.

TO

SAMUEL SMITH, M.P.

———

REPRINTED BY
AMERICAN WOMEN REMONSTRANTS TO THE
EXTENSION OF SUFFRAGE TO WOMEN.

# FEMALE SUFFRAGE.

1, Carlton Gardens,
*April* 11, 1892.

Dear Mr. Samuel Smith,

In reply to your letter, I cannot but express the hope that the House of Commons will not consent to the second reading of the Bill for Extending the Parliamentary Suffrage to Women, which will come before it on the 27th instant.

The Bill is a narrow Bill, inasmuch as it excludes from its operation the entire body of married women; who are not less reflective, intelligent, and virtuous, than their unmarried sisters, and who must I think be superior in another great element of fitness, namely the lifelong habit of responsible action. If this change is to be made, I certainly have doubts, not yet dispelled, whether it ought to be made in the shape which would thus be given to it by a halting and inconsistent measure.

But it is a change which obviously, and apart from disputable matter, ought not to be made without the fullest consideration and the most deliberate assent of the nation as well as of the Parliament. Not only has there been no such assent, but there has not been even an approach to such consideration. The subject has occupied a large place in the minds of many thoughtful persons, and of these a portion have become its zealous adherents. Just weight should be allowed to their sentiments, and it is desirable that the arguments on both sides should be carefully and generally scrutinised: but the subject is as yet only sectional, and has not really been taken into view by the public mind at large. Can it be right, under these circumstances, that the principle of a change so profound should be adopted? Cannot its promoters be content with that continuance and extension of discussion, which alone can adequately sift the true merits of their cause?

I offer this suggestion in the face of the coming Election. I am aware that no legitimate or effectual use can be made of it for carrying to an issue a question at once so great and so novel; but I do not doubt, considering the zeal and ability which are enlisted in its favour, that the occasion might be made available for procuring an increase of attention to the subject, which I join with them in earnestly desiring.

There are very special reasons for circumspection in this particular case. There has never within my knowledge been a case in which the franchise has been extended to a large body of persons generally indifferent about receiving it. But here, in addition to a widespread indifference, there is on the part of large numbers of women who have considered the matter for themselves, the most positive objection and strong disapprobation. Is it not clear to every unbiassed mind that before forcing on them what they conceive to be a fundamental change in their whole social function, that is to say in their Providential calling, at least it should be ascertained that the womanly mind of the country, at present so largely strange to the subject, is in overwhelming proportion, and with deliberate purpose, set upon securing it?

I speak of the change as being a fundamental change in the whole social function of woman, because I am bound in considering this Bill to take into view not only what it enacts, but what it involves. The first of these, though important, is small in comparison with the last.

What the Bill enacts is simply to place the individual woman on the same footing in regard to Parliamentary elections, as the individual man. She is to vote, she is to propose or nominate, she is to be designated by the law as competent to use and to direct, with advantage not only to the community but to herself, all those public agencies which belong to our system of Parliamentary representation. She, not the individual woman, marked by special tastes, possessed of special gifts, but the woman as such, is by this change to be plenarily launched into the whirlpool of public life, such as it is in the nineteenth, and such as it is to be in the twentieth century.

So much for what the Bill enacts: now for what it involves, and involves in the way of fair and rational, and therefore of morally necessary, consequence. For a long time we drew a distinction between competency to vote and competency to sit in Parliament. But long before our electorate had attained to the present popular proportions, this distinction was felt to involve a palpable inconsistency, and accordingly it died away. It surely cannot be revived: and if it cannot be revived, then the woman's vote carries with it, whether by the same Bill or by a consequential Bill, the woman's seat in Parliament. These assertions ought to be strictly tested. But, if they cannot be confuted, do not let them be ignored.

If the woman's vote carries with it the woman's seat, have we at this point reached our terminus, and found a standing ground which we can in reason and in justice regard as final? Capacity to sit in the House of Commons now legally and practically draws in its train capacity to fill every office in the State. Can we alter this rule and determine to have two categories of Members of Parliament, one of them, the established and the larger one, consisting of persons who can travel without check along all the lines of public duty and honour, the other, the novel and the smaller one, stamped with disability for the discharge of executive, administrative, judicial, or other public duty? Such a stamp would I apprehend be a brand. There is nothing more odious, nothing more untenable, than an inequality in legal privilege which does not stand upon some principle in its nature broad and clear. Is there here such a principle, adequate to show that when capacity to sit in Parliament has been established, the title to discharge executive and judicial duty can be withheld? Tried by the test of feeling, the distinction would be offensive. Would it stand better under the laws of logic? It would stand still worse, if worse be possible. For the proposition we should have to maintain would be this. The legislative duty is the highest of all public duties; for this we admit your fitness. Executive and judicial duties rank below it: and for these we declare you unfit.

I think it impossible to deny that there have been and are women individually fit for any public office however masculine its character; just as there are persons under the age of twenty-one better fitted than many of those beyond it for the discharge of the duties of full citizenship. In neither case does the argument derived from exceptional instances seem to justify the abolition of the general rule. But the risks involved in the two suppositions are immeasurably different. In the one, individual judgment and authority plainly would have to distinguish between childhood and manhood, and to specify a criterion of competency in each case, which is now more conveniently fixed by the uniformity of law. In the other, a permanent and vast difference of type has been impressed upon women and men respectively by the Maker of both. Their differences of social office rest mainly upon causes, not flexible and elastic like most mental qualities, but physical and in their nature unchangeable. I for one am not prepared to say which of the two sexes has the higher and which has the lower province. But I recognize the subtle and profound character of the differences between them, and I must again, and again, and again, deliberate before aiding in the issue of what seems an invitation by public authority to the one to renounce as far as possible its own office, in order to assume that of the other. I am not without the fear lest beginning with the State, we should eventually be found to have intruded into what is yet more fundamental and more sacred, the precinct of the family, and should dislocate, or injuriously modify, the relations of domestic life.

As this is not a party question, or a class question, so neither is it a sex question. I have no fear lest the woman should encroach upon the power of the man. The fear I have is, lest we should invite her unwittingly to trespass upon the delicacy, the purity, the refinement, the elevation of her own nature, which are the present sources of its power. I admit that we have often, as legislators, been most unfaithful guardians of her rights to moral and social equality. And I do not say that full justice has in all things yet been done; but such great progress has been made in most things, that in regard to what may still remain the necessity for violent remedies has not yet been shown. I admit that in the Universities, in the professions, in the secondary circles of public action, we have already gone so far as to give a shadow of plausibility to the present proposals to go farther; but it is a shadow only, for we have done nothing that plunges the woman as such into the turmoil of masculine life. My disposition is to do all for her which is free from that danger and reproach, but to take no step in advance until I am convinced of its safety. The stake is enormous. The affirmation pleas are to my mind not clear, and, even if I thought them clearer, I should deny that they were pressing.

Such being the state of the evidence, and also such the immaturity of the public mind, I earnestly hope that the House of Commons will decline to give a second reading to the Woman's Suffrage Bill.

I remain, dear Mr. S. Smith,

Very faithfully yours,

W. E. GLADSTONE.

BULLETIN No. 10

# FIFTEENTH ANNUAL REPORT

ILLINOIS ASSOCIATION
OPPOSED TO WOMAN SUFFRAGE
1523 DEARBORN AVENUE
CHICAGO

# The Illinois Association Opposed to Woman Suffrage

---

### OFFICERS

*President,*
Mrs. Caroline F. Corbin

*Vice-Presidents,*

| | |
|---|---|
| Mrs. S. M. Nickerson | Mrs. James M. Walker |
| Mrs. R. J. Oglesby | Mrs. T. B. Blackstone |

Miss J. C. Fairfield.................................*Secretary and Treasurer*
1523 Dearborn Avenue

### EXECUTIVE COMMITTEE

The Officers and,

| | |
|---|---|
| Mrs. B. F. Ayer | Mrs. R. N. Isham |
| Mrs. John de Koven | Mrs. Francis Lackner |
| Miss Mary Pomeroy Green | Miss Larrabee |
| Mrs. Geo. W. Kretzinger | Mrs. J. H. Roseboom |
| Miss M. D. Hutchison | Mrs. Orson Smith |

Mrs. John C. Welling

# Fifteenth Annual Report

Ladies:

Our work for the past year has been mostly as heretofore, the distribution of literature, original and selected. Our Bulletins issued every three months, go regularly to about one thousand of the best newspapers in this country, from New York to California, from Maine to Florida, and to the Legislatures, Libraries, and to clergymen. In addition to these we send out in packages, when asked for them, as we are at the rate of from one to five a week, in all more than twenty thousand copies. These are scattered to every state in the Union. This may be done with a comparatively small membership, since we make no account of conventions or public meetings of any sort, but it gives us in the end a large and interested audience. The money called for is, likewise, nothing like that involved in the report of the meeting of the National Woman Suffrage Association recently held in Frankfort, Ky., which deplored the existence of a deficit of $60,000 for salaries and traveling expenses alone. So far as we know, not one of the dozen and more states which have formed Committees or Associations for the opposition of Woman Suffrage have ever been obliged to report a deficit in expenses, but most, if not all of them have a small but efficient balance on the opposite side. In a country where the public income often runs into many millions, it is important, we think, to consider this question of reckless expenditure.

Our watchfulness of the wide field suggested by this report brings many queries to mind, a few of which I feel moved to present to your attention this morning. Perhaps the first one may well be: Why is this agitation in favor of Suffrage called pre-eminently the woman movement, as though advocated by all women and supported unanimously by them? Why should not the movement, slow, perhaps, of growth, but supported by some of the largest and most important States of the Union, which opposes the thrusting of political duties and responsibilities upon women, without their demand or consent, be likewise recognized as a woman movement?

It has good grounds for its opposition, based as it is upon the universal dictum of nature and civilization, which recognizes that the work of woman is distinct from that of man, and can never be usurped by him, nor the continuance and moral uplift of the race achieved without it; and we affirm that if any movement should practically be known as the woman movement, it is that affirmative one which upholds woman as the origin and moral savior of the race.

Why is the common reply of men, even of some noted members of those arrayed upon our side of the question, when appealed to for votes for women, that "when the majority of women demand the ballot it will be given them."

We believe this reply to be insincere, and based wholly upon false and fallacious grounds. It implies that the men of our earlier days were actuated wholly by selfish and insincere motives when they kept the ballot in their own hands and that it would be simply a matter of gallantry to bestow it upon women. We deny this assumption altogether. We believe that men in the beginning justly regarded a free government as the work of men and that they kept the management of it in their own hands, in order that the time and labor of women might be relieved of such work so that they might have more time for those labors which nature has made inseparable from their constitution and of which men can never relieve them. It is this fact, patent to all men and women, which makes the foundation of the home and which suffragists universally ignore in practice. A recent suffrage writer puts the doctrine thus: "We women owe nothing to our husbands or children, because we have duties only to ourselves. The individual is an end in himself and ought not to be considered merely as the means of creating another individual. Love and maternity should be only episodes in the life of women." But, somehow or other, the slight episodes of love and maternity seem to get in the way of woman's success, and though every woman in the world claimed the right of doing man's work if she pleased, we affirm that men have no right to yield to her clamor, till they are willing and able to bear and rear half the children from which the next generation shall be recruited, and to be responsible in their own persons for the labor and duties of the moral and affectional world.

The work of the sexes is co-ordinate, one cannot be complete without the other. The original Creator devised the plan of co-operation and upon it based the equality, the oneness of the married state, and men have no right, much less the ability, to controvert it.

A certain religious paper of the East, of high character, while carefully maintaining its neutrality as a matter of policy, points out that "men have hitherto been the granters of the ballot to such women as have gained it, that it has been so far in States where women have been decidedly in the minority, and that as the agitation has pursued its way into the more populous states, the opposition to it has been more stubborn." This is true and also that women are everywhere more strenuously objecting to having political obligations thrust upon them against their will and in opposition to the more advanced educators and scientists who are directing their best and most salutary work; and that women by a large majority deem that the men who favor the ballot for the female sex, lower their own dignity in the State and belittle their own importance as the true makers and enforcers of law.

Why, we ask in all seriousness, should it be considered justice to woman to double her labors and responsibilities, while it halves those of men, as making women equally responsible with men for the political duties involved in the ballot would do. The holding and managing of caucuses, conventions, primaries, courts and legislatures, are all involved in the simple casting of a ballot and these are labors which call forth the extreme of man's physical and intellectual power. Who would consider it wise or just to exact of him, besides, the bearing of children, the training of them in obedience, purity, knowledge of right and wrong and all those moral virtues which the State requires that he shall learn in the first twenty-one years of his life, in the home and at the hands of his parents, especially his mother?

The attempt to assert the economic and industrial equality of women with men must necessarily result in failure. Nature has given her a physical constitution, adapted to her work as woman, and this fact makes her forever of less value as a worker in material things than man. She has not the strength, the endurance, the equal flow of vitality which the world's work demands. Meantime her power, drawn off from the labor which Nature assigns her, leaves the world depleted by just so much of moral strength and all the best educators and scientists declare, lowers the entire race in its affectional, social and moral achievements. Instead of going forward we go backward. This is ever the result of founding a people upon an individual rather than upon a family basis.

If woman's work in the home were always properly performed, there would be far fewer bosses, ringsters and grafters in the world at large. It is a case where prevention is much better than cure.

The United States census shows that of all the women now employed in doing the outside work of the world, a very large proportion are girls not yet of voting age, and who, as they marry, as many of them do, will be supplanted by other girls not yet women, but still in that unformed age when the experiences of womanhood and its duties are still before them. We affirm that it is neither right nor just to place their opinions and needs in opposition to those of mature women who know by experience the wants of the sex.

Perhaps the most important question of all remains to be answered. Whence arose this heresy that all the American woman needs for her perpetual glorification is the right to vote, and how does it happen that such success as it has attained, is on the western shore of our continent? Also does it tend to the confirmation of the early ideas of this American people, that the family rather than the individual is the basis of free government, or does its spread incline to destroy the sacredness of marriage, lessen the natural increase of the race and destroy those moral ideals upon which the wonderful and almost incredible advance of our government has mainly been founded?

A short and simple answer to these questions, but one abundantly vindicated by the testimony of the past sixty or seventy years, is that the doctrine of woman suffrage came first from Europe and was an offshoot of the rising agitation of Communism and Socialism; that it was introduced into New York by the Woman Suffrage Convention of 1848, called by Mrs. Elizabeth Cady Stanton and a few of her friends. Since then it has been agitated in the East by a growing party of radicals often with atheistic tendencies. In the latter part of the last century it was taken up by Populism, itself a party with Socialistic tendencies, and thus became a political issue in the West. When Populism died it was believed by many people that Woman Suffrage died out with it, but they had not reckoned upon the determined vitality of European Socialism. This party, having seized upon the great continent of Australia known a half century ago as Botany Bay, a penal colony of England, and ready for any form of European heresy which might be brought to it, sought with some success to establish there a Socialist colony, in which the doctrine of the individual rights of men and women should overthrow the doctrine of the family as established in the beginning.

Before time had elapsed to give this colony a fair trial it came across the Pacific and joined hands with the remnant of Woman Suffrage left by Populism and the two, together with Mormonism, which still cherished its doctrine of plural wives, gained an ascendancy in five of our least organized and least civilized Western States. None of these States, however,

# HIDDEN FROM HISTORY

## From N. Y. MAIL AND EXPRESS,

### May 12th, 1897.

The progress that woman's suffrage has made in New Zealand is causing considerable agitating talk in England, especially in view of the fact that the women are voting against the extreme temperance party. In 1893 the New Zealand parliament established full female suffrage, equivalent to that of the men, and it also passed a law giving absolute right of local control, even to the extent of the entire prohibition of the liquor traffic.

The first Parliament and the first local control elections in 1894 were in accordance with the expectations of the reformers, for the women electors came strongly to the poll. They were almost universally in favor of the limitation of the liquor licenses. They supported the advanced radical candidates. The social question came to the front, and men of dubious morality stood little chance in that election. The progressive party and its friends congratulated themselves on the fact that the accession of women to politics was a great gain for the democrats and social reform. But on the second election which has recently taken place, all these calculations were disturbed. Previous to the election extensive canvassing was done by the publicans and prohibitionists. Organizations were formed in all directions; every elector, male and female, was canvassed. Temperance literature was scattered broadcast. The liquor sellers formed what they called Liberty Leagues all over the island and boomed their side. Three distinct issues were presented to the electors: one that the liquor traffic should continue as it is at present, the number of licenses remaining unchanged ; another, that these licenses should be greatly reduced, and the third issue was that there should be total prohibition of the sale of intoxicants. In no one district was the reduction of licenses carried, or were licenses altogether refused. This extraordinary result has only been attained by the shifting of a large part of the women's votes from the temperance to the liquor party, in exact opposition to their votes of three years since.

Sir Robert Stout, writing in the Australian "Review of Reviews" says: "It cannot be said that purity of administration or the character of the candidates loomed larger in the eyes of women than in those of men. The prediction that party zeal and partisan feeling would not blind them to the defects of the character of candidates has not been fulfilled. A few members have been returned to the House whose character for sobriety does not stand high, and women were found supporting them just as much as men. It cannot be said that women were anywise different in their voting from their husbands and brothers. They were carried away just as much by party cries as the men were, and party dominated them. That the influence of women in politics and their voting will not be different from that of their husbands and brothers may be regarded as a foregone conclusion."

For more leaflets, send to 13 Elk Street, Albany, N. Y.

## FROM THE OUTLOOK.

### March 31, April 7, April 14.

A PETITION is being extensively circulated in the State of New York, to be presented to the approaching Constitutional Convention, asking to strike out the word "male" from the provision regulating suffrage. This amendment, adopted, would confer suffrage upon the women of the State. . . . . . . . . . .
. . . . Woman has the suffrage in Washington and Colorado; she has suffrage on certain matters in several of the States; many women who have no political ambition are yet desirous of suffrage on school and excise questions; but it is at least doubtful whether any line can be legitimately drawn between topics on which women may and topics on which they may not vote. The movement for woman suffrage cannot be laughed down; it is not a proper theme for satire. Nor can it be disapproved on the ground that women are incompetent to exercise the suffrage. He would be a singular woman-hater who would affirm that the average woman is not as capable of voting intelligently and uncorruptly as are the average voters in our great cities or those in the Black Belt. Woman's capacity to deal with public questions was assured when education was guaranteed her. If there are some distinctively feminine qualities which might make mischief at the ballot-box, there are other distinctively masculine qualities equally mischievous. American democracy cannot refuse the ballot to woman on the ground of her incompetence. Universal suffrage ignores distinctions of class, sect, position, even learning. If it recognizes a distinction of sex, it must have a clear reason to show for so doing. . . . . . .

If, therefore, suffrage were a privilege and women were deprived of it, justice would combine with chivalry in demanding that it be given to her. But suffrage is not a privilege to be enjoyed! it is a duty to be performed; often a burden to be borne. This fundamental truth needs constant reiteration.

The question whether women shall vote is not, Shall a privilege be extended to them of which they are now deprived? but, Shall a duty be laid upon them from which they are now exempt?

For it must not be forgotten that if a woman *may* vote she *must* vote. And not only must she vote, she must acquaint herself with public questions and be prepared to vote upon them independently and intelligently. America has already too many selfish, indifferent, and unintelligent voters. She has too many men who might exercise a wide influence on the votes of others, who do not even take the trouble to cast their ballot. If the suffrage is extended to women, and they do not accept it as a sacred duty, the only result will be a great accession of unintelligent voters, swayed by party passion, domestic influence, or sectarian and ecclesiastical counselors, and a great abstention from the polls of the women whose votes would really count on the side of wisdom and virtue. It is only as the women of education and culture accept the suffrage as a sacred duty, and bring to bear upon the performance of that duty the same conscientious spirit which they bring to bear upon their present life-problems, that the extension of the suffrage could be of any benefit to them or to the State.

The question, then, to be considered is this: Is it the duty of women to take up the political burdens of the State? We say this is the question for the women to consider, because if the time ever comes when a majority of the women of this country think that they ought to assume a share of political responsibility, the men will not refuse it to them.

. . . . . . . . .

If the women of the State of New York do not wish to assume the responsibilities of the suffrage, it is high time they bestirred themselves to say so. For the women who do want the ballot are naturally enthusiastic; the women who do not want it are naturally apathetic; and a little enthusiasm is more than a match for a great deal of apathy. The woman suffragists are, quite properly, pushing very vigorously to get signatures to their petition for the extension of the suffrage; the women who do not want to vote are, naturally enough, staying at home, and paying little or no attention to the matter. Under these circumstances thousands of signatures are attached to the petition by persons who do not consider seriously the effect of the political revolution which would be involved if the petition should be granted. The unwisdom of conservative opposition to this movement has, moreover, greatly strengthened it. It has been gravely argued that women are incompetent to vote; this has been asserted in an age and country which confers the ballot on thousands of foreigners and millions of negroes who cannot read the ballot put into their hand. The ballot is falsely treated as a kind of symbol of citizenship; the deprivation of it as a denial of equality. Women are told that by that deprivation they are classed with idiots, the insane, criminals, and children. All this stirs their resentment, as it ought to do. Educated women demand the ballot, not because they really want to vote, but because they want this symbolic and official recognition of their competency and character. Meanwhile the men, who have to decide this question, are waiting to see what the women want. Convince the voters of this State that the women want the ballot, and it will instantly be given to them. Few husbands would deny it to the wife if she wanted it; fewer sons to the mother. The question is really one for the wives and the mothers to determine.

The danger is that it will be determined by the enthusiasm of the few and by the apathy of the many.

. . . . . . . . .

In our judgment, then, the women of this country can no longer treat the woman suffrage question with indifference. They can no longer regard it as the pet notion of a few impracticables, who accord a harmless entertainment to the public by a pure doctrinaire agitation. The question of woman suffrage is fast becoming, if it has not already become, a practical question. The women who do not believe that the advantages of woman suffrage would counterbalance the disadvantages, who treasure their present exemption and desire to be exempt in the future, or who have never really given the subject any serious consideration, are brought by the present condition of the problem to a point where they can continue their indifference no longer, but must seriously consider the issue for themselves and their daughters, and determine whether their influence shall be cast for or against the extension of the ballot. The time is already at hand when *no* influence is practically *an* influence in support of the movement. . . . . . . . . .

There is no advantage in a mere extension of the suffrage. If one million of voters can decide a question, there is no necessary advantage in summoning two million voters to decide it. There is, on the contrary, some disadvantage, since it involves double the amount of human energy. It must be made to appear that this enlargement of the political tribunal is either of advantage to the new voters as an education, or to the community as an accession to its wisdom. These are the two questions which the women of the State of New York have first to determine. . .

And these are followed by another. If the women of the State are to assume the duty of suffrage, they must either add it to their other duties, or must lay aside other duties to take up this new duty. Which alternate will they accept? Doubtless there are a considerable number of idle women who could take on new duties without being overburdened. But we do not believe that the proportion of idle women is any larger than that of idle men; we doubt if it be as large. The women in agricultural districts are generally overworked. In towns and cities domestic cares are for many less exacting; but, relieved from household drudgery, women have taken upon themselves the sweet offices of charity and religion. They are increasingly the directors and managers of charitable, educational, and religious institutions. They are the almoners of bounty made possible only by the concentration of masculine energy in the accumulation of means out of which that bounty can be bestowed. In determining the question whether they wish to vote, the women are to consider whether they are prepared to add the duty involved in intelligent and conscientious voting to their present duties, or to lay aside some of their present duties as less sacred or less important than that of participation in the science and art of politics.

It is a great mistake to suppose that similarity of function is necessary to equality of position or influence. . . . We look with suspicion upon the well-meant movement which, under the appearance of conferring upon woman a right and a symbol of equality with man, imposes upon her the performance of duties hitherto accepted and assumed by men. We believe that the division of labor which makes man the breadwinner and the administrator of the State, and gives to woman the administration of the home and of those wider domesticities which are of kin to the home, — the hospital, the school, and the like, — has its reason in the eternal laws of God, and that no reform is for either her welfare or that of the community which, in its eagerness to affirm the equality of the sexes, confounds their social functions and endeavors to make them duplicate each other. Nor is this general law modified by the fact that in exceptional cases each has nobly assumed and fulfilled the duties which naturally would devolve upon the other.

Published by the Protest Committee by permission of "The Outlook."

*Reprinted for the Massachusetts Association opposed to Extension of Woman Suffrage.*

# HIDDEN FROM HISTORY

## FROM "THE WORLD," LONDON,
### July 19th, 1899.

### WOMAN AND WHINE.

The world's women have spoken their mind and departed from our midst, and one is at last able to sit down calmly to recall the prevailing note of the International Congress. Day after day the clatter of tongues went on. Five meetings concerned with as many different subjects would proceed simultaneously, and eager women would dodge from one to the other for fear of missing a single idea, making rushes now and again to luncheon parties, receptions, or evening "at homes." It would be difficult to name a subject, from shoes and ships and sealing-wax to cabbages and rings, which did not come within range of the feminine tongue. And yet it is not easy to say what is the outcome of it all. This is perhaps partly due to the multiplicity of the problems which the ladies set themselves to solve; partly, perhaps, to the exuberant verbosity of speakers who found themselves face to face with the chance of a lifetime. For it not infrequently happened that an enthusiastic speaker had reached her time-limit before she had finished her exordium; and you can hardly criticise a sermon of which you have heard no more than the text.

But now that the dust has settled and the tumult subsided, the note that remains in our ear is not, as might be supposed, one of jubilation and triumph at the amazing progress of womanhood to the goal of emancipation, a career, and an income. The note is rather one of complaint, of dissatisfaction, of a wistful regret. Of all the speeches which assailed our ears, that of Mrs. Fenwick Miller will linger longest in our memory. Women are elevating the newspapers, purifying the Post-Office by their presence, and earning very respectable salaries. But just as Mr. Henry George was startled to find that the tramp had appeared in the free and glorious United States, so Mrs. Fenwick Miller is troubled that in the newer and nobler world of which woman is the guiding spirit the lazy husband shows, as it were, the slippered foot. The husband of the woman with a career takes it for granted that his wife should go careering and earn an income; he himself lies upon the sofa at home, reads novels and smokes cigars. He does not even mind the baby and order the dinner. And Mrs. Fenwick Miller complains bitterly that so many women are handicapped by the obligation to support lazy husbands. Now, this aspect of the case is really a very serious one, for it suggests a difficulty which will certainly have to be faced by the careering sex. There are, to put it frankly, not enough careers for everybody to have one. And if our women despatch our telegrams, write our novels, tend our libraries, run our farms, and heal our diseases, there will be by so much the less room for men in the world of work. The lazy husband will find ample apology in the fact that his wife insists upon doing the work which should have fallen to his share.

Perhaps, however, we are not progressing so much as we imagine. It is true that the speakers at the Congress laid almost irritating stress upon the "enormous strides made by women." (It is not an attractive picture of the present-day woman!) But it is not easy for the individual to determine whether the social movement in which he is borne along is a forward one or a backward one. And we have no little apprehension that the appearance of the lazy husband denotes a retrogression to barbarism rather than a progress towards the millennium. In savage countries the men do not work. It is the women who bear the burdens and till the ground, while the men sit calmly by and enjoy their leisure until such time as they feel like killing somebody. With civilization came the belief that women should have the easier time, while men did the work. But women, not knowing when they were well off, demanded a reversal of the position. It must be allowed that men showed no particular eagerness to renounce the responsibility of earning an income for their womenfolk to spend. When, however, women had seized upon the positions which their husbands had found anything but easy, one may understand that the husbands were quite ready to accept the situation, and return to the barbaric practice of making the women do the work.

Likewise we may understand the feelings of the woman who, having got what she wanted, finds that she does not want it at all. She does not intend, however, to enjoy her newly won privilege of earning the income of the family without effectual protest, as we gather from a horrifying suggestion which fell from Mrs. Fenwick Miller's lips. It appears that women, if they do not get all they want, more particularly the Parliamentary franchise, are advised to take it out of their husbands at home. The horrors of civil war would be nothing to those of a struggle waged by means of ill-cooked fish, half-cooked *entrees*, and indigestible joints. The power of a wife to make her husband uncomfortable is almost unlimited, and his discomforts would come from so many quarters that he would not know whose hand was smiting him. If only the members of the discontented sex could decide exactly what they want, and organize a domestic campaign to get it, the lazy husband could not hold out for a week. The careering wife would be admitted to the House—if she were not previously turned out of the home.

# Household Hints

**National Association OPPOSED to Woman Suffrage**

Headquarters
268 Madison Avenue
New York, N. Y.

Branch
726 Fourteenth Street, N. W.
Washington, D. C.

**Votes of Women can accomplish no more than votes of Men. Why waste time, energy and money, without result?**

# Vote NO on Woman Suffrage

BECAUSE 90% of the women either do not want it, or *do not care*.

BECAUSE it means *competition* of women with men instead of *co-operation*.

BECAUSE 80% of the women eligible to vote are married and can only double or annul their husbands' votes.

BECAUSE it can be of no benefit commensurate with the additional expense involved.

BECAUSE in some States more voting women than voting men will place the Government under petticoat rule.

BECAUSE it is unwise to risk the good we already have for the evil which may occur.

# HIDDEN FROM HISTORY

# How Suffrage Pickets Were Suppressed by Real Men.

*(From "The Rights of Women." By M. Ostragorski, Chapter 2.)*
This book secured first prize by the Paris Faculte de Droit.

---

"On the eve of the French revolution, a great voice arose in favor of the political emancipation of women. The voice was that of Condorcet.

"In 1789, at election time, several pamphlets appeared demanding the admission of women to the states general, and protesting against the holding of a **national assembly** from which half the nation was excluded."

One of these, written by Olympe de Gouges, called "Declaration of the Rights of Women," states that:

"All male and female citizens, being equal in the eyes of the law, ought to be equally admissible to all **dignities, posts,** and **public appointments,** according to their capacity."

"The Constituante Assembly, however, was not to be persuaded. If in the ranks of the assembly there were some illustrious or notable men willing to free women from their social and political subjection, like Sieyes, the Abbe Faucher, and others, the great majority would not hear of women's political rights. Men so divergent in their opinions as Mirabeau and Robespierre met together at this point."

"Having flung themselves into the revolution with an ardor and an enthusiasm not devoid of grandeur at the outset, the **women soon lost all** balance, intellectual and moral. The Terrorists, themselves, **were disgusted in the end,** if not by their excesses, at least by the habit into which they fell, of **exciting the people, of remonstrating with the men in office,** and of **promoting disorder in the streets.** Upon the defeat of the Girondins, the Montagnards were not slow in getting rid of **their sinister allies.** On the 28th brumaire, 1793, when a band of **red-capped viragoes forced their way into the lobby of the Communal Council chamber,** Chaumette, the procurer general, apostrophised them in the severest terms.

"'What, shall these degraded beings who have shaken off and violated Nature's laws, be suffered to enter a place entrusted to the guardianship of citizens? Since when have women been allowed to adjure their sex and turn themselves into men?

"'A few days later Amar, in the name of the Committee of Public Safety, asked the convention to take measures against **female politicians.**

"'Should women enjoy political rights and mix themselves up with the affairs of the government? Universal opinion scouts the idea.'

"**The convention thereupon decreed the suppression of female clubs and societies,** and subsequently prohibited any **public assemblies of women. The female politicians completely disappeared."**

---

**The More a Politician Allows Himself to be Henpecked
The More Henpecking We Will Have in Politics.**

---

**A Vote for Federal Suffrage is a Vote for Organized Female Nagging Forever.**

---

**Issued by
REPUBLICAN SECTION, NATIONAL ASSOCIATION
OPPOSED TO WOMAN SUFFRAGE,**
Metropole Hotel, Chicago.

(OVER)

**HIDDEN FROM HISTORY**

# What Happens to Miss Representatives

## Suffrage Champions Lose in Primaries

(*Special to the Pittsburgh Dispatch.*)

CHARLESTON, W. Va., June 1—A surprising feature of the result of the State-wide primaries developed as the tabulation votes on the counties and districts proceeds, that every one of the Senators or members of the House of Delegates standing for re-election, who voted for woman suffrage at the recent special session of the West Virginia Legislature, has been defeated for renomination. Conspicuous among these who thus went down to defeat is Fred L. Fox, Democrat, of Sutton, who has represented the Tenth Senatorial District in the upper house since 1912, and has been the recognized floor leader for the Democratic membership in all sessions of the Legislature since probably his first term.

(OVER)

# How Women Can Best Serve the State

AN ADDRESS

BEFORE THE

STATE FEDERATION OF WOMEN'S CLUBS

TROY, N.Y., OCTOBER 30, 1907

BY

MRS. BARCLAY HAZARD

REPRINTED BY COURTESY OF
THE NEW YORK STATE ASSOCIATION OPPOSED TO WOMAN SUFFRAGE
BY
THE ILLINOIS ASSOCIATION
OPPOSED TO THE EXTENTION OF SUFFRAGE TO WOMEN
597 DEARBORN AVENUE, CHICAGO

## HOW WOMEN CAN BEST SERVE THE STATE

Mrs. President and Ladies:

The Twentieth Century opens with government by party, the almost universal rule in all civilized countries, Russia alone excepted. Even the Kaiser, reigning by right Divine, does not venture on pushing any very important measure unless he is sure of the preponderance of the Reichstag. Naturally, in a Republic, the strength of party government has "grown with our growth and strengthened with our strength." Our parties have grown from the smallest of beginnings to the most formidable of organizations. No longer does the voter on election day cast his vote for an elector who, exercising his own best judgment, shall choose a President for him, but for an elector who casts his vote for the man whom the party he represents has already chosen. Theoretically, nothing could be better than party government, especially where the parties are pretty equally divided. The "Ins" are to be kept in the path of virtue by the "Outs," who in their turn will endeavor to so shape their policies as to insure for themselves recognition and return to power from the people. Unfortunately, human nature being what it is, this theory has not worked out in practice, and many a party politician will welcome a national misfortune, provided it bring obloquy to the other side. Nor is this a new development. Macaulay, in his lay of Horatius, makes the appeal for the old days (old even in those days of fable), "When none were for a party and all were for the State." It is evident, therefore, that we must accept partisanship, political trickery and office-seeking as necessary evils inseparable from modern conditions, and the question arises what can be done to palliate the situation. To our minds, the solution has been found by the entrance of women into public life. Standing in an absolutely independent position, freed from all party affiliations, untrammeled by any political obligations, the intelligent, self-sacrificing women of to-day are serving the State (though many of them hardly realize it) as a third party whose disinterestedness none can doubt.

To do men justice, they have welcomed the new element. Governors have gladly appointed women to positions on Boards of Education, of Charities and Corrections, and on Sanitary Commissions. "It is such a relief," said one Governor lately, "to be able to pick out the best worker in that particular line and know that one is neither giving offense nor raising false hopes by doing so."

The advantage of complete political independence enjoyed by women so appointed, can not possibly be over-estimated. Only those who have been so placed (and doubtless there are many such in this audience) can begin to realize what it means to be able to plead for a cause or a reform in administration, and to know that such a plea will be considered on its merits alone, with no ulterior thought of what may be the motive of the pleader or what "pull" may lie back of the petition. This attitude of entire disinterestedness is, above all things, useful when appropriations have to be obtained from legislatures. Some years ago, an appropriation for absolutely necessary improvements to one of the asylums for the criminal insane was "held up," session after session. The parties were very evenly divided, and each wanted to trade appropriations with the other. The deadlock was at last broken by two women, who appeared before the committee, and in a simple but convincing manner explained the unnecessary sufferings of the poor creatures who could not make their wrongs known. The bill was reported favorably and went through at once. The chairman of the committee thus explained the matter: "When those women told us just how things were and what was really needed, we knew they were telling us the truth, for they had nothing to gain, one way or another." "When I look at my poor lunatics in their nice clean cells," one of these two women wrote, some time later, "I am so thankful to be a woman; to be able to *work* for the *work* and not to be suspected of wanting any political advantage out of it." Unquestionably, had the poor lunatics been capable of understanding the situation, they would have been thankful likewise. More than one probationary officer in New York City has expressed gratitude that she could not be said to belong to Tammany, nor the County Democracy, nor yet the Republicans, and when aid was needed for her protégés, could approach all organizations indifferently, relying only on the genuineness of her case.

Organization being the order of the day, the majority of women do their share of public service through an organization, rather than by individual effort. In organization, the same principle of power through independence holds good. A "Good Government" club or a "Civic Betterment" club, composed of women, exercises its influence for good because it expresses in its highest terms the best public opinion—that is, public opinion divorced from political or party questions. It is for this reason that such clubs command respect and secure respectful hearings. When, for instance, the

Woman's Municipal League of New York City, goes to Mayor McClellan, and says: "Never in our memory have the streets been so dirty," the Mayor can not reply: "Well, you are a Tammany organization; why don't you see your friend Murphy?" Nor can he allege: "As Republicans, it is evident you are determined to find fault with everything a Democratic administration may do." On the contrary, he is obliged to take it as a disinterested protest and act accordingly, and *that*, I am happy to say, was just what he *did* do! This co-operation of organized women in public life is still so new that it is no wonder that the pioneers make some mistakes. The only matter of surprise is that they do not make more. Fortunately, the conservative women connected with such movements realize that what is at stake is not so much present measures as the whole status of women as public servants. Feeling this, they advocate a caution which frequently irritates their more strenuous sisters. For example, recently (so very recently that the city shall be nameless) a Good Government club, after much agitation, secured the appointment of four police matrons, such appointments being made after the usual municipal-politics manner. Ere long, complaints come in; and a few weeks ago a committee from the club found itself waiting on the police commissioner and relating its grievances. One matron, it was alleged, was rarely sober; another had been known to purloin trifles from helpless prisoners. The third had a violent and ungoverned temper, while the fourth was just plain incompetent. The police commissioner listened quietly, and then said: "I have no doubt, ladies, that what you tell me is exactly so, but you see these women are all appointed by 'Big Dick Smith,' and we can't offend him; but," he added, brightening up, "if you will press the matter, agitate it in the newsapers, I will discharge the women on account of pressure from your organization. I will even go farther—I will appoint any four women your club suggests." Delighted, the committee hurried back to the board of directors to report, and found themselves confronted with this situation: The club would certainly agitate, and do all it could to bring about the discharge of undesirable city employés, but recommend others it could not, one of its cardinal policies being, "Measures, not men." Some of the most active and enthusiastic workers deeply lamented this attitude, which they felt deprived the club of an opportunity to do an excellent and greatly needed piece of work. That it was a wise stand, however, who can doubt, who realizes that only in that way can absolute independence be maintained.

My understanding of the subject allotted to me to-day is, women in public life as distinguished from women in charitable life or mission enterprise. Yet, in these days of interdependent work and effort, it is very difficult to draw the line where the one begins and the other ends. How, for instance, shall we classify the "Consumers' League"? It began in the philanthropic desire of a few women to safeguard and alleviate the lot of that singularly helpless body of workers—young shop girls. At first, it hardly went beyond inducing employers to provide seats for the girls when they were not actively engaged in their work, seeing that they had proper sanitary conveniences and an adequate luncheon hour. Now the work has grown until it has become a state question, involving factory inspection and including much legislation affecting the working hours and conditions for women and children. Another example of the way in which sociological work transforms itself into practical problems is to be found in the legislation arising out of the investigations of the household research department of the Woman's Municipal League in New York City. The director of the department, Miss Frances A. Kellor, under a fellowship from the University of Chicago, began ten years ago a study of women detained in prisons and reformatories. In prosecuting this work, she often stayed for weeks and months in the prisons as a guest of the wardens, and was thus enabled to make friends with the inmates and secure their confidence. When she came to collate and arrange the notes thus taken, she was herself surprised to find how many women dated their downfall from the abominable conditions prevailing at the employment agencies where they had gone for work. These facts Miss Kellor placed before some active workers, and the consequence was that, with her co-operation, an association was formed (the treasurer of which I have the honor to be), with branches in Boston, Philadelphia and New York, the object being to improve the conditions under which an unemployed and untrained woman must seek work, and at the same time to try to attract these young women from the over-crowded, poorly-paid trades into the well-paid, under-manned line of domestic service. I am sure it would interest you all, could I take the time to tell you how we first secured an employment-agency law for the State of New York, and how then, finding that the discredited agents simply moved across the ferry, we applied to the energetic women of New Jersey, and how they, with our aid, secured the passage of an excellent agency bill through the last legislature. Meanwhile, the Philadelphia ladies had drawn Pennsylvania into line. It is much easier to get a law passed than to get it enforced, and we felt that, as an organization, we had our hands full in investigating complaints and keeping the commissioner of licenses up to his work; but we have not been allowed to pause in our labors. Our work with the employment agencies has brought us in touch with the immigrant girl and woman, and we had forced upon our attention the terrible dangers which surround her. It was owing to investigations undertaken by us that Congress last year passed the bill rendering liable to deportation any girl found in a disorderly house within two years after landing. Another phase of the immigration question which was forced upon our attention was the shameful way in which the foreigners were treated (usually by their own countrymen) in the matter of remitting money to their home people. In New York City there existed very many fake banks. The so-called banker, usually an Italian or a Hebrew, had no capital beyond a few foreign coins, which he placed in a bowl in his window, yet he undertook to forward money entrusted to him to any part of the world. Needless to say, it never reached its destination, and when the hapless victim returned to complain, he either found the "banker" flown or was met with ridicule or threats. One poor man, for example, was told he had better not make a fuss about the matter, as it was against the law to send money out of the country, and if he complained to the police he would be himself arrested. The victims were indeed quite helpless. The district attorney's office, which has always most loyally and willingly stood by us, could do nothing, as the evidence that the money was *not* received was in Europe. These precious scamps added to their nefarious gains by posing as steamship ticket sellers, their qualifications consisting of a poster of some steamship line, though in one case, a colored lithograph of a battleship was forced to do duty. Of course, they could not sell tickets, but they sold what they called orders for tickets, which, upon being presented on the other side, were, naturally, useless. I would not harrow your feelings, even if I had the time to spare, by narrating some of the stories that have come to us, for pitiful they were beyond words to describe. The steamship companies were only too anxious to break up the ticket business, but found themselves in the position of interested parties before the Legislature, so once again we profited by our inestimable privilege of freedom from all trammels, and our bills were passed by the last Legislature. One of these bills, No. 515,845, is an amendment to the banking bill, and provides that all "firms or corporations" taking deposits to be sent abroad, and selling steamship tickets, must file a bond for $15,000.

The other bill, No. 1553, is an amendment to the penal code to prevent fraud in the sale of transportation tickets. Both these laws came into effect on September 1st of this year, and we are now engaged in looking after their proper enforcement.

I have dwelt at length on the work of the research department, not because I think it an exceptional board—I have no doubt that equally good work is being done in every city in the state—but because the work accomplished seems to me a good illustration of the great advantage possessed by women in their present political status. I find among my more radical friends an objection to our method of work, which for some unknown reason, they term indirect. "Yes," they say, "you have done a great deal, and you have got all you want from Congress and the Legislature, but these indirect ways are so undignified—how much better to have direct influence." My answer to that is: If we are *anything*, we are direct; if we stand for anything in public life, it is for direct methods and straightforward action—it is the men who need the lobby, not we. It is the men who, because they belong to this party, must placate some men on the other side, not we. It is the men who go to their party leader and through him get at the committee they wish to influence, not we. We go straight to the governor, attorney-general, or chairman of the committee, as circumstances require. We have no favors to give and none to ask. We make a plain statement of our case, backed up by as carefully-arranged evidence as we know how to prepare. We answer the questions asked us and take our leave. If there is anything indirect in this procedure it lies beyond my powers of discernment.

As I pause in my writing at this point, it occurs to me in what a different spirit I have put what I had to say than would have been the case twenty-five years ago. Then, I should have thought it necessary to begin my paper with an elaborate defense of the propriety of woman appearing in public life at all. I should have felt it imperative to express a belief that it would not unfit them for their domestic duties. Now, I have taken it as a matter of course that we all agree that bridge, lectures, theatres, or even prayer-meetings, are more likely to distract a woman from her home pursuits than the arduous path of public service. For public work is hard work. Those who follow it must be content to receive "more kicks than ha'-pence." It is a self-effacing work. We women who are in it are too busy with our work to talk about it. We have among us women who are capable of drawing up a brief for the attorney-general, or an abstract of evidence for the governor, but we have very few speakers and no agitators. Only women who love the work for its own sake will ever be tempted into our ranks. Yes, the position of woman has changed much in the last quarter of a century. She has now every legal right necessary for her protection, and, crowning mercy, she has acquired them without being called upon to lay down her independence! I often think of a meeting I once attended in California, where some of our strenuous sisters were demanding what they chose to call "rights." At the close I was asked to make a few remarks. In reply, I gave a brief digest of the laws of California concerning women. There was a dead pause after I had finished speaking, which was suddenly broken by a shrewd old woman from Southern Missouri, who drawled out with the true "bush-whacker" intonation: "Wal, gals, I reckon your quarrel is with the Lord and not with the law."

And now in closing, I want to say a few words to young women, especially—to those young women who are to-day coming forward to take up the task that we older workers must ere long lay down. Do not be beguiled by any specious arguments about the so-called equality of women into forgetting your true position. Do not let yourself be imposed upon by change, masquerading as progress. Above all, I beseech you, let no hope of personal gain, no restless ambition to play a part in factional public life, induce you to surrender the all-powerful, absolutely unique position we pioneers have secured for you. Let your watchword be "Power through Independence"—that is our last word to you from the conservative women represented by our organization.

---

### NEW YORK STATE ASSOCIATION OPPOSED TO WOMAN SUFFRAGE

#### OFFICERS

PRESIDENT:
Mrs. FRANCIS M. SCOTT

1ST VICE-PRESIDENT:
Mrs. ARTHUR M. DODGE

VICE-PRESIDENTS:

Mrs. ELIHU ROOT
Mrs. RICHARD WATSON GILDER
Mrs. WILLIAM A. PUTNAM
Mrs. PHILIP SCHUYLER VAN PATTEN
Mrs. GEORGE DOUGLAS MILLER
Mrs. WILLIAM P. NORTHRUP

TREASURER:
Mrs. FRANCIS S. BANGS

SECRETARY:
Mrs. GEORGE PHILLIPS
337 West End Avenue, New York

CHAIRMEN OF AUXILIARIES:

Mrs. WILLIAM A. PUTNAM
70 Willow St., Brooklyn

Mrs. PHILIP SCHUYLER VAN PATTEN
146 Prospect Ave., Mt. Vernon

Mrs. W. WINSLOW CRANNELL
9 Hall Place, Albany

Mrs. WILLIAM P. NORTHRUP
80 Jewett Avenue, Buffalo

FERGUS PRINTING COMPANY, CHICAGO.

JAMES T. GARDINER, an eminent scientific and business man, spoke in regard to what he has observed in his constant visits to Kansas as to results of woman suffrage.

"The first year or two, women took little interest in the municipal elections. Then one party put up a man of questionable reputation as mayor, the other party nominated a man of spotless character. Soon the latter's friends found that the other party were enlisting all the negro women of the city to their cause by sympathy and by bribes. We then saw that all would be lost if we could not arouse our wives and sisters to their duty as enfranchised women to vote for the pure election. They at first demurred, but we showed them what a disastrous effect upon the city it would be in every way should the other candidate be elected. Soon they became interested and began canvassing around amongst their neighbors. Constantly they increased in enthusiasm and numbers, until finally people who had been friends and neighbors for years would not speak, and the whole history of each candidate, with that of their ancestors and followers, was discussed in every household, even before its youngest members. Women had caught the fever of politics and it raged high and furiously. For over a month before election day, the whole dirty stream of politics flowed over my hearthstone, washing away all the quiet, happiness and peace which had reigned there before. And, as a climax, on election day we saw our wives and daughters driving through the city, picking up women of the lowest possible class and morality, and then walking with their arm around them to the polls to see that they voted rightly. Every means of intimidation, bribery and cajolery which had been used by men was employed unhesitatingly by women on election day, and yet when the votes were counted the result was no different than if they had remained quietly at home, without the ballot. The effect on Leavenworth society has been most disastrous."

Such is the fear of the Anti-Suffragists of what would occur to New York State, should women vote.

Officers of the Anti-Suffrage Association of the 3rd Judicial District of the State of New York:

    MRS. J. V. L. PRUYN,
           *President.*

    MRS. WILLIAM J. WALLACE,
           *1st Vice-President.*

    MRS. WM. BAYARD VAN RENSSELAER,
           *Secretary.*

    MRS. JOSEPH GAVIT,
           *Treasurer.*

    MRS. W. WINSLOW CRANNELL,
           *Chairman.*

    MRS. ERASTUS CORNING,
    MRS. J. HOWARD KING,
    MRS. JOEL R. REED,
    MRS. WILLIAM CASSIDY,
    MRS. WM. O. STILLMAN,
    MRS. FREDERICK TOWNSEND,
    MISS LUCY A. PLYMPTON,
           *Executive Committee.*

Apply for more papers to Anti-Suffrage Association, 13 Elk Street, Albany, N. Y.

By Wm. Coady.

Ms. 19th Amend
to Const.

JOINT RESOLUTION OF THE SENATE
AND HOUSE OF DELEGATES OF MARYLAND,
REJECTING AND REFUSING TO RATIFY
AN AMENDMENT TO THE CONSTITUTION
OF THE UNITED STATES, PROPOSED BY
CONGRESS, TO THE LEGISLATURE OF
THE SEVERAL STATES.

JOINT RESOLUTION # 2.

JOINT RESOLUTION of the Senate and House of Delegates of Maryland, rejecting and refusing to ratify an amendment to the Constitution of the United States, proposed by Congress, to the Legislature of the several States.

WHEREAS, The General Assembly of Maryland has received official notification of the passage by both Houses of the Sixty-sixth Congress of the United States of a proposal to amend the Constitution of the United States, in the words following, to wit:

RESOLVED, By the Senate and House of Representatives of the United States of America in Congress assembled (two-thirds of each House concurring therein), that the following Articles is proposed as an amendment to the Constitution, which shall be valied to all intents and purposes as part of the Constitution when ratified by the Legislature of three-fourths of the several States:

ARTICLE.

"The right of citizens of the United States to vote shall not be denied or abridged by the United States or by any State on account of sex.
"Congress shall have power to enforce this Article by appropriate legislation."

BE IT RESOLVED BY THE GENERAL ASSEMBLY OF MARYLAND, That we deny that the Congress of the United States has any lawful right or power to propose such an amendment to the Constitution of the United States; we deny that the Legislatures of three-fourths of the States have any lawful right or power to adopt such an amendment; and we deny that such an amendment would be validly a part of the Constitution of the United States if thus adopted, for the following reasons:

The avowed purpose of the people of the United States in adopting the Federal Constitution was to establish a perpetual Union of States.

In order that this great purpose might be accomplished, it was essential that each State should be preserved as an indestructible political unit.

In the oft quoted words of the Supreme Court of the United States, their purpose was to establish "an indestrictible Union composed of indestructible States".

For "without the States in union there could be no such political body as the United States".

It is manifest, therefore, that when the people, in this same Federal Constitution, conferred upon Congress and the Legislatures of three-fourths of the States the power to "Amend" that Constitution, it could not have been their intention to authorize the adoption of any amendment or any measure under the guise of an amendment, which would wholly or partially destroy the States, by taking away from the States any one of their functions, essential to their separate and independent existence as States.

The right of a State to determine for itself by the vote of its own people, who shall vote at its onw State, county and municipal elections is one of those functions.

When we surrender to any outside power the right to say who shall vote at our state elections, we surrender the right to determine who shall govern, the State, and, without the rigjt of local self-government, we cease to be a State and become a mere province, with far less power to determine our own destiny than we had prior to the American Revolution, under that charter granted by the British Crown.

RESOLVED, FURTHER, That the General Assembly of Maryland could not exercise the power to ratify this so-called nineteenth amendment, conferred upon it or supposed to be conferred upon it, by the fifth Article of the Constitution of the Unites States, without violating, in most flagrant fashion, the Constitution of our own State.

The Constitution of Maryland limits the rights of suffrage to men. The people of Maryland have not conferred upon their General Assembly any right to amend that Constitution by extending the franchise to women.

Yet this proposed nineteenth Amendment to the Federal Constitution if adopted and held valid, would, in effect, amendment the Constitution of the State of Maryland in that respect and establish woman suffrage in this State, ~~wou~~ without the consent, and it may be contrary to the wishes of a majority of both the men and women of Maryland.

We conceive that the Members of this General Assembly would be false to their duty to their own people, if not to their official oaths, if they should vote to ratify the proposed Amendment.

THEREFORE, BE IT FURTHER RESOLVED, That the General Assembly of this State, hereby rejects the said nineteenth Article, proposed as an amendment to the Constitution of the United States, and, on behalf of the State of Maryland, refuses to ratify the same.

RESOLVED, FURTHER, That we solemnly protest to the Legislatures of those State have heretofore voted to ratify such Amendment against their action is thus seeking to force this measure upon our people, without their consent, and we earnestly appeal to the Legislatures of those States who have not as yet voted to ratify it, not to do so.

AND BE IT FURTHER RESOLVED, That the Governor be requested to forward a copy of the foregoing preamble and resolutions, duly attested, to the ~~Section~~ Secretary of State for the United States, our Representatives and Senators in Congress, to the Governors of each of the States and to the presiding officers of each House of the Legislatures thereof.

APPROVED March 26, 1920.

My dear Mrs. Cameron:—

I am inclosing the platform of THE SOUTHERN WOMEN'S LEAGUE FOR THE REJECTION OF THE SUSAN B. ANTHONY AMENDMENT TO THE CONSTITUTION OF THE UNITED STATES, and am asking your careful consideration of the same, with the firm belief that the principles so contained will appeal to the hearts and the understanding of all patriotic and loyal men and women of the South.

The membership of this League is composed of representative women from all the Southern States— and is organized for the purpose of arousing the women of the South to the dangers of WOMAN'S SUFFRAGE THROUGH A CONSTITUTIONAL AMENDMENT.

We appeal to you to aid us in furthering the purpose of this League. First, by endeavoring to arouse the interest of the women of your state, who have hither-to been inactive- Second, by sending us the names of such women, as might be induced to organize against this the adoption of this iniquitous, unwise, and unnecessary Amendment.

We will take pleasure in sending literature, and in giving any possible assistance that might be desired.

With grateful appreciation for any timely aid that you might render, I am,

Very sincerely yours,

(Mrs.) Sarah Calhoun Winter
Member of Executive Committee.

Headquarters— 1008 Bell Bldg.,
Montgomery, Ala.

THE SOUTHERN WOMEN'S LEAGUE
FOR THE REJECTION OF THE
SUSAN B. ANTHONY AMENDMENT

# HIDDEN FROM HISTORY

Jeffersonville, Twiggs, County, Georgia,
June 28, 1918.

To the Honorables Hoke Smith and Thos. W. Hardwick,
United States Senators from Georgia,
Washington, D.C.

We the undersigned citizens of Twiggs County, Georgia, are individually and directly opposed to the passage of the Susan B. Anthony Amendment to the Constitution of the United States, thereby granting equal suffrage. In our opinions this is a question which should be settled by and through the action of each State for itself, and the enactment of such a law would deprive the States of the rights of being Commonwealths. To give equal suffrage in the South would only open the way to race riots, murder, and a repetition of the "Reconstruction Days of the Sixties". We most earnestly appeal to you to do what you can for our defense and protection in this most signal injustice.

Mrs. W.R. Carswell,
  (Sec. Anti-Suf. League
    of Twiggs Co.)
J.H. Balcom
Mrs. W.M. Whitehurst
Mrs. J.M. Wall
Mrs. J. Hunter Johnson,
  (Vice-Pres. Anti-Suf.
    League Twiggs Co).
I.G. Phillips
A.K. Smith
  (Editor Twiggs Co. Citizen)
Mrs. Mark O'Daniel,
  (Pres. Anti-Suf. League
    of Twiggs County).
A.F. Martin, Jr.
Mrs. Annie S. Adams
W.M. WHITAKER
Miss Janet Faulk
G.J. Holloman
F.C. Balcom
T.E. Methvin
Rev. J.T.B. Anderson,
  (Baptist Pastor).
Mrs. J.T.B. Anderson
J.L. Griffin
C. Ives
T.J. Cannon
Dr. W.H. McCrary
A.F. Martin, Sr.
J.F. Balcom
W.V. Wood
W.J. Gallemore
J.W. Walters
J.S. Baker
J.K. Hartley, M.D.
W.L. King

J. Hunter Johnson
B.R. Jones
Mrs. B.R. Jones
E.E. Sauls
A.M. Gates
W.T. Chappell
J.K. Burns

Judge E.D. Shannon
Mrs. L.E. Shannon
S.T. Carswell
J.M. Wall
F.Y. Stokes
W.C. Faulk,
  (Ordinary,
    Twiggs County).
R.R. Slappey
J.W. Land

S.J. Faulk
B.S. Faulk
T.J. Faulk
Jas. B. Shannon,
  (Representative
    Twiggs County).
John Hatfield
G.B. Hambrick
C.C. Humphries
C.G. Parr
Mrs. C.G. Parr
Miss Lily B. Wall
W.H. Califf
J.R. Wimberly, P.M.
Dr. J.S. Slappey
W.B. Gettys,
  (Pres. Gettys Lbr. Co).
J.S. Bridges
G.T. Chapman
J.C. Shannon, Sr.,
  (Pres. Twiggs Co. Bank)
J.S. Bookmore,
  (Cashier Twiggs Co. Bank)
M.S. Faulk

Mrs. J.E. Powell
F.E. Wimberly
H.L.B. Hughes
T.S. Tharpe, Member County Board of Roads & Revenues
Linton Hatcher   "   "   "   "   "   "
F.J. Ray         "   "   "   "   "   "
S.M. Gallemore
R.L. Thompson

W.H. Whitehurst
C.R. Faulk
J.I. Newby
J.H. Horn
W.O. Johnson
H.A. Rogers M.D.
W.B. Wimberley
S.E. Simes
J.T. McCormic
Dr. W.A. Newson
H.F. Griffin Sr.
W.M. Marchman
Col H.F. Griffin Jr
W.G. Mercer
J.G. Slappey Jr.
W.F. Shanen
J.H. Solomon,
J.M Whitehurst,
  (Cashier F.&M. Bank)
H.T. Pope
Joel Whitehurst
Miss S.Z. Solomon
  "  Daisy W. Whitehurst
S.E. Jones
A.E. Coombs
J.R. Fountain
J.I. White
B.E. Davidson
James P. Califf
J.H. Vaughn
Col E.A. Harison
E.G. Griffin Sheriff
Rev L.E. Brady
L.F. Carson
H.V. Jackson
W.J. Tompson

I hereby certify that the above is a true and correct copy of the original petition.

W. M. Whitehurst

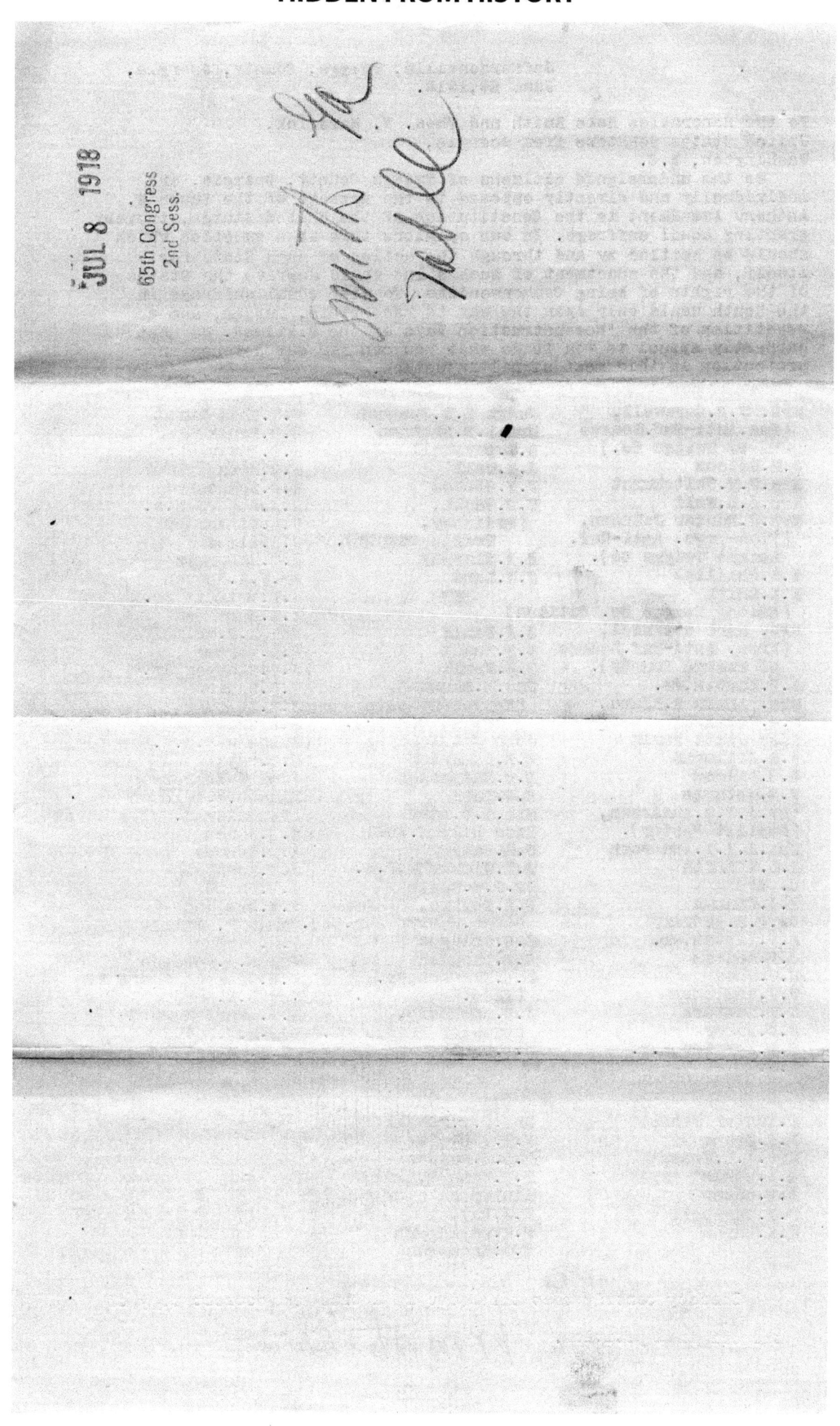

# LETTER FROM MRS. CLARA T. LEONARD,

## IN OPPOSITION TO WOMAN SUFFRAGE,

### First Woman Member of the State Board of Health, Lunacy, and Charity of Massachusetts.

The following letter was read by Thornton K. Lothrop, Esq., at the hearing before the Legislative Committee on Woman Suffrage, January 29, 1884: —

The principal reasons assigned for giving suffrage to women are these:

That the right to vote is a natural and inherent right of which women are deprived by the tyranny of men.

That the fact that the majority of women do not wish for the right or privilege to vote is not a reason for depriving the minority of an inborn right.

That women are taxed but not represented, contrary to the principles of free government.

That society would gain by the participation of women in government, because women are purer and more conscientious than men, and especially that the cause of temperance would be promoted by women's votes.

Those women who are averse to female suffrage hold differing opinions on all these points, and are entitled to be heard fairly and without unjust reproach and contempt on the part of "suffragists," so called.

The right to vote is not an inherent right, but, like the right to hold land, is conferred upon individuals by general consent, with certain limitations, and for the good of all.

It is as true to say that the earth was made for all its inhabitants, and that no man has a right to appropriate a portion of its surface, as to say that all persons have a right to participate in government. Many persons can be found to hold both these opinions. Experience has proved that the general good is promoted by ownership of the soil, with the resultant inducement to its improvement.

Voting is simply a mathematical test of strength. Uncivilized nations strive for mastery by physical combat, thus wasting life and resources. Enlightened societies agree to determine the relative strength of opposing parties by actual count. God has made women weaker than men, incapable of taking part in battles, indisposed to make riot and political disturbance.

* Mrs. Leonard was characterized by the late Senator George F. Hoar as "the highest living authority on private and public charities."

2

The vote which, in the hand of a man, is a "possible bayonet," would not, when thrown by a woman, represent any physical power to enforce her will. If all the women in the State voted in one way, and all the men in the opposite one, the women, even if in the majority, would not carry the day, because the vote would not be an estimate of material strength and the power to enforce the will of the majority. When one considers the strong passions and conflicts excited in elections, it is vain to suppose that the really stronger would yield to the weaker party.

It is no more unjust to deprive women of the ballot than to deprive minors, who outnumber those above the age of majority, and who might well claim, many of them, to be as well able to decide political questions as their elders.

If the majority of women are either not desirous to vote or are strongly opposed to voting, the minority should yield in this, as they are obliged to do in all other public matters. In fact, they will be obliged to yield, so long as the present state of opinion exists among women in general, for legislators will naturally consult the wishes of the women of their own families and neighborhood, and be governed by them. There can be no doubt that in this State, where women are highly respected and have great influence, the ballot would be readily granted to them by men, if they desired it, or generally approved of woman suffrage. Women are taxed, it is true; so are minors, without the ballot; it is untrue to say that either class is not represented. The thousand ties of relationship and friendship cause the identity of interest between the sexes. What is good in a community for men, is good also for their wives and sisters, daughters and friends. The laws of Massachusetts discriminate much in favor of women, by exempting unmarried women of small estate from taxation; by allowing women, and not men, to acquire a settlement without paying a tax; by compelling husbands to support their wives, but exempting the wife, even when rich, from supporting an indigent husband; by making men liable for debts of wives, and not *vice versa*. In the days of the American Revolution, the first cause of complaint was, that a whole people were taxed but not represented. To-day there is not a single interest of woman which is not shared and defended by men, not a subject in which she takes an intelligent interest in which she cannot exert an influence in the community proportional to her character and ability. It is, because the men who govern, live, not in a remote country with separate interests, but in the closest relations of family and neighborhood, and bound by the tenderest ties to the other sex, who are fully and well represented by relations, friends, and neighbors in every locality. That women are purer and more conscientious than men, as a sex, is exceedingly doubtful when applied to politics. The faults of the sexes are different, according to their constitution and habits of life. Men are more violent and open in their misdeeds; but any person who knows human nature well, and has examined it in its various phases, knows that each sex is open to its peculiar temptation and sin; that the human heart is weak and prone to evil without distinction of sex. It seems certain that, were women admitted to vote and to hold political office, all the intrigue, corruption, and selfishness displayed by men in political life would also be found among women. In the temperance cause we should gain little or nothing by admitting women to vote, for two reasons: first, that experience has proved that the strictest laws cannot be enforced if a great number of people determine to drink liquor; secondly, because among women voters we should find in our cities thousands of foreign birth who habitually drink beer and spirits daily without intoxication, and who regard license or prohibitory laws as an infringement of their liberty. It has been said that municipal suffrage for women in England has proved a political success. Even if this is true, it offers no parallel to the condition of things in our own cities: first, because there is in England a property qualification required to vote, which excludes the more ignorant and irresponsible classes, and makes women voters few and generally intelligent; secondly, because England is an old, conservative country, with much emigration and but little immigration. Here is a constant influx of foreigners: illiterate, without love of our country or interest in, or knowledge of, the history of our liberties, to whom, after a short residence, we give a full share in our government. The result begins to be alarming — enormous taxation, purchasable votes, demagogism, — all these alarm the more thoughtful, and we are not yet sure of the end. It is a wise thought that the possible bayonet or ruder weapon in the hands of our new citizens would be even worse than the ballot, and our safer course is to give the immigrants a stake and interest in the government. But when we learn that on an average one thousand immigrants per week landed at the port of Boston in the past calendar year, is it not well to consider carefully how we double and more than double the popular vote, with all its dangers and its ingredients of ignorance and irresponsibility? Last of all, it must be considered that the lives of men and women are essentially different. One sex lives in public, in constant conflict with the world; the other sex must live chiefly in private and domestic life, or the race will be without homes and gradually die out. If nearly one-half of the male voters of our State forego their duty or privilege, as is the fact, what proportion of women would exercise the suffrage? Probably a very small one. The heaviest vote would be in the cities, as now, and the ignorant and unfit women would be the ready prey of the unscrupulous demagogue. Women do not hold a position inferior to men. In this land they have the softer side of life, — the best of everything. There are, of course, exceptions — individuals — whose struggle in life is hard, whose husbands and fathers are tyrants instead of protectors; so there are bad wives, and men ruined and disheartened by selfish, idle women.

The best work that a woman can do for the purifying of politics is by her influence over men, by the wise training of her children, by her intelligent, unselfish counsel to husband, brother, or friend, by a thorough knowledge and discussion of the needs of her community. Many laws on the statute

4

books of our own and other States have been the work of women. More might be added.

It is the opinion of many of us, that woman's power is greater without the ballot or possibility of office-holding for gain, when, standing outside of politics, she discusses great questions upon their merit. Much has been achieved by women in the anti-slavery cause, the temperance cause, the improvement of public and private charities, the reformation of criminals, all by intelligent discussion and influence upon men. Our legislators have been ready to listen to women, and carry out their plans when well framed. Women can do much useful public service upon boards of education, school committees, and public charities, and are beginning to do such work. It is of vital importance to the integrity of our charitable and educational administration that it be kept out of politics. Is it not well, that we should have one sex who have no political ends to serve, who can fill responsible positions of public trust? Voting alone can easily be performed by women without rude contact, but to attain any political power women must affiliate themselves with men; because women will differ on public questions, must attend primary meetings and caucuses, will inevitably hold public office and strive for it; in short, women must enter the political arena. This result will be repulsive to a large portion of the sex, and would tend to make women unfeminine and combative, which would be a detriment to society.

It is well that men after the burden and heat of the day should return to homes where the quiet side of life is presented to them. In these peaceful New England homes of ours, great and noble men have been reared by wise and pious mothers, who instructed them, not in politics, but in those general principles of justice, integrity, and unselfishness, which belong to and will insure statesmanship in the men who are true to them. Here is the stronghold of the sex, weakest in body, powerful for good or evil over the stronger one, whom women sway and govern; not by the ballot and by greater numbers, but by those gentle influences designed by the Creator to soften and subdue man's ruder nature.

(Signed) CLARA T. LEONARD.

*Issued by the Massachusetts Association Opposed to the Further Extension of Suffrage to Women.*

Pamphlets and leaflets may be obtained from the Secretary,

Room 615,
Kensington Building,
687 Boylston Street, Boston, Mass.

# HIDDEN FROM HISTORY

## Alabama Male Association Opposed to Woman's Suffrage

Jas. B. Ellis, President,
Selma, Ala.

Martin L. Calhoun, Sect'y.-Treas.
Selma, Ala.

Hon. W. B. Craig, 2nd Vice-President
Selma, Ala.

(Address all communications to the Secretary.)

---

PLATFORM:—THE ALABAMA MALE ASSOCIATION OPPOSED TO WOMAN'S SUFFRAGE:—
Stands for HOME and NATIONAL DEFENSE against Woman's Suffrage, Feminism and Socialism. For MAN-POWER in Government, believing that Democracy must be STRONG to be SAFE. For the PRESERVATION of the established foundations of the American Republic as a Model for the World. For the RECOGNITION and ENFORCEMENT of the INHERENT RIGHT of EACH STATE to control the question of Woman's Suffrage for ITSELF. For EFFICIENCY and PROGRESS without Waste and Duplication in Government. For the CONSERVATION of the BEST WOMANHOOD of all conditions and stations in life, along NON-PARTISAN lines, so that the interests of Womanhood, Childhood and Civilization may be advanced FREE from the strife and division of politics, factions and parties. For the retention of the BEST IDEALS of the past, adapted to the advantages and opportunities given women under modern conditions, so that the FUNDAMENTAL PRINCIPLES of Morality, of Patriotism and of World Progress may be more firmly established in the present and future generations.

---

Selma, Ala. September 23d 1918

Senator, Duncan U. Fletcher, U.S.S.
Washington, D.C.

My dear Senator:-

I note the Senate anticipates taking action action at an early date upon the proposed Susan B. Anthony Suffrage Amendment.

The proposed submission of this Amendment seems so foreign to the democracy taught us by Morgan and Pettus, who gave their life as a service, that the South might live, that I can not believe any Southern Senator could lend it support. If the South yields its control of suffrage to the Federal Gcovernment, all the efforts of the manhood of the past will have been in vain. I am not afraid of our government, but I do not want to be placed in a position where we will always have to trust the party in power to be merciful to us- the South had to take a dose of that medicine once and it was very, very bitter.

Equity demands no fairer solution of the question of woman suffrage than each state be permitted to solve the issue for itself and if we take away this right from the states they lose their identity and become mere parcels of a central government.

President Wilson has stated," when the soldiers come back from Europe they will be heroes; we will have to treat them different; they will expect something". Among "those soldiers" will be thousands of negroes, trained in military efficiency and the use of high power rifles, with the possibility of the ballot in their hands, I ask in all seriousness- what will become of white supremacy in the grand old South ? There is a grave responsibility resting upon our representatives and we can only plead and trust they will not betray us. I can see no possible good in the Amendment, but there is ample opportunity for much harm.

Will you help defeat it when it comes up.

Very cordially yours,

*Martin L. Calhoun*
Sect'y-Treas.

CITY OF MACON, COUNTY OF BIBB,

STATE OF GEORGIA.

TO THE CONGRESS OF THE UNITED STATES:

The petition of the undersigned respectfully shows:

1.

That there is pending before Congress a bill to amend the Constitution of the United States, the purpose of which is to confer the right of sufferage upon the women of our Country.

2.

The women of Georgia whose names are signed hereto, and on the list of he petitioners hereto attached, wish hereby to register their solemn protest against the said proposed amendment to our National Constitution. We believe that the proposed amendmend is dangerous and hurtful to the best interests of our Country and especially to the South, in that the inevitable result of the legislation proposed would be to destroy white supremacy and States' rights.

Believing that the best interests of the homes, of society, of he State, and of the Nation, demand that this proposed legislation should be defeated, we, therefore, hereby earnestly petition the Senators of the United States and the Representatives in Congress to vote against this amendment that is fraught with so much danger to the peace and happiness of our Section.

Mrs Lee Worsham — Miss
Miss Annie Smith
Mrs Farrell
Mrs Lutie Westcott
Mrs Harry Wright
Mrs Lillian Wright
" Bernice Wright
Mrs Archie Shake
Mrs Frank Rogers
Mrs B. A. Watters
Mrs F. L. Watters ch Tatnall | Daisy Ward colored
Mr P. H. Ward
Mrs Helen Ward
Mrs John C Walker
Mrs John M Walker
Mrs Beulah Radcliffe ch N.H. Boulevar
" F. C. Hurley chgman Broad St Cart moon
Mrs E. H. Lafayette
Mrs Sarah Hyon
Mrs C. Jones
Mrs J. Wilcox
Miss Ellen Cox
Mrs Nancy Pitton

Mrs. Ross Bowdre
Mrs. Philo Paughton
Mrs. Bruce Carr Jones
Mrs. Thos. N. Baker
Mrs. Bernard S. Gostin
Mrs. Edwin S. Davis — Mrs. E. S. Davis
Mrs. R. J. Taylor — R. J. Taylor
Mrs. B. T. Adams
Mrs. Mary A. Patterson
Mrs. W. E. Godfrey
Mrs. Jenkins
Miss Ella Jenkins
Miss Maxine Humphries
Mrs. A. C. Williams
Miss Marie Blackstone
Mrs. Clara Jossey
Mrs. Neil Bussell — Mr. N. Bussell
Mrs. Louise Hopkins
Miss Stella Daniels
Mrs. Louise Raineault
Mrs. W. B. Daniel

Mrs. Thos. Jackson
Mrs. E. Middlebrooks
Mrs. L. Mitchell
Mrs. Walter Lowe
Miss Mrs. Foster
" Nettie Mau Foster
Mrs. W. Turner
" Duncan Brown
Mrs. Ashwell
Mrs. Low
Mrs. Jessie Bates
Mrs. Daisy Price
Miss Joe Perkins
Mrs. Alex Howell
Mrs. Pat Ward
Mrs. Beulah Radcliffe
" F. W. Hardy Jr
" H. C. Sutton
Mrs. Arthur Hooker
Miss Sheridan
Mrs. George Hatcher
Mrs. Cruell
Mrs. Clarence Henry

Mrs. Lloyd Moore
Miss West
Mrs. Royal
Miss Maurine Foster
Mrs. Irwin
Mrs. L. Taylor
Mrs. McMillan
Mrs. Egell
Mrs. Strauss
Mrs. Sayer
Mrs. A. Long
Mrs. C. Meek
Mrs. L. Mullins
Mrs. A. Bramen
Mrs. J. Steele
Mrs. V. Inman
Mrs. L. Sucker
Mrs. R. Collins
Mrs. L. Brady
Mrs. Joe Allen

Mrs Llewellyn Hodges
Mrs Alice Miniberly
Mrs John Sandford Beadsley
Mrs Llewellyn Hoch
Mrs. E. J. Peacock
Mrs B. E. Toole
Mrs P. Dougeas Feagin
Mrs DuPont Guerry
Mrs J. P. Goston
Mrs H. D. Adams
Mrs N. N. Solomon
Mrs H. A. Burkal
Mrs. W. E. Shelverton
Miss J. B. Johnson
Mrs. A. K. Troutman
Miss Julia Dickinson
Mrs. B. F. Sutton
Mrs James B. Hall
Mrs E. L. Vickery
Mrs H. Llewellyn

# HIDDEN FROM HISTORY

MRS. F. A. MILLARD, PRESIDENT, BURLINGTON     MISS ALICE FRENCH, 1st VICE-PRES, DAVENPORT     MRS. F. I. HERRIOTT, TREASURER, DES MOINES     MISS MARY CHITTENDEN, SECRETARY, BURLINGTON

## IOWA ASSOCIATION OPPOSED TO WOMAN SUFFRAGE

1032 NORTH FOURTH STREET
BURLINGTON, IOWA

**HON. PRESIDENT**
MRS. SIMON CASADY
DES MOINES

**HON. VICE-PRESIDENT**
MRS. D. B. HENDERSON
DUBUQUE

**VICE-PRESIDENTS**
MRS. W. N. FORD
SIOUX CITY

MISS KATE VAN DUZEE
DUBUQUE

**DIRECTORS**
MRS. WALTER I. HAYES
CLINTON

MRS. CLARA COOLEY BECKER
DUBUQUE

MRS. JOHN BLUNT
WEST UNION

MRS. MAUD WHEDON SMITH
WINTERSET

MRS. GLENN AVERILL
CEDAR RAPIDS

MRS. DRAYTON W. BUSHNELL
COUNCIL BLUFFS

MRS. H. L. WATERMAN
OTTUMWA

MISS MARGARET G. DOLLIVER
SIOUX CITY

MRS. W. F. McFARLAND
MRS. J. J. FLEMING
BURLINGTON

MRS. GEORGE STEWART
FT. MADISON

MRS. MARY E. STEWART
DES MOINES

MRS. M. B. HUTCHISON
OTTUMWA

September 21, 1918.

Hon. Duncan U. Fletcher,
United States Senator,
Washington, D.C.

Dear sir;

    We women of Iowa who realize through our State's recent rejection of woman suffrage by popular vote, that we have been relieved of the burden and protected from the strain of political life, do earnestly beg of you to stand by us, by the decision of our electorate, and by the Constitution of the United States in rejecting the Anthony Amendment, thus permitting the voters of each commonwealth to determine for itself, according to its own necessities the vital question of whom it shall enfranchise.

    The projection of this suffrage question into the maelstrom of problems that today demand the legislator's supreme effort, is but another evidence of the ruthless selfishness that elsewhere throughout the world is manifesting itself in strikes and revolutions, and it is taking advantage of a world that is fighting for life itself.

    To force this question "as a war measure" is as cowardly as it is illogical, for we women should all be free both as individuals, and as organizations, to do our part in this war, and we should not be forced to lay aside these duties in order to fight this tool of socialism, feminism, and pacifism in the legislatures of the various states, as we inevitably must and will of the amendment be passed by Congress.

    We women sincerely appreciate all past opposition to this unjust amendment, and hope for the protection of your vote,

    We submit this plea from,

IOWA ASSOCIATION OPPOSED TO WOMAN SUFFRAGE

*Mrs. F. A. Millard*
President.

(KKV)

## NEW JERSEY ASSOCIATION OPPOSED TO WOMAN SUFFRAGE

Miss Dayton, *Honorary President*
Trenton
Mrs. Carroll P. Bassett, *President*
Summit

*Vice-Presidents*
Mrs. Thomas J. Preston
Mrs. Garret A. Hobart
Mrs. E. Yarde Breese
Mrs. John R. Emery
Mrs. Theodore C. Woodbury
Miss Clara Vezin
Miss Henrietta O. Magie
Miss Anne MacIlvaine
Mrs. Hamilton Fish Kean
Mrs. William Libbey
Mrs. Horace F. Nixon
Mrs. Henry M. Darcy
Mrs. Sherman B. Joost
Mrs. Henry L. Seligman
Mrs. Thomas B. Adams
Mrs. Robert C. Maxwell
Miss Elizabeth DeH. Kean

Mrs. A. P. McMurtrie, *Recording Secretary*
Mrs. Isaac C. Ogden, *Corresponding Secretary*
31 Highland Avenue, Orange
Mrs. Charles R. Smith, *Treasurer*
421 Ellison Street, Paterson
Mrs. O. D. Oliphant, *General Secretary*

Miss Clara Vezin
*Chairman of Legislative Committee*
712 Grove Street　　　　　Elizabeth, N. J.
Telephone 859

Office of President, Summit, N. J.

September 24th, 1918.

Hon. Duncan U. Fletcher,
　Senate Office Building,
　　Washington, D. C.

My dear Senator Fletcher,-

　　　The women of America who have dedicated themselves to the task of winning the war and are working most unremittingly to that end are now forced to pause and consider this burden which a minority of women seek as a right.

　　　When the notorious Hearst papers are sufficiently interested in securing votes for women to spend the time and money required to procure the mammoth petition recently presented to Congress, when pronounced pacifists, socialists and pro-germans are almost a unit behind the suffrage propaganda, it seems not only unwise but dangerously unpatriotic for Congress to force upon unwilling and admittedly unprepared women of the country, a suffrage, fraught with gravest peril, during the crisis confronting the nation.

　　　Should we not avoid any action which is certain to hamper the noblest service that women can render,- the rearing of great citizens in their homes?

　　　I therefore respectfully urge you to vote against the Susan B. Anthony Amendment! While every energy should be devoted to winning the war can the country afford to force this decision upon the forty-eight states and encourage the contests and bitterness which are inevitable?

　　　　　　　Very sincerely yours,

　　　　　　　(Mrs Carroll P.) Margaret K. Bassett,
　　　　　　　　President - New Jersey Association
　　　　　　　　　Opposed to Woman Suffrage.

*To the* Hon. Henry W. Blair, *U. S. Senator from New Hampshire:* —

Dear Sir, — During the last week of the last session of Congress I received, under cover of your own frank, a copy of your Report of the Select Committee on Woman Suffrage, delivered to the Senate of the United States, December 8, 1886. In it you make a lengthy quotation from a pamphlet of mine, entitled "Letters from a Chimney Corner." It appears to me that in the argument drawn from this quotation you mistake utterly the point at issue, and it is my purpose in this letter to direct your attention to this mistake, and to put the argument upon its proper basis. I shall also comment upon certain other considerations put forth therein.

The quotation referred to is too long for the limits of a letter like this. The argument briefly is, that neither the man nor the woman is individually the representative of the *genus homo*, but that, according to nature and revelation, the two united make one, and that to each constituent of that union certain distinct powers and properties belong, each dependent upon the other, in a minor way, for proper fulfilment. You say, "If upon this account woman is to be denied suffrage, then man equally should be denied the ballot, if his highest and final estate is to be something else than a mere individual."

Now, marriage is that partnership upon which the right order of society and the right perpetuation of the species depends. The question is, whether each partner shall keep to that line of labor which Nature has marked out, or whether of woman shall be demanded, not only her own share of the labor, but also a large part of that which belongs to man. For, let us notice, that while it may be granted that woman has the physical capacity to cast a ballot, man has not the physical capacity to bear

2

and nourish children. Nature has made it forever impossible that he should perform that office. If, therefore, he demands of her that she shall participate in those external and general duties, such as labor for the support of the home and for the direction of the State, which his natural constitution, physical and intellectual, fit him for, while he cannot by any possibility relieve her of those most necessary offices and duties which Nature demands of her, he commits a palpable and monstrous injustice.

Nor does it help the matter to say, as you do, that, because woman's nature is purer and nobler than man's, the state would be benefited by her participation in political affairs. If men are not capable of managing the affairs of the state according to the highest and best ideas of the race, that is, of both men and women, will you permit me respectfully to inquire what proper and adequate share of this world's work they *can* perform? What is their natural place in the order of society? Are they mere hewers of wood and drawers of water? They cannot bear citizens; they cannot care for them in infancy and rear them to manhood. If they cannot govern them with wisdom and justice when they are produced ready made to their hands, what is their reason for being? When a man stands up in the United States Senate and makes such a statement as that, in regard to the men of this republic, it appears to me that he compromises his own self-respect, and the respect due to the dignified and honorable body to which he has been elevated.

You say that you have only proposed the measure because women have asked you to do it. The same plea was made by your great progenitor in the Garden of Eden; but it did not avail him. Moreover, in the case of Adam, it was true. In the present instance the plea contains but the minimum of truth. There are fifteen millions of women in this country (I quote your own statistics) of voting age. Will you kindly inform us what proportion of that fifteen millions you have heard from?

3

You say that these women are being governed without their consent. Is it possible that you can sincerely believe that fifteen millions of American women *could be* governed without their consent? Do you not rather feel assured that if a bare majority of that number did not consent, for what appear to them to be good and sufficient reasons, to be governed by indirect rather than direct representation, there would be a revolution within twenty-four hours? With every right of agitation at their command which man possesses,— free speech, free assembly, the right of petition, a press ever ready to disseminate their views, and many privileges of courtesy besides, that men lay no claim to, — what power could withstand the moral force of any demand which these fifteen millions should unitedly make?

With what show of reason do you compare free-born American women to the degraded and ignorant slaves on Southern plantations, and speak of men as their masters? As a matter of fact the power of men over women is not greater than that of women over men. Nature lays the infant man a helpless creature in the lap of his mother. He is in her power for life or for death, and for the first ten or fifteen years of his existence, and that during the forming and determining period of his career, a period, too, in which he is answerable to no other law than that of his home, her power over him, physical, intellectual, and moral, is so nearly supreme, that no power which he can arrogate over her in later years can overbalance it. Under ordinary circumstances the faithful, intelligent mother may make of her son, in all the essentials of manners and morals, whatsoever she will. If American men were to-day the narrow-minded, tyrannical, vicious creatures they are charged with being by the woman suffragists, unfitted to be legislators for the whole nation, it could only be because their mothers had misunderstood or neglected the opportunities which Nature puts into their hands. Such a charge is a tremendous indictment against the motherhood of the nation, and, if it could be sustained, ought of itself to bar women from all legislative functions until they can better fulfil that which Nature demands of them in child-bearing and rearing. Moreover, it is the function of slaves to labor; but it is this nation's pride and boast that in no other country that the sun shines on are there so many homes supported by the loyal and untiring industry of men, where women are kept in ease and comfort, in order that they may give their time to the higher duties of rearing children and planning and carrying on enterprises of charity, philanthropy, and reform; and the influence of these homes upon public sentiment is the one irresistible power in American social and political life. Plainly, if any portion of the American people are slaves, it is not the women.

But let us return to the question of the physical adaptability of women to the duties of voters. If women vote, they must also hold office and assume the working duties incident to political campaigns. It appears from the published record of your life that you commenced your political career at about the age of thirty. For the next ten or fifteen years you were actively in politics. Now, will you tell me if you think it would have been convenient or agreeable during those years, when you were laying the foundations of your political success, to have been also engaged in bearing and rearing a family? Could you have done what you found it necessary to do politically, and at the same time have attended properly to your duties as wife and mother? You will say that the very suggestion is indelicate, and I agree with you, but the fault is in the situation as proposed by you. The duties and offices of motherhood are all sweet, and pure, and holy, when kept within the sacred precincts of the home. Brought out into the garish light of publicity, what do they become?

Nor will it avail you to say that some part of these offices may be delegated to servants. There are too many mothers of that sort in the country now; no political measure can be a wise one which tends to increase their number.

You say in your Report that there are many women who are not wives and mothers. Very true, and when women vote and hold office, there will be more of them. A true regard for the best interests of society demands that their number shall be reduced by all natural and reasonable means; but when political rewards are offered as the price of services in public life, do you not believe that many, and those not of the weak and ignorant, but of the more gifted and intellectual, will be tempted to forego marriage and motherhood for the sake of winning them? Woe betide the land which thus offers its political trusts as premiums for childless women! The morals of society are corrupt enough now. What do you suppose they will become when not to be married, not to be a mother, is the prerequisite for a woman's success in a chosen and tempting career? History gives abundant evidence that women are not naturally of purer instincts or more capable of self-control than men. It is only as they are subject to men as in heathen countries, or yield themselves to the elevating and purifying influence, of Christian teaching concerning marriage and the home, that they rise to a higher moral level. Emancipated from these restraints, the intensity of their nature often betrays them into surpassing depths of depravity. I speak advisedly, therefore, and in the light of thirty years' profound and prayerful study of social problems, when I say that the direct tendency of woman suffrage would be to form a class of women such as held high court in Greece in the days preceding its downfall; women brilliant and intellectual, but wholly wanting in that steadfast faith and abiding virtue which characterize the Anglo-Saxon ideal of womanhood, I may say the Christian ideal as well, — the wife and mother. Are American men prepared to relegate the wives and mothers of this republic to a secondary and subservient place, and share the political leadership of this great and free country with an oligarchy of Aspasias?

6

You say that the passage of the proposed resolution would not commit any person to the support of woman suffrage in the end. But what does it do if passed by both houses? It sends the discussion of this question, backed by the authority of Congress, into every State of this Union. A score or two of the professional advocates of woman suffrage will beat up the entire territory, and, by their noisy persistence, will necessitate either that women shall take the field upon the other side, or else let the question go by default. Home-loving women — the women who stay in their homes and fulfil the duties of their vocation, and these women are in the great majority in all our States and Territories — have little taste for public strife, and few gifts with which to win battles in the public arena. Still, if needs must, they can and will defend their homes; but, believe me, they will not exonerate from blame those legislators who, by the advocacy of measures like this which you propose, have thrust the hard necessity upon them.

Do you ask me, then, what shall men do, in regard to this cry, which is coming up all over the land, for purer politics, a worthier conduct of affairs? Men know very well what they ought to do about it. They ought to live daily and hourly in the fear of God and for the honor of good women. They ought steadfastly to practise those principles of purity, honor, uprightness, and patriotism which it is the duty of every Christian home to inculcate. It is very true that the duty is now too often imperfectly performed in our homes; but, believe me, the remedy for this evil does not lie in the direction of woman suffrage. It is by inciting and helping woman to the more faithful discharge of her own duties that legislators will honor her far more than by dragging her out of the quiet of her own domain, and setting her to perform their neglected and unfulfilled tasks.

Instead of fifteen millions of women voters vainly trying to do the work which God demands of men, there should be fifteen millions of happy homes in this broad, fair land; homes supported by the fathers' labor, made to glow with heaven's own light by the mothers' tender love and care; homes where children are being reared who shall become just and upright men, and faithful, conscientious women; where those virtues are being taught which are the only enduring bulwarks of a free, republican government. It is to build up such homes, not to break down their walls, and quench the light upon their hearthstones, that legislation ought to be directed.

There are other and weightier arguments against woman suffrage, but these are such as are suggested by the text of your Report. I commend them to your earnest consideration before you again address the United States Senate as the Champion of Woman.

Very respectfully yours,

CAROLINE F. CORBIN,
*Author of "Letters from a Chimney Corner."*

[Reprinted by Massachusetts Association opposed to the Extension of Suffrage to Women.]

# HIDDEN FROM HISTORY

MRS. FRANK FOXCROFT, Chairman
25 HILLSIDE AVENUE
TELEPHONE CAMBRIDGE 5706

MISS ALBERTA M. HOUGHTON, Treasurer
58 GARDEN STREET

MRS. CHARLES B. GULICK, Secretary
59 FAYERWEATHER STREET

## CAMBRIDGE BRANCH
OF THE
## MASSACHUSETTS ANTI-SUFFRAGE ASSOCIATION

CAMBRIDGE, MASS., February 15, 1916

To the Senate and House of Representatives of the United States:

The Cambridge Branch of the Massachusetts Anti-Suffrage Association, including in its membership more than 1,400 women of voting age, and representing a membership of 36,761 in the State at large, respectfully petitions your honorable bodies not to give your approval to the proposed woman suffrage amendment to the Federal Constitution.

We believe that the basis of the suffrage should be determined by each State for itself; and that it should not be changed except by the votes of the qualified electors of each State.

In view of the fact that the eleven States which, during the last four years, have rejected suffrage amendments to their Constitutions, have a combined population nearly five times as large as the combined population of the eleven double-suffrage States, we hold that it would be wrong to sanction a measure, the avowed purpose of which is to enable the minority to override the majority, and to do this without submitting this revolutionary change to the voters in any State.

Believing that we express the views of the vast majority of American women, we ask you to vote against the proposed amendment.

*Lily Rice Foxcroft*
Chairman.

*Alice Hathaway Gulick*
Secretary.

By Mr. Lodge

Petition of the Cambridge Branch of the Massachusetts Anti-Suffrage Association, of Cambridge, Massachusetts, remonstrating against an amendment to the Constitution extending suffrage to women

FEB 19 1916

# HIDDEN FROM HISTORY

# LETTER TO Rev'd DR. J. M. BUCKLEY.

When about thirty years of age I accepted for a time the doctrine of woman suffrage, and publicly defended it. Years of wide and careful observation have convinced me that the demand for woman suffrage in America is without foundation in equity, and, if successful, must prove harmful to American society. I find some worthy women defending it, but the majority of our best women, especially our most intelligent, domestic, and godly mothers, neither ask for nor desire it. The instinct of motherhood is against it. The basal conviction of our best manhood is against it. The movement is at root a protest against the representative relations and functions by virtue of which each sex depends upon and is exalted by the other. This theory and policy, tending to the subversion of the natural and divine order, must make man less a man, and woman less a woman. A distinguished woman advocate of this suffrage movement says, "We need the ballot to protect us against men." When one sex is compelled thus to protect itself against the other, the foundations of society are already crumbling. Woman now makes man what he is. She controls him as babe, boy, manly son, brother, lover, husband, father. Her influence is enormous. If she use it wisely, she needs no additional power. If she abuse her opportunity she deserves no additional responsibility. Her womanly weight, now without measure, will be limited to the value of a single ballot, and her control over from two to five additional votes forfeited.

The curse of America to-day is in the dominated partisan vote, the vote of ignorance and superstition. Shall we help matters by doubling this dangerous mass? Free from the direct complications and passions of the political arena, the best women may exert a conservative and moral influence over men as voters. Force her down into the same bad atmosphere, and both man and woman must inevitably suffer incalculable loss. We know what woman can be in the "commune", in "riots", and on the "rostrum".

Woman can, through the votes of men, have every right to which she is entitled. All she has man has gladly given her. It is his glory to represent her. To rob him of this right is to weaken both. He and she are just now in danger through his mistaken courtesy.

JOHN H. VINCENT.

Topeka, Kansas, April 18, 1894.

# LIBERTY ABOVE EQUALITY
## BY JOHN CORBIN

IT is a self-evident truth, or so Thomas Jefferson held, that all men are created equal. With similar solemnity, as one who says an undisputed thing, Jefferson's greatest disciple declared: "Democracy rests upon the equality of the citizen." These be winged phrases; but, as it happens, they fly in directions precisely opposite. Wilson was demanding a rigid exclusion of Chinese and Japanese laborers—in whose increasing presence among us, as he clearly saw, the vigor and virtue of our free institutions would suffer. He was asserting not universal equality, but an irreconcilable difference. By precisely the same logic, we should be justified in discriminating against unassimilable people of any race or color. Which of the phrase-tipped shafts comes nearer the bullseye of our Americanism?

The question is pertinent to the cause of the forgotten folk who are remembering themselves as the middle class—the newly poor brainworker who finds himself taxed and otherwise put upon to provide ever widening opportunities for those who were once called the poor. If the brainworker is to feed his mind with the knowledge of books, his life with human contacts; if he is to have children and hand on the education and the larger tradition which he received—if, in short, he is to fill the position and do the work which is owing to himself and to the nation—it must be by a frank recognition of inequalities and distinctions. He must have a life scaled higher in opportunity, and in expense, than the life of the man whose capacity is for merely manual labor. That can be right only if Thomas Jefferson was wrong—if some men are destined from birth to higher privileges and opportunities. But then this land of liberty is not, and never can be, the land of equality. Somewhere between the two sayings, which were proffered as equally axiomatic, there is room for a deal of close thinking.

Our revolutionary forefathers had precious little use for the words with which we now concern ourselves, equality and democracy—those of them, at least, who fought for independence instead of writing about it. The word on their lips was liberty. This fact, and the quaint predicament of the Wilson-Jefferson phrase, suggests that equality and liberty are distinct principles—perhaps contradictory.

Jean Jacques Rousseau, deeply as he is despised for the looseness of his thought, had considered this matter more closely than his disciple, Thomas Jefferson. He knew that there is no such thing as absolute equality. In his *Discourse upon Inequality,* which exercised a vast revolutionary force both on the France of 1789 and on the America of 1800, he admitted at the outset what he called the "inequality of nature." Some men are created taller than others, and stronger; intellectually more able, morally more elevated. These inequalities of nature Rousseau sadly dismissed as irremediable. As for social equality, which means, basically, equality in property, he knew that it did not exist in any state—that it could not exist in life as we know it or can conceive it. But he felt that it ought to exist; and to picture it more vividly he assumed a state of primitive nature in which there was as yet no such thing as property—because tools and weapons had not been invented, and because land was so plentiful that no one thought of appropriating any tract as his own. In this state, as Rousseau pictured it, the father had no care for the mother or claim on her, the mother no care for their child.

Such a state is unknown to nature. The fox owns his hole; the trout owns his favorite bend in the brook, and will fight for it. Among the higher animals, of whom man is one, the possession of females is a primordial instinct, as is the love of parents for offspring. Rousseau was aware that his "state of nature" was conjectural, so he passed on to the American Indians, whom he praised as leading the most perfect known life—the nearest approach to the life of social equality. Jefferson knew the noble red man as his master did not; yet he repeated this verdict so explicitly and so often that we are forced to conclude that he believed it. "Those societies (as the Indians) which live without government, enjoy in their general mass an infinitely greater degree of happiness" than was possible "under the English system of government"; and he called it "a problem not clear to my mind" whether the "unrestraint" of Indian life were not preferable to the restraints imposed by even his own loose construction of the American Constitution. This is the intellectual milieu which gave birth to the most frequently quoted of our political axioms.

At best it is a "glittering generality," as Rufus Choate called it—a verbal tom-tom with the beating of which our leaders inspire us to follow them where they will. It has nothing to do with the concrete realities of any situation in which, as a nation, we have ever found ourselves. The granting of an equal vote to the negroes whom our fathers so nobly fought to free was as misconceived philosophically as it has proved impossible in practice. When the Declaration of Independence passes from Jeffersonian generalities to a plain statement of the cause for which the fathers were in revolt, it becomes manifest that "equality" was to them neither "natural" nor social. They stood for taxation through representatives, for trial by jury—for a merely political equality. In plain terms, "equality" meant that an Englishman in America was as good as an Englishman at home. Democracy most of them scorned; but their freedom, certainly, rested upon the equality of the citizen.

Even political equality is an ideal—a thing to be longed for, striven for, rather than a possible fact. If anyone thinks otherwise, let him look about him. Repeatedly we have seen important legislation, from prohibition to woman's suffrage, carried by organized, wire-pulling minorities without reference to the will of the people. Even in the courts, equal justice is defeated. The murderer who can retain the ablest counsel and a staff of alienists has a decided advantage over the murderer who is poor—and so he gaily spends his life in escaping from sanitarium to sanitarium, in retrial after retrial, to the vast expense and chagrin of the community.

Why do we who profess equality permit such abuses? Because we love another and greater ideal, irreconcilable with the ideal of equality. The desire for personal differences and distinctions, of which property is but one, is intrinsic in the scheme of things. In all life that rises above the brute struggle for food and shelter, the prime motive is to prove oneself unequal and superior—to realize all native qualities and aspirations. Man wants the mate of his choice against all the world, wants to work for her and to pass the fruit of his toil to their children. He wants to sing his songs, build his railways, lead his fellow men. Unless the way is open to do so he is not a free man. Not equality, but liberty, is the master passion of our race.

Like equality, to be sure, liberty is something less than absolute. The moment a man takes a mate, he is bound to her by one of the strongest ties of which he is capable. Their children subject them both to bonds equally strong. And so it goes, throughout civilized life. The things which freedom gives us with a seeming-generous hand, the things for which alone we hold that freedom is precious, enmesh our insurgent spirits with silken strands. Liberty imposes obligations against which instinct often rebels, but against which the true man is powerless. We live in ceaseless conflict, within ourselves and within the community.

Only a strong man can contain such a conflict, control it. And so, as Montesquieu pointed out, and as Rousseau conceded,—though to do so disillusioned him,—there are peoples for whom self-government is no blessing—inferior peoples. Liberty is a tonic to strong, selfmastering races, and to them alone. To Montesquieu and Rousseau this idea could only be an abstraction. In our American problem of immigration, Woodrow Wilson was face to face with the concrete reality. He cast about it the bright woof of a casual phrase but did not pause to weave it into the close web of thought. To him and to his hearers the phrase was doubtless inspiring merely as an echo of Jefferson.

And always liberty is in conflict with the ideal of equality—which, though we outrage it in every act of life, we feel to be somehow noble and sacred still. In Rousseau's earliest essay, he found in the human desire for distinction—found in the spirit of liberty—only an ignoble vanity, to which he attributed all the corruptions of society; and he never quite lost his infatuation for the equality of red Indians and his wonderful state of nature; but when he came to analyze civilized life in *The Social Compact* he recognized a new set of facts. His reasoning was often loose, but his perceptions were those of a man of genius. Wherever " the forces of life " are unchecked, he says, they tend to destroy equality; but the social pact works powerfully to arrest the tendency, substituting for the inequalities of nature a moral and legal equality. " Unequal in physical

## LIBERTY ABOVE EQUALITY

force or in genius," men are only "equal by the conventions of the law." So equality became, to Rousseau as to us, a legal convention. Liberty was something more—an active principle. Yet it had definite limitations. "To obey every appetite is to be a slave to mere impulse," but if one lives under the self-imposed laws of a sovereign people the laws "become instruments of a truer and higher freedom." Equality is of the law but liberty is the distilled essence of civilized living. And so, having begun as an individualist uncompromising and absolute, Rousseau became an uncompromising and absolute champion of the sovereign state, a precursor of the Prussian. "As nature gives to each man absolute power over all his members, so the social compact gives the body politic an absolute power over all its units."

The justification of the state is that it gives the highest liberty which is possible to the civilized individual—scope to talents that, without it, would be thwarted. Equality itself becomes a mere convention of the law in order that each man shall live his life to the utmost—for himself and for the state. In our thoughtless moods we vaunt our liberty; but when the day of trial comes we know that liberty is the most austere of masters, to whom true men give to the utmost in service and sacrifice. No principle in a republic is more basic than this, that the absolute right of an individual to take wealth and power out of the national stock is proportioned to the vigor and ability with which he uses it for the national good.

The *Discourse upon Inequality* was the prime motive force in the upheaval of 1789—in which Jefferson, though American Ambassador, took an active part. But when the Revolution had progressed to the point of organizing a Government of its own it drew its philosophic inspiration from the maturer *Social Compact,* and the result was a State exerting a sovereignty rigid and absolute. Jefferson, meantime, had returned to America. He escaped the Terror, but he missed also the more deeply philosophic influences of his master—both as expounded in *The Social Compact,* which he does not appear to have read, and as exemplified in the constitution of the First Republic. Republican sovereignty as administered by Robespierre no doubt confirmed his belief in "unrestraint" and red Indians. Meantime in America, as it happened, Washington and Hamilton were organizing a Government which, though perhaps unconsciously, was in general accord with the ideas of *The Social Compact*. To them citizenship implied service; government was a function austere and noble. But to Jefferson their every thought was anathema. They were " tyrants," " monarchists," " monocrats " and what not—Washington and Hamilton. Eventually, thanks to the blunders of the Federalists who succeeded Washington, Jefferson brought off his " Revolution of 1800 "—the foundation of the Democratic party —which he never ceased to laud as an event equal in importance to the Revolution of 1776. In so doing, he fixed upon our political thought a wholly doctrinary and largely false conception of republican institutions, exalting above the mature theory of Rousseau, above the organized practice of the founders of our nation, a nebulous dream of equality.

For our present purpose all this is of importance chiefly as applying, not to individuals but to groups— if you will, to classes; for they also in a republic are subject to a conflict between the principles of equality and liberty, subject to the necessity of using the national resources for the general good. The laborer claims a right to hours that enable him to give the needed strength to his work and to have due leisure for self-development; to wages that enable him to maintain his efficiency and to provide normal opportunities for those who depend on him—to rise out of his class, if he is able, to any height. On what principle, if not those we have adduced, can he justify this claim— equality as to the laws of the game with liberty to play it to the utmost? The capitalist claims the right to a life which shall keep him in touch with the world he so largely controls, the right to bend to his purpose as large a portion of the wealth of mankind as he can rightfully amass; and all this we have freely granted him. No claim is made for the brain worker. He is forgotten so fully that if he also asserts his right to survive and to serve, according to his needs and the needs of the state, men rub their eyes.

Today the cause of the middle class has—very suddenly, as it seems—become the cause of the state. The proletarian is rising with an insistent demand that equality be granted him not only in politics but in industry—that all of wealth and all of social amenity—all of civilization, in short— which the race has achieved through the disciplined liberty of the individual be subjected, day by day, to the will of the industrial voter. With class warfare already upon us, the

## LIBERTY ABOVE EQUALITY

blindest can see in the middle class a powerful and indispensable ally—with whose aid the ideals and the institutions of the fathers may still be preserved and without whom the liberties of all will crumble.

No precise count or classification of the middle class exists; like so many of the rest of us, the census taker has forgotten them. Yet in a general way we can estimate who and what they are. Very largely they are Americans of the older stock. Edward Alsworth Ross, Professor of Sociology in the University of Wisconsin, estimates that fully one quarter of our population are descended from the Puritans who sought the wilderness between 1618 and 1640—the men who have caused New England to be humorously styled the "brain orchard" of the nation. One sixth of our population at the time of the Revolution were of the scarcely less able Scotch-Irish stock; and, until recent decades, they also have multiplied mightily. It is conservatively estimated that of the Americans of today some 40,000,000, or over 42 per cent. of our white population, are descended on both sides from Colonial ancestors. Some of these no doubt are degenerate; the great majority are still educated, energetic. In the nineteenth century also our immigration was from a stock of prime vitality. Professor Ross estimates that those of German ancestry comprise 25 per cent. of our present population. The immigration of Scandinavians up to 1910 numbered almost two millions, and of Celtic Irish over four millions; with their descendants they doubtless number 8 per cent. of the population. In all 75 per cent. of native Americans come from the Nordic peoples. In addition there were, in 1910 upward of two million recent immigrants born in Europe, including 1,221,000 from England, Scotland and Wales. In purely British stock alone, as W. S. Rossiter has pointed out, we outnumber the British Isles and Canada combined, with some 55,000,000 as against some 50,000,000—the scale being turned against us by 5,000,000 Australian Britons and a smaller number in South Africa.

In all of these national groups in America there are, of course, many who cannot be included in the middle class; but the fact remains that over three-quarters of all Americans are from nations predominantly of the North European stock. They readily fall into the spirit of our life and the abler of them, being equal before the law and individually free, rise easily into the middle class. As the United States is the richest of modern countries in material resources, so also it is the largest single reservoir of the Nordic stock. And the middle class is its brain power. Is it not an omen, a portent, that more and more the middle class is submerged by the unregenerate hordes of new immigration from the east and south of Europe—that we make it a virtue to teach them the phrases of democracy, equality?

Wherever civilization has reached its pinnacles, it has been under the leadership of this northern man—the Aryan, as he is more familiarly, though less accurately, known—in Assyria, in Persia, in Greece, in Rome, and now again in the nations of the north and west of Europe. And wherever the Aryan civilization has reached its utmost heights it has developed free institutions. Yet freedom has not meant stability: the power of self-control has not endured. In Greece the rise of democracy and in Rome the rise of the Republic was speedily followed by a decline—a tragic and arresting phenomenon. It would be interesting to know why. Historic records are meager, yet two factors may still be distinguished—the wasting of the best blood and its weakening through intercourse with alien peoples.

As to Greece we can be sure only of the former cause—civil war, adventurous mercenary expeditions and the migration of men of intellect to alien Mediterranean ports. Before Hellas could achieve unity, its best were no more. But there must also have been a corruption of those who lived on in Greece. How soon this happened we do not know; yet it is worthy of note that, as early as 450 B. C., Athenians found it necessary to pass a law limiting citizenship to men both of whose parents were citizens. Even in the age of Pericles, it would seem, the danger of an admixture of alien blood was serious. Today among the people who speak the language of Homer there is only a thin trickling of the ancient blood.

The case of Rome is clearer. When the old Romans ceased to labor with their own hands, their place was supplied by slaves—who were furnished in abundance, and from a great variety of races, by ever widening conquest. It was the custom to select the slaves on each estate from different nationalities, so that language would prove a barrier to intrigue and insurrection—and thus the way was paved to an eventual admixture of widely divergent races. Men of the Latin stock, meantime, extinguished one another in fierce civil war and in wholesale proscriptions. The virtues of family life sank in luxurious idleness and debauchery—the most sordid and hideous race suicide. From the lack of men of the ancient stock, Roman citizenship was thrown open to freed men—an actual if not a doctrinary equality. In the first century of our era, Tacitus noted that the people of Rome were almost entirely of the class of emancipated slaves. Freedom died with the Roman stock, in the birth of the new equality. Roman institutions remained, and enough of the original race to administer them; but among the people as a whole the Aryan spirit was submerged. Only an Empire was possible. Many causes have been alleged for the decline of the Empire, but this is probably the most fundamental. Only of late have students of history taken note of all this and there is doubtless truth in what they say, that the determining factor in history is not war, politics or economics, but race. Or, to paraphrase another publicist, liberty rests upon the superiority of the citizen.

In the modern world once again the Nordic race has developed free institutions. There is no abatement of the warlike spirit, or of the racial devastation which it works. From the ethnological point of view the recent war was a civil conflict, and the slaughter of the best blood was unprecedented, appalling. We of the new world fought as the Nordic has always fought when he felt that his liberty was in danger; but fortunately our losses in battle were relatively few. Yet we suffered a far greater loss through the war, which few have noted—still suffer it, and shall do so for decades to come. It is the loss of children who should be but will not be born. And these are almost wholly children of the middle class.

For a generation before the war, race suicide had been noted—and noted as a middle-class phenomenon. Though analyzed statistics are lacking, it is probable that among highly educated and professional people—the finest flower of the nation—it has progressed farther even than in France. Before the war a Harvard professor calculated that if the university were limited to the sons of graduates it would have to close its doors within a century. During the war the proletariat continued, as always, to swarm; being organized, it was able, on the whole, to maintain the normal proportion of wages to the price of commodities. But those dependent upon salaries have been forced lower and still lower in the scale of living, both during and since the war. Men and women of today who are hard put to it to feed and clothe themselves and maintain the dignity of their standards do not bring children into the world to increase their hardships—and to suffer from them, as children must, tenfold. Our middle class has little of the ancient lust of conquest and delight in military adventure— though it fights with the best when it must and dies with the age-old heroism. Its ruling passions are those of peace. Thanks to the diffusion of knowledge, and of spiritual comprehension, it stands on a higher plane than has ever before been possible to it, in the history of the world. Yet even in normal times of late, and especially under the impact of war, it has suffered diminution of its best blood as surely as those of the ancient world suffered through orgies of civil strife and debauchery.

The reason for this loss is much more nearly the same in modern and ancient times than appears on the surface. In Greece and Rome, the excesses of warfare and of debauchery were a result of slave labor; for, except the pursuit of philosophy, the youth of the dominant stock had little else to do. Americans of the middle class are more fortunate in having to work for their livelihood; yet an important—perhaps the fundamental—cause of their decline lies in the age-old problem of the manual laborer—with us the problem of a disguised slavery, the " new " immigration.

As early as 1891 General Francis A. Walker noted the sterilizing power of immigration. " Not only did the decline in the native element as a whole take place in singular correspondence with the excess of foreign arrivals, but it occurred chiefly in just those regions to which the newcomers most frequently resorted." " When the country was flooded with ignorant and unskilled foreigners, Americans instinctively shrank from the contact and the competition thus offered them." Other causes may be noted. The burden of taxation and of the cost of living fall most heavily upon the middle class. Meantime their standards are advancing. There has been a wide increase of reading, of devotion to music and playgoing, of knowledge of the great world and of interest in society and fashion—in brief, all the phenomena of a rapidly diffusing civilization. In individual instances the resulting limitation of the family is often selfish and wilful; but on the whole, the lifting of the cultural standards of the middle class is the result of a sound and salutary instinct, calculated to give it precisely the breadth of outlook and tonic mentality which has always been its greatest need. And at the worst this cause is secondary. The primary cause is immigration, the results of which are so immediate and definite that, as General Walker found, they could be checked off "in those States and in the very counties" into which immigration flowed.

All this became evident even under the old immigration from Northern Europe, which reached its crest in 1882 and then steadily subsided. By 1896 a widely different immigration had come to surpass it in numbers, floods of "Mediterranean" and "Alpine" peoples from southern and eastern Europe and Asia Minor, including half a million largely Mongolian in blood—Portuguese, Sicilians, South Italians, Greeks, Slovaks, Lithuanians, Poles, Syrians, Armenians—people that, having been basely subjected throughout history, still live in mediaeval filth and squalor, with little sense of the dignity of life or the nobility of womanhood; people who have no experience of free institutions and probably little or no capacity for them.

Our tolerance of the new immigration has two sets of causes, ironically contrasted. The chief consideration, from our side of the water, has been the profit that is to be made out of laborers who will submit to an un-American standard of living—and of wages. Hand in glove with this is the profit which steamship lines find in a multitude of steerage passengers. These are no mere allegations but facts familiar to all sociologists—who make use of them nowadays mainly as socialistic propaganda. A vigorous contributory cause has been the effort of philanthropic Jews to relieve their nationals from the persecutions of central Europe, and to open up to them the blessing of our land and its institutions —a movement that has been more successful, far, than Zionism. "Not only Jerusalem is the golden." These forces of our own ruthless greed and of an intelligent race philanthropy have found a strong ally in our national sentimentality—which propagandists from the basic industries, from the steamship companies and from the friends of Russian and Polish Jews have not been slow to foster. The "blessing of democratic institutions," they tell us, is a solvent in which all races rise to any desired height. In praise of our "melting pot," Israel Zangwill wrote a whole, long play, which had a wide appeal to our self approbation. Even the politicians have joined the fulsome eulogy—for many of them find in the increasing hordes of ignorant voters an inexhaustible source of power. One and all point out—and not without truth—that in patience and endurance, as also in thrift, these aliens are our superiors—neglecting to add, of course, that these very qualities, coupled with their lower standard of conduct and thought, will enable them eventually to dispossess us of our birthright. They subtly suggest that, by relieving us of the merely manual task, they leave us free to advance in prosperity and in the enjoyment of it—but do not point out the inevitable end of that enjoyment! They appeal mightily to our " reason " in suggesting that the only quick solution of the servant problem is in rapidly increasing immigration. No doubt the wise ones said the same in Rome! Industrially and politically we are committing the age-old Nordic folly. And we not only give these " wage slaves " full citizenship but proclaim them in all ways our equals—blandly assume that we have " Americanized " them when we have taught them our patter of equality and democracy.

The peoples of the old immigration spoke various languages, had various national characters and traditions; but racially they were for the most part close kindred—to one another and to us. The melting pot has melted nothing—biologists know that it can melt nothing. Widely divergent races may mingle but they do not blend. And the result of their mingling is mongrelization—the progressive debasement of both stocks which has made the " free institutions " of Central and South America a jest. In becoming Americans, immigrants of the northern race have sloughed off their superficial and merely national differences, but in the process they have realized more fully their unity and harmony of race. For the first century of its life our nation, though traveling the dangerous, untrod paths of democracy, has been the world's paragon of stability—as the nations to the south of us have been a byword of facile revolution. And now we also have started in the way that, in the slow lapse of centuries, can only end in mongrelization.

Meantime there is a near danger, not racial but political—a danger of revolution, which the public has strangely misconceived. Nowhere is the force of racial instinct more clearly evident than in the popular conception that the really dangerous radicals are foreigners. In point of fact, alien propagandists have been relatively few and, except in the incitement of sporadic violence, impotent. As for the great masses of immigrants, they have been too ignorant, too hard-working, too much bent upon the week's wage, to give thought to revolution. Even in the steel strike, which was essentially a strike of " new " immigrants, the revolutionary element was negligible. The organizing leaders, Fitzpatrick and Foster, were Americans—and revolutionists. So everywhere, the radical element which is dangerous consists of Americans born and bred.

And with the leaders we have furnished the inflammatory idea, without which revolution is impossible—we ourselves, the American people. Professing the Jeffersonian doctrine of universal equality, we have carried it to its political consummation in universal franchise. Whether right or wrong, that step cannot be retraced. If we proceed by the ancient logic, however, one more step is inevitable. Like our political government, our industries, and their invested capital, will be administered democratically. For, though we persistently blink the fact, the basic principle of Socialism is the doctrine of equality. By the logic of our own teaching, industry must be controlled by all workers—including the " wage slaves " of the new immigration.

Now in industrial democracy there are many plausible and perhaps fruitful ideas. Even the American Federation of Labor, once so solidly conservative, has declared in favor of " democratic control " of the railways, and by an overwhelming majority. It is a confident prophet who will say that our great industrial units may not some day have a definite power over government as it affects their special interests. But if this new order is to be ruled by its educated brain force, and not by the voice of the ignorant and racially inferior laborer, it can only be by a candid recognition of the special services and responsibilities of the middle class.

Many questions arise of the when, the how, and the wherewithal—questions which, far from being answered, have not yet been clearly put. But beneath them all lies this necessity: the Jeffersonian bubble of equality must be pricked. Above equality is liberty, and liberty rests upon the superiority of the citizen.

JOHN CORBIN.

# The women of Massachusetts opposed to Woman Suffrage ask your consideration of the accompanying appeal from their sisters of Illinois, as it expresses fully their own convictions on the subject.

---

*To the Honorable the Senate and House of Representatives of the State of Illinois,*                                                  *Greeting:*

The undersigned, viewing with apprehension the persistency with which certain measures, inimical to those institutions in which our dearest interests are involved, are urged upon your honorable body, avail ourselves of the immemorial and inalienable right of a free people to lay our grievances before the government under which we live, and to petition for a respectful consideration of the same.

We are women of Illinois, mothers, sisters, daughters, wives of citizens of this our beloved State, to whom are committed by government, usage, and our own consent, the right to represent us in the councils of the State, and to propose and frame such political measures as are necessary, not only for our own, but for the general safety and prosperity.

Making due allowances for the conditions which have come down to us from the past, and for the imperfection which necessarily pertains to all human action, we have found no reason to complain of the manner in which these representative rights have been used. If a wrong existed, we have seen again and again that if our just claims were urged upon these, our natural representatives and agents, they have not failed generously to respond to such petitions; so that in our own State of Illinois the rights of women, in regard to such interests as those of property and the guardianship of children, are already equal to those of men. And if any other wrongs remain upon the statute books, we feel assured that they can easily be redressed by measures similar to those already employed. So far, therefore, as these our natural representatives are concerned, we have no real or just cause of public grievance.

But of late years, certain women have arisen and have formed themselves into a sect, and have zealously propagated their ideas, which we believe to be false and unnatural; and have urged them upon men, from the public platform, through the public press, invading legislative halls and the councils of the church, and not refraining from sending their aggressive literature into our very homes.

Their leaders waylay the men of other households than their own upon the streets and in public places. They have even the effrontery to claim that they are speaking in our behalf, and uttering the counsels of our secret hearts, which we, the said mothers, sisters, daughters, wives. have neither the intelligence nor the courage to urge for ourselves.

They have called us slaves, and compared us to the ignorant and degraded negroes on Southern plantations.

They belittle our home interests, which are dearer to us than our very lives; for which many a time and oft we cheerfully put our lives in peril. They treat with scorn and contempt our prerogatives as wives and mothers and home-loving women. In all these and various other ways they behave in such a manner as to bring reproach upon the ancient good repute of womanhood.

All this we have borne for many years in silence, not deeming it the part of modest and dignified matrons to engage in unseemly strife; but so persistent are these women in their misrepresentations of us and of our sentiments that our patience is exhausted, and we feel it a sacred duty to lay before our law-makers and the world our just complaint, and the arguments and exhortations by which we are able to enforce it upon the public hearing.

We believe that Almighty God formed men and women of one flesh, that they might dwell together in peace and unity; and that neither man nor woman attains the highest estate of humanity except through such union as he has ordained.

We believe that the offices and functions of the two are different in kind, but equal in power and honor.

We believe that while men find their appropriate sphere of activity in the out-door world of wage-labor, commerce, enterprise, and the administration of civil, judicial, and ecclesiastical law, women have a no less exhaustive and honorable field of usefulness in the administration of domestic and social affairs. Nor are these latter duties, when properly understood and performed, of less, but, if possible, of *greater* moment to the welfare of the race. They are the fountain and source out of which all other conditions of life proceed, and when the fountain is not kept pure and sweet, all the streams which flow therefrom will be turbid and impure.

We believe, therefore, that neither men nor women have any reason or right to complain of, or desire to change, these great assignments of duty which nature has wrought into the very fibre of the physical and intellectual being of the sexes; but that the proper course for each is to accept the fiat of nature with a reverent spirit, and seek to exercise their best powers so as to achieve the greatest possible amount of good to the race, each in their own appropriate manner.

We believe that as men have by no means reached an ideal development of the State, although they are sincerely struggling toward that achievement, so in social and domestic life there are still many reforms to be accomplished, which demand the utmost devotion and energy of women and afford ample scope for their highest ambition. We rejoice that through that great movement for the higher education of women, which began at the outset of our career as a nation and which has been forwarded mainly by those who have desired to make women more happy and useful in their own sphere, all branches of learning, language, mathematics, science, are now open on practically equal terms to the youth of both sexes. But as there is still special training for boys in such branches as manual labor, technology, engineering, and political economy, so we hope to see the day when there shall be special schools or classes for girls, wherein such subjects as the chemistry of foods, scientific methods of cookery, the laws of drainage and ventilation, the appliances for heating and lighting our homes, the laws of physical health and beauty, kindergartening, trained nursing, and in short all the vast and varied knowledge which bears upon the home and tends to make it more and more the fitting birthplace and nursery of the race shall be freely imparted to the future wives and mothers of our land.

Nor is society so free from evils, inherited from an earlier stage of civilization, and others incidental to the rapid influx of emigration from foreign shores, that women can afford to hold their charitable and philanthropic responsibilities lightly, or to crave other and more arduous duties.

We believe that it is a mistaken idea that for women to advance they must become more like men. No doubt there are individual women to whom, from peculiarities of their nature or circumstances, public duties may be fitting and appropriate; but these are exceptional  In the order of Christian civilization, the great mass of women must always be homekeepers. It is this unnumbered multitude of tireless, loving workers for human advancement and happiness who must always form the highest exponent of womanhood, the truest criterion of its requirements and destiny; and these, from the nature of the case, must always be womanly women.

Such is our faith. We believe that you share it with us, and that you deprecate, as we do, the addition to our already sufficiently heavy burdens, of the duties and cares of the State. We beg you, therefore, as the highest representative body of men in the Commonwealth, that you will continue to the end the good work which you have so well begun, and record yourselves on every and all occasions as unalterably opposed to any change in the status of women before the law, which shall impose upon them those public and civic duties which belong to men.

We ask this for our protection, for the protection of the social and domestic interests of the Commonwealth, and in the name of those tender and holy memories of home which are our common heritage and joy.

WOMEN REMONSTRANTS OF THE STATE OF ILLINOIS.

## MASSACHUSETTS ASSOCIATION OPPOSED TO THE FURTHER EXTENSION OF SUFFRAGE TO WOMEN.
## 1897.

### BY-LAWS.

1. The name of the society shall be: The Massachusetts Association Opposed to the Further Extension of Suffrage to Women.

#### MEMBERS.

2. Any woman living in Massachusetts, and over twenty-one years of age, may become a member of the Association by sending her name to the General Secretary, or to the Secretary of any Branch Association.

#### STANDING COMMITTEE.

3. There shall be a Standing Committee of all persons who signed the original call for the Association, of the Officers and Executive Committee, of the Chairmen of the several Branch Committees, and of such other persons throughout the State as may be approved by the Executive Committee.

The Standing Committee shall meet annually in May to hear the reports of the Executive Committee and of the Treasurer; for the election from their own number of Officers, and an Executive Committee for the ensuing year; and for such other business as may come before them.

#### OFFICERS.

4. The Officers shall be a President, two Vice-Presidents, a Secretary, and a Treasurer.

The President shall call meetings when necessary, shall preside at them, and shall have the general oversight of the work. In case of the absence or disability of the President and Vice-

Presidents, a Chairman *pro tempore* may be appointed. The President shall be *ex officio* a member of the various committees.

The Secretary shall keep records of all meetings, shall send notices of the Annual and of Executive Committee meetings, take notes of the same, either herself or by an assistant, correspond with Branch Committees, and in general be the means of communication between Executive Officers and Committees.

The Treasurer of the Association shall be elected annually at the meeting of the Standing Committee, shall receive all money contributions, shall pay bills duly approved by the Secretary, shall make an annual report to the Association, and present a statement to the Executive Committee quarterly, or oftener if requested. The Treasurer may have authority to appoint an Assistant Treasurer, subject to the approval of the Executive Committee.

### EXECUTIVE COMMITTEE.

5. The Executive Committee shall hold office for one year, or until their successors are appointed, shall conduct the business of the Association, shall hold meetings monthly, or as often as shall be deemed necessary, and shall appoint sub or special committees at discretion.

A vacancy may be filled by the vote of a majority of the Executive Committee, who shall appoint a special committee to nominate a new member and report at the next meeting.

Five shall constitute a quorum, unless otherwise ordered.

The officers of the Executive Committee shall be the President, the Vice-Presidents, and the Secretary of the Association.

Members of the Committee who have served two years or more, and who do not desire reëlection, may be regarded as Honorary Members of the Executive Committee.

### SUB-COMMITTEES.

6. Three Sub-Committees, on Organization, Printing, and Education, shall be appointed yearly by the Executive Committee, and special committees may also be appointed at any time.

### BRANCH COMMITTEES.

7. Branch Committees may be formed in cities and towns at the discretion of the Executive Committee.

Each Committee shall have a Chairman and a Secretary, who shall report to the General Secretary at intervals agreed upon between the Secretary and each Branch Committee.

8. These By-Laws may be amended at the request of the Executive Committee at any Annual Meeting, or at a special meeting of the Standing Committee called for the purpose by the President. Due notice of any proposed change must be sent at least a week before the meeting to each member of the Standing Committee, and not less than twenty-five members must vote upon the proposed amendment.

---

Pamphlets and leaflets may be obtained from the Secretary of the Association.

Mrs. Robert W. Lord,
56 St. Stephen Street, Boston.

# HIDDEN FROM HISTORY

# Massachusetts Association Opposed to the Extension of Suffrage to Women.

---

This association was formed by women who believe that a more systematic resistance should be made to the appeals and claims of Woman Suffragists.

At a meeting held in Boston last May, a Standing Committee of one hundred chose an Executive Committee for active work. *1895*

We urge on all women interested in the welfare of their State the clear and imperative duty of helping to form public opinion on this important question.

To those of doubtful mind we recommend our pamphlets and leaflets by

>Francis Parkman, Massachusetts,
>Judge Lowell, Massachusetts,
>Richard H. Dana, Massachusetts,
>Professor W. W. Goodwin, Massachusetts,
>George G. Crocker, Massachusetts,
>Mrs. Clara T. Leonard, Massachusetts,
>Mrs. J. H. Robbins, Massachusetts,
>Mrs. K. G. Wells, Massachusetts,
>Mrs. A. D. T. Whitney, Massachusetts,
>Francis M. Scott, New York,
>Mrs. Schuyler Van Rensselaer, New York,
>Mrs. Richard Watson Gilder, New York,
>From "The Outlook," New York,
>Professor E. D. Cope, Pennsylvania,

And other writers. For sale at W. B. Clarke's, 340 Washington Street, and the Old Corner Bookstore.

Women of twenty-one years of age and over who desire to join our Association are requested to send their names and addresses to our Secretary, Mrs. Guild, or to any of the undersigned members of the Standing Committee.

We have no membership fee; but subscriptions, whether annually or as donations, will be gratefully received by our Treasurer, Mr. Laurence Minot, 39 Court Street, Boston.

>Mrs. James M. Codman, Brookline, Mass.
>Miss Sarah H. Crocker, 319 Commonwealth Avenue, Boston, Mass.
>Mrs. James C. Fisk, 32 Quincy Street, Cambridge, Mass.
>Mrs. Charles E. Guild, Secretary, Edgehill Road, Brookline, Mass.
>Miss E. H. Houghton, 1000 Massachusetts Avenue, Cambridge, Mass.
>Miss Elise Johnson, Weymouth, Mass.
>Mrs. Francis C. Lowell, 159 Beacon Street, Boston, Mass.
>Mrs. Oliver W. Peabody, 25 Commonwealth Avenue, Boston, Mass.
>Mrs. Philip H. Sears, 85 Mt. Vernon Street, Boston, Mass.
>Mrs. William T. Sedgwick, 32 Chestnut Street, Boston, Mass.
>Mrs. G. H. Shaw, 23 Commonwealth Avenue, Boston, Mass.
>Miss E. P. Sohier, 79 Beacon Street, Boston, Mass.
>Mrs. Henry M. Whitney, Boylston Street, Brookline, Mass.
>Mrs. Clara T. Leonard, Springfield, Mass.
>Miss Anna L. Dawes, Pittsfield, Mass.
>Mrs. Nathaniel Paine, 72 Elm Street, Worcester, Mass.
>Mrs. Charles T. Hubbard, Main Street, Taunton, Mass.
>Miss Julia Delano, 20 Hawthorne Street, New Bedford, Mass.
>Mrs. John F. Pearson, 7 Pond Street, Newburyport.

# HIDDEN FROM HISTORY

## MASSACHUSETTS ASSOCIATION
## Opposed to the Extension of Suffrage to Women.

This Association has been organized by women who believe that the further extension of Suffrage to Women is unwise and inexpedient.

A Standing Committee has been formed, from which the following Executive Committee was chosen.

| | |
|---|---|
| MRS. JAMES M. CODMAN, | MRS. FRANCIS C. LOWELL, |
| MRS. J. RANDOLPH COOLIDGE, | MRS. OLIVER W. PEABODY, |
| MRS. JAMES M. CRAFTS, | MRS. PHILIP H. SEARS, |
| MISS SARAH H. CROCKER, | MRS. WILLIAM T. SEDGWICK, |
| MRS. JAMES C. FISK, | MRS. G. H. SHAW, |
| MISS E. H. HOUGHTON, | MISS E. P. SOHIER, |
| MISS ELISE JOHNSON, | MRS. HENRY M. WHITNEY. |

MRS. CHARLES E. GUILD, *Secretary and Assistant Treasurer*,
Edge Hill Road, Brookline, Mass.

No fee is exacted from members of the Association, although money is needed to carry on its work, and voluntary contributions of $1.00 and upwards will be gratefully received.

Women of twenty-one years of age or over who desire to join this Association are urged to sign this paper, or to send their names and addresses to the Secretary, or to any member of the Executive Committee.

| SIGNATURE. | ADDRESS. |
|---|---|
| | |

PLEASE AFFIX MRS. OR MISS TO NAME

(OVER)

## MASSACHUSETTS ASSOCIATION OPPOSED TO THE FURTHER EXTENSION OF SUFFRAGE TO WOMEN.

### OFFICERS:

*President*, Mrs. J. ELLIOT CABOT, Clyde Street, Brookline, Mass.
*Vice-Presidents*, Mrs. CHARLES E. GUILD, Edge Hill Road, Brookline,
   Mrs. HENRY M. WHITNEY, Boylston Street, Brookline.
*Secretary*, Mrs. ROBERT W. LORD, 56 St. Stephen St., Boston.
*Treasurer*, Mr. LAURENCE MINOT, 39 Court Street, Boston.

### EXECUTIVE COMMITTEE:

Mrs. JAMES M. CODMAN, Walnut Street, Brookline, Mass.
Mrs. C. H. COLBURN, 228 Beacon Street, Boston.
Mrs. J. RANDOLPH COOLIDGE, 147 Beacon Street, Boston.
Miss SARAH H. CROCKER, 319 Commonwealth Avenue, Boston.
Mrs. JAMES C. FISK, 32 Quincy Street, Cambridge, Mass.
Mrs. C. D. HOMANS, 184 Marlborough Street, Boston.
Miss ELIZABETH HOUGHTON, 1000 Massachusetts Avenue, Cambridge.
Miss ELIZABETH JOHNSON, Weymouth, Mass.
Mrs. FRANCIS C. LOWELL, 159 Beacon Street, Boston.
Mrs. PHILIP H. SEARS, 85 Mt. Vernon Street, Boston.
Mrs. G. H. SHAW, 23 Commonwealth Avenue, Boston.
Miss E. P. SOHIER, 79 Beacon Street, Boston.

### HONORARY MEMBERS OF EXECUTIVE COMMITTEE:

Mrs. OLIVER W. PEABODY, Milton, Mass.
Mrs. JAMES M. CRAFTS, 59 Marlborough Street, Boston.

The present membership of this Association is 3575, representing 121 cities and towns.

2

The officers of the Association are a president, two vice-presidents, a secretary, and a treasurer, who, with an Executive Committee, are elected annually by the Standing Committee, which meets in May. This Standing Committee consists of the members who signed the original call to the Association, the chairmen of the Branch Committees, and any other persons who, for special interest or service, may be elected as members.

This Association was formed to oppose the further extension of political duties to women. It represents the belief that the ballot is not necessary to equality of position or of influence; that nature has established the basis for the present division of labor between men and women; and that the general suffrage of women would involve a dangerous political change and social readjustment. The Association is in full sympathy with the highest ideals of educational and professional opportunities for women, and it claims that these can best be attained without her ballot.

Believing it to be the duty of every woman who is opposed to woman suffrage to testify to her opinion, this Association gives her the opportunity.

**Three Kinds of work.** The work of this Association is of three kinds. The legislative, which provides that the views of the opponents of women suffrage shall be properly presented to **Legislative work.** members of the Legislature, and includes the sending to them of literature; the appearance of speakers before special legislative committees; the employment of counsel when necessary to oppose suffragist petitions; and the endeavor on the part of constituents to keep their legislators informed of the anti-suffrage opinions of their own neighborhood.

**Educational work.** The educational work seeks to increase general interest in this subject, and to educate and stimulate public opinion to an opposition based on intelligent conviction, by means of articles in the public press and magazines, by short addresses or lectures, and the gathering of audiences to listen to them, or to extemporaneous speakers, and by the collection and distribution of these articles and addresses in printed leaflets and pamphlets.

**Constructive work.** The constructive work, which must include more or less educational work, aims to extend the organization throughout the State by increasing the membership, and establishing a system of Branch Committees which shall work, each in its particular locality, in any and all of these three lines of activity, and pre-eminently for *the increase of membership*, as it is most important that the latent anti-suffrage sentiment of the State, in order to be effective, should make itself felt through a strong and formal organization.

## 3

**Membership.** Any woman of twenty-one or over may join the Association, and thereby only pledges herself as in sympathy with its creed and work. In joining, no publicity is incurred, as the names of members are kept on file for reference only.

**Fees, subscriptions, and donations.** No annual fee is required for membership. Every member is, however, urged, when it is within her power, to give some active aid to the Association, either in gaining new members or in money contribution. Any sum, however small, will be most gratefully received; and annual subscribers are particularly desired, as thereby a certain fixed income is assured.

**How to organize and form a committee.** The best way to start a committee in any locality has been found to be as follows: To first call together, by personal invitation or note, in some private house, a small number of women (who may previously have been interested in the subject by reading literature or by conversation) to listen to an explanation of the aim and work of the Association, by a speaker whom the Executive Committee will gladly send. As a result of that meeting (either at the time or later) a committee called a " Branch Committee " of three or more should be chosen, with power to add to their number, two of whom will consent to serve as chairman and secretary. The best number for a Branch Committee is not less than three nor more than seven. When practicable, it is wise to have a representative from every church in the community on this committee, as thereby the communication with the whole people is more easily established.

It is also recommended that the committee have regular monthly or bi-monthly meetings, to which the active associate workers shall be expected to send a report of work done. These Branch Committees should be to surrounding towns and villages what the Executive is to the Branch Committees, — a centre for reference and information.

**Further steps in organization.** A larger meeting should soon be called, where again the Executive Committee would provide speakers, to which the women of the community, except the pronounced suffragists, should very generally be asked; and at that meeting those present should be urged to become members, and to take membership postal cards to gain new members. A paper for signatures of those present, membership postal cards, and literature for distribution should be provided, and will be furnished by the secretary to any applicant.

**Membership cards.** The membership postal cards are of two sizes, one having room for twenty and the other for ten names,

4

and contain explicit directions for their use. In giving out these cards it is advisable to set a definite date for their return; and if a name or two can be obtained to head the list, it may often be easier for a new worker to get the card filled.

*Solicitation of names of members.* In the systematic canvass of any locality for membership, it is desirable to divide it into definite parts (the postal routes, for example, have been successfully used in one town), to call in a sufficient number of helpers, and to have a carefully prepared list of suffragists. By these means the visitors are spared the awkwardness of calling on people who are unknown to them, or whose sentiments are not known.

*Finances.* It is hoped that the Branch Committees may find it possible to raise money enough to pay their own expenses, and to send an annual contribution, however small, to the general treasury.

*Hints on methods of work.* All unnecessary friction with suffragists is deplored. Public debates have been tried, and the result, in the judgment of the Executive Committee, has been to excite ill feeling, and to make few converts for either side. Our work must be pushed steadily and quietly, without malice toward those who differ from us; and our aim must be to gain our members, not through instinct or prejudice, but from intelligent conviction; and our converts should be from every walk in life, — the professional woman, the bread-winning woman, as well as the so-called woman of leisure.

*The relation of the Executive to Branch Committees and members.* The Executive Committee wishes to leave its Branch Committees and the members of the Association the widest liberty for work and action compatible with a few very broad and general limits. They are ready at any time to give any member advice or help, to send literature and speakers on application, and to take a hearty interest in the work and the workers everywhere. They will have regular communication with Branch Committees through quarterly reports made by those committees, and will also welcome informal and unofficial correspondence.

*By-Laws and annual publications.* A copy of the By-Laws of the Association will be sent to any member on application. And a paper, "The Remonstrance," and a Report are printed yearly and sent to every member of the Association.

The present membership of this Association is 3575, representing 121 cities and towns.

Pamphlets and leaflets can be obtained from the secretary, Mrs. Robert W. Lord, 56 St. Stephen Street, Boston.

BULLETIN No. 16

# MATRIMONY

# AND THE BUILDING OF HOMES

---

"What universal panacea have you for the evils that affect society in these days?" scornfully asked an advocate of Woman Suffrage of a dozen young women who had met to discuss those phases of modern reform which particularly affect women. The instant reply by one of the members was:

"Matrimony and the Building of Homes."

It was one of those sudden clashes which can never be foreseen nor accounted for, but which, like the flint and the steel, strike out a spark of genuine fire. It has seemed to the writer of this article worthy to introduce a subject particularly germane to much of the discussion of woman's work which, in these days, is so frequent.

From the early days of Christianity until modern times, marriage has always been considered a binding sacrament, and divorce, as now understood, has been unknown. Since the transformation of rules and ordinances, which occurred in the sixteenth century, marriage has been less sacred, and its great purposes have been gradually lost sight of. In these days of so-called emancipation, a new-fangled scheme of economic reform has arisen, and for its own purposes has attempted to pander to the passions of the human race, by throwing marriage overboard altogether. Economics, it has been affirmed, have no relation to religion, or to speak more plainly, to superstition; all social rights and obligations are wholly separate from it, and the old idea that duty and responsibility are in any way connected with the earning and distribution of our daily bread is wholly outgrown. We affirm that this is a view as entirely false and hurtful to the cause of labor, as any promulgated in the old capitalistic time. Any reform in manners and morals that is not founded upon and does not command the assent of the whole nature of the race, social and religious, as well as economic, is false and metricious. Certainly that relation which was made the only provision in nature for the continuance of the human race, and its progress from generation to generation, cannot, in any true philosophy, be left out of the account. Matrimony, therefore, and the building of homes, becomes not at all a negligible matter, but one of great responsibility and its permanence becomes of the first importance to human rights, individual and especially social.

The first question which arises, perhaps, is whether marriage is to be regarded as formed solely or even primarily for the pleasure of two human beings, male and female, or whether its ulterior purpose is of deeper import, more important indeed and more lasting than any human passion can be. Many are the people, both men and women, so imperfect in their nature, being either above or below the median line of humanity, that however they may be deceived by the mirage of youthful passions, they can never be united to any one in a tie which shall be of itself lasting in this world, and let it be remembered that marriage belongs only to the time when death shall part them. Many more know so little of themselves, of the world at large, and, under present very general circumstances, of the conditions which they are assuming, that their state is certainly, to say the least, pitiable. Shall they, therefore, be set free of all the human responsibilities of marriage, and their children, if any have been born to them, be turned over to a materialistic and changeable State, for rearing and instruction? Or, shall the other alternative be adopted, and the two, feeling their responsibility to the world pressing hard upon them, compromise the idea of individual happiness in this state of life, and be mutually governed by a sense of duty, and the responsibility of giving to the world the best service in race continuance, of which they are capable?

It is out of these imperfect homes, and the lessons of self-surrender and patient bearing of crosses, and the strong putting down of those clashings of spirit which come from differences of desire and ambition, that often arise some of the sweetest and truest and most self-sacrificing natures that the world knows, or the strongest and most aspiring. Those nurtured by mother love or led by examples of determined fatherhood, often set forward the youthful soul as no other agency known to man can do. It is the history of the ages that the atmosphere of the home, however imperfect that home may be, is the truest and most inspiring of all for the human soul to breathe and grow on. It is the condition ordained by God for that purpose, and no institution advanced by man, however perfect by man's standard, has ever yet been found that could rival it.

Many, perhaps more than are ever suspected, adopt this course and find that it entails upon them no more disappointment or sacrifice than is incumbent upon almost any other lot in this necessarily imperfect and struggling life. With the new force, namely, Socialism, that has arisen to menace our nation, another view of the relations between the sexes has sprung up. Its main tenet is that men and women are essentially the same, and that whatever difference may exist between them physically and mentally, has been bestowed simply for their own desires and convenience, and everything beyond this momentary gratification may be counted of slight importance. Its final outcome may be given over to the State—whatever that may be—for future care and rearing. It is for the present life only, not by any means for the future life, which, probably to their minds, has no existence, that this race has sprung into being. Its various units, therefore, are to receive "equal work, equal pay, equal political privileges," and, to quote the language with which this article commences, this condition of equality is to constitute a "panacea for all the evils which afflict modern society." Is this view of the relations between men and women the right one? Is it founded upon unchanging natural principles, or is it only a mere fad of the day, having its source in the excitable brain and the passionate nature of mankind, and destined to die as the evening moth perishes before the morning light?

That there are many evils which affect society in this day need not be denied, but there are none which the Creator has not forseen and provided for, by means already recognized as a part of His great, original work. Perhaps the most encouraging feature of the time is that never before, as since the reign of material science began, was human attention so widely and emphatically called to these evils as now. The surprising increase in wealth, also, in this great, new country has its share in the uprising, and the sources of power in the home, the Church, and in society at large have been resolutely set towards their mitigation and cure. Everywhere we see evidence of this increasing change, and all within the natural laws of growth and progress, with no apparent need of revolution or wild upheaving. Even in the most exasperating forms of venal politics, the true remedy might be found in the early use of the opportunities afforded by the home, and, in the methods enjoined upon it by its Creator. Instead of better man-made laws, we need especially a wider and more thorough use of those powers which the Maker from the first put into the hands of women. It is for this reason that all the plans for the improvement of the condition of the child, the better hygiene and sanitation of the home, the widening and uplifting of earlier education, have either proceeded from sensible and well-intentioned women, or they have been the best helpers of such progress. They have learned, in the thorough teaching of experience, that it is not better laws that we need so much as better men, and that good men and good women are alike the product of good and well-administered homes.

# HIDDEN FROM HISTORY

One of the greatest failures of the cry against venal legislation, is its insincerity and its loud-mouthedness. There has probably never been a State held up to greater obliquy than Illinois. Its corruption and dishonesty have been heralded all over the world, yet a critical investigation of its law books will show that it stands in the front ranks for intelligent and philanthropic laws with the best of Eastern and Western communities. It is among the first half dozen of our most forward states, probably even more nearly at the front than this assertion would indicate. There is a potent reason for giving it the bad name which it has been called to bear. The following true story will help to explain my meaning:

Some years ago, the son of a loudly-proclaimed Socialist, known on both continents, was sitting at the dinner table of an intimate friend of his, and exploiting Socialist ideas. He was himself a man of great wealth and power, though of moderate ability. "But it is not possible that you believe such principles as you are advocating," said his host, in some astonishment. "No, of course not," he said, "but they are just such principles as are calculated to catch the crowd, and, in this country, where the 'people,' together with such enthusiasts and rattle-brains as they can sway, control the votes, and, through them, the offices."

That evening's conversation showed plainly that in a country where there are many millionaires who could not grasp the power, or lead the brilliant lives of ambitious politicians, men with far less ability, together with money and specious talk, may be depended upon to lift themselves, or, at least, attempt to lift themselves, into high places. A millionaire, or a smooth-tongued orator, who would never think of rising to be the President of the United States, or first on the list of our foreign Ambassadors by honest worth, may, by adroit methods, and the votes of demagogues, become either.

There will be found many men of small caliber and disappointed ambitions among these modern self-styled reformers, who seek the good of the nation far less than their own personal honor and preferment. It is such men that are the bane of our country far more than any laws or lack of laws on our legislative records.

Chicago, February, 1913.

(Issued by the Illinois Association opposed to Woman Suffrage. Price of all Bulletins, $2.50 per hundred.)

# MEN!

## ARE YOU POLITICALLY A "SUBJECT SEX?"

".... Various organizations of women, which probably do not represent 10% of the sex, maintain at times a veritable reign of terror in legislative bodies by pretending to speak in the name of all women. In consequence half the country is now bedevilled by some form or other of harem government which is in no respect a true expression of public opinion..... The statute books are loaded down with foolish laws dictated by a few crusading women and enacted by a spirit of "The ladies— God bless them!"

(*New York World*, Mar. 14, 1915. *Editorial*)

BULLETIN NO. 3.

# Men and Women

ILLINOIS ASSOCIATION OPPOSED TO WOMAN SUFFRAGE

1523 DEARBORN AVENUE

CHICAGO

# HIDDEN FROM HISTORY

## MEN AND WOMEN

The almost universal answer of men when asked to express an opinion in regard to woman suffrage is, that it is a question which women must decide for themselves. Anti-Suffragists have always felt this to be a great mistake. They have contended from the first, that to make so radical and far reaching a change in the electorate of the country, to place upon the shoulders of all women the heavy additional burdens of political duties, is a measure which must affect seriously the rights, duties and responsibilities of every citizen, and in fact the whole social structure. Men have hitherto seemed strangely blind to this view of the case, or perhaps they were only waiting for the full outcome of argument and experiment in the matter. But in the past few years there has been a very decided awakening on their part. Prominent men here and there have indeed been urging the dangers of such a radical and unnatural change. Last winter at the legislative hearing in New York, such men as Elihu Root, Nicholas Murray Butler, President of Columbia University, Rev. Dr. Lyman Abbott, the late Richard Watson Gilder, and others equally well known in political, educational and literary circles, came out squarely on the Anti-Suffrage side. And now we have a Protest from Massachusetts, signed by one hundred and fifty prominent men including as the Boston **Herald** says in noticing it, "substantial leaders in the educational, religious, business and legal world." The protest reads as follows:

### To the People of Massachusetts.

"We the undersigned, believing that the success of the present agitation in favor of Woman Suffrage, would be prejudicial to the best interests of the Commonwealth, do hereby affirm our opposition to the further extension of suffrage to women."

The Protest is still being circulated and the list of names is rapidly growing.

In calling attention to this very significant fact, we desire also to speak of the increasing interest among men in their own personal relations to politics. Men are taking their political duties much more seriously than they did fifty years ago, and are spending much effort to bring honesty, purity and intelligence into politics, as the only way to preserve the strength and stability of the Republic. This can only be taken to mean on their part, a determination to give more time, more study, more consecrated zeal, to political duties, than ever before, and these increased burdens, women must share if they become factors in political strife.

On the other hand, women are growing more widely and deeply interested in the duties which belong naturally and inalienably to them. When labor questions which affect women-workers arise, to shock the public sense, and disturb the public peace, they are asking themselves, why it is that when women have so much justly to complain of, as workers outside the home, there is so much difficulty in obtaining women helpers in the home, where there is crying need of every one of these complaining strikers. Less exacting work, under more comfortable conditions and with much better wages, are offered them only to be scornfully rejected. Why this should be so, is a very important question, and one which men never can solve. That it in no way depends upon the ballot, is noticed by Dr. Jacobi a well known suffragist, in her book on **woman suffrage** entitled **Common Sense.** She says "Notwithstanding the suppression of Woman's civil rights, and their absolute exclusion from even a dream of a political sphere, the women of France engage more freely than anywhere else in business and industry" and it might be added, with greater success. But at what a cost? The French nation to-day stands appalled at the lack of increase in its birth rate, and the large increase in its infant mortality, which result from the employment of its women in work outside the home. Why should women clamor for municipal house keeping when they have not yet solved questions of such deep importance, so closely related to their own home housekeeping.

Another pressing fact which the new woman is urgently called upon to consider and deal with is, that largely for want of time and education along those lines, women are not paying adequate attention to the intimate training of their children in purity and self knowledge, and this leads by a very short and direct route to a state of social morals, against which scientists, physicians, clergymen and reformers are crying out. As social philanthropists carry their investigations below the surface of society, they **first** institute juvenile courts, and homes and schools for abnormal children, but they soon find that all these do not stay the flood of vice, crime, disease and degeneracy which is being poured out upon society from the homes of the rich and the poor almost equally, where no proper instruction is given concerning honesty, purity and morality. These laborers in the field of reform will almost unanimously tell you that the seeds of social evils are sown in the first decade of a child's life, a time when the law takes no cognizance of its moral training, when even the church works at arms length if at all, when the mother in the nursery and at the crib side, is the only potent moral agency which the child knows.

Dr. Evans, Chicago's able and faithful Health Commissioner has lately said:
"Nearly all our economic problems would find solution, and many of our hospitals and grave yards would lose a large percentage of their occupants if women from highest to lowest, were educated to do, and did do, their duty in their homes."

With such a statement as this ringing in our ears, is it a time to lay upon the shoulders of women new and untried duties, for which the great majority of them feel no call, no adaptation which in fact they believe to be incompatible with all that is highest and best and most necessary to the welfare of the race, in their own lives.

The American Republic stands before the world as the supreme expression of masculine force, a force which has made of agriculture a learned profession and doubled and trebled the productivity of the soil, which girdles the earth with its commerce, which digs from its hidden depths unprecedented mineral wealth, which solves the mighty engineering problems involved in the building of transcontinental railroads, and an inter-oceanic canal for the whole world's need, conducts negotiations with foreign powers, and raises and commands armies for defense against all enemies. All these are purely masculine enterprises. They require exclusively masculine brains as well as brawn. The Republic gives wisely therefore, into the hands of men, the sole power to make the laws, to execute the laws, to judge the laws under which they shall be conducted.

On the other hand American women at their best have a realm of labor and authority equally dignified and important, but which is governed by influences almost wholly above and beyond the dictation of statute books. They are known the world over as the brilliant exponents of freedom, purity, self control, and all the higher and finer graces of life. They are the unique and forceful expression of the domestic, social and philanthropic phases of the human soul. Having scarcely yet burst the chrysalis of old, enthralling customs and traditions, not yet wholly accustomed to the use of their new wings, they have still achieved an enduring triumph in their peculiar field which gives them leadership throughout the civilized world. They have an influence over the men of their own nation, such as the women of no other country possess. They owe this influence in a large degree to the fact that they are spared the hard, material labor to which men in the pursuit of their natural career, devote themselves, and are thus given leisure and opportunity for the culture of those tender, spiritual graces for the possession of which men set them upon a pedestal and so reverence them as to be willing to grant them what ever favors, legislative or otherwise, they, as a sex, desire.

All this is in the large. It is the Ideal of American attainment and points the way to the supreme achievement of glory and grace, in national life. But let the Republic beware. A chain is no stronger than its weakest link, and the attempt to make statesmen of women would, we believe, set back the hands upon the dial of progress, would reduce the virile force of the Republic to the standard of the weaker sex, and seriously lower its power and prestige among the nations of the earth.

CHICAGO, March, 1910.

BULLETIN No. 8

JUNE, 1911

# MEN FOR THE STATE
# WOMEN FOR THE HOME

ILLINOIS ASSOCIATION
OPPOSED TO WOMAN SUFFRAGE
1523 DEARBORN AVENUE
CHICAGO

## MAN FOR THE STATE; WOMAN FOR THE HOME.

The attention of the public has several times been called to the fact that for the past thirty years the first and most definitely announced of the principles declared in all Socialistic platforms has been that of woman suffrage, or "universal suffrage without distinction of color or sex." It should be fully understood why this principle is of so much account to Socialism, and what are the distinctions between the settled orderly form of this American Republic, everywhere conceded to be the most stable and successful form of popular government the world has ever seen, and that wholly untried system advocated by Socialists. While the Republic has more than a century of success at its back, it should be remembered that Socialism represents a social theory such as has never yet been embodied as a whole in any, even a tentative form of government. It advocates, as if new, certain principles which underlie all Christian governments, with theories of making them practical which in one form or another have been tried and found wanting in almost every century since Christianity existed. Chief among these newly resurrected, but really old and untenable theories is the doctrine of the so-called enfranchisement of women, that is, the identity of woman with man as a political unit, and in making this assertion we come at once upon the reason why a well-known Socialist admits plainly that Socialism is not based upon the natural law of evolution, which has hitherto reigned supreme through all the increasing changes which have marked the progress of the race, but demands a "new law of development."

In the old order, from the beginning down to the present day, the duality of the race has been an accepted fact; the work of man pertaining always to the material or intellectual world, especially the world of government, that of the woman making ever for the continuance of the race, and especially in later times through her educating influence in its early years, to laying the foundation of its moral and spiritual career. In these two spheres of action, the work of natural and social selection has had free play, and the progress of the social side of life as expressed in the political world has testified to a way of evolution prescribed by nature, and carrying the race forward from the patriarchal through the monarchical, to the latest, or democratic form of government.

But Socialism proposes to change all this. The family has hitherto been regarded as the unit of the State. It has ever been the social form from which all progress, all uplift have been evolved. But Socialism makes the individual, whether male or female, the unit of society. It refuses to recognize the natural work of woman as of equal value with that of man, and as between fatherhood and motherhood, puts the highest value upon material and political labor of which it gives to woman an equal share, making the continuance of the race of slight importance, and the building up of its social and moral welfare a matter to be left wholly to chance. Marriage and the home are left out of the account, indeed they are abolished altogether, as we shall see later, and the enfranchisement of women, as it is persuasively called, is to prevail to its fullest extent. That is, woman is to be free and irresponsible in her sexual choice as the men of Socialism are, and the voice of passion is to override the voice both natural and divine which makes in sexual, as in all other relations of life, self-sacrifice, self-discipline and spiritual aspiration the price of all true and lasting success.

It is the tempting lure of "equality" which the Socialist holds out to the men and women whom it seeks to inveigle into its wholly unwarranted scheme of progress, and to this so-called "equality" between the sexes, political equality, or "woman suffrage," is imperatively necessary. It is an integral part of Socialism, which simply cannot exist without it. It is wholly opposed to that natural law which has lifted the race up from unredeemed nature to the civilization of the present time, and promises through the active benevolence, the intelligent seeking for higher things which mark the present century, to bring the race still farther forward upon its upward way.

The business world, no less than the political, has a share in this promise, if it holds to natural law, and we have before us a prominent example of the result of obliterating the sphere of woman, and leaving her necessary work to be altogether neglected, or to be done by hirelings. France has boasted for years that her married women were the natural business partners of their husbands and has gained a wide repute by means of their system and cleverness in the business world. But at what a cost! The nation is moribund to-day, for the want of well-reared men and women. Her morals are the world's byeword, and her population is decreasing till a very important part of the work of her dignified body of deputies consists in the comparison of nursing bottles, and the attempt to devise some statutory means of increasing the number of her babies and lengthening their lives.

Similar will be the result in every country which insists upon ignoring the value of woman's natural work, and lays upon her shoulders burdens which properly belong to men. Nature will teach them by the most unsparing methods that child-bearing is not a joke, nor an antiquated, and therefore outgrown idea, but an incontrovertible fact upon which the whole social polity is founded.

It is the family which gives to woman the true recognition of her equality with man, the indisputable importance of her work to the whole world. Miss Ellen Key, who advocates "the enfranchisement of women" is one of many European writers who has recently proclaimed to the world by her writings, variously translated, the right of the unmarried woman to all the mental and moral rewards consequent upon child-bearing, but she fails to carry out her reasoning to its natural conclusion.

If she may have one child by an unmarried father, that is but the beginning of her career. Must the next, and the next, for her appetite will no doubt grow by what it feeds upon, have the same father. But if so, is not this practically marriage, against which she is protesting, or shall there be a different father for each child. In that case how does the woman's position differ from promiscuity, which is indeed about what Socialism demands for all its followers. But the whole tendency of the race for ages has been towards the abolition of promiscuity, and the establishment of the continence and sobriety of passion, inculcated by true marriage, as the highest form and that most advantageous to the world, of race continuance.

Man, on the other land, belittles himself foully when he imposes upon women the duties which belong wholly to himself. From the woman who "enfranchises" her degenerate husband from the support of his family by her own labor over the wash tub, to the middle class wife who makes money-getting of greatest consequence in her life, or the daughter of the capitalist who expends the millions which she has inherited upon a man who lives at her expense a life of idleness or dissipation, the result is the same. The woman becomes the worker, the slave, the man declines to a position which deprives him of the larger half of his manliness, his courage, his ambition.

This is the condition which woman suffrage everywhere confronts and with some curious results. In the new government which is to abolish classes and establish a true democracy we are told in a published interview from Mrs. Harriet Stanton Blatch, that the children will be borne by the poor and uneducated women, to be reared by the more cultivated. Why may not the world claim to have the children of educated and refined women as its heritage, instead of only those borne under less favorable circumstances. Dr. Anna Shaw, president of the National Woman Suffrage Association, in a similar interview says that the rearing of children will be solely an affair of the state. How unfortunate that the state cannot **bear** the children which it thus conveniently accepts the responsibility of rearing. Mr. Jack London in his War of the Classes (Pages 260-64) faces the difficulty boldly, like a man! Acknowledging with lengthy particularity that the principle of continuance and progress under which the world has hitherto evolved itself is wholly contrary to the new principles announced, he calls for some good Socialist to "devise and put into execution" some "new law of development" which shall prevent equality and the abolition of classes from resulting in race deterioration and decay!

We await this attempt to put the Almighty out of commission, and supersede His plan of the evolution of a race, by a better and man-made one, with curiosity, and indeed with interest.

of small consequence both as regards to their population and influence, seriously alarmed the more conservative East by their radical action. But when to the list was added California, although the majority by which the bill was carried was much smaller than that of the other Socialistic measures which accompanied it, an energetic opposition was aroused, the result of which cannot yet be confidently foretold. Certain it is that it has given many hitherto careless observers, serious pause.

Whoever studies deeply the history of the woman suffrage movement is likely to call to mind the eternal difference in the characteristics of sex, as maintained from the days of Adam and Eve down, and to repeat with a new sense of its vital truth the last and most disagreeable line of Mr. Rudyard Kipling:

*"For the female of the species is more deadly than the male."*

He will also be convinced that when men try to put the two sexes upon an identity never contemplated by Nature in the beginning, the time has arrived for the impartial thinker to cry "Beware!"

Chicago, December, 1911.

*From the Chicago Record-Herald, May 17, 1911.*

# Woman Suffrage.

CHICAGO, May 16—To the Editor: When political privileges are given to women, voting isn't all of it, unless one wishes to become simply like the "dumb driven cattle" of whom the poet speaks. Surely we have enough of that kind of voters now. But when men take upon themselves the responsibility of making and executing the laws of a great country like this, they surely find it a task which requires their utmost courage, judgment and labor. Primaries, caucuses, conventions, courts and legislatures are all involved in the simple casting of a ballot, and these are all men's work, the work of the outdoor world. They make an inalienable distinction between the man and the brute. It is his highest prerogative, physical and intellectual, the one which makes him a man, a being worthy to stand upon an equality with woman.

Woman has her own ultimate status as the mother of men, the exemplar and expounder of all noble, moral and spiritual gifts, her crowning adornment at the hands of her Maker. If you give her besides the uttermost gift of man, his power to rule, you destroy the equality between them. What have you left him, as his distinguishing trait? He sinks at once to the level of the working woman's inefficient husband, the commercial woman's errand boy, the worthless dissipated duke of the multi-millionaire's heiress. What true woman would ever, even for bread and butter's sake or for the sake of a strawberry crown, marry a man so shorn of his manhood? What woman wants a man whose power of law-giving is no more than equal to her own? She has her great gift from God's own hand, which man has no power to take from her except at his own eternal loss. Equally inalienable is his birthright. If he were thoughtlessly or foolishly to rob himself of it, what would become of that mutual homage and respect which is the natural bond between the sexes? No, let him keep for himself something by which we may still reverence him, the horns of Moses, his manly power of law-giving!

OPPOSED TO WOMAN SUFFRAGE.

# MINORITY REPORT

OF THE

## COMMITTEE ON WOMAN SUFFRAGE,

IN OPPOSITION TO THE BILL REPORTED TO THE MASSA-
CHUSETTS LEGISLATURE OF 1885.

THE undersigned, a minority of the committee, respectfully dissents from the conclusion of the majority, and for the following reasons: —

The petitioners ask for municipal suffrage for women, which is at present withheld by men, in whom the functions and duties of municipal government have by general custom been vested. To effect this change, or some such change, they have for years sought legislative action, and to this end your aid is now invoked.

Sincerely respecting the earnestness, the ability, and the undoubted honesty of the petitioners, I am not unmindful that they represent a small minority of the women of the Commonwealth, although they appear to have captivated by their eloquence a majority of your committee. It seems fitting that a minority report should be given representing the vast majority of the women of the State who claim exemption from the duties of citizenship, preferring to have their rights maintained and vindicated by the men of Massachusetts, whose zeal for the highest welfare of their mothers, sisters, wives, and daughters is surpassed by no other State in the civilized world.

This vast majority of the women of our State, whose wishes it seems but just to present, are absorbed in carrying out plans for benefiting the poor and the ignorant, public and private charities, social obligations, as well as household duties, and the upbuilding of our homes, which, according to De Tocqueville, are the true foundations of the American Republic. They believe that they serve their country more faithfully with their present opportunities than would be possible if the ballot were thrust upon them. They are women so intelligent that they do not wish to assume the active duties of citizenship without studying the situation and attempting to solve the problems of statesmanship, a work so difficult that they believe it to be entirely impracticable for them to do it without neglecting the duties nearest to them, the efficient administration of domestic, social, and philanthropic activities, which are essential to the well-being of the State. They recognize themselves as unprepared by inclination, by education, and by nature for the duties of electors; and they claim that to inflict these responsibilities upon them, because a small fraction of the sex desire it, would be unjust and oppressive.

Believing, as I do, that four fifths of the women of this Commonwealth do not desire this change, then by every principle of justice their judgment should rule; and so far as relates to the duty of the present session of the legislature there can be no question of the imperative nature of our obligation to take no precipitate action against the wishes of the vast majority of those most interested and who most desire that no present change be made in our legislation upon the subject.

2

Would not an examination of our existing laws show that men are not unmindful of the rights of woman? that the enactments for her protection, socially, morally, and pecuniarily, are abundant, and that if others are needed they will, judging by the past, be cheerfully made? Our legislators will not neglect the best interest of their own mothers, sisters, wives, and daughters, and they cannot legislate for them without also protecting every widow and unmarried woman in the Commonwealth.

Would the ballot promote domestic happiness? In the early days of woman suffrage in Wyoming I saw much of it; but I saw nothing I would like to see transferred to Massachusetts. I knew an intelligent, contented family there in which the husband was nominated for a justice of the peace (a trial justice with us), and on the following day the wife was nominated for the same office by the opposing party. The wife was elected. Can any one suppose the happiness of that family was increased by that event?

Would the ballot strengthen woman's influence? Upon this subject one who is widely known, and everywhere honored for her valuable services upon the State Board of Health, Lunacy, and Charity, Mrs. Clara T. Leonard, in a letter to the Committee on Woman Suffrage of last year, says:—

It is the opinion of many of us that woman's power is greater without the ballot or possibility of office-holding for gain, when, standing outside of politics, she discusses great questions upon their merit. Much has been achieved by women in the anti-slavery cause, the temperance cause, the improvement of public and private charities, the reformation of criminals, all by intelligent discussion and influence upon men. Our legislators have been ready to listen to women, and carry out their plans when well framed. Women can do much useful public service upon boards of education, school committees, and public charities, and are beginning to do such work. It is of vital importance to the integrity of our charitable and educational administration that it be kept out of politics. Is it not well that we should have one sex who have no political ends to serve who can fill responsible positions of public trust? Voting alone can easily be performed by women without rude contact; but to attain any political power, women must affiliate themselves with men; because women will differ on public questions, must attend primary meetings and caucuses, will inevitably hold public office and strive for it; in short, women must enter the political arena. This result will be repulsive to a large portion of the sex, and would tend to make women unfeminine and combative, which would be a detriment to society.

Will the public welfare be advanced by giving the vote to woman? Miss Mary E. Dewey, in a remonstrance bearing the names of many well-known women, says:—

We believe that the common good will be lessened by the voting of women on political questions. We believe in a wise division of labor, based on natural fitness, inherited capacity, and functional occupation; and just as it would not be wrong, but very unwise, for men habitually to exercise their indisputable right to manage the details of the kitchen and nursery, so we urge that it would be a great mistake for women to mix in the technical turmoil of politics and cast votes. Our influence will be stronger and truer exerted in ways more congenial to us than the ballot box.

Therefore, we pray you not to impose an undesired and undesirable obligation upon one half the community whom you represent, and whose wishes you are here to consider.

The Rev. Brooke Herford, at our last hearing, said:—

The exercise of woman suffrage in municipal elections in England has not been conducive to the intelligence of town councils. In Manchester ignorant and disreputable men have been voted into office by woman suffragists solely because these men would support a further advance of woman suffrage.

The effect of the experiment in Utah has been the reverse of that hoped for and expected. Instead of checking and restricting polygamy, it has nurtured and spread the red roots of that cancerous growth until the adjoining territories have become badly infected. There the women added their influence to that of their vicious male companions. A Mormon patriarch, with five wives and twenty marriageable daughters, is at least twenty-five times harder to handle than he would be if woman suffrage were suppressed in Utah.

It is probable that in our State, in the smaller towns and villages, the voting of women would be attended with no objectionable results, for in them intelligence so largely predominates that doubtless the influence of any woman caring to vote would be in the direction of sobriety and good order. But to increase the number of legal voters in the large towns and cities of the Commonwealth, where ignorance and vice assume such alarming proportions, by adding the suffrage of the worst of the women to the least intelligent of the men, would, in my judgment, be hazardous in the extreme.

What class of women most desire the ballot? We are frequently told by the advocates that Beacon Street does not favor suffrage. In other words, the rich do not want it. This is doubtless true, for they well know that the parlor and the library would be very largely outvoted by the basement. That the great majority of the reading, thinking, middling class of women do not want it is evident, and is generally admitted by the friends of suffrage.

Then who does want it? This, we think, is satisfactorily answered by Mrs. Kate Gannett Wells, whose earnest work for the advancement of her sex is widely known, in an opinion given before the Committee on Woman Suffrage in 1884: —

It is argued that for various reasons we need not fear that the unintelligent will vote. This must remain a matter of opinion between us and those who differ from us. I can only say that my experience has led me to the contrary conclusion. I had occasion one winter to be connected with some work at the North End. The women were too careless and wretched in their lives and in their dress to be here described. They talked with each other in little groups; many a one spoke of the time when she could vote as the only vengeance left her to exercise upon the wealthy classes. Woman suffrage, they said, would give the unskilled workwomen more ample wages, for they could vote themselves what they needed. Again, I was in a house where workingmen came for their daily dinner. The men were also talking on this subject, and said that the women must vote, "for we want the eight-hour law, and can get it through the women. They must make the State give us work. The women must see to it that we have work, and only work for eight hours." These are but two instances, though I think they could be multiplied a hundredfold; yet are they not indications of the way in which woman suffrage may be urged to forward some special party measure? Once let the great mass of uneducated women be added to the great mass of already uneducated men voters, and the State will slowly but surely be shaken under the varying demands made upon it for bread, work, money, leisure, and all kinds of laws to favor all kinds of persons. When those times come, there will be more bitter animosities of women against women, of secret warfare, of despicable wire-pulling, and of exercise of the power of personal charms as a weapon of persuasion, than now exist among men.

It is generally conceded by the business men of the State that the great political problems of the future are likely to be those of finance and the relations of labor and capital. The consideration of these subjects will require an amount of experience and careful attention, cool deliberation, and a freedom from passion very rarely found among men. The ablest of the women, as I have before indicated, have little time for giving the attention needful for such problems; and the least able of the women are not peculiarly fitted by nature, education, or temperament for such difficult work.

Then what can be gained by increasing the vote of this State?

Will the cities be better governed?

Will morality and good order be advanced and strengthened?

In view of the indisputable testimony accumulated upon this subject, I do not believe it is wise to put this experiment to the test in the populous places of this Commonwealth, where of all places the danger is the greatest.

The experiment already made in this direction in Massachusetts has not been successful. Some years ago we were asked to test this question by granting the women the right to vote upon the school question. The eloquent speeches then made led us to expect a great deal from this, the first extension of suffrage. We were told the women were everywhere anxious for the privilege, and their voice and influence would soon place the educational system of the State upon a higher and far better plane of usefulness. But the result has been a great disappointment. Instead of an enthusiastic interest, we have found apathy and indifference. In his official statement the Secretary of the Commonwealth shows that last year while 3,471 women registered only 1,789 voted.

In 1883, 2,778 registered and 1,333 voted.

In 1882, 2,570 registered and 1,181 voted.

In 1881, 3,032 registered and 1,437 voted.

In one county last year 68 obtained the right to vote, but only 3 exercised it. This could not have been caused by "the oppressive restrictions to registration" so much complained of; for, having registered, why did they not deposit their ballots?

In this city, with 1,000 female voters, they have not been able to retain one woman on the Boston School Board.

In the entire State, outside of Boston, there were last year less than 800 "female voters," and we find 100 women serving on the various school boards, and 47 of these women are on the school boards of towns in which there is not a single woman voter.

These facts confirm my belief that the women of Massachusetts, who are the leaders in elevating their own sex, who are foremost in promoting organized charity, who minister to the sick, who enlighten the ignorant, who train the children of the State for future usefulness and honor, do not desire the ballot. Will it not be better to defer action upon the bill reported by the majority of the committee until the women of the State want it entered upon our statute books?

I believe the present distribution of public duties is not disadvantageous to women or to society, and that it is founded upon the broad principle of justice to both men and women; and no sufficient cause has been shown for any such radical change in our laws as the petitioners pray for, and as a majority of the committee propose; and therefore, in my judgment, the bill which they report should be rejected, and the petitioners have leave to withdraw.

WILLIAM H. TAPPAN.

Result of Vote: Against Woman's Suffrage . . . . . . 130
In favor of Woman's Suffrage . 61

BULLETIN No. 15

# MODERN THOUGHT

There are three phases of modern thought, which however they may differ in other respects, all unite in their earnest advocacy of woman suffrage, namely, Progressivism, Socialism and the propaganda of the Industrial Workers of the World.

The modern progressive party, through its public tactics, however it may urge on the side, certain tentative and wholly theoretical economic measures, makes this doctrine a leading one in its claim for public support. Socialism has put it forward as its first demand in every platform which it has issued for the last quarter of a century. The "Industrial Workers of the World" is a comparatively new party, ostensibly devoted to the interests of the working people and the equal rights of all, both men and women. It is in fact Socialism gone to seed; that is Socialism which has reached its last and reproductive stage, the stage wherein talk gives place to action. It is therefore as might be expected, more pronounced in theory than any of the old parties.

The **Chicago Tribune** of December 1st, 1912, has an editorial entitled "Emotional Unionism" describing the Industrial Worker whose companionship it is evidently a little ashamed of, in which he and the movement which he represents are set forth in the following terms.

"When a national organization, nation-wide in its scope, inscribes the word revolution upon its banner, its leaders, theories and literature become of public interest, the Industrial Workers of the World is such an organization.

"The extent to which the activity of the I. W. W. is regulated by emotion, passion and prejudice, rather than by clear thinking is evinced by its literature. The entire literature of this movement which promises to right all the wrongs of humanity by means of revolution over night, consists of half a dozen pamphlets. Each of these represents the central idea that employers and employes have nothing in common, and the workers should aim to wrest all control of industry from the hands of its present possessors. All the I. W. W. leaders are swayed by emotion rather than reason. They are men of no education or have a smattering of education, which is worse than none at all. They are men who have sprung from the most desperate, the most hopeless strata of the working class. The program of the I. W. W. with its direct means of getting even with society, appeals to these men largely because it offers an opportunity to wreaking vengance.

"There is another important feature about the I. W. W. agitators. The majority of them, in fact almost all of them—are men without family ties. They know of no responsibilities or obligations," which of course includes the repudiation of marriage and the home. "'The majority of them are absolutely' non-moral. This emotional unionism with its recklessness, open appeal to vengeance upon industry, upon their employer, is just the sort of unionism which the great masses of unskilled workers who have real grievances against present industrial conditions, understand most easily. The I. W. W. by devoting itself entirely to these unskilled and exploited masses, bids fair therefore to become the vortex of industrial turmoil in this country."

Thus far the **Tribune**. The question that we now desire to ask is, Why is it that these three classes, the Progressivists, the Socialists and the I. W. W.'s all base their proposed Social reform upon Woman Suffrage, or to use the most euphemistic language at hand, "equal work, equal pay and equal political privileges for both sexes."

And first let us notice that **there are** three classes and what they stand for. Progressivism in general regards marriage and the institution of the Home as a mere social incident, founded upon any present whim or desire. It thus opens a wider door for divorce, and attaches little opprobrium to the breaking of the relations between the sexes, whatever may be the consequences to such children as may have been born of the sexual relation. It encourages the labor of woman in fields hitherto regarded as the express heritage of men, as mill work, factory work, commercial enterprises and the like, to the robbery of female employments, which call for womanly traits; and instead of curbing these growing inclinations of the day, and encouraging womanly virtues, it scoffs at the home and lures girls more and more into the life of cafes, restaurants, hotels, places which all tend to bring about equality between men and women and the adoption of masculine habits, even in such personal matters as smoking, drinking and the like.

Socialism is quite as publicly advocated, makes even a more scornful jest of marriage and the home and has been for more than fifty years, corrupting the American mind on the matter of those well-known virtues of patience, honesty and upright rule, upon which our government was founded.

The I. W. W. has attracted attention within the past few years, and largely by the importation of such foreign words and ideas as "sabotage," which may be understood as the wooden shoe of the peasant kicking down the institutions reared by intelligence and spiritual aspiration to strengthen and solace the soul of man, or "syndicalism" which we of an earlier time knew by the more easily understood term of governmental communism, making its way to the front of the "advanced" system of modern thought, a growing multitude forging itself into a mass of immoral citizens ready to substitute a bullet for the ballot; and here let us say, that while a person without intelligence may innocently be unintelligent, a person who is "non-moral" must necessarily be **immoral,** because to be without morals is necessarily an immoral quality.

These advocates of modern thought range in their sphere of action from the highest to the lowest human beings, but each and every class of them founds itself from the beginning to the end upon the one doctrine of Woman Suffrage. And why? For two reasons. In the first place that all human beings, men and women as well, may be equal upon the material plane, equal as workmen, equal in opportunities, equal in political privileges. It is an egregious folly and mistake, born of ignorance and low ideals, to imagine that political privileges are withheld from woman because she is not capable of exercising them, however unsuitable they may be to her physiological make-up. They belong to man together with his physical and intellectual strength, because in no other way can he be the equal of that bright and spiritually minded creature whom God made in the beginning to be his help meet and equal,—the mother of the race.

For a second reason, this reversal of Woman's place in Nature, this placing her upon a forced and unnatural equality with man, promises to the unthinking multitude a solution of certain economic difficulties, of which a true observation and reason shows at once the folly and the absurdity. The quieter and more thoughtful of the race see in the elevation of the child through a truer education and mothering, the rising up of a new contingent of both men and women, to whom a better sense of the real objects of Nature from the first, shall come; the work of constantly elevating and purifying the unselfishness of the race, and giving to the world a new sense of the honor and the glory of the spiritual as above the material side of life. And this is a work to be done by woman and woman only. She may, indeed must, have the cordial and unselfish co-operation of the father of the race but he alone can never accomplish without her intuition and direction, the work which it is given her by Heaven to do, and which increases in amount and value with each generation and to which the attention of the philanthropist is called in this age as never before. It is a work which joins the two sections of the race in a tender and elevating co-operation and gives a new meaning to the old prophecy, "And a little child shall lead them."

Chicago, December, 1912.

Issued by the Illinois Association Opposed to Woman Suffrage
1523 Dearborn Avenue, Chicago.

# MR. DEPEW ANSWERED.

### His Address to Women Graduates Criticised by an Albany Woman.

### A FLIGHT OF IMAGINATION.

Mr. Depew was guilty of one, Mrs. W. Winslow Crannell says, when he suggests that man does his work better than woman does hers, and that women have always labored and are still laboring under a terrific disadvantage.

*To the Editor of The Albany Argus:*

The Hon. Chauncey M. Depew, in an address to the forty-seven women who received their diplomas as bachelors of law from the University of the City of New York on April 29, said in part: "The familiar idea through all time has been that the sphere of woman was in the house and in the domestic circle." This Mr. Depew deprecated— "Fortunately for our country and our times," he said, "women are in evidence in every department of our American life."

Mr. Depew, as an argument to advance his theory, said: "In the complex conditions of our civilization there are as many women as men dependent upon their own resources to make a living, or their own brains and judgment to protect and care for property. That women fail to receive the same remuneration as their brothers, that their services are rewarded with starvation wages, and that the courts are crowded with cases of women of property being defrauded, deceived and robbed, is due to the continual working of that senseless and vicious maxim, written large over the doors of employment and education: 'You cannot pass these portals without becoming unsexed.'"

# HIDDEN FROM HISTORY

## 2

I confess myself puzzled by Mr. Depew's own words, for just before saying this he said, as we have quoted above, that "women are in evidence in every department of our American life. They are in literature, in journalism, in the professions, in the trades, in art, and especially in education."

Will Mr. Depew kindly explain then what "doors of employment and education" are closed to women? Those doors, that opened, would relieve them from the terrible condition which he pictures above? Has Mr. Depew forgotten that he said in an address before the Working Women's Protective Union: "There are one hundred thousand working women in this city, and they get on an average only about two or three dollars a week, and they have no other means of support. For two thousand years Christianity has been endeavoring to ameliorate and elevate the condition of women. Among savages they are beasts of burden; among barbarians and Mohammedans they are toys and slaves; but among us, notwithstanding that my friends, the Woman Suffrage Association, have not got all they wanted, woman has every right that man has and every privilege, except the right to vote, and the right to vote would not protect her in just the things that we are looking after to-night."

As the society to whom he spoke has for its object "especially to provide women with legal protection from the frauds and impositions of unscrupulous employers," were not " the things " referred to the same as those to which he refers in his later address?

Mr. Depew said also: " If a brother and sister equally equipped go out into the world for employment, there are ten places open for the brother where there is one for the sister." Does not that fact find solution in the assertion that the men do the work better than women? Mr. Depew continues: "If there are a thousand hands eagerly stretched out for work which requires only a hundred, they underbid one another to the point of starvation. Women have always labored and are still laboring under this terrific disadvantage. Had every avenue of employment and every vocation been thrown open to her, that saddest poem in literature, 'The Song of the Shirt,' could never have been written."

That is a flight of imagination hardly consistent in so thorough a man of business as Mr. Depew. First, I would like to ask Mr. Depew what " avenue of employment and vocation" is not thrown open to women? And next, if there are "avenues of employment and vocations" open to men which are not open to women, and which, if opened to women would work such wonders as Mr. Depew hints at, why men are unemployed or employed at starvation wages, or why they commit suicide because they can find nothing to do?

There are many unwritten poems that are as sad as "The Song of the Shirt," sunken deep in the hearts of men who have faced want and penury, not through an unwillingness to work, but because of the "thousand hands eagerly stretched out for the work which requires only a hundred."

Mr. Depew, after several flights of imagination nearly equal to the above, says: "When the question of woman suffrage was up in Albany last winter, there were more women who appeared against it than in favor of it. It was the old cry that for women to vote would unsex them. I am not here to advocate on this platform woman suffrage, but I have seen hundreds of women educating and caring for their children, and maintaining worthless husbands." Does Mr. Depew forget that if the women do so it is simply out of their own desire, as the laws of New York State relieve a wife from the support of her husband, while they compel the husband to support the wife? Mr. Depew continues, "The only thing I have known these husbands to do was to vote." The thing for Mr. Depew to advocate under these circumstances is the relieving of such men of the privilege of voting. He cannot, in the face of what he has said before, believing that to add to the already overtaxed women he speaks of, the necessity for educating themselves up to the needs of their country in order to vote intelligently, would in any way ameliorate their condition. Mr. Depew adds: "I know ladies who manage large properties, carry on extensive charities, employ great numbers of men as superintendents, gardeners and workmen, and yet the superintendents, the gardeners and workmen enact the laws which govern and tax the woman whose income, energy and intelligence support them all, and she has no voice in the matter." That reads well; but does Mr. Depew intend to imply that when suffrage is given to the wives, daughters and sisters of the great number of superintendents, gardeners and workmen that a better condition of things would prevail for that woman?

Mr. Depew is mistaken when he says that the opposition to woman suffrage is founded on "the old cry" of unsexing women. The condition of things to-day in the political, social and moral world is such as to appall the earnest thinker. In the political world the ballot of every man whom Mr. Depew employs, no matter what his degree of intelligence regarding any one theory of government and another may be, has as much influence upon public policy as does that of Mr. Depew; and men whose utmost notion of fidelity to duty at the polls is to cast their ballot as the "boss" bids outnumber Mr. Depew and the men of his intelligence largely. If this is not so, why do we suffer from corrupt legislation? Mr. Depew derides the attitude of our forefathers regarding women. The people derided the fundamental principle established by our forefathers that the nation's safety must depend upon restricting the suffrage to those who should be, presumably, most competent to exercise and gave suffrage to thirteen millions of men without any restrictive clause as regards intelligence. Does Mr. Depew believe that when as many millions of women possess the power of influencing public policy by their ballot that either the women or the State will be benefited? Does he not know, judging by what universal male suffrage has done for the country, that universal female suffrage would be a hazardous experiment to try? Inasmuch as Mr. Depew says that "women have every right that man has and every privilege except the right to vote."

There are social and moral reforms that women understand, and for which no legislation is needed; or, if it be shown that there is, can be obtained without woman's ballot; these reforms are still to be made. Here is an avenue for the unrest that threatens to "create a new order of things." For these women who do not find their greatest pleasure as well as their greatest duty in the care of their homes, the strengthening and comforting of their husbands to fit them for their outside duties, the education and Christian influencing of their sons and daughters, together with the charitable work that pleads for recognition, there are, as Mr. Depew has said, "every right that man has, and every privilege" awaiting them. They may join their sisters "in literature, in journalism, in the professions, in the trades, in art, and in education," but it were well for wise men and women to pause to ask themselves seriously what condition of things would obtain if all women were given suffrage, before they hold up "the right to vote" as a panacea for want of employment, for low wages, for unrest, and unhappiness.

MRS. W. WINSLOW CRANNELL.

ALBANY, N. Y., *May 1, 1896.*

# HIDDEN FROM HISTORY

## MR. GLADSTONE ON WOMAN SUFFRAGE.

Extract from his Letter to Samuel Smith, M. P.

"There has never within my knowledge been a case in which the franchise has been extended to a large body of persons generally indifferent about receiving it. But here, in addition to a widespread indifference, there is on the part of women who have considered the matter for themselves, the most positive objection and strong disapprobation. Is it not clear to every unbiased person, that before forcing on them what they conceive to be a fundamental change in their whole social function, at least it should be ascertained that the womanly mind of the country is in overwhelming proportion, and with deliberate purpose, set upon securing it? * * * * * * * * * * * * * * * I think it impossible to deny that there have been and are women individually fit for any public office however masculine its character; just as there are persons under the age of twenty-one better fitted than many of those beyond it for the discharge of the duties of full citizenship. In neither case does the argument derived from exceptional instances seem to justify the abolition of the general rule. I for one am not prepared to say which of the two sexes has the higher and which has the lower province. But I recognize the subtle and profound character of the difference between them, and I must again, and again, deliberate before aiding in the issue of what seems an invitation by public authority to the one to renounce as far as possible its own office, in order to assume that of the other. * * * * * * * * * * * * * As this is not a party question, or a class question so neither is it a sex question. I have no fear lest the woman should encroach upon the power of the man. The fear I have is, lest we should invite her unwillingly to trespass upon the delicacy, the purity, the refinement, the elevation of her own nature, which are the present sources of its power. * * * My disposition is to do all for her which is free from danger and reproach, but to take no step in advance until I am convinced of its safety. The stake is enormous. The affirmation pleas are to my mind not clear, and, even if I thought them clearer, I should deny that they were pressing.

* * * * * * * * *

Very faithfully yours,

W. E. GLADSTONE."

# MRS. CREIGHTON'S APPEAL.

[Mrs. Creighton is the wife of the Bishop who has recently been translated from the diocese of Peterborough to that of London. She is noted for her executive ability, as well as her literary talent. Her History of France and England and her historical biographies are well known. The following extracts are taken from her article on Female Suffrage in the Nineteenth Century:]

The advocates of female suffrage seem to labor under two delusions: First, that the vote is a good in itself; and, secondly, that change is necessarily progress, and must be welcomed, at any price, by all who do not wish to remain hopelessly behind. Mrs. Ashton Dilke, indeed, acknowledges that the vote is not an end in itself, but only a means to an end. But she does not say to what end; she only says that, without a vote, we "risk the loss of all those improvements in the position of our sex" which have been obtained. Such a statement implies a hostility between the sexes from which society seems to be happily free; and it is not easily to believe that the day will ever come when men will take away from women what has been proved to be good both for them and for the whole community. There is surely no need to feel that we have won a position from an active foe, which we must maintain at the risk of our lives.

The vote is supposed to have a certain magical power. Mrs. Dilke even knows why it was originally given, and when she says that the vote "was certainly originally intended to give effect to the opinions of the quiet orderly citizen instead of leaving power in the hands of the strong and warlike," she has solved a problem which has long baffled the ingenuity of the constitutional historian. The attitude of many of the advocates of female suffrage seems to suppose an ideal woman, working side by side with an ideal man in an ideal system of politics. But we have to do with realities; there is a great deal of work to be done, and the practical question is how to do it. It has yet to be proved that giving women the vote will enable them to do better in the future the work which they have neglected in the past.

There is no magic about the vote; it is merely a necessary part of the machinery of government. The act of voting is not, as some would wish to make it, the chief way in which the individual can share in the work of the State for the good of all. The question is not whether women are not as qualified to vote as men. We are very tired of the rich and cultivated lady who may not vote whilst her coachman may. If the vote was the privilege of the wise and the educated, many women might justly claim it. But it is the propelling power of a part of the machinery of government which has always belonged to one sex.

The present organization of society offers an abundant field for the energies of women. The fields are white for the harvest, and the reapers are few. The pursuit of female suffrage as the first aim offers a wrong ideal to women; the desire to play an active part in politics make them neglect their own work. It is perfectly true that women in the last few years have formed political organizations for the purpose of influencing public opinion; but many of them regard such organizations as only a temporary nature, justified by a period of exceptional difficulty. I am not concerned with defending the wisdom or expediency of such societies; but it is no discredit to those who have joined them if they frankly admit that their experience of the results of their activity does not make them wish to extend it universally. There is much to be said for women discussing amongst themselves political and social questions, investigating points concerned with the labour and education of women, and suggesting grievances to be remedied. Their formulated opinion will be sure to meet with respectful attention. But the more women stand apart from the machinery of party organization, the more weighty and influental will be the expression of their opinions.

The more women take an active part in politics the more considerations of sex will be used as one of the means of obtaining political influence. We may try to change society, we cannot change nature; sex will remain. The advocates of female suffrage, indeed, speak of women as a class, and as such demand that they be represented in Parliament. We answer that they are not a class but a sex, and that our representative system knows nothing of classes as such. We urge that women should be content to continue working side by side with men, possessing their own duties and their own opportunities. We think that the questionable advantage of a direct representation of such interests as women may be supposed to have made peculiarly their own, would be dearly bought by an experiment which would shake the very basis of human society.

The present need is that women should do their own work better. For the married and the mothers the path is comparatively plain, but no one could say that they have yet risen to a full sense of their responsibilities in training useful members of the community. For those who, from circumstances or choice, are compelled to carry on their struggle alone the opportunities of doing useful work are unlimited. I am not speaking now of paid work; there the question is more difficult, and the possession of the franchise would not solve it. But the community can never have too large a number of devoted and unselfish workers in every line. The women who show their capacity for such work never fail to get it. But women need to train their practical abilities, to show their capacity. We want more women guardians, more women on school boards, more women who will investigate the existing conditions of society. What the future may need we cannot say, and it would be rash to say that the time may not come when in an ideal political system the ideal woman may work side by side with the ideal man.

The power of woman's influence cannot be measured. When I speak of influence, I do not mean a conscious definite desire to guide another in some particular direction, but the effect produced upon man by a nature which he believes to be purer, nobler, more unselfish than his own. Sex is a fact—no act of Parliament can eliminate it—and woman, as woman, must be a power for good or evil over man. In her hands rests the keeping of a pure tone in society, of a high standard of morality, of a lofty devotion to duty in political life.

It is given her to make or mar a man's life; she may not care for the power—she may wish she did not possess it; but she cannot escape from its responsibilities. Would not the wise course be, to try to make herself such a woman that her influence may lift all those with whom she comes in contact? She need not have wealth or position to do this. Beside the struggling, toiling women are struggling, toiling men; each lonely worker is a power in her little sphere; she will be a greater power if she is not struggling for her rights, but is trying to live her own life nobly and unselfishly.

Mrs. Dilke says that we who do not want the vote are like those who will not open the door to go into a concert hall to hear beautiful music, but content themselves with the faint echoes that reach them through the windows. We might retort by saying that those women who, not content with what they have, still demand the franchise, are like those who, deaf through misfortune or their own fault, stand within the concert hall but cannot hear the music.

# HIDDEN FROM HISTORY

# Mrs. Lyman Abbott on Woman Suffrage.

**ADDRESS BEFORE THE
ANTI-WOMAN SUFFRAGE ASSOCIATION OF ALBANY, N. Y.**

So much has been so well said on Woman Suffrage that I hesitate to speak to you on the familiar topic, but a new voice under new circumstances may sometimes give a new significance to old ideas, and at the present moment, when the forces demanding the suffrage for women are so active and so aggressive, we, whose convictions are opposed to any extension of the suffrage, should be ready to give reasons for our opinion and should be sure that we use the best methods for our defense.

These two aspects of our subject I wish you to consider with me this morning: First, What are the grounds of our opposition to the suffrage, and, Second, What methods should we use to protect ourselves and our yet uninterested sisters from the infliction of the great injustice.

At the outset let us understand that suffrage is not a right; it is an obligation. The ballot is not an expression of opinion; it is an act of the will. If suffrage were a natural right no restriction could be put upon it, every human being could demand it without qualification of age, intelligence or property; it only becomes a right when it becomes an obligation, and that is determined by circumstances. When our Fathers decided to take the government of the colonies from Great Britain they took upon themselves an obligation to organize and maintain the government, and suffrage is an adjunct of the government, it is not "merely dropping a paper in a box," and they assumed the right to associate with them in the government such others as they deemed it wise to choose. Unfortunately they did not, I think, sufficiently guard the obligation, and further action after the civil war increased the difficulties resulting from their error. Through this measurably unrestricted male suffrage serious complications have arisen which have been disastrous, especially in the South. The ignorant have been made the tool of the vicious, the weak have been oppressed by the strong, and progress in virtue and wisdom has been hampered if not halted in some of our Southern states. Much effort has been made to remedy the evil, but it is not easy to take away the suffrage once given, and too often the men who have attempted to restrict it have been actuated by prejudice and greed, and have failed to secure a just regulation of the abused right, for, what has been imposed as an obligation has become a right, and ignorance always misinterprets its rights. This experience should be a lesson to us. If suffrage is imposed on women, the vicious in our great cities, the ignorant, of whom the numbers in the black race and among the so-called poor whites in the South cannot be here reckoned, would be used by unscrupulous partisans for their own selfish ends, and the women of moral purpose and intelligence would be forced to turn aside from the tasks already pressing heavily upon them, not merely to drop a paper into a box, but to enter into a contest in party affiliations as undesirable as their labor would be futile. The number of vicious women—so registered—in the City of New York is variously estimated from thirty to sixty thousand and it has been recently claimed by a prominent suffragist that every one of these women, voluntarily giving themselves to vice, is an argument for woman suffrage, "sixty thousand arguments." How can it be that sixty thousand acknowledged law breakers should become, by the use of the ballot, sixty thousand virtuous law makers. Educative the ballot may sometimes be, but how would it be reformatory?

The influence of woman should be felt in municipal affairs, but she can fulfill her duty there better without than with the ballot. Disentangled from party affiliations she can more efficiently labor for the best things; freed from the dust raised by party conflicts her vision will be clearer; untrammeled by party obligations she can choose her allies, and her influence on legislators will be greater because her motives can not be questioned. The fact that she does not vote is a strength to her, and, may I add, I believe that the men to whom we must look to settle this question for us, will the more thoughtfully and seriously consider it on our behalf because they realize that we are not asking anything for ourselves, nor for a class, but are concerned alone for the race as a whole, and think we need for all the purposes of good on power which we do not now possess.

Exemption from voting does not mean that woman does not have some power to change the things that are wrong. With the influence that she has she can do very much to change the unjust conditions under which "people are freezing, starving, sickening; girls are trying to live honestly on a dying wage, children are overworked so that men and women die of old age at thirty-five and war is going on here and there." This is the graphic statement recently made of the evils which woman, the mother, has not only the right but the sacred duty to attack, and for it she has all the power necessary, she requires only the will to do it. And she is doing it bravely. I will not stop to name the groups of women who are at work to relieve those who are suffering from unjust conditions—the neglected children, the girls in factories and shops, the feeble driven to the wall by circumstance, the weak oppressed by the strong, the prisoners to be redeemed from their sin; and not only are these women striving to relieve the suffering from present unjust conditions but they are working to change the conditions. They seek prevention as well as cure. Tens of thousands of women in our state and as many in other states singly and in associations, are eagerly, wisely and efficiently working for the improvement of conditions which are unjust, and many unjust conditions have by their influence been removed. They have been vigorously doing things without thinking of the ballot and have accomplished more than they have taken time to recount.

If any of us are not having our share in this crusade let us at once find a place where our influence will be felt, to abolish child labor, to keep women from that labor that undermines their health so that they bring into the world children who will by the greed of selfish men and women —for women have their part in making the ill conditions— be put to work still further to deplete the equipment they have inherited.

The kitchen and nursery are an important part of woman's domain not to be despised but rather to be respected, but they are not the limits of her opportunities or her duties.

When the babe leaves the nursery the mother's work for him is but just beginning. All his growing interests are hers; his plays, his school, his companions, his religion must be her daily increasing care. His protection is not now so easily provided for as it was. Bars at the windows, a fender before the nursery fire, a gate at the stairs—ah! would it could always be so simple to save him from disaster. But now how complicated her problem and, yet how inspiring thus to guard and guide that life for which she is jointly responsible so that there shall be a sound mind and a pure spirit in a sound body.

And as for the kitchen and what it represents, what woman is equal to it all? What greater problem could a woman desire? All that a college girl can get in her four year's course is not sufficient for its demands in science and in art. Who has the training in power of adaptation and in executive action which a well-regulated home calls for? Having ability for this she has ability for anything, and lacking power to manage a small kingdom she need not ask for a larger.

It is said that woman needs the ballot to give expression to her opinion. I have said before it does not express an opinion it asserts a will. The will may be in harmony with the opinion, and it may not. There may be no opinion back of the ballot. An opinion is the off-spring of reason, feeling affects the will. Crowds of voters at every important election are carried by the appeal to their feelings which govern their will or are carried by the force of another's will. Women are more easily swerved by their emotions and would be more at the mercy of the will of others.

Fortunately woman has not all the work to do either inside the home or out of it. Man has some capabilities and has proved that he can govern fairly well. In spite of great faults yet uncorrected, the advance in morals and intelligence during the last century has been unprecedented. This is unquestionably the best age and under manhood suffrage, with all the ill-conditions yet to be bettered, no country stands so free from abuses to-day as ours. And woman has much to thank her brother for. In spite of all the clamor for "equality" we have to thank him that we are still a "privileged" class, and the sarcastic toast, "Woman once our superiors now our equals" is not yet applicable. Men have saved women from themselves. In demanding exemption from governmental obligations we do not acknowledge our inferiority, we do insist that difference in sex—a fundamental fact which I assume without discussion—requires different condiditions; we emphasize this difference but we emphatically deny that it implies inferiority on one side or the other, altho as woman's share in life is finer and more delicate than man's, if there is superiority on either side it is on her side. In specializing their duties she has the most to do with those that relate to the inner and higher life and he with those that relate to the outer and the grosser. As one has well expressed it: "Man builds the scaffolding for the convenience and the protection of woman who builds the temple." I am free to acknowledge that many men are my superiors, but I deny that man is the superior of woman. And woman should not admit inferiority by making man and man's work her standard—not what man can do should be her aim but what woman can do. It was a great mistake of the past which thrust women into employments which should have been left to men, it has resulted in serious complications and evils which social scientists are now trying to unravel and to remedy. Our concern is to secure the best that can be for the race, man, woman, child equally, If we believed that best could be secured by unrestricted suffrage we should cheerfully accept the burden, but is our firm belief, founded on careful study of history interpreted by the best thought of the most unselfish thinkers, that no gain would be made and much evil would be incurred by any further extension of the suffrage, and especially by involving woman in governmental duties.

And now what course shall we take to protect ourselves and those yet without thought on the subject from the imposition of this evil? What shall be our methods? Reason not sentimentality should be our motto. It is easy to say that all things could be made right by the vote of women: we must show that this is a fallacy. We must by thought and study be prepared to use pen and voice and especially the press and our own carefully prepared literature to prove that our contention is right.

We must not be led into hysterical quarrelling with our opponents. If we are accused of unrighteous alliances let us refrain from making doubtful assertions in reply. Our temper must be calm, our statements guarded and our attitude dignified. The methods in detail must change from time to time, but the spirit need not change. When the "entering wedge" of a demand for the suffrage for tax paying women is presented, we must recognize that it is an entering wedge and combat it with vigor. Property qualification is not in harmony with our democratic government and would not be argued for by the women who have heretofore demanded that there should be no class distinction in relation to voting except as they intend it to be followed by the demand for full suffrage. This we must understand and meet.

We have every reason to be encouraged, but the encouragement should lead us to greater and more serious effort and not to inertia. The position of defence is never easy, and our duty requires patience that is not experience, it calls for readiness which is not aggressive, and vigorous expression of our views which must never be acrimonious. Assured that we are right we may pursue our way always with caution but certain of success.

---

For leaflets apply to Mrs. Geo. Douglas Miller, 125 State street, or, Mrs. W. Winslow Crannell, 9 Hall Place, Albany, N. Y.

## MUNICIPAL SUFFRAGE FOR WOMEN — WHY?

### BY FRANK FOXCROFT.

I PUT the question in this form, because it is clear that, when so revolutionary a change is proposed as that of doubling the electorate in municipal affairs by giving the ballot to women, the burden of proof rests with those who advocate the change. They must be prepared to show that great advantages would accrue, either to women or to the community at large, from the change proposed. I am inclined to think that either would be sufficient. If they can show that women would derive great benefit from the use of the municipal ballot, the community would be willing to take some risk to bring about that result. If they can show that the community at large would gain greatly, the great mass of women, who now shrink from the responsibilities of the suffrage, would overcome their reluctance. But I submit that one or the other of these propositions must be clearly proved, before any legislature can be justified in enacting a law giving municipal suffrage to women.

Touching the first proposition, what evidence is forthcoming? There is declamation in plenty; vague generalizations about the rights of women; a tedious reiteration of the misapplied principle that "taxation without representation is tyranny"; even, now and then, a faint echo of the generally abandoned claim that the suffrage is a natural right. But when it is asked precisely what are some of the wrongs under which women suffer in town and city government as at present conducted, at precisely what points the by-laws of towns or the ordinances of cities bear unjustly upon women as women, and in precisely what ways women are to gain from being permitted to vote at town and city elections, there is silence all along the line. No one yet, to my knowledge, has ever formulated a definite, concrete, reasonable statement of this kind. Until such a statement is made, and adequately supported by argument, the question why municipal suffrage should be extended to women — so far as the interests of women themselves are concerned — remains unanswered.

But how about the interests of the community? In what particulars would cities and towns be benefited by the bestowal of the ballot on women? The question cannot be answered by contrasting the best and most intelligent women with the worst or least intelligent men. The ballot, if it is given to women, will be used by all sorts of women, just as it is now by all sorts of men; and if, as must be confessed with shame, it is usually more difficult to bring out and concentrate the votes of the best sort of men than those of the baser sort, somewhat the same difficulty may be anticipated with regard to women. The practical question is: *Will the average woman vote more steadily, more intelligently, with a clearer knowledge of men and affairs, and with a wiser adaptation of means to ends than the average man?* It will not serve to say that she will vote almost as steadily, intelligently, and wisely as the average man; or that, in course of time, after she has freed herself from the handicap of inexperience, and has so readjusted her other duties as to give herself ample time for this, she will vote just as steadily, intelligently, and wisely. If the community is to gain from her use of the ballot, the average woman must vote *more* steadily, intelligently, and wisely than the average man. Otherwise, at the best, the general average will be only what it was before.

Here again what is needed is a definite and concrete statement. In precisely what particulars — with reference to precisely what problems of municipal government — are women likely to act more wisely than men? Here, for example, is a list of the standing committees of the Boston Board of Aldermen: —

Armories and military affairs.

County accounts.

Electric wires.

Faneuil Hall and county buildings.

Lamps.

Licenses.

Markets.

Railroads.

Public improvements, with subcommittees upon paving, sewers, bridges, ferries, sanitary regulations, street cleaning, and street watering.

The list might be extended to include the special committees and joint standing committees,* but, as given, it fairly represents the practical matters which engage the attention of city governments. Will any advocate of municipal suffrage for women run his finger down the list and place it on those items regarding which the votes of women aldermen would be likely to be more intelligently and wisely given than those of men! If this cannot be done, then the question as to the second proposition goes unanswered, just as the question relating to the first proposition did.

In a word, it not only has not been shown that the municipal ballot in the hands of women would be a benefit to women, or a benefit to the community, but scarcely any attempt worth mentioning has been made to show it. Yet this is the really crucial and determining point.

---

*The joint standing committees are these: Appropriations, art, assessing, auditing, baths, building, cemeteries, city clerk, city messenger, claims, clerk of committees, collecting, elections, engineering, finance, fire department, health department, hospitals, institutions, lamps, legislative matters, library, markets, music, ordinances, overseeing of the poor, parks, police, printing, public buildings, public grounds, public lands, registry, schools and schoolhouses, statistics, streets, street laying out, treasury, vessels and ballast, water, weights and measures, wire department. The joint special committees are these: Fourth of July, June Seventeenth, Labor Day, Mayor's address, Memorial Day, rules and orders. The special committees are these: Inspection of prisons, rules and orders, and state aid.

---

*Printed by the Massachusetts Association opposed to further Extension of Suffrage to women.*

Pamphlets and leaflets may be obtained from the Secretary of the Association, MRS. ROBERT W. LORD,

P. O. Box 2262, Boston.

# NOBLESSE OBLIGE

## By MARY A. JORDAN

### OF SMITH COLLEGE

THE woman who opposes the extension of the suffrage to women is likely to find herself in a peculiarly ungracious position. Her attitude is almost certain to be interpreted as that of a protected and privileged person, so well off herself that she is easily indifferent to the needs of women less favorably placed. She is bluntly asked in the last resort: "Supposing you do not want or need the suffrage yourself, why do you object to our having it?" In another form the same criticism is made by some exceptionally high-minded men as well as by some most thoughtful women as they question, "Why do you resist the implication of the most obvious equity?" or, "Why will you be blind to the practical and educational benefits the suffrage would confer on women?"

I am sure the thoughtful woman does not live to whom these questions do not bring keen pain. Nor does careful explanation of her reasons meet with much sympathy. In proportion as men are thoughtful, sympathetic, and competent judges of social movements, they are likely to think time wasted in combating the demands of a few women for the suffrage, on the ground that whatever the whole class of women decide that they want, men will be only too glad to give them, even though the desired thing should be clearly unrelated to the end for which it is proposed. With the passing comment that this position is the most final assertion of feminine inferiority, however well meant in the particular instance it may be, I will try to show why the trained and thoughtful woman must persist in her opposition to the extension of the suffrage to women, and must persist in proportion to the thoroughness of her training and to the accuracy and efficiency of her thinking.

And first of the demand for equity. I take it that this means in general that women should have full opportunity to secure the widest and most fundamental well-being. To this I suppose no enlightened person will dissent. But I conceive that the claim for equity is intended to cover very different and far less obvious demands. There is a deep underlying conviction on the part of women who ask for the suffrage that men are as men better off in the world than women, that they enjoy themselves more, and, by some curious distortion of the moral forces of the universe, find themselves literally the lords of creation. There is also a strong belief among women that an active part in the process we call government has had much, possibly most, to do with putting men in this position, and in keeping them there. This belief is summed up in the assertion that society is organized by men for men, and that laws are made by men for men. In regard to the belief that men are better off and happier than women, it is contrary to probability. There are not facts to support it. As a belief it, for the most part, begins and ends with women who are discontented with their lot as women, and who thus far are a small proportion of the whole number. There is little reason for thinking that men are happy because they are lords of creation, but much for believing that as far as they are happy they are lords of creation. In the same view it may be more than suspected that women are not happy because they are satisfied, as often as dissatisfied because they are unhappy. The inequity of expecting many women to make themselves unhappy because some others are dissatisfied needs no comment.

But with regard to the value of the suffrage in securing and maintaining the position of men, it must first be noticed that the suffrage is at best but one of many means to an end, and it may easily be shown that the well-being of men is dependent, not upon the right of suffrage, but upon a share in the blessings of that for which the suffrage, in any form, exists, — good government. Men have been quite as powerful, quite as happy, quite as virtuous, without the suffrage as with it. Indeed there are men who undertake to be powerful, happy, and even virtuous in spite of the suffrage. There are men who look on it as a dull tool, others refuse to use it, and a growing class look upon it as a heavy concession made to the tardy education of social dullards and savages.

Concerning the faith that the possession of the suffrage has directly enabled men to better their conditions, it should be remarked that in no case has the improvement in conditions been the result of an extension of the suffrage. Nor has it come through the use of the suffrage as an instrument. In individual cases calamity has not been arrested nor much mitigated by the possession of the right; political defeat has been less bitter to the voter only where he was enough of a philosopher to recognize the true value of his vote, and to estimate judicially the meaning of a majority.

Finally, it is said that men make the laws for men. As far as the effort has been to accomplish the well-being of men by legal enactment, it must be admitted that the failure has been conspicuous. The student of things as they are is driven to the conviction that legal enactment touches very few of the most important issues of life. Furthermore, men have made many laws for women, not indeed for women as women, as the phrase goes now, whatever it means, but for women as human beings, in the nature of the case entrusted with important services to the social organism. In some communities at least, women are highly protected by law. A married woman's earnings are her own in a sense that her husband's are not his. A young woman has the right to be paid where a man is compelled to wait. The working day for women has been restricted. Seats must be provided in stores and suitable conditions in factories where women are employed. The wages of a wife cannot be attached for her husband's debts. Failure to pay the wages due to a woman up to $50.00 makes all a man's property liable to execution and he himself to imprisonment without bail. No woman can be arrested in a civil action, or held by an execution, except under the most stringent provisions. The rights of a married woman in property and in dower are so generous in some parts of the United States as to be unfair to other heirs. Now, the point for consideration here is not that these enactments are all wise, or all well-considered, or that they singly or together effect the changes that are contemplated at present by women who demand the ballot, but that they have been effected by men not themselves directly interested, and that each and all of them have at some time been advocated by women as ends for which it was particularly necessary that they should have the ballot.

A standing reason for demanding the ballot, on the part of many women, is that it is needful for the protection of their in-

4

terests as property-holders and wage-earners. Here it is supposed popularly that men have profited by their possession of the suffrage. There is no greater fallacy among those left untold by Aristotle and by Bacon. The ballot has not kept the privileges of property, nor raised the wages of labor for men. It is a significant fact that the organizers and members of Labor Unions are all voters. Would such efforts at control of the market be needed if the ballot were a means to the same end? The despairing men who see the value of their corner lots going down before an unexpected tide of fashion, or their homes left in an ugly and disagreeable neighborhood to switching-yards and round-houses, all are voters. The stately gentlemen who have improvements voted on their property until it is assessed beyond its rental, all have the suffrage. In such cases they are at the disadvantage of not being in the majority, or of being confronted by what no votes can change, no law control. Economic laws, public taste, moral motive, are beyond the province of the ballot.

It must be conceded that in cases where the way a man uses his right of suffrage may be made to serve some ulterior end, he becomes of more importance thereby. It is possible that the politics of a candidate for school inspector may determine his appointment or even his election. But this is corruption; this is the intrusion of politics into places where politics should have no weight. I cannot believe that this use of a vote would ever be seriously put forward by a woman as good reason for her having one to prostitute. But granting that she contemplated this use of it in the last resort, how would her case radically differ from the one that she resents now? It is true that one aspect of disadvantage under which she thinks she works, as compared with men, would have been removed, but another would have been substituted in its place, and a much more influential one. For she would appear as the representative of a class and of a principle, not as she does now, as an exception, to be treated on the merits of the case. Consider for a moment the facts. In this country there are four million working women. Half a million are teachers; a million and a half are in domestic service; two million are in the manual industries. Of the three hundred and sixty-nine groups of industries represented in the United States only nine are without women. Five per cent of the wage-earning women have a tenure of work above five years, the other ninety-five per

## 5

cent live in homes during their term of outside employment, and at the end of five years return to homes. Fifty per cent of the women workers use their earnings for home support, and over sixty per cent, besides their trade, help with housework at home. These are plainly not the conditions of permanent workers, nor of skilled workers. Yet even here, when a woman succeeds in these untoward conditions in making herself a skilled worker, she often earns as much as a man or, in case of piece work, more. Otherwise she falls under the action, not of an unjust discrimination against her sex, but of an inexorable economic law, — that quick and easy trades are overstocked, and therefore poorly paid; that skilled trades take time and attention, which she ceases to give just as her work becomes valuable. Finally, more than half the wage-earning women in this country are under twenty-one, so that to be practically useful for them as wage-earners, the suffrage would have to be extended to them as infants, instead of as women. That any one should seriously advocate the desirability of influencing this ninety-five per cent of wage-earning women, now accepting their lot temporarily, to make it permanent, is out of the question. It could not result in the happiness of women nor in the welfare of society.

Again, what would be gained for good government by adding to the bulk of votes either by the repetition of those already cast, or by the foredoomed effort to form and conduct a Woman's Labor Party? The working women are only a tenth of the whole number. Is it likely that the rest would sympathize with them in case their economic interests were definitely opposed to those of men? In view of the differences of opinion and of practice now existing among men on the labor question, is there any reasonable certainty that all women, or even the majority of them, would generally think more accurately or more reasonably than any but the best men, and so justify the complication created by their share in the machinery of the suffrage? Indeed, is there any reasonable certainty that women would be more likely to agree upon any question than men are? Would they strike out any new, any better way of looking at public questions? Or in case they did, would they be any more competent to make their view prevail than are the best men now? From these considerations it seems clear that the ballot will complicate, not simplify, the economic conditions of all wage-earning women, and will put

## 6

on the already burdened woman, who becomes a permanent wage-earner, an embarrassing and formidable addition to her task of maintenance and progress.

There remains to be considered the plea that the ballot should be given to women on account of its practical and educational influence. It is very honestly believed by the advocates of this extension of the suffrage, that some women will be by its exercise made more competent, more earnest, and more responsible. It is felt that the failure to require formally of women an ardent and constant interest in questions of government and of public policy, reacts unfavorably upon certain characters, making them, more than they would otherwise be, unpractical, if not willful ; and indifferent, if not frivolous. The exercise of the suffrage is expected to impart weight and dignity, soberness and gravity where levity has been most apparent. It is thought that other women deserve, and need as much as they deserve, the suffrage as a door into an experience for which all their powers fit them. All women, it is asserted, would with proper education and practice perform their part here well enough to justify the change, and some women would do exceptionally well. From this field they have been inequitably excluded too long. To the arguments from the steadying effect of the suffrage on women, it must be replied that the woman who has been light-minded, without the ballot, is more likely to use it carelessly than to change her mind. It is hardly likely that the ballot has any magic of purity or of earnestness about it. Nor is there any reason to suppose that it will do any more for the individual woman than for the individual man. For the individual man the ballot takes its place in a series of symbols beginning with first trousers. For the individual woman there is an ideal series of equal value where the ballot can be shown to be as superfluous as it is out of place. But of this later. Meantime, what of the exceptional woman who has a taste for the management of business, a taste for affairs ? Is she to be shut up to the narrow influence of an insignificant life because she has, from choice or from necessity, stepped out from the one assigned to women ? My answer is that it is her own fault if her life is insignificant, and that the ballot would hinder, not help her, in the effort to make it significant. And whether or not she has her way, simply because it is her way, and because she has set her heart on it, I am profoundly indifferent ;

## 7

for her satisfaction, as far as it calls for radical changes in the relation of women to an ideal society, is at once undesirable and perverse.

The ballot is superfluous for women because their interests are indissolubly bound up with those of civilized society. It is superfluous because women always have accomplished, do now bring about, and always will effect more without it than it has ever compassed. They have the right of petition, of organization, and of moral initiative. All that the ballot is fabled to insure, for the individual or for the sex, is really controlled by these influences. Women undoubtedly have a work to do in settling the vexed questions of economics, personal happiness, and of government; but it will not be done by the use of less than the best tools at their disposal, nor by competing with any part of society for the largest share of awkwardness and blunder. The ideal series of which I spoke, and in which the ballot is as superfluous as it is out of place, cannot be better stated than by T. H. Green as the possession of the " will to know what is true, to make what is beautiful, to endure pain and fear, to resist the allurements of pleasure in the interests of some form of society."

## OBJECTIONS TO LICENSE SUFFRAGE FROM A NO-LICENSE POINT OF VIEW.

*Address of Mr. Frank Foxcroft, of Cambridge, before the Massachusetts Legislative Committee, 1898.*

DIFFERENT considerations influence the advocates of license suffrage for women. Every year certain members of the Legislature support it who are not suffragists in any general sense of the word, but who believe that it would be a good thing for temperance if the women voted on this question. I respect the motives of these men, but I do not approve their judgment. I approach this question as a No-license man, and it is because I believe that giving women the ballot on the license question would be a bad thing for No-license that I oppose it.

It is assumed that the majority of women would vote for No-license. But this is only an assumption. It must be remembered that what is asked is not that certain selected classes of women, but all women, shall be empowered to vote: not only the intelligent, but the ignorant; not only the women of the Christian Temperance Unions, but the women of the slums and the saloons.

For the sake of the argument, however, let us grant the assumption that the majority of women would vote for No-license: what then?

As matters now (1898) are, about four fifths of the towns and cities of Massachusetts are carried for No-license. The number varies slightly from year to year, but that is about the average ratio. I claim that in these towns and cities we have an ideal condition for the enforcement of No-license. We have first of all a majority of the male voters declaring that they want No-license. We have this same majority of male voters choosing the officers who are to enforce the law, and able to punish promptly any unfaithfulness on their part. I claim that the introduction of the women's vote, so far as these four fifths of Massachusetts cities and towns are concerned, would only weaken and confuse the situation.

I think of this with reference to the city where I live. I am from Cambridge, where I have been for seventeen years a member of the No-license Citizens' Committee. For twelve consecutive years we have carried Cambridge for No-license. Our majorities have ranged from 400 to 1,900. Yet there is scarcely an election which we have carried in which we have not owed our victory to the support of moderate men who, as a matter of general principle, are scarcely No-license men at all. This certainly has been true of all our close elections. These men have voted with us because they have been convinced by the practical workings of the system that it is best for Cambridge. One reason for their support has been their knowledge that they had the control of the situation in their own hands, and that if No-license did not work well or was not properly enforced, they could vote License in again. Now, suppose that by means of the women's vote, you take away that assurance: what happens? We lose some hundreds of men's votes, which are potent, not only for voting No-license but for securing its enforcement, and we get in place of them some hundreds of women's votes, which are potent only as regards voting for No-license and powerless as regards its enforcement.

There is another consideration with reference to No-license communities. All of us who have had any direct share in No-license work know how hard it is to keep public sentiment keyed up on such a question for a series of years. There is a disposition to take it for granted that the election will go all right any way, and it is hard to convince individual voters of the importance of every separate vote. If it came to pass that the vote of the women was generally relied upon to carry this question, there would be, I am confident, an appalling increase of indifference on the part of men voters, and we might have some painful surprises.

So far, then, as concerns the towns and cities now usually carried for No-license, numbering, as I have said, about four fifths of the whole, the vote of women, assuming that a majority of them would vote for No-license, is clearly not needed, and I am sure that it would work injury, for the reasons which I have stated.

And what of the other places, now usually voting for License? With the reinforcement of the women's vote, it might be possible to carry some of them for No-license. But have you reflected upon the situation in that event? You would have a majority of the men-voters voting for License, but balked of obtaining it by the vote of the women. You would have this License majority of men voters electing the officials who are to enforce the law. By the wishes of which body of voters would the officials be likely to govern their conduct: that body which elected them and had the power to depose them? or that body which had no control over them? Would it not be inevitable, under such conditions, that the enforcement of No-license would become a mockery and a farce?

It is for these reasons, then, because I believe that the voting of women on the license question would work injury in the places now carried for No-license, while at the best in the other places it could only bring in a nominal No-license, half-enforced and demoralizing to the public conscience, that, as a temperance man and a No-license man, I oppose License suffrage for women.

*Printed by the Massachusetts Association opposed to further Extension of Suffrage to Women.*

Pamphlets and leaflets may be obtained from the Secretary of the Association, Mrs. Robert W. Lord,
P. O. Box 2262, Boston.

# OF NO BENEFIT TO WOMAN.

## She is a Far Greater Power Without Suffrage.

*Reprinted from the Boston Sunday Herald.*

*To the Editor of The Herald:—*

The question of woman suffrage can no longer be treated with indifference — it has already become a practical question. If women are to assume the duty of suffrage, they must either add it to their other duties or lay aside other duties to take up this new duty. Would either alternative be just to the women themselves and the community at large? It is for us to decide. Indifference is practically an influence in favor of the movement; we should seriously, in the light of a sacred duty, consider what the issue portends for ourselves and our fellow-beings.

"Rights" is a word of much sound, but little meaning — since everybody's rights stop where another's commence, if there be a conflict between them. We are to consider a question of rights, woman's rights, the suffragists call it, but let us look into it and we see a threefold aspect: The rights demanded by the women who advocate suffrage; the rights of those women who oppose the movement; the rights of the community at large, the Commonwealth, the nation.

We are to determine whether the claim of the first class to a natural, inherent right to vote, and its demand to exercise that right, are: First, just; second, expedient; that is, not in conflict, but in harmony, with the rights of the others.

The suffragists claim the franchise for women on the following grounds:—

*First,* That the right to vote is a natural and inherent one, of which they are deprived.

*Second,* That women are taxed but not represented, contrary to the principles of free government.

*Third,* That society would gain by the participation of women in government, in that they would purify politics; the cause of temperance would be promoted by their vote; woman's voice would abolish war; the franchise would be to woman an educational factor.

1

2

*Fourth*, That a majority of women not wishing the franchise is no reason for depriving a minority of an inborn right.

*Fifth*, That women are physically and intellectually as capable of the duties of the franchise as are men.

The first two proposals come under our first head — justice; the rest under the second — expediency; and so we will consider them. As to the justice of their claim to an inherent, natural right of which they are deprived, we answer that the right of suffrage is not inherent or inalienable. In all political history there is not one phase which could be construed into meaning that men have the right of suffrage because they are human beings. Society does not exist by the consent of those who enter it. Our government was established long before the present generation existed; so the consent of the governed must be taken for granted (except as changes are made by constitutional methods) until a rebellion arises.

A government exists to secure the safety and best welfare of all who look to it for protection. The assumption that suffrage is a natural right is anti-republican, since the very essence of republicanism is that power is a trust to be exercised for the common weal, and is forfeited when not so exercised, or when exercised for private or personal ends. To deny this is to imply that our government is a pure, unmitigated democracy, which may be interpreted in two ways — either as tantamount to no government, or as the absolute despotism of the ruling majority in all matters. This is not American republicanism certainly, since republicanism has always aimed to restrain the absolute power of majorities and protect minorities by constitutional provisions.

Suffrage cannot be the right of the individual, because it does not exist for the benefit of the individual, but for the benefit of the state itself. "Unless a doctrine is susceptible of being given practical effect, it must be utterly without substance" (Cooley's Constitutional Law); and this doctrine of inherent right cannot be given practical effect, since this would imply that minors, insane, idiots, Indians and Chinese (now wholly or partially restrained) would have a right to exercise the franchise. A gift from nature must be absolute, and not contingent upon the state to prescribe qualifications, the possession of which shall be the test of right of enjoyment; and no restrictions of age or education could be put upon it, such as now exists. Liberty itself must come from law, and cannot, in any institutional sense, come from nature. Rights, in a legal sense, are born of restraints, by which every one may be protected in their enjoyment within prescribed limits. In prescribing limitations, the framers of the Constitution showed that they did not consider suffrage an inherent right. The article of the bill of rights which refers to inalienable rights has nothing whatever to say about suffrage.

The suffragists claim that women are taxed without representation. Those advancing this argument exhibit their entire lack of understanding of the theories of taxation and suffrage, and prove that they, at least, are not yet ready to enter intelligently into politics.

### 3

We have founded our government on manhood suffrage, not because our male citizens own more or less property, or any property at all, but because they are men; because behind the law must be the power of enforcing it. Without sufficient force to compel respect and observance, laws would be dead letters. To make laws that cannot be enforced, is to bring a government into ridicule and contempt, and invite anarchy! The insuperable objection to woman suffrage is fundamental and functional, and nature alone is responsible for it, since she has created man combatant and woman non-combatant.

The reason we have adopted as the basis of our political system that the will of the majority must prevail over that of the minority, is that we recognize the fact that the majority can, if the minority rebel, compel them to acquiescence. Therefore suffrage has been given to men, because they can back laws by force enough to compel respect and observance. It becomes thus a duty to be performed, not a privilege to be enjoyed, and women are exempt because of what it would entail; their present position in the state, as its mothers and educators of future citizens, being held as more than equivalent to any political service.

The duty of voting is in no sense dependent — in this state at least — upon the fact that the voter pays taxes or owns property. A man who has no property has the same voice in voting as a millionaire! Property of a town, city, or state is justly liable for the current expenses of the government which protects such property, and thus increases and preserves its value. The only question the law asks is: "Is there property?" If so, it imposes a tax. The laws of taxation are general, and not particular, taxation being simply a compensation to the government for protection of property, that such property may have value. Woman's property receives exactly the same protection as man's and she benefits as much thereby; there is therefore no injustice to her.

Minors are taxed without being able to vote, and there are more minors than voters. Men between eighteen and twenty-one could quite as justly as women consider themselves wronged, for they are by a large majority capable of voting intelligently; so also could those who are taxed upon property placed where they cannot vote. Women enjoy all the rights of citizens, protection of property, use of public institutions, roads, gas, postal facilities, etc. A vote would not protect her property, since two women with no property interests could more than annul her vote by theirs. There is not a single interest of women which is not shared by men. What is good for men — what protects their interests, also protects woman's. We may look to men to further what in their judgment seem the best interests of life and property, and in doing this they protect both man's and woman's interests because they are inseparable.

Since women have not — for men have not — any natural right to vote, and cannot claim it on the ground of taxation without representation, it remains to be seen whether they can demand it on the ground of expediency. The pointing out of benefits always rests with those who demand a radical change in a system of government;

not pointing out only, but proving. Will the franchise extended to women — first, benefit the whole community? second, gain definite benefits for women, which cannot be obtained in the existing order of things?

The remonstrants to woman's suffrage cannot find stated in all the suffragists' arguments one definite, certain benefit to result to either state or woman. On what grounds of expediency do the suffragists demand the ballot? First, that society would gain because woman would reform politics.

The cause of temperance would be promoted by their vote. Woman's voice would abolish war. Second, that women would gain since the ballot would be to them an educational factor. The problem of woman's wages would be solved.

Would women reform politics? Let us see! In our country it is not a question, as it is in England, of the relatively intelligent and responsible women being allowed a share in the government. Such a system as England has adopted in restricting the use of the ballot (by women) in municipal affairs to those who pay rates and taxes in their own names, if applied here would limit the women voting in our larger cities to a few hundred at most. You see that what the suffragists propose here is a far different matter. If the franchise were granted to women in America, all women of legal age, sound mind, and not disfranchised for special causes (now applying to men) could vote. Not only the intelligent and those unburdened by home and business duties, but all women without respect to race, character, or intelligence.

We must not overlook or leave out the densely ignorant, the supinely indifferent, the trivial, the " occupied" women — out and out bad women (60,000 in New York city alone). The suffragists say, "Yes, that is true also of men;" but it is surely evident that existing evils should not be added to simply because they exist, or that two unintelligent, bought, or corrupt votes are worse than one — on the simple ground of unnecessary outlay of means and energy, if nothing else. If the great mass of ignorant women's votes are added to the great mass of ignorant men's votes, there will be constant unwise demands for work, money, bread, leisure, in short, "all kinds of laws to favor all kinds of persons." Colonel Higginson (who makes no positive claims for woman suffrage, save on the ground of natural right) acknowledges that " the ground taken that woman as woman would be sure to act on a higher plane than man as man, is now urged less than formerly, the very mistakes and excesses of the agitation itself having partially disproved it," and again " while the sympathies of women are wholly on the side of right, it is by no means safe to assume that their mode of enforcing that sentiment will be equally judicious."

As for temperance — there must be taken into consideration not only its advocates, and on the other hand those women who favor license through depravity (the most difficult class to deal with, *vide* kitchen bar-rooms in no-license cities), but the countless number of foreign-born women brought up where liquors are used, and not abused, who would feel themselves cramped in their liberties under a no-license law.

"Woman's voice would abolish war." The Civil War was stimulated and encouraged by women in the North; and it is generally conceded that but for the women of the South it would have sooner ended. A suffragist is responsible for the statement that a mayor of a leading southern city lays the survival of dueling anywhere in the South to the sustaining public sentiment of women. I cannot better sum up the illusive nature of the benefits proposed by the suffragists than in again quoting from Colonel Higginson. In an article devoted to "Too much prediction," he says: "I am persuaded that at present we indulge in too many bold anticipations!"

We come to the question of the gain to woman personally. Is there anything to be gained which cannot be brought about with the existing franchise? The suffragists say: 1. Women will be educated by the ballot. 2. The problem of woman's wages will be solved. In regard to their first claim we need only ask, Has the ballot proved of much educational value to men; then what are the probabilities as regards women?

The problem of woman's wages! The ballot could not help the working girl in the way the suffragists claim, since legislation affects the business of the country only in a general way, helping or hurting all the workers alike in any special industry. The question of wages is one of supply and demand simply! So the general wages of women will always depend greatly on the amount of skill acquired by the mass of them. What especially affects woman's wages is the temporary character of her work! The average age of working women is twenty-two years, as determined by government investigation. You see what this means — that the ranks are constantly being filled up with raw, untrained girls, while those who have attained to some degree of skill are constantly dropping out.

The natural expectation of every normal girl should be that sooner or later she will marry and leave her work; therefore, there is not that incentive that men have to become highly skilful; and the character of her work is, consequently, not so high, generally speaking, as men's, lacking, as they do, two factors, time and incentive, to develop great skill. Then, since the majority of women take up work with the intention — conscious or unconscious — of devoting only a part of their lives to it, they naturally gravitate to such work as can be most easily made a temporary occupation, and competition comes in to help complicate the wage question.

The problem therefore resolves itself into this — how to regulate justly the distribution of wages between a sex which works throughout life and a sex which works with only temporary expectations, looking toward withdrawal in a few years from the labor market, and withdrawing to take with it its acquired skill, leaving only inexperience in its stead. The wiser of the suffragists acknowledge that the suffrage will not of itself solve the problem of wages, dependent as it is on other than political considerations. The wisest and best of our women are studying what can be done for the working girl.

They hope that organization among workers, and the coöperation of all intelligent women may do much. Let all thoughtful women consider how they may best contribute their share, and, leaving the duties of political life to those whom they now burden, devote what of energy, time, and ability they have to the solution of this problem, which the ballot cannot help to solve.

We have left one argument for granting woman the suffrage, namely, that a majority of women not wishing to vote should not be a sufficient reason for depriving a minority of an inborn right. We have summed up the other arguments for the franchise and shown what is to be said in their refutation; but this last argument, it seems to me, contains the gist of the whole question, that is, wherein the demands of the suffragists and the anti-suffragists clash. We have shown their error in claiming the franchise as an inherent right, but even were we to grant that such a right existed, it would still be perfectly within the power of the state to deprive women of this right, if by granting it the general good would be imperilled. We know that the State holds authority to deprive citizens of the right of property, of liberty, of life itself, if the common weal demand it. The family is the safeguard of the state, and the granting of the suffrage to women tends to weaken this mainstay of the nation by bringing into it elements of discord and disunion; therefore the state would be more than justified in denying women even an inherent right which might prove thus disastrous.

To the rest of the argument we answer that a majority of women believe that their inherent rights and privileges would suffer if the duty of voting were imposed upon them, for the following reasons: Because suffrage involves office-holding, which is inconsistent with the duties of most women; because they feel that their obvious duties and trusts — as sacred as any on earth — already demand their best efforts; because the duties cannot be relegated to others; because political equality will deprive woman of special privileges hitherto accorded to her by law; because they hold that the suffrage would lessen rather increase their influence for good.

Suffrage involves office-holding. If women vote, they ought also to hold office, and assume the working duties incident to office. A system which tends to the dissolution of the home is more perilous to the general good than any other form of danger, and office-holding is, on the face of it, incompatible with woman's proper discharge of her duties as wife and mother. There is too little stress laid on this. No theory of womanly life is good for anything which undertakes to leave out the cradle.

We cannot ignore the fact that nature has imposed upon women the duty of bearing and rearing the race, and in so doing, has unfitted her (for a number of years at least) for holding political office.

Many women there are, it is true, who are not wives and mothers; and, if women vote, there will be more of them. When political rewards are held out as the price of services in public life, many women — and those of the brightest — will be tempted to forego marriage and motherhood for the sake of winning them. Well may we say with Mrs. Corbin: "Woe betide the land which offers its political trusts as premiums for childless women!" What will become of the morals of society when not to be married, not to be a mother, is the prerequisite for a woman's success in a chosen career?

The trusts of woman now are as sacred as any on earth, and man cannot relieve her of them. If, therefore, he demands of her participation in such duties, political or general, which his natural constitution fits him for, while he cannot relieve her of those most necessary duties which nature demands of her, he commits towards her a monstrous injustice. This is what imposing the suffrage on women would amount to; for, if woman may vote, she must vote. It is a mere sophism to say that the simple dropping of a ballot is all that is required of her. If the suffrage is extended to women, they must accept it as a duty, bringing to bear on it the conscientious spirit which they bring to bear on their present life problems.

It would be well to consider, too, if they would be prepared to give up the special privileges which in Massachusetts they possess:—

Unmarried women and widows of small estate are exempt from taxation.

Women, and not men, are allowed to acquire a settlement without paying a tax.

Husbands are compelled to support their wives, but wives (even when rich) are exempt from supporting an indigent husband.

Men are liable for their wives' debts, but women are not made liable for their husbands'.

Women are excused from jury duty.

Woman is exempt, except in actions for tort, from arrest previous to judgment and execution.

She has the advantage of man in regard to policies of life insurance.

The husband is liable for criminal acts committed by his wife in his presence, yet no such counterbalancing liability exists for her.

A father must support his children during their non-age, even when they have property of their own. A widowed mother is not under such obligation unless she have sufficient means, and her children have none of their own.

Women can more easily than men acquire citizenship of the United States.

Finally we oppose the suffrage for women, because we feel that we have more influence without it. There is not a single subject in which woman takes an intelligent interest in which she cannot exert an influence in the community proportionate to her character and ability. Without the ballot, women have obtained more than mere justice in Massachusetts. The number of women who want the ballot for itself is reduced to a mere handful when we take away those who are working for temperance, or other worthy causes. How much more would be gained by advocating these causes on their own merits!

The influence of woman standing apart from the ballot is immeasurable. Men look to her then (knowing that she has no selfish, political interests to further) as the embodiment of all that is truest and noblest. She has influence with all parties alike; if a voter, she would have only the influence of her own party, even the woman's vote being divided against itself. We believe that it is of vital importance that our sex should have no political ends to serve!

Our legislators have shown themselves ever ready to listen to women, and much has already been achieved by the intelligent influence of women in the anti-slavery cause, the temperance cause, the improvement of public charities, and the reformation of criminals. It is of the utmost importance that charitable and educational administration be kept out of politics, and to woman is given this trust. In whatever tends to protect and elevate woman, to secure her rights in the true sense of the word, to open up to her new paths of usefulness, all true-hearted men will join with women! In such work there is no difference of purpose.

Childhood is hers to influence and mold, and what greater power for good could there be given her? Let all true women, loyal citizens of our republic, look to the best performance of the trusts which are naturally theirs, striving for no false "equality" since there is no question of comparison between men and their duties and women and theirs. They are not "like in like" but "like in difference," each supplementing the other, rising or falling, but always together.

MARY A. J. M'INTIRE.

# Of What Benefit to Woman?

### The First Question

THE question of woman suffrage cannot be treated with indifference — it is a practical question. If women are to assume the duty of suffrage, they must either add it to their other duties or lay aside other duties to take up this new duty. Would either be a good thing for women or for the community at large?

"Rights" is a word of much sound, but little meaning — since each one's rights stop where another's begin, if there be a conflict between them. We are to consider a question of rights, woman's rights, the suffragists call it, but let us look into it and we see a three-fold aspect: The rights demanded by the women who advocate suffrage; the rights of those women who oppose the movement; the rights of the community at large, the Commonwealth, the nation.

### What the Suffragists Claim

The suffragists claim the franchise for women on the following grounds: —

*First*, That the right to vote is a natural and inherent one, of which they are deprived.

*Second*, That women are taxed but not represented, contrary to the principles of free government.

*Third*, That society would gain by the participation of women in government, in that they would purify politics; the cause of temperance would be promoted by their vote; woman's voice would abolish war; the franchise would be to woman an educational factor.

*Fourth*, That women are physically and intellectually as capable of the duties of the franchise as are men.

*Fifth*, That the fact that a majority of women do not wish the franchise is no reason for depriving a minority of an inborn right.

### Suffrage not a Natural Right

The first two proposals come under one head — justice; the rest under a second — expediency; and so we will consider them. As to the justice of their claim to an inherent, natural right of which they are deprived, we answer that the right of suffrage is not inherent or inalienable.

Suffrage cannot be the right of the individual, because it does not exist for the benefit of the individual, but for the benefit of the state itself. A gift from nature must be absolute and not contingent upon the state to prescribe qualifications, the possession of which shall be the test of right of enjoyment; and no restrictions of age or education could be put upon it, such as now exist. In prescribing limitations, the framers of the Constitution showed that they did not consider suffrage an inherent right. The article of the bill of rights which refers to inalienable rights has nothing whatever to say about suffrage.

## The Ballot Needs Force Behind It

The suffragists claim that women are taxed without representation. Those advancing this argument exhibit their entire lack of understanding of the theories of taxation and suffrage. We have founded our government on manhood suffrage, not because our male citizens own more or less property, or any property at all, but because they are men; because behind the law must be the power of enforcing it. The insuperable objection to woman suffrage is fundamental and functional, and nature alone is responsible for it, since she has created man combatant and woman non-combatant.

The reason we have adopted as the basis of our political system the principle that the will of the majority must prevail over that of the minority is that we recognize the fact that the majority can, if the minority rebel, compel them to acquiescence. Therefore, suffrage has been given to men, because they can back laws by force enough to compel respect and observance.

## Voting Has Nothing To Do With Taxation

The possession of the ballot is in no sense dependent upon the fact that the voter pays taxes or owns property. A man who has no property has the same voice in voting as a millionaire. Property of a town, city, or state is justly liable for the current expenses of the government which protects such property. Woman's property receives exactly the same protection as man's, and she benefits as much thereby; there is therefore no injustice to her. A vote would not protect her property, since two women with no property interests could more than annul her vote by theirs. There is not a single interest of woman which is not shared by men. What is good for men — what protects their interests also protects woman's interests.

## The Question of Expediency

Since women have not — for men have not — any natural right to vote, and cannot claim it on the ground of taxation without representation, it remains to be seen whether they can demand it on the ground of expediency. Will the franchise extended to women — first, benefit the whole community? second, gain definite benefits for women, which cannot be obtained in the existing order of things?

The remonstrants to woman's suffrage cannot find stated in all the suffragists' arguments one definite, certain benefit to result to either state or women. On what grounds of expediency do the suffragists demand the ballot? First, that society would gain because woman would reform politics. The cause of temperance would be promoted by their vote. Woman's voice would abolish war. Second, that women would gain, since the ballot would be to them an educational factor, and that through the ballot the problem of woman's wages would be solved.

### Would Women Reform Politics?

Would women reform politics? Let us see! In our country where manhood suffrage exists it follows that, if suffrage belongs to women at all, it belongs to all; suffrage must be given to all women or none, and such is the final proposition of the suffragists. If the franchise were granted to women in the United States, all women of legal age, sound mind, and not disfranchised for special causes (now applying to men) could vote; not only the intelligent and those unburdened by home and business duties, but all women without respect to character or intelligence.

### What Would Women Gain?

We come to the question of the gain to woman personally. Is there anything to be gained which cannot be brought about with the existing franchise? The suffragists say: First, Women will be educated by the ballot. Second, The problem of woman's wages will be solved. In regard to their first claim we need only ask, Has the ballot proved of much educational value to men; then what are the probabilities as regards women?

### As To Woman's Wages

The problem of woman's wages! The ballot could not help the working girl in the way the suffragists claim, since legislation affects the business of the country only in a general way, helping or hurting all the workers alike in any special industry. The question of wages is one of supply and demand simply! So the general wages of women will always depend greatly on the amount of skill acquired by the mass of them. What especially affects woman's wages is the temporary character of her work! $49\frac{3}{10}$ per cent. of female workers are under 25 years of age; $32\frac{4}{10}$ per cent. of female workers are under 21 years of age, as determined by government investigation. You see what this means, that the ranks are constantly being filled up with raw, untrained girls, while those who have attained to some degree of skill are constantly dropping out. The natural expectation of every normal girl should be that sooner or later she will marry and leave her work; therefore, there is not that incentive that men have to become highly skillful.

The problem, therefore, resolves itself into this — how to regulate justly the distribution of wages between a sex which works throughout life and a sex which works with only temporary expectations,

4

looking toward withdrawal in a few years from the labor market, and withdrawing to take with it its acquired skill, leaving only inexperience in its stead. The wiser of the suffragists acknowledge that the suffrage will not of itself solve the problem of wages, dependent as it is on other than political considerations.

## The Majority or the Minority

There remains one argument for granting woman the suffrage, namely, that the fact that a majority of women do not wish to vote is no sufficient reason for depriving a minority of an inborn right. This argument contains the gist of the whole question, that is, wherein the demands of the suffragists and the anti-suffragists clash. We have shown their error in claiming the franchise as an inherent right, but even were we to grant that such a right existed, it would still be perfectly within the power of the State to deprive women of this right, if by granting it the general good would be imperiled. The State holds authority to deprive citizens of the right of property, of liberty, of life itself, if the common weal demand it. The family is the safeguard of the State, and the granting of the suffrage to women tends to weaken this mainstay of the nation by bringing into it elements of discord and disunion; therefore, the State would be more than justified in denying women even an inherent right which might prove thus disastrous.

## Why the Majority of Women do not Want the Ballot

We contend that a majority of women believe that their inherent rights and privileges would suffer if the duty of voting were imposed upon them, for the following reasons: Because suffrage involves office-holding, which is inconsistent with the duties of most women; because they feel that their obvious duties and trusts — as sacred as any on earth — already demand their best efforts; because the duties cannot be relegated to others; because political equality will deprive woman of special privileges hitherto accorded to her by law; because they hold that the suffrage would lessen rather than increase their influence for good.

Suffrage involves office-holding. If women vote, they ought also to hold office, and assume the working duties incident to office. A system which tends to the dissolution of the home is more perilous to the general good than any other form of danger, and office-holding is, on the face of it, incompatible with woman's proper discharge of her duties as wife and mother.

Many women there are, it is true, who are not wives and mothers; and, if women vote, there will be more of them, but laws are made for the average individual, and the average woman is occupied in her house with the cares of a wife, a mother, and a home-maker.

The trusts of woman now are as sacred as any on earth, and man cannot relieve her of them. If, therefore, he demands of her participation in such duties, political or general, as his natural constitu-

5

tion fits him for, while he cannot relieve her of those most necessary duties which nature demands of her, he commits toward her a monstrous injustice. This is what imposing the suffrage on women would amount to; for if woman may vote she must vote. It is a mere sophism to say that the simple dropping of a ballot is all that is required ot her. If the suffrage is extended to women, they must accept it as a duty, bringing to bear on it the conscientious spirit which they bring to bear on their present life problems.

## Rights and Exemptions Given by Massachusetts Law to Women and not to Men (1909).

Under the Common Law and the Laws of the United States and of Massachusetts many rights and exemptions are given to women which are not given to men.

Citizenship is acquired more easily by women than by men, as "All persons born or naturalized in the United States, and subject to the jurisdiction thereof, are citizens of the United States and of the State wherein they reside" (U. S. Const. 14th Am.), and "Any woman who is now or may hereafter be married to a citizen of the United States and who might herself be lawfully naturalized shall be deemed a citizen." — U. S. Compiled Statutes, sec. 1994.

Women are not obliged to do jury duty. — R. L. ch. 176, sec. 1.

Women are not allowed to do military duty. — Acts 1905, ch. 465, sec. 2.

Women are not obliged to pay a poll tax. — R. L. ch. 12, sec. 1.

The property of a widow or of an unmarried woman above the age of twenty-one years to the amount of $500 is exempt from taxation provided her whole taxable estate does not exceed $1000. — R. L. ch. 12, sec. 5, cl. 9.

Women, by residing in a city or town for five consecutive years, and married women if their husbands have settlements, will gain settlements, entitling them to support in case of need in such city or town, although they have paid no taxes. Men, on the other hand, must pay taxes three out of five consecutive years of residence in order to gain such settlement. — R. L. ch. 80, sec. 1, cls. 1 & 6.

Women who are employees are exceptionally provided for and protected by the statutes regulating labor. — R. L. ch. 106, secs. 36–41; Acts 1904, ch. 397; Acts 1907, ch. 413; Acts 1908, ch. 645.

In general the welfare of women and children has been increasingly regarded. — Acts 1905, ch. 251; Acts 1905, ch. 269; Acts 1904, ch. 397; Acts 1907, ch. 413; Acts 1907, ch. 367.

Women are exempt from arrest in civil actions except for tort, but after judgment has been obtained against them they may be committed for contempt of court upon failure to pay. — R. L. ch. 168, sec. 3.

Married women are exempted from punishment for many criminal and tortious acts committed by them in the presence of their husbands, there being "a presumption of law that acts done by the wife in the immediate presence of her husband are done by her under coercion from him." In the absence of evidence to rebut this presumption the husband is held and the wife excused. — 145 Mass. 307.

A husband is bound to support his wife and children, and is liable for debts incurred by his wife in the purchase of necessaries. — 101 Mass. 78; 114 Mass. 424. See also R. L. ch. 212, sec. 45 as amended by Acts 1905, ch. 307.

During the pendency of a libel for divorce, the court may require the husband to pay into court an amount which will enable the wife to defend or maintain the libel, and may require him to pay the wife alimony during the pendency of the libel. — R. L. ch. 152, sec. 14.

A justice of the Superior Court may, if he deems it advisable, appoint an attorney to investigate and report to the Court in relation to any suit for divorce or any suit to have a marriage declared void, and may direct such attorney or any other attorney to defend the suit. — Acts 1907, ch. 390.

The rights of the husband and wife in relation to the control of their minor children have been made substantially equal, and now in any controversy between the parents relative to the final possession of the children, the welfare and happiness of the children shall determine their custody or possession. — R. L. ch. 152, sec. 28.

A married woman may now hold both real and personal property free from the control and debts of her husband. — R. L. ch. 153, secs. 1 & 7.

A married woman may now make contracts and sue and be sued, except that husband and wife cannot make contracts between themselves or sue each other. — R. L. ch. 154, secs. 2-6.

A married woman may now carry on business on her own account. — R. L. ch. 153, sec. 10.

The wife upon the decease of her husband may remain in his house for six months without being chargeable for rent. — R. L. ch. 140, sec. 1.

The wife upon the decease of her husband may be given an allowance for necessaries out of his property. The amount of this allowance is fixed by the Probate Court according to her circumstances and condition in life, and is paid to her in preference to the payment of his debts. — R. L. ch. 140, sec. 2.

Aside from these advantages to the wife, the rights of the surviving husband or wife in the property of the one who has deceased are now practically the same. If there is no will, or if the provisions of the will have been waived, the husband or wife, if there are issue surviving, will take one third of the personalty and realty; if there are no issue surviving, then the husband or wife will take $5000 and one half of the residue of the personalty and one half of the realty. — R. L. ch. 140, sec. 3. See 201 Mass. 59.

### Woman's Influence Without the Ballot

From this summary it will be seen that without the ballot women have obtained more than mere justice.

We oppose the suffrage for women, because we feel that we have more influence without it. There is not a single subject in which woman takes an intelligent interest in which she cannot exert an influence in the community proportionate to her character and ability.

If the suffrage movement were to disband to-day and no woman ever vote, not a single great interest would suffer. None of woman's wide philanthropies would be harmed; women's colleges would be unaffected; the professions would continue to give diplomas to qualified women; tradesmen would still employ women; good laws would not be repealed, and bad laws would be no more likely to be framed; literature would not suffer; homes would be no less secure; woman's civic work would not cease.

The influence of woman standing apart from the ballot is immeasurable. Men look to her then (knowing that she has no selfish, political interests to further) as the embodiment of all that is truest and noblest. She has influence with all parties alike; if a voter, she would have only the influence of her own party, even the women's vote being divided against itself. We believe that it is of vital importance that our sex should have no political ends to serve.

In whatever tends to protect and elevate woman, to secure her rights in the true sense of the word, to open up to her new paths of usefulness, all true-hearted men will join with women. In such work there is no difference of purpose.

Childhood is hers to influence and mold; and what greater power for good could there be given her? Let all true women, loyal citizens of our republic, look to the best performance of the private and public trusts which are naturally theirs, striving for no false "equality," since there is no question of comparison between men and their duties and women and theirs. They are not "like in like" but "like in difference," each supplementing the other, rising or falling, but always together.

---

*Issued by the Massachusetts Association Opposed to the Further Extension of Suffrage to Women.*

Pamphlets and leaflets may be obtained from the Secretary,

Room 615,
Kensington Building,
687 Boylston Street, Boston, Mass.

## OPINIONS OF EMINENT PERSONS AGAINST WOMAN SUFFRAGE.

DANIEL WEBSTER. "The rough contests of the political world are not suited to the dignity and the delicacy of your sex. . . . It is by the promulgation of sound morals in the community, and more especially by the training and instruction of the young, that woman performs her part toward the preservation of a free government."

REV. HORACE BUSHNELL, D.D. "Hitherto it has been an advantage to be going into battle in our suffrages with a full half . . . as a corps of reserve, left behind, so that we may fall back on this quiet element . . . and settle again our mental and moral equilibrium. Now it is proposed that we have no reserve any longer, that we go into our conflicts taking our women with us, all to be kept heating in the same fire for weeks or months together. . . . Let no man imagine . . . that our women are going into these encounters to be just as quiet, or as little moved as now, when they stay in the rear unexcited, letting us come back to them often and recover our reason. They are no more mitigators now, but instigators rather, sweltering in the same fierce heats and commotions, only more tempestuously stirred than we." *Women's Suffrage; the Reform against Nature.*

FRANCIS PARKMAN. "It has been claimed as a right that woman should vote. It is no right, but a wrong, that a small number of women should impose on all the rest political duties which there is no call for their assuming, which they do not want to assume, and which, if duly discharged, would be a cruel and intolerable burden."

MRS. CLARA T. LEONARD, Massachusetts Board of Health, Lunacy and Charity. "The best work that a woman can do for the purifying of politics is by her influence over men, by the wise training of her children, by her intelligent, unselfish counsel to husband, brother, or friend, by a thorough knowledge and discussion of the needs of her community."

REV. EDWARD EVERETT HALE, D.D. "I am now asked to confer the responsibility of suffrage upon women. This means, of course, that they are willing to accept all the responsibilities of public-spirited men. To which request I reply that I do not think they want to do these things, and second, that I do not think they would do them well."

LE BARON R. BRIGGS, President of Radcliffe College. "As to public life, I am still so conservative as to hold that a political competition of both sexes is less likely to elevate men than to degrade women, and that the peculiar strength of refined and earnest womanhood is exercised in ways less public. I fear the loss of the best that is in woman, and, with it, the loss of a power that is hers and hers alone."

JACOB A. RIIS. "I do not think the ballot will add to woman's real power which she exercises or can exercise now."

CARL SCHURZ. "Is it not certain that so tremendous an addition to the voting force as the granting of unqualified woman suffrage would effect, would involve at least the possibility of a dangerous increase of those evils which the best thought of the country is at present painfully struggling to remedy?"

MRS. KATE GANNETT WELLS. "In the present constitution of events, of facts, physiological, social, financial, moral, and political, it is inexpedient for government to grant universal female suffrage."

CARDINAL GIBBONS. "If woman enters politics, she will be sure to carry away on her some of the mud and dirt of political contact."

HON. MOSES HALLETT, United States District Judge for Colorado. "Our state has tried the female suffrage plan a sufficiently long time to form a fair idea of its workings. I am not prejudiced in any way, but honestly do not see where the experiment has proved of benefit. . . . It has produced no special reforms and it has had no particular purifying effect upon politics. There is a growing tendency on the part of most of the better and more intelligent of the female voters of Colorado to cease exercising the ballot. . . . If it were to be done over again, the people of Colorado would defeat woman suffrage by an overwhelming majority."

HON. THOMAS F. BAYARD, Secretary of State. "There never was a greater mistake, there never was a falser fact stated than that the women of America need any protection further than the love borne to them by their fellow-countrymen. Do not imperil the advantages which they have; do not attempt in this hasty, ill-considered, shallow way to interfere with the relations which are founded upon the laws of Nature herself."

MISS PHOEBE W. COUZINS, Lawyer, Missouri Commissioner for the World's Fair, and platform speaker for woman suffrage for 20 years. "I do not believe that women are constructed by nature for the rough and tumble fight of the political arena. . . . Women are easily influenced. They do not stop to think of the consequences of their acts, and in their hands the ballot would become a most dangerous weapon. . . . I am through forever with woman suffrage."

ABRAM S. HEWITT. "After carefully considering all the arguments advanced by the advocates of woman suffrage . . . I do not think, from the organic difference between men and women, that it will ever be shown to be for the advantage of women that they should be forced to take part in political controversies. In fact, I think it would be a great misfortune to them, as well as to the human race."

Hon. CHARLES J. BONAPARTE. "The suffrage is not a mere privilege. It is a public burden, and when it is proposed to make your mothers and sisters and other ladies of whom, perhaps, you may sometimes think, share this burden, the question is properly not whether women should be allowed to vote, but whether they should be obliged to vote."

Prof. EDWARD D. COPE. "The first thing that strikes us in considering the woman suffrage movement is that it is a proposition to engage women once more in that 'struggle' from which civilization has enabled them in great measure to escape; and that its effect, if long continued and fairly tried, will be to check the development of woman as such, and to bring to bear on her influences of a kind different from those which have been hitherto active."

Miss DOROTHEA L. DIX. "Distinctly and emphatically, Miss Dix believed in woman's keeping herself aloof and apart from anything savoring of ordinary political action. . . . She must be the incarnation of a purely disinterested idea appealing to universal humanity, irrespective of party or sect." *Life of Dorothea Lynde Dix,* by Francis Tiffany.

Dr. S. WEIR MITCHELL. "The best of the higher evolution of mind will never be safely reached until the woman accepts the irrevocable decree which made her woman and not man. Something in between she cannot be."

RICHARD H. DANA. "The truth is, the ballot for women is not needed . . . and if they were ever called upon to combine and work in antagonism to the men, which they must do if their vote is really needed, the evils of the conflict would strike at the very foundations of our social system."

Prof. WILLIAM T. SEDGWICK. "Why should the great majority of women, who, as everybody knows, are either indifferent or opposed to woman suffrage, be forced to accept it against their will when there is no sound evidence that any material good is likely to accrue either to themselves or to the state?"

Bishop JOHN H. VINCENT, Founder of Chautauqua. "When about thirty years of age I accepted for a time the doctrine of woman suffrage, and publicly defended it. Years of wide and careful observation have convinced me that the demand for woman suffrage in America is without foundation in equity, and, if successful, must prove harmful to American society."

Miss JEANNETTE L. GILDER, Founder of *The Critic*. "In politics I do not think that women have any place. Neither physically nor temperamentally are they strong enough for the fray. The life is too public, too wearing, and too unfitted to the nature of women. It is bad enough for men . . . and it would be worse for women. I believe not only that the ballot in the hands of women would be a calamity, but I believe that it would prove a boomerang."

JOHN BOYLE O'REILLY. "Woman suffrage would be the constitutional degradation of women; it would be an appeal to the coarser strength of men; and I profoundly believe that it would result in social disorder and disrespect of law."

GAIL HAMILTON (Miss Mary Abigail Dodge). "My earliest instinct and my latest judgment combine in maintaining that women have a right to claim exemption from political duty and responsibllity, and that men have no right to lay the burden upon them. If the public work is ill done by men, the remedy is to do it better, not to shift the weight to shoulders already heavily laden, and whose task they do not propose in any respect to lighten."

REV. JAMES M. BUCKLEY, D.D. "Should the duty of governing in the state be imposed upon women, all the members of society will suffer. . . . The true woman needs no governing authority conferred upon her by law. In the present situation the highest evidence of respect that man can exhibit toward woman, and the noblest service he can perform for her, are to vote NAY to the proposition that would take from her the diadem of pearls, the talisman of faith, hope, and love, by which all other requests are won from men, and substitute for it the iron crown of authority."

HON. HENRY B. BROWN, Ex-Justice of the Supreme Court of the United States. "It is a mistake to suppose that either men or women have a *natural right* to vote. We are bound to distinguish between natural and political rights. They may be said to have a natural right to protection in their persons, their property and their opinions, but they have no natural right to govern or to participate in the government of others."

REV. THEODORE L. CUYLER, D.D. "There is full scope for woman's patience, power, purity and prayers without attempting to override that divine arrangement which never fitted her to be a soldier, a sailor, a civil engineer, a juryman, a magistrate, a policeman, a politician."

HON. ELIHU ROOT, Secretary of State. "I am opposed to granting suffrage to women because I believe it would be a loss to women and an injury to the state, and to every man and woman in the state. . . . I think so because suffrage implies not merely the casting of a ballot, but entering upon the field of political life; and politics is modified war. In politics there is struggle, strife, contention, bitterness, heart-burning, excitement, agitation — everything which is adverse to the true character of woman. In my judgment, this whole movement arises from a false conception of the duty and the right of men and women. . . . It is a fatal mistake that these excellent women make when they conceive that the functions of men are superior to theirs and seek to usurp them."

4

# HIDDEN FROM HISTORY

JENNIE JUNE (Mrs. Jane C. Croly), "Mother of Clubs," Founder of the New York Sorosis, and President of the New York Women's Press Club. "The best way for women to approach politics is to let them entirely alone. In all the fifty years that in one way or another I have worked, I have never identified myself with suffrage nor politics."

ROSSITER JOHNSON. "The most civilized portions of mankind have not yet outgrown the measurement of force for the ultimate settlement of every great question, and the unit of force is the man capable of bearing arms. . . . The government set up, and the policy adopted, may not be the best possible; but, if a majority of the men stand behind them, we shall at least have stability, and that is the most necessary element in any government. . . . To make any party victorious at the polls by means of blank-cartridge ballots would only present an increased temptation to the numerical minority to assert itself as the military majority. . . . If an election is carried by a preponderance of votes cast by women, who is to enforce the verdict? When a few such verdicts have been overturned, we shall find ourselves in a state of anarchy."

THE ENGLISH REMONSTRANCE (*Nineteenth Century*, June, 1889). "To sum up: we would give the women their full share in the state of social effort and social mechanism; we look for their increasing activity in that higher state which rests on thought, conscience, and moral influence; but we protest against their admission to direct power in that state which *does* rest upon force — the state in its administrative, military, and financial aspects — where the physical capacity, the accumulated experience, and inherited training of men ought to prevail without the harassing interference of those who, though they may be partners of men in debate, can in these matters never be partners with them in action. . . . Nothing can be further from our minds than to seek to depreciate the position or importance of women. It is because we are keenly alive to the enormous value of their special contribution to the community that we oppose what seems to us likely to endanger that contribution. We are convinced that the pursuit of a mere outward equality with men is for women not only vain but demoralizing. It leads to a total misconception of woman's true dignity and special mission. It tends to personal struggle and rivalry, where the only effort of both the great divisions of the human family should be to contribute the characteristic labor and the best gifts of each to the common stock."

| | |
|---|---|
| Mrs. Humphry Ward | Mrs. George J. Goschen |
| Mrs. Leslie Stephen | Mrs. Frederic Harrison |
| Mrs. Thomas H. Huxley | Mrs. Matthew Arnold |
| Mrs. William E. Forster | Mrs. Max Müller |
| Lady Frederic Cavendish | Mrs. J. Richard Green |
| Hon. Emily Lawless | Mrs. Walter Bagehot and others |

5

VICTORIA, Queen of England. "The Queen is most anxious to enlist every one who can speak or write to join in checking this mad, wicked folly of 'Woman's Rights,' with all its attendant horrors, on which her poor, feeble sex is bent, forgetting every sense of womanly feeling and propriety."

JOHN BRIGHT. "When women are not safe under the charge or care of fathers, husbands, brothers, and sons, it is the fault of our non-civilization and not of our laws. As civilization founded on Christian principles advances, women will gain all that is right for them to have, though they are not seen contending in the strife of political parties. In my experience I have observed evil results to many women who have entered heartily into political conflict and discussion. I would save them from it."

WILLIAM E. GLADSTONE. "A permanent and vast difference has been impressed upon women and men respectively by the Maker of both. I for one am not prepared to say which of the two sexes has the higher and which has the lower province. . . . I am not without the fear, lest beginning with the state, we should eventually be found to have intruded into what is yet more fundamental and more sacred, the precinct of the family, and should dislocate, or seriously modify, the relations of domestic life."

HERBERT SPENCER. Herbert Spencer, in *Justice*, maintains that there are fundamental reasons for keeping the spheres of the sexes distinct. He had formerly argued the matter "from the point of view of a general principle of individual rights," but he finds that this cannot be sustained, as he "discovers mental and emotional differences between the sexes which disqualify women for the burdens of government and the exercise of its functions."

Mrs. HUMPHRY WARD. "Women should not vote on questions in the solution of which they can never play a responsible part. Fancy a female general, a female admiral! Fancy a railroad run by women, roads built or mines worked by them! If there is this inevitable physical limitation to a woman's activity . . . is it just that she be given a vote on matters that involve these activities? The national government . . . is concerned in all of these things, and is maintained by the votes of the male portion of the population, which thus indirectly decides on the army, the navy, the railroads, and the scores of material interests in which women cannot by nature take an active part."

GOLDWIN SMITH. "Political power has hitherto been exercised by the male sex; not because man has been a tyrannical usurper and has brutally thrust his weaker partner out of her rights, but in the course of nature because man alone could uphold government and enforce the law. Let the edifice of law be as moral and as intellectual as you will, its foundation is the force of the community, and the force of the community is male."

6

# HIDDEN FROM HISTORY

QUARTERLY REVIEW, *Women at Oxford and Cambridge*, October, 1897. "Either sex is an appalling blunder, or else it must have been intended that each sex should have its own work to do, not merely in the physical economy of the race, but also in the social and intellectual world. . . . Woman, alike in body, mind, and character, 'is not lesser man, but other.' At the moment, many able women think that it is possible to follow masculine ideas in education, in habit, in practical life, and yet to be true to their own nature. In the long run this is impossible."

Other notable persons who have remonstrated against woman suffrage are President Grover Cleveland, Mrs. Margaret Deland, President Arthur T. Hadley of Yale University, Miss Ida M. Tarbell, Bishop David H. Greer of New York, Miss Caroline Hazard, President of Wellesley College, Rev. Dr. Lyman Abbott, Miss Agnes Irwin, Dean of Radcliffe College, Charles Dudley Warner, Mrs. Mary E. Wilkins Freeman, Felix Adler, Madame Louise Homer, President William DeWitt Hyde of Bowdoin College, Mrs. Kate Douglas Wiggin, Bishop William C. Doane, Mrs. Clara Louise Kellogg Strakosch, Hon. Charles C. Nott, Chief Justice United States Court of Claims, Mrs. John Ware, Andrew S. Draper, New York State Commissioner of Education, Miss Carolyn Wells, Rev. Dr. Theodore T. Munger, Miss Mabel T. Boardman, Edward W. Bok, Mrs. Andrew Carnegie, Richard Watson Gilder, Mrs. Celia Thaxter, President Henry P. Judson of the University of Chicago, Marion Harland (Mrs. Virginia Terhune), Governor Woodrow Wilson of New Jersey, Mrs. Schuyler Van Rensselaer, Bishop Arthur C. A. Hall of Vermont, Mrs. Grover Cleveland, Hon. Edgar Aldrich, United States District Judge for New Hampshire, Mrs. Mary Anderson de Navarro, Rev. Dr. Washington Gladden, Mrs. Rebecca Harding Davis, Winston Churchill, Mrs. Josephine Daskam Bacon, Rev. Dr. Charles H. Parkhurst, Miss Adeline Knapp, Prof. William K. Brooks of Johns Hopkins University, Mrs. Helen Watterson Moody, Octave Thanet (Miss Alice French), Mrs. Adeline D. T. Whitney, James Bryce, William E. H. Lecky, Miss Octavia Hill, Frederic Harrison, John Ruskin, Sir E. Ray Lankester, Gilbert K. Chesterton, Rudyard Kipling and Lord Cromer, "Maker of Modern Egypt."

Other prominent Massachusetts men who have expressed their opposition to woman suffrage are Governors Eben S. Draper, Curtis Guild, Jr., W. Murray Crane (now United States Senator), Roger Wolcott, William E. Russell, George D. Robinson and William Gaston, United States Senator Henry Cabot Lodge, President A. Lawrence Lowell of Harvard University, President Charles W. Eliot of Harvard University, President Franklin Carter of Williams College, President Mark Hopkins of Williams College, President George Harris of Amherst College, President Frederick W. Hamilton of Tufts College, President Henry Lefavour of Simmons College, President L. Clark Seelye of Smith College, President Albert P. Fitch of Andover Theological Seminary, Principal Alfred E. Stearns of Phillips Exeter Academy, Bishop William Lawrence, Archbishop William H. O'Connell, George G. Crocker, Congressman William C. Lovering, Prof. Charles Eliot Norton, Major Henry L. Higginson, John Fiske, James Ford Rhodes, Charles F. Donnelly, Judge

7

Francis C. Lowell, Charles Warren, Prof. Charles J. Bullock, Morgan Rotch, William D. Sohier, Rodney Wallace, Rev. Joshua P. Bodfish, Samuel J. Elder, Dr. Edward M. Hartwell, Arthur Lord, Charles T. Gallagher, Albert C. Houghton, William B. Plunkett, James M. Prendergast, John N. Cole, Henry L. Pierce, William F. Wharton, Solomon Lincoln, Henry M. Whitney, Rev. John O'Brien, Henry H. Sprague, T. Jefferson Coolidge, Thomas Russell, Prof. William B. Munro, Charles Francis Adams, Prof. Francis J. Child, Elisha Morgan, Jeremiah W. Coveney, Dr. J. Collins Warren, John R. Thayer, W. Lyman Underwood, Dr. Henry P. Walcott, Frederick P. Fish, Melvin O. Adams, James P. Munroe, Robert Winsor, Edwin F. Atkins, Theodore Lyman, John F. Fitzgerald, Dr. William L. Richardson, Walter Clifford, Timothy G. Spaulding, Robert Luce, John T. Burnett, Laurence Minot, John A. Sullivan, Moses Williams, Thomas L. Livermore, Robert M. Morse, Levi J. Gunn, Dr. Walter Channing, Francis H. Appleton, Thornton K. Lothrop, Judge William C. Loring, Charles F. Choate, Arthur H. Lowe, Prof. F. Spencer Baldwin, Dr. William J. Councilman, Frank Foxcroft, Rev. Octavius B. Frothingham, Prentiss Cummings, Prof. William W. Goodwin, Congressman Robert O. Harris, Prof. Paul H. Hanus, William A. Gaston, District Attorney Richard W. Irwin, Dr. Dudley A. Sargent, Frederic J. Stimson and many others.

---

### WOMAN SUFFRAGE IN COLORADO.

"I have voted since 1893. I have been a delegate to the city and State conventions, and a member of the Republican State Committee from my county. I have been a deputy sheriff and a watcher at the polls. For twenty-three years I have been in the midst of the woman suffrage movement in Colorado. For years I believed in woman suffrage and have worked day in and day out for it. I now see my mistake and would abolish it to-morrow if I could.

No law has been put on the statute book of Colorado for the benefit of women and children that has been put there by the women. The child labor law went through independently of the women's vote. The hours of working-women have not been shortened; the wages of school-teachers have not been raised; the type of men that got into office has not improved a bit.

Frankly, the experiment is a failure. It has done Colorado no good. It has done woman no good. The best thing for both would be if to-morrow the ballot for women could be abolished."

Mrs. FRANCIS W. GODDARD,
*President of the Colonial Dames of Colorado.*

DECEMBER, 1910.

---

*Printed by the Massachusetts Association Opposed to the Further Extension of Suffrage to Women.*

Pamphlets and leaflets may be obtained from the Secretary, Room 615, Kensington Building, 687 Boylston Street, Boston, Massachusetts.

JANUARY, 1911.

## OUGHT WOMEN TO VOTE?

REPRINTED, BY PERMISSION, FROM THE GUIDON OF MANCHESTER, N. H.

AMONG the questions to be submitted to the voters of New Hampshire, on the 10th of March, not the least interesting is the one of woman's suffrage. Ought women to vote? At the risk of being considered ungallant and being forever included in the class called "old fogy," we answer that question, No.

We have read with a great deal of care the abundant literature the suffragists have supplied during the last few months, and must confess that to our minds the petitioners should be given leave to withdraw, — with all the honors of war, however, for they have fought a gallant fight, but they have not proved their case.

The first argument usually adduced why women should vote is that in intelligence they are equal to men; that in conscientious discharge of duty they are equal, if not superior; that in the moral and economic condition of the country they have as much concern as have their husbands, sons, and brothers. Granting all this, still it does not follow that women should vote. It only proves that they would do as well as the men, not better. We still have the abiding belief that there is enough intelligence, honesty, and morality among the male portion of the community to regulate its affairs without having to call in the help of the women, by giving them the unrestricted privilege of voting.

"Privilege" of voting? we hear some one say, "the right," you mean. No, we do not mean the right. Those who set out to have women vote achieved a master stroke when they invented the term "woman's rights," for where is there a living man who will dare refuse woman her "rights?" And how many a doughty champion she can enlist when her rights are endangered or assailed! In such a conflict we, certainly, would not wish to be numbered among the cads. We simply hold that voting is not an absolute right of women nor is it an essential part of citizenship. The constitution of our country guarantees to her citizens only "the right of life, liberty, and the pursuit of happiness." Nowhere is it said that the right of voting is included. Universal suffrage never prevailed in this or in any other country. The separate states may make and do make the conditions necessary for voting. Sometimes the state requires the ownership of a certain amount of property as a qualification to vote; sometimes it is the ability to read and write; then there are such conditions as a residence in one place for a given time, registration, and the like. If the state wishes to add the qualification of sex, this, in itself, is no infringement on right.

But why should sex disqualify one from voting? Man and woman God created us, and it is neither possible nor desirable that we should overcome the barrier of sex. That sex is an obstacle to voting is seen from the nature of woman and the conditions required for civil government. The last resort of law is force. Now, woman by her very nature is pacific and is incapable of maintaining those laws when necessity arises. Woman's peculiar attribute is that of maternity, and by reason of it she enjoys privileges and immunities which are denied to men. Her sphere is the family, and love, not force, is the source of her power. She is exempt from the duty of holding public office, from the discharge of judicial and police functions, and from military service. None of these could be performed by women without violating the proprieties and safeguards of female purity and delicacy.

Aside from the question of right and of justice, there is the question of policy and expediency.

It is alleged by those asking for this suffrage that women are under certain legal disabilities which are unjust and burdensome. We answer, men are by no means insensible to the rights and privileges of their mothers and wives, sisters and daughters, and are ready to redress any wrongs to which they may be subjected in a legal sense as promptly and effectively as they would resent any wrong inflicted upon them in the social or moral order.

It is claimed that woman, by her vote, would correct the great evil of intemperance. We wish she could; that in itself would be sufficient to overcome almost any objection to her claims to suffrage, but we have no confidence in the promise. Men have voted for prohibition before this, but they have not legislated men into temperance. The suffrage of either men or women or of both is powerless to restrain the animal appetites. Reformation of society comes from elevating the moral tone of the individual, and herein lies the greatest power of woman. This power is exercised in the home, not in political assemblies nor at election booths.

It is urged that politics would be purified and elevated by presence of women. In theory this is all very fine, but any one who knows what practical politics are knows that these entail the caucus and too often the bar-room. Instead of lifting men up, she herself would be dragged down by such association. Then there would be a new element of discord introduced into the family. For the one woman who would vote from conviction when that conviction was at variance with her husband's, nine others would follow blindly the dictation of their spouses, and the consequence would be that the baser element of society would prevail. We believe, moreover, that the vast majority of women do not want to vote, nor would they exercise the privilege, were it granted to them. For this is the case where a restricted suffrage is already allowed them.

Our last appeal is to history. The suffrage movement is now about fifty years old. During that time four states have given women unrestricted suffrage. These states are Utah, Idaho, Wyoming, and Colorado. A number of other states have accorded them the right to vote for school committees, library trustees, or some similar offices. Within the last six years the suffrage cause has met defeat sixty times in twenty-eight states. We naturally ask, What has woman's suffrage accomplished in the states where it has prevailed? " By their fruits ye shall know them," said a good Authority, many years ago. Has this movement met the expectation of its friends and justified its promises? Utah still smells rank of Mormonism, though women have been voting there for many years. Wyoming is notoriously an ill-governed state, where gambling and vice are actually licensed by law. The recent election of a United States senator in Denver, where the members of the legislature sat with revolvers on their desks, does not reassure us as to the prevalence of law and order in Colorado. Idaho has not, so far as we know, any special claim for a model government. We have not heard of any emigration of women from other states into these Utopias where their sex is expected to enjoy all the liberty and bliss promised from the exercise of unrestricted suffrage. But we have heard of election methods in these districts which make our own campaigns seem like Quaker meetings. Our politics are bad enough, but if we would be spared this new misery let us add to our litany: " From campaigns of hysteria, hatchets, and hullabaloo, O Lord deliver us." We sincerely trust that on this question of women's voting, sensible men will vote No.

*Printed by the Massachusetts Association opposed to Extension of Woman Suffrage.*

Pamphlets and leaflets may be obtained from the Secretary of the Association,

Mrs. Robert W. Lord,
P. O. Box 2262, Boston.

## PAPER BY J. NEWTON FIERO AT ANTI-SUFFRAGE MEETING, MAY 11TH, 1894.

It were a rash man to attempt "By either force or skill to turn the current of a woman's will," and it must therefore be conceded on all hands that when the majority of the women of New York favor the extension of suffrage it will speedily become an accomplished fact. Since men will grant this privilege when women demand it, as they have conceded heretofore more than could be reasonably required, through their disposition to treat the gentler sex not only with justice but in a broad-minded and liberal spirit.

The question is not whether men will exclude women from a right to which they are absolutely entitled, but a broader and more comprehensive one. Will women be benefited by the suffrage, or will its exercise tend to their real disadvantage? If it is to be valuable to them, men will yield it with pleasure. If it is to be injurious or disadvantageous to them, then men will refuse to grant the dangerous privilege even though it is claimed as a heaven-born right, and refuse it because of their interest in and respect for women.

The average man, as in duty bound, treats this question in its relation to him as a son, a husband or a father, and as he regards women in the light of mother, wife or daughter, and cannot escape looking at the question from the point of view that he owes a duty of care and protection to what is physically, at least, the weaker sex. True, many women are both independent and self-supporting, but the discussion of this subject must proceed with reference to the condition of the great mass of women and to their relations to each other and to the race, and not solely with a view to the interests of the minority who are self-supporting, or for any other reason indifferent to the attention, protection and courtesies of the sterner sex.

As was justly observed on a very recent public occasion by a polished and accomplished orator, the question is from its nature one of extreme delicacy and cannot be treated in many of its aspects with the frankness its importance demands, since much must be left unsaid that has an important bearing upon the determination of the question, but its main features, as to the benefits or disadvantages of the suffrage to the gentler sex, are open to full discussion.

# HIDDEN FROM HISTORY

Woman is not qualified for the ballot or likely to be benefitted by its exercise for physical and physiological reasons:

Plato in his ideal Republic, in order to arrive at a conclusion as to the propriety of woman's sharing in the duties citizens owe to the state, asks, "Is she capable of sharing, either wholly or partially, or not at all, in the actions of men," and seems to regard her right to participate in the affairs of Government to be determined by the answer of the question he proposes: "Whether she can share in the toils of war and the defense of the country?"

The right to take part in the political affairs is one of the same class of duties as the performance of duty as jurors in courts of justice, and service, voluntary or compulsory, in the army and navy, and from time immemorial the person exercising political control in time of Peace have been held responsible for the preservation of the Government by force of arms in the time of war.

The protest against the suffrage rightly speaks of its burdens and responsibilities, since with the right to vote is closely connected the enforcement of purity of the ballot, the inquiry into the honesty and capability of public officials and the proper administration of affairs of Government. To all these, women are manifestly and confessedly unequal. Physically, women are not fitted for the task of protecting and upholding any form of Government. They may be active in putting it in operation by their ballots but must yield the burden and cast aside the responsibility when the circumstances demand strength and endurance in camp or on the battlefield. These are, however, necessarily and logically connected with the right to the ballot and are burdens and responsibilities which must reasonably be assumed as inseparable from it. Women must therefore recognize the natural limitations upon her strength and fitness to discharge the duties of citizenship.

From what may reasonably be termed a business standpoint, involving the legal rights of women, there is certainly little to be desired by way of improvement or reform and nothing to be gained by her active participation in politics. The old restrictions upon the rights of women to hold property independent of their husbands and to deal with it in the same manner as men have been entirely swept away, and women stand before the law in every respect entitled to at least the same rights and privileges as the sterner sex. In addition there is a survival of all the old rules devised as a protection to women, well illustrated by the retention upon the statute books of the right of dower which every married woman has in the real estate of her husband, so that he is unable to dispose of his real property without her consent, and the right on the part of the wife to demand and receive from the husband support and maintenance according to his rank and station in life and his ability to provide for himself and family. Thus, in no respect is woman hampered by law as regards material affairs, but rather highly favored by its provisions and the reason so frequently and persistently alleged that women should be granted the ballot, that she may be able to protect herself in her property rights, is entirely dissipated by the progress of modern law reform in the direction of legal emancipation of women, so that in truth and fact she is entitled not only to absolutely control her own property but to certain rights in that of her husband, of which she cannot by any act of his be divested or deprived.

In the natural course of events and order of things the right of suffrage, by means of which women is expected to provide for and protect herself at the polls, must react against her so far as her legal rights are concerned, by compelling men to lay aside all considerations of compliment, chivalry or courtesy and assert their rights, to at least an equality with reference to property interests. It can scarcely be possible that women can at the same time appeal to the sense of justice in men by reason of their helplessness and in the same breath insist upon their rights at the ballot box which are to be enforced by their political power.

There still remains the sentimental side of the question,—difficult of treatment and scarcely possible of adequate presentation,—well expressed in a recent pithy discussion of the question in these words, "It seems a pity that the barriers to harmony and sympathy between men and women, which have been building for the last fifty years, should be increased by this new effort, in as much as the sexes cannot exist without each other as long as the world lasts. American women, of all others, should shrink from encouraging distrust in their husbands and fathers and looking upon them as they are learning to do in the light of lineal descendants of the forty thieves."

If women are no longer to rely upon the fact that they are to be treated with consideration because they are the weaker sex physically, but insist upon certain alleged rights and privileges because they may be able at the ballot box to govern and control Legislation, they must certainly expect but scant courtesy outside of matters of strict justice and can scarcely be reasonably expected to receive at the hands of men that chivalrous treatment with regard, not only to their rights but as to their privileges, which is now so cheerfully accorded them. In this aspect, assertion of power must, in every respect, be disadvantageous to women, since they are certainly not so well qualified to carry on the machinery of politics and the administration of the affairs of Government as are men, by reason of their nature, education and experience.

It is insisted that the advent of women in the field of active political life would tend to purify elections and reform legislators, which is by no means likely, since it is much more probable that in the contact with political methods at the polls and in the details of legislation, women would be dragged to the political level of men than elevate the existing standard of political morality. Even where it otherwise, it would seem that the price would be too great to pay for a reform of this character, if, in order to accomplish it, women must not only exercise the right of suffrage, but as its logical outcome, must attend the primaries, arrange for local assemblies and political meetings, be active at the caucus and upon the stump and take upon themselves not only the right and privileges but the burdens and responsibilities of the ward politician as well as of the statesman.

It is for these, among other reasons, that women have not heretofore desired, and do not, as to the majority, now insist upon the right of suffrage, and this question must ultimately turn, not upon whether suffrage is their natural right or whether it may prove expedient to the administration of governmental affairs, but upon its effect upon women as such, whether beneficial or the contrary, and until the gentler sex are fully satisfied that they will receive some substantial and material benefit from the burdens and responsibilities of the suffrage, the majority will continue to protest against having cast upon them a right which will subject them to personal annoyance, serious inconveniences and material disadvantages, without corresponding benefits. Until such time, Man as the natural guardian and protector of woman will insist upon shielding her from burdens and responsibilities fit to be borne alone by that sterner sex which is endowed by nature in such a manner as to be physically adapted to govern as statesman, or, if need be, maintain as soldiers the integrity of the political institutions for which it should be solely responsible.

---

Apply for more papers to Anti-Suffrage Association, 13 Elk Street, Albany, N. Y.

63rd Cong. }
1st Sess.  }

TO THE FEDERAL CONGRESS OF THE UNITED STATES OF AMERICA, IN WASHINGTON ASSEMBLED:-

We the undersigned citizens of Newport in the county of Sullivan and state of New Hampshire, representing women of every station in life, trusting in God and vitally interested in the preservation of the traditional American home, are opposed to the extension of suffrage to our sex.

With the demands of society, the calls of charity, the church, and philanthropy constantly increasing, we feel that to add the distracting forces of political campaigns would wreck our constitutions and destroy our homes.

At all times we are ready to give our full portion of love and sacrifice for the life of the nation and the good of mankind, but we look upon the attempt now being made by some to crowd the obligations of suffrage upon us, as a move to change our natures and destroy us for that wider field of influence and usefulness which in America has always belonged to woman.

THEREFORE we respectfully petition your Honorable Body, and ask that you will vote against all measures which may come before you looking to the extension of the franchise to women.

Dated at Newport, N.H. this 7th day of July 1913.

Isabella C. Edgell (Mrs George S.)
Alice R. Mooney (" Chas. E.)
(Mrs) Barbara Bartlett
"  Abbie J. Glynn
"  Hazel R. Trask
"  Jennie Read Goodale
"  Bertha W. Hadley
"  Luella E. Kempton
"  Bessie H. Varney
"  Clara E. Reed
"  Nellie W. Whittemore
"  Laura R. Hall

Mrs E. B. Carey
Mrs N. P. Moore
Mrs. B. C. Wright
Mrs A. W. Hartt
Mrs F. C. Foster
Mrs J. M. Barton
(Miss) Florence F. Barton
Mrs. John C. Silsby
Mrs John G. Pike
(Miss) Lillian M. Upham
(Miss) Hattie F. Reed

# HIDDEN FROM HISTORY

Laura R. Hall  (Miss) Hattie H. Reed
Mrs Allie M. Deck  Mrs H. L. Reed
Maine E. Ennis  Mrs. E. G. Heath
Mrs J. A. LaCroix  Mrs Jas Cupples
Mrs H. M Stevens  Mrs E C Bull
Mrs Lillian M. Cain  Mrs Minnie Lewis
Mrs Estella Hitchcock  Mrs Geo. A. Wilmarth
" Flora L. Fletcher  (miss) L. Marguerite Wilmarth
" Etta B. Haven  (miss) Bertha P. Wilmarth
" Florence S. Martin  (miss) Mary J. Marshall
Julia Loabembach  Mrs John Puck
Mrs K. A. Gilman  Mrs Abbie Glasson
Mrs. J. C. Ketchen  (miss) Alice Bruce
Blanche Morse  Mrs H. G. Marshall
Mrs C C Straw  Giuseppina Bonaccorsi
Mrs. W. Frank Dickey  Mrs Eliza B. Rogers
Mrs R. G. Errett  Miss Ellen H. Rogers
Mrs L. D. Perkins  Ethelyn C. Morse
Mrs F. E. Barden  Mrs. Myron W. Tinney
Mrs F. P. Murphy  (Mrs) Zilpha M. Cain
Mrs Maria Hebrick  (Mrs) Martha B. Stetson
(Mrs) Mabel Babcock  Mrs Lizzie B. Cutting
Mrs Dora Deming  Mrs Lovisa A. Dodge
Mrs L. D. Kempton  Mrs K. E. Huntoon
Mrs Lucena D. Chapin  Mrs. Emma A. Paul
Mrs Henry J. Sawyer  Mrs Lillie H. Reed
Mrs Lillie Derrick  Mrs Mary C. Glynn
Emma W. Chellis  Mrs Maude F. Lewis
Mrs Martha J. Tandy

Mrs. H. R. Jordan.
Newport, N.H

Mrs. Wm Geo. Ellis.
Mrs. G. B. Lear
Mrs. Clarence D. Mooney.
Mrs Tyler L. Barker.
Mrs. R. H. Tenney
Mrs. W. W. Safford
Mrs. Dana G. Mooney.
" Jennie Winn
" Deloy P. Leachieu
" G. A. Smith
" Mrs Frank Jordan
" Fred Jenkins
Mrs. Arthur S. Currier
Mrs. Oley G. Lear
Mrs. C. H. Gile
Mrs. H. P. Chapman.
Mrs. Perry Jameson
Mrs. George Wells
Mrs. E. A. Paul
Mrs. H. E. Dodge.
" John Gage
Mrs. George W. Tilton
Mrs. J. W. Johnson
Mrs. M. G. Kempton.
Mrs. J. W. Thompson
Mrs. Mary G. Paul.

Mrs Mary Glyn
" Leggie Reed.
" James Jordan
" Peter Wright
" Mrs S. H. Jordan
" C J George
" J B Cooper
" L S Dolloff
" Nellie Blanchard
" Ruth Stark
" Alice King
Mrs. M. S. Colby.
" Albert Hildreth
" Jo LaCroix

Mrs. Mary F. Paul.

Mrs. W. P. Bronson    Newport N.H.
Mrs. W. H. Davis      Newport N.H.
Mrs. G. A. Tenney,    Newport, N.H.
Mrs. C. E. Pollard    Newport, N.H.
Mrs. F. C. Foster     Newport, N.H.
Mrs. L. E. Huntoon    Newport N.H.
Mrs. M. G. Carleton         "        "
Mrs. A. Wood                Newport N.H.
Mrs. A. H. Jurard     Newport, N.H.
Mrs. Frank Johnson    Newport N.H.
Mrs. Oliver _____    Newport N.H.
Mrs. Eugene York      Newport N.H.
Mrs. Emma Spooner     Newport N.H.
Mrs. G. A. Fairbanks  Newport, N.H.
 "   F. A. Reed            "     "
Mrs. H. C. Reed
Mrs. N. A. Reed       - Brooklyn N.Y.
Mrs. ___ Paul         Newport N.H.
Mrs. Wm H Dewey       Newport N.H.
Mrs. J. A. Robbins    Newport N.H.
Mrs. G. H. Hervey     Newport, N.H.
Mrs. G. W. Endicott   Newport N.H.
Mrs. E. B. Earl       Newport N.H.
Mrs. H. _____        Newport N.H.
Mrs Rose A Barton     Newport N.H.
Miss Elizabeth Barton Newport N.H.
Mrs. N. A. Persons    Newport N.H.
Miss Elvira M. Bartlett Newport N.H.
Mrs. _____ Burley    Newport N.H.
Mrs. Eliza S. Tenney, Springfield, N.H.

Mrs. Eliza S. Tenney, Springfield, N.H.
Mrs. Henry Bellair — Newport, N.H.
Mrs. G. W. Nourse       "        "
Mrs. Fred Craig         "        "
Mrs. C. J. Heath        "        "
Mrs. E. M. Howe         "        "
Mrs. C. J. Belknap      "        "
Mrs. W. J. Teague    Concord, N.H.

+ Jennie E. Felch
  Addie C. Symonds
  Jennie W. Eaton
  Hazel M. Stofford
  A. Lou Breed
  Nellie S. Breed
  Clara N. Ford
  Laura Block
  Lizzie Eaton
  Mattie B. Marshall

  Mrs. Isabelle Walker
(Miss) Mamie C. Maley
   "   Kathryn Conroy
   "   Anna Donovan
   "   Marie J. Donovan
  Mrs. Cynthia A. Whipple
  Mrs. M. A. George
  Mildred M. Conner
  Josephine W. Conner
  Mrs. Georgie Ryder
  Mrs. C. G. Hutton
  Mrs. E. L. Robinson
  Mrs. Betsey S. Stickney

Mr E L Robinson
Mrs Betsey S. Stickney
Mrs Lorinda A Putney
Ginny Russell
Mrs. Fermor H. Feathers
Mrs Laura A. Chase
Mrs. Eleanor E. Austin
" Nellie S. Blake
C. Maude Parker
Flora J. Parker
Marymith B. Giling
Idao Bartlett
Ada M. Hadley
Belle Richardson
A Olive Richardson
Celinda Bean
Florence Winter
Mary Borton
Lottie E. Farmer
Louise Lussier
Blanch E. Lussier
Eva Chatfield
May Daudrow
R. A. Corrow
Ada Crane
Edla M. Hadley
Calista E. Condon
Kitty M. Bull

## NEW YORK STATE ASSOCIATION OPPOSED TO WOMAN SUFFRAGE

*WHEREAS*, it is proposed by those advocating suffrage for women to introduce at this session of Congress a bill providing for an amendment to the Federal Constitution, giving women the ballot, and

*WHEREAS*, it is our best judgment that according to the Constitution and fundamental principles of our government, it is the sole province of each state to decide this question for itself, and

*WHEREAS*, in most of the states where this question has been submitted to the people, their verdict has been adverse to granting suffrage to women,

We, the undersigned, believing that the passage of such a bill would be antagonistic to the sovereign rights of the several states, hereby earnestly protest against such action and respectfully petition the members of both Houses of the Congress of the United States to reject any bill which has for its object the forcing of woman suffrage upon unwilling states by means of a federal constitutional amendment.

| NAME | ADDRESS |
|---|---|
| Mr. Richard Keppler | 427 Grove St. Brooklyn |
| Mr. Charles Keppler | 427 Grove St. " |
| Mr. J. W. Heinrich | 39 Stanton St. Woodhaven L.I. |
| Dr. Joseph J. Koob | 401 Grove St. B'klyn N.Y. |
| Mr. Oscar Erhard | 1266 Madison St. Bklyn |
| William Scholer | 1385 Putnam Ave Bklyn |
| L. Otto Sturtevant | 309 Wyckoff Av. |
| Oscar P. Kimmel Ph.G. | 762 St. Nicholas Ave Bklyn |
| Rudolph A. Zipple | 59 Maiden Lane, NY City |
| Fred J. Kirchner | 287 Wyckoff Ave Bklyn |
| Joseph Loeb | 402 Grove Str |
| William Schelling | 204 Menahan St |
| Chas Giesing | 425 Grove Str. B'n |
| Jacob Croissant | 270 St. Nicholas Ave |
| Henry Knett | 315 Wyckoff Ave |
| Henry Skulz | 396 Menahan St |
| Henry Borignaux | 236 Wyckoff Ave |
| Harold Levine | 1163 - 43rd St. |

(Over)

# PETITION

### From the Women Voters Anti-Suffrage Party of New York
#### TO THE
#### UNITED STATES SENATE

Whereas, This country is now engaged in the greatest war in history, and

Whereas, The advocates of the Federal Amendment, though urging it as a war measure, announce, through their president. Mrs. Catt, that its passage "means a simultaneous campaign in 48 States. It demands organization in every precinct; activity, agitation, education in every corner. Nothing less than this nation-wide, vigilant, unceasing campaign will win the ratification," therefore be it

Resolved, That our country in this hour of peril should be spared the harassing of its public men and the distracting of its people from work for the war, and further

Resolved, That the United States Senate be respectfully urged to pass no measure involving such a radical change in our government while the attention of the patriotic portion of the American people is concentrated on the all-important task of winning the war, and during the absence of over a million men abroad.

| NAME | ADDRESS | SERVICE |
|---|---|---|
| Jean McA. Staples | 528 Richmond Ave. | National League for Woman's Service |
| Mrs. G. K. Staples | 528 Richmond Ave. | |
| Betty A. Keeley | 200 Niagara St | National League for women service |
| Mable Spawton | 410 Hoyt St | " |
| Emma Burris | 1698 Main St | National League for woman service |
| Ruth L. Staples | 528 Richmond Av | Gov't Service |
| Mrs. H. C. Wood | 75 Hampshire St | Bureau of Aircraft Production |
| Elizabeth Cohen | 426 Wilson St. | Red Cross |
| Evelyn Cantor | 205 Hickory | Red Cross |
| Mrs. G. L. Tucker | 168 Delaware ave | |
| Bessie Murtaugh | 215 Northland Ave | Red Cross |
| Mrs. Frances Drenthom | 39 Bennett St. | Red Cross |
| Mrs. Lou Jackson | 424 Jefferson St | |
| Mrs. L. Licht | 424 Jefferson St | |
| Helen Stern | 195 Amherst St | " |
| Mrs. H. C. Stern | " | " " " |
| Ethel Stearns | " | " " " |

## WOMEN VOTERS' ANTI-SUFFRAGE PARTY

Co-operating
with established parties
against radicalism.

ROOM 809    280 MADISON AVENUE
NEW YORK CITY

Telephone
Vanderbilt 3780

September 2, 1918.

Dear Mrs Doane

As you know, one result of the Woman Suffrage gain in this State last November is that every sort of pressure is being brought to bear to throw the weight of New York State into the balance for a suffrage federal amendment, forcing "suffrage first" on all the other States.

Should such an amendment go through, the entire country would be threatened with an immediate, intensive suffrage campaign to compel a ratification by the legislatures in 48 States at a time when all legislative bodies and all loyal men and women should be giving their best endeavors absolutely and undividedly to the problems of the war.

Will you help New York to do its part to prevent this unwarranted distraction?

We need enrollment,
We need your co-operation,
We need your contribution

in carrying on the work we know you want done. Will you secure what signatures you can between now and September 9th, returning the list to this office on that day?

Sincerely yours,
Mary G. Kilbreth, Congressional Chairman.

Did you see the Open Letter
to the President in the "Times"
and "World"? A second of the          Checks made payable to
series will appear this week           Mrs. Harald deRaasloff, Treasurer.
and others as we receive the
money.

---

## PETITION

### From the Women Voters Anti-Suffrage Party of New York
### TO THE UNITED STATES SENATE

Whereas, This country is now engaged in the greatest war in history, and

Whereas, The advocates of the Federal Amendment, though urging it as a war measure, announce, through their president, Mrs. Catt, that its passage "means a simultaneous campaign in 48 States. It demands organization in every precinct; activity, agitation, education in every corner. Nothing less than this nation-wide, vigilant, unceasing campaign will win the ratification," therefore, be it

Resolved, That our country in this hour of peril should be spared the harassing of its public men and the distracting of its people from work for the war, and further

Resolved, That the United States Senate be respectfully urged to pass no measure involving such a radical change in our government while the attention of the patriotic portion of the American people is concentrated on the all-important task of winning the war, and during the absence of over a million men abroad.

| NAME | ADDRESS | SERVICE |
|---|---|---|
| Mrs Howard F Doane | 500 W. 111" St. | Volunteer Canteen |
| Mrs M. L. Pray | 500 W. 111 St. | Red Cross |
| Alexander Cleland | 17 E. 41st St | Director W.C.C.S. Units 3 + 9 |
| John G. Tietz | 17 E. 41st St | Asst Director " " |
| Helen Gunbrach | 301 West 106" St | Canteen Volunteer |
| Emma B. Ruppel | 69 W. 93 St. | Canteen Volunteer |
| Miss Shearman | 840 Park Ave. | Canteen Service |

# HIDDEN FROM HISTORY

| Name | Address | Service |
|---|---|---|
| A. Louise Brownson | 276 State St., Flushing, L.I. | U.S. Government |
| Caroline S. Brownson | 276 State St. Flushing, N.Y. | Volunteer Canteen service |
| Mary S. Baskerville | 611 W 110 St. | Vol. Canteen |
| Ageda M. Fitzpatrick | 611 W. 110 St. | " " |
| Edith Hopkins | G. Hopkins, Dwight & Co | " " |
| Mrs. Hue Stuart Baird | 137 W. 85 St. | V.C. Canteen |
| Edith A. Higgs | 500 West 111 St | American Red Cross |
| Harriet de L. Higgs | 500 West 111 St | Red Cross |
| P. Jackson Higgs | | Air Service U.S.A. |

## WOMEN VOTERS' ANTI-SUFFRAGE PARTY

Co-operating
with established parties
against radicalism.

Telephone
Vanderbilt 3780

ROOM 809  280 MADISON AVENUE
NEW YORK CITY

September 2, 1918.

As you know, one result of the Woman Suffrage gain in this State last November is that every sort of pressure is being brought to bear to throw the weight of New York State into the balance for a suffrage federal amendment, forcing "suffrage first" on all the other States.

Should such an amendment go through, the entire country would be threatened with an immediate, intensive suffrage campaign to compel a ratification by the legislatures in 48 States at a time when all legislative bodies and all loyal men and women should be giving their best endeavors absolutely and undividedly to the problems of the war.

Will you help New York to do its part to prevent this unwarranted distraction?

We need enrollment,
We need your co-operation,
We need your contribution

in carrying on the work we know you want done. Will you secure what signatures you can between now and September 17th, returning the list to this office on that day?

Sincerely yours,

Mary G. Kilbreth, Congressional Chairman.

Did you see the Open Letter
to the President in the "Times"
and "World"? A second of the
series will appear this week
and others as we receive the
money.

Checks made payable to
Mrs. Harald deRaasloff, Treasurer.

---

# PETITION

### From the Women Voters Anti-Suffrage Party of New York
#### TO THE UNITED STATES SENATE

Whereas, This country is now engaged in the greatest war in history, and

Whereas, The advocates of the Federal Amendment, though urging it as a war measure, announce, through their president, Mrs. Catt, that its passage "means a simultaneous campaign in 48 States. It demands organization in every precinct; activity, agitation, education in every corner. Nothing less than this nation-wide, vigilant, unceasing campaign will win the ratification," therefore, be it

Resolved, That our country in this hour of peril should be spared the harassing of its public men and the distracting of its people from work for the war, and further

Resolved, That the United States Senate be respectfully urged to pass no measure involving such a radical change in our government while the attention of the patriotic portion of the American people is concentrated on the all-important task of winning the war, and during the absence of over a million men abroad.

| NAME | ADDRESS | SERVICE |
|---|---|---|
| Stephen H. Olin | Rhinebeck N.Y. | |
| Emeline H. Olin | " | " |
| Letitia Bowe | | " |
| Helen Gray Huntington | Staatsburgh New York | |

# PROTEST AGAINST WOMAN SUFFRAGE.

ADDRESS DELIVERED BY
## The Rev. FATHER WALSH, of Troy.

*At a Mass Meeting called by the Anti-Women's Suffrage Asssociation of Albany, N. Y.*

---

LADIES AND GENTLEMEN.—A gentleman of our city with more tact than intelligence, on being asked to express an opinion on woman suffrage, met his questioner with this remark: "This is a woman's question and must be decided by women."

Unhappily for women, though it is a woman's question, it is to be decided by men only—by men in the Constitutional Convention, and by the men voters afterward, if this Convention decide to adopt it. For this reason men will by courtesy and necessity take part in these preliminary meetings whether called to promote or defeat female suffrage.

Before this audience of the gentle women of this city, convened for the purpose of voicing opposition to any amendment to the Constitution investing women with the right of suffrage, I crave a religious reverence for woman. In opposing what we believe to be a movement calculated to degrade woman, we are impressed altogether by the danger lurking under an assumed privilege, and right, which threatens the position and character of this being, whom we would have like Cæsar's wife — without suspicion or reproach.

No one here can forget his indebtedness to woman. To her as mother, sister, wife or friend, we owe the tenderest emotions of life—the noblest elements of character—the purest aspirations and the sweetest sympathy in joy and sorrow. Into her arms we are born. Watching her lips we begin to speak; led by her hand we learn to walk in obedience of law. In painting, sculpture and poetry, she gives us ideals of innocence and beauty. Innocence is a woman; chastity is a woman; charity is a woman. I and you do not wish to lose this ideal woman.

I belong to a church where woman has been clothed with high responsibilities, and even the right to vote. In all our religious orders of women, sometimes all the subjects, and sometimes a few, exercise this right in the selection of their superiors.

Is there then inconsistency in my present position?

In the sphere of morals, to vote or not to vote, is a neutral duty. It is the surroundings which may lead to demoralization and degradation—not the mere act of casting the ballot. If I can be convinced that the right of suffrage granted to women may be exercised as innocently, as harmlessly, amidst all the filth, obscenity, blasphemy and perjury of our modern polling-booth as in the peace, solitude and purity of the cloister, then I am willing to be recorded as in favor of woman suffrage.

If I can be convinced that this enfranchisement of woman is needed to idealize woman still more, or make her more womanly, or secure her in greater purity and innocence, or deepen her sympathetic and religious nature, or strengthen her maternal and domestic instincts, then I will gladly lift my voice, and exert my influence, in behalf of granting this boon to woman.

I have yet to learn that a single advocate of female suffrage has contended for the measure for the reason that its concession will improve and strengthen and safeguard the female character. Much declamation is indulged in on the plea that it is a hurtful discrimination between "male" and "female" in the Constitution — or that women will never enjoy the full measure of liberty till they can vote, or that women owning property are unjustly taxed by others; and they have a fondness for the axiom, "No taxation without representation."

Can there be serious disagreement as to the result of her enfranchisement? Rum and politics are the ruin of vast numbers of our citizens. Incurable and deepening corruption is the condition of politics to-day. Polling places are pestilential spots, seething with perjury, bribery, unclean language and rowdyism. I have never yet cast a ballot that I did not blush for shame because of this temporary association. I have no hope that these evils will ever be cured till some limitation is placed on the farce of universal suffrage. Parties ambitious of political ascendancy or continuance in power will perpetuate them.

These female suffrage fanatics say: "Let the women vote and healing will come to the festering and hideous sores of politics. Let the woman bring all her refinement and delicacy, and intelligence and sympathy down into this noisome vortex, and she will bring peace, orderliness and purity out of confusion, chaos and uncleanness."

Ah! They know little of human nature who talk in this fashion. The best element among our male voters has tried to improve the shame. Have they succeeded? They were so apathetic, owing to repeated failures, that Governor Hill twice in his messages tried to induce the Legislature to enact laws making the suffrage a duty, and not merely a right. And where strong influential men have failed, will women succeed? Who here would wish to see his mother, wife or sister, enter our polling places? And you really believe that the most of the female voters would be proof against bribery, and intoxicants, and, in time, more degrading and iniquitous crimes? They read the history of woman with false lights, who cannot recognize, in her affiliation with public affairs, the marked cause of her deterioration in personal character. There are some few exceptions; but from Deborah to Cleopatra, and Elizabeth of England, and Catharine of Russia, and to the princess claiming the right to the throne of Hawaii, there is an insolent cruelty, and a moral debasement, that shames the worst male profligacy.

Within her own sphere, woman's influence is beneficial and uplifting. When ambition or accident has carried her beyond her sphere, the transfer has wrought evil to man, and wreck to woman. This, then, is my first reason of opposition to female suffrage—in the present debased and corrupt condition of politics, I fear that female participation in the franchise must entail consequences fatal to the legitimate work and destiny of women.

My second reason is close to this. Has not partisanship in politics been carried already to a ruinous extreme in this country? Is not our boasted national unity a farce and a fiction? Have not recent Congressional debates, and measures, affirmed that we are hopelessly divided into opposing industrial camps, and recent political contests proved the fierce enmity of our battling political hosts? I believe that our prosperity, and vitality, depend on the coalition and pacification of these hostile forces. I believe that we should be a party to no legislation which would tend further to separate us, and increase the din of battle.

I believe that other more vital interests which cluster about the home, the church, and the school, demand that our large female population be kept aloof from these rivalries and contentions, as a refuge and restraint in the day of our direst distress, and with the fervent hope that their unbiased influence may beget a generation of citizens who may be willing to put the nation before the individual, and men and principles ahead of party.

If we clothe our women with the franchise, we increase a thousand-fold all the evils and injustice and blindness and selfishness of partisanship. Into the nation we throw a solvent that will be felt down in its lowest foundations. Already, with only men to vote, the heat of a political fight will divide families, and strain and snap friendships of a life-time. Bring women into the strife, and what home will be secure against discord, and what friendship safe from wreckage?

The more sacred duties of home, religion, and education, will be sacrificed to the more engrossing excitements of politics; and we will have a grotesque, ill-formed nation, where women are never mothers, and where men will know more of the tariff and the election law than of God and the ten commandments. That morbid condition is universal enough now among men. Do you want it also to brand women?

My third reason, which is also my last, though these are only three of a series which might run into many were I the only speaker, is based upon other material. The remark has been made editorially by one of your journals, that this question of female suffrage is not to be determined by female superiority or inferiority as compared with males. The issue at best is ungallant and ungracious, and yet I cannot avoid it. I would regret to find the question settled without a reference to this issue of comparative ability. Legitimately, it never should be raised; and it would not now if women were not insisting on trespassing on exclusive male territory. Fortunate would we be if we could imitate the gallantry of Horace Greeley, who, when asked "who was the cleverer, man or woman?" replied, "It depends very much on what man or woman you mean."

If the franchise is conferred on woman, it should co-ordinately confer on her the right to hold any office for which she may vote. If you separate the two, female agitators will never sleep till they worry you into granting this substantial sequence of the franchise. If you now permit her to vote, sooner or later this is the very serious condition you must face. In such an event, her sex should be no bar to her being a governor, a chief justice, United States Senator, or any official within the jurisdiction of the people, or other appointing power of this State. If being eligible to these offices, the mother's and wife's ambition covets them against the protest of husband and children—what then? If to prevent her election, husband and children must vote against her—what then? If during the tenure of office, the duties or functions of motherhood demand her retirement—what then? If, in the distribution of official patronage, she ignore husband and sons—what then?

Women agitators call the franchise, by a gross misnomer, a natural right. The refutation of the absurdity lies in the obtrusive antagonism between this alleged *natural* right and other *real natural duties*. Frances Power Cobbe, a vigorous female agitator, confesses there is a period in a woman's life when the duties she owes her sex force her to a complete abandonment of the duties she owes the commonwealth. Is not this a singular anomaly? Because female suffragists will not heed the voice of nature they are unsexing themselves.

It is this possibility of female office-holders that forces on us the feature of female capacity.

Dr. Wm. A. Hammond, the distinguished nerve and brain specialist, after writing harshly of the original female suffrage agitators as short-haired women and long-haired men, says that a woman's brain evolves emotion rather than intellect; and whilst this feature fits her admirably as a creature burdened with the preservation and happiness of the human species, it painfully disqualifies her for the sterner duties to be performed by the intellectual faculties. The best wife and mother and sister would make the worst legislator, judge and police.

The excessive development of the emotional in her nervous system, ingrafts on the female organization, a neurotic or hysterical condition, which is the source of much of the female charms when it is kept within due restraints. In emergencies, or difficult situations, or moments of excitement, or under continued strain, it is liable to explode in violent paroxysms, when all the mental and physical faculties are perverted, and thrown into a condition of startling turbulence. Every woman, therefore, carries this power of irregular, illogical and incongruous action; and no one can foretell when the explosion will come.

A woman lives more in her emotions, and will judge more as she feels than as she thinks. She is bereft of the "judicial mind." She has no idea of abstract justice. Her likes and dislikes are paramount with her. She will sacrifice life, duty, family and character, if necessary, to the man she loves; and punish severely those, who, innocent of crime, may have only aroused her prejudices. A man will judge of things as they are without reference to himself. Only the exceptional woman can do this. Men are strong in those virtues that grow out of the nature of things—women in those that are found in mere sentiment or right feeling.

These differences make their union necessary. They were never intended for rivals. They are complementary to each other, like the voices in a choral harmony; and their wants and differences are the bond of their union. If nature makes them differ, so must the spheres of their action vary.

If an abnormal female ambition, blind to these essential and God-given unlikenesses, craves for activity in an unhealthy, masculine field, let the strong, virile opinion of the State, rebuke the yearning as it would that of an unthinking, wayward child.

Gladly do I endorse your own resolution when you say:

"It is our fathers, brothers, husbands and sons who represent us at the ballot-box. Our fathers and our brothers love us; our husbands are our choice and one with us; our sons are what we make them. We are content that they represent us in the corn-field, on the battle-field and at the ballot-box, and we them in the school-room, at the fire-side and at the cradle, believing our representation even at the ballot-box to be thus more full and impartial than it would be were the views of the few who wish suffrage adopted, contrary to the judgment of the many.

"We do, therefore, respectfully protest against any legislation to establish 'woman suffrage' in our land, or in any part of it."

---

Anti-Suffrage papers and pamphlets can be obtained, and Protest signed, at headquarters, 70 North Pearl Street, ground floor, under the Kenmore Hotel, Albany.

# *Please Leave A Review!*

Reviews are an important way for others to learn about products by Danica De La Mora and your input is important to us. Please return to your place of purchase and let us know how you liked this product.

---

## *Follow Danica De La Mora*

**Facebook:** Danica.Delamora
**Twitter / X:** @DanicaDeLaMora
**Pinterest:** MsDanicaDeLaMora
**Instagram:** MsDanicaDeLaMora

www.DanicaDeLaMora.com

---

## *Browse Other Books & Products by Danica De La Mora*

*First Wave Feminism: The Tsunami That Submerged the Republic*

*Timeless Teachings from Mrs. Stroupe's Blackboard:
Inspirational Wisdom Through the Ages*

*Digital Dignity (For the Lady):
Contemporary & Online Dating with Old World Class*

*Digital Dignity (For the Gentleman):
Contemporary & Online Dating with Old World Class*

*The Digital Dignity Dating Calendar*

*The Digital Dignity Dating Journal*

*The Digital Dignity Vault: A Safe Place for Your Digital Passcodes*

*... And More!*

# About the Authoress

**Danica De La Mora**

For more than a decade, Danica De La Mora has been following a plant-based lifestyle, building on her collection of knowledge through extensive study and education lectures by doctors who are at the forefront of nutritional research. She is a graduate of the Plant-Based Nutrition program by the Center for Nutrition Studies at Cornell University.

She also holds a degree in Communication and Film Studies from St. Andrews University and is a graduate of the Barbizon modeling academy. She has a background in graphic design, multiple forms of editing, DVD authoring, film transfer and preservation, videography, photography, and photograph restoration, as well as print media production, having been reared in a family who owned print publications all over the Southeastern United States.

Ms. De La Mora has been strongly influenced by her family. She is experienced in Latin and ballroom dancing, as well as music, with her grandmother's ownership of a prestigious etiquette and dance school for 50 years and her father having placed fourth in the world on accordion out of thousands of contestants. In addition to her own research and experience with relationships, she has obtained substantial knowledge through her mother's wide-ranging background involving social work, alcoholism treatment, psychology, and print media publishing. Her grandparents' loving and traditional marriage of nearly 60 years provided her with an excellent foundation for understanding successful relationships and gender polarities.

Ms. De La Mora advises groups and individuals of all ages who are interested in refining themselves with a traditional and conservative elegance. She leads them down the path of optimal nutrition so that they may regain health, prevent disease, and enjoy long-term weight management. She also counsels ladies and gentlemen in their romantic relationships and helps them find the fulfilling lives that they were destined to enjoy.

From the manner in which one conducts oneself to the manner in which one presents oneself, elegance is everything!

www.DanicaDeLaMora.com

A Timeless Treasures Publication.
www.TimelessTreasuresStudio.net

www.ingramcontent.com/pod-product-compliance
Lightning Source LLC
Chambersburg PA
CBHW081144290426
44108CB00018B/2433